Songs without Music

Philosophy, Social Theory, and the Rule of Law

General Editors

Andrew Arato, Seyla Benhabib, Ferenc Fehér, William Forbath, Agnes Heller, Arthur Jacobson, and Michel Rosenfeld

Songs without Music

Aesthetic Dimensions of Law and Justice

DESMOND MANDERSON

University of California Press

BERKELEY   LOS ANGELES   LONDON

University of California Press
Berkeley and Los Angeles, California

University of California Press, Ltd.
London, England

© 2000 by the Regents of the University of California

Library of Congress Cataloging-in-Publication Data

Manderson, Desmond.
    Songs without music : aesthetic dimensions of law and justice /
Desmond Manderson.
        p.   cm.—(Philosophy, social theory, and the rule of law ; 7)
    Includes bibliographical references and index.
    ISBN 0-520-21688-1 (alk. paper)
    1. Law and aesthetics.   I. Series.
K487.A3M36   2000
340'.11—dc21   99-38447
                                                                    CIP

Manufactured in the United States of America

09   08   07   06   05   04   03   02   01   00

10   9   8   7   6   5   4   3   2   1

To Mum
and in memory of Harry Blackmun

Contents

Preface and Acknowledgments

Songs without Music is about the aesthetic dimensions which lie at the heart of law and justice. Aesthetics is the faculty which reacts to the images and sensory input to which we are constantly exposed and which, by their symbolic associations, significantly influence our values and our society. "Legal aesthetics" suggests that the discourse of law is fundamentally governed by rhetoric, metaphor, form, images, and symbols.

Mapping this space involves three dimensions. First (in the first three chapters), an aesthetic methodology, sensitive to the form and imagery of legal texts, can illuminate both the meaning and force of law. Second (in the "Requiem" and "Variations"), an aesthetic epistemology helps illuminate the social values which find expression in law as well as the form they take. Social conflict is not just an argument about reasons; it is also a battleground of symbols. Third (in the last two chapters), taking aesthetics seriously is shown to have normative implications. If we thought that symbolism and imagery were not just failures in law's rationality but part of its power, what would the legal system look like? The thesis contrasts a variety of modern legal theories and argues that each show a commitment to particular aesthetic values. I conclude by attempting to conjoin the ideas of legal pluralism with the changing aesthetic tenor of the times, in order to find new approaches to law and new metaphors through which to give them life.

These dimensions are developed using a range of analytical tools of growing significance in legal theory, including semiotics, legal history, literary studies, and poststructuralist philosophy. At the same time, each chapter focuses on a different case study of legal discourse, including the history of the English statute, capital punishment, illegal drugs, and contemporary legal theory.

A complex interrelationship of meaning and structure is fundamental to this approach to law. By treating a text, legal or otherwise, as merely a sequence of logical propositions, readers miss its formal, metaphorical, and symbolic meanings. In the pages that follow, therefore, aesthetic as well as logical techniques are used to develop this argument. Each chapter is based on a different musical form, and each uses music as comparison and exemplar. *Songs without Music* has been designed not only to talk about aesthetic meaning but to embody it.

The use of music throughout these *Songs* requires further elaboration. In the beginning was the word, but before the word came the voice, raw and unformed, just a potential awaiting exploration. The idea of many voices — of poly/phony — runs through this work like a refrain, and, of the many voices summoned up, the most insistent and the most protean is that of music. If this opus is about law and meaning, then music is its *leitmotif*.

There are at least three aspects to this attempt to use music to convey meaning. The first is structural. Each chapter is structured as a kind of textual equivalent to a different musical form, and often on the basis of a particular example of it. Each is meant to be, then, a kind of song without music. I am thinking here of the famous *Songs without Words* of Felix Mendelssohn, who may or may not have been a distant ancestor of mine. Mendelssohn, at any rate, was my father's name and my own secret patronymic.

Chapter 4, to give one example, is organized around Mozart's Requiem and has sections entitled "Agnus Dei," "Dies Irae," and so on. These sections parallel the organization of a requiem and at the same time capture the essence of the arguments I make there.

Chapter 1, which is modeled on the C-major prelude of Bach's *Well-Tempered Clavier*, is a more complex example. The chapter evinces a pattern of unfolding and emergence which reflects both the organization of the first prelude and the Foucauldian argument about the emergence of modernism which I relate to it. Several characteristics that the chapter shares with the prelude and with Foucault's interpretation of modernism will help to draw out these connections. First, that of unity, an expression of an aesthetic ideal. Like the prelude, the chapter is not divided into distinct sections but evolves continually from point to point. Second, that of identity, an exemplification of modernity's focus on individualism as the unit from which societies are not so much built as accreted. Just as the prelude is built on a musical unit or atom of eight notes whose pattern is constantly repeated throughout the piece, so too the chapter is built of paragraphs each of which is about the same number of lines long. The paragraph is like a block of Lego—or like the individuals in a modern society—out of the very commensurability of whose members infinite structures may be built. Third, that of duality, which reflects the dichotomization at the heart of the modernist dilemma: between form and content, self and other, reason and the aesthetic. In the prelude, the eight-note unit is played twice, identically, in every bar—in fact, the idea of a double is of more general significance in the scheme of the *Well-Tempered Clavier*. The chapter, for its part, uses paired paragraphs whose arguments respond to and balance each other. They form bars of two units each, and in twinned lockstep the chapter thus proceeds. Finally, that of a calculus of gradual changes and shifts—a Foucauldian interaction between identity and duality. The prelude is not static; it uses the formula of units and bars to build ever bigger structures in a continuing process of expansion and change. In the chapter, too, units form larger units in a continuing process of exegetical building. The seamless feeling given by the form masks a layered structure of some care, and this structure creates a form which both disciplines and contributes to the content of the chapter.

The second aspect of the use of music as a voice which articulates what I mean by the aesthetic is thematic. The musical compositions which are the focus of each chapter have specific relevance to the arguments developed there. "Motet," for example, centers on a comparison between the history of the English motet from 1200 to 1500 and the history of English legislation over the same period. The same formal and stylistic changes took place in each discipline, suggesting a parallel change in the worldview of both. Musical themes are brought to bear very differently in the Requiem, the Latin text of which expresses certainty in God's infallible judgment of the dead. This acts in ironic counterpoint to the U.S. judicial system's failed attempts, in the area of capital punishment, to replicate such certainty in deciding who will live and who will die. And in "Quartet," to give another example, both the history and musical content of Messiaen's remarkable composition are used to help talk about the dangers of modernism and the paradigm shift to postmodernity which we are undergoing.

The third way in which music expresses meaning is emotional. Each piece of music provides its corresponding chapter with a distinct character. "Prelude" attempts to capture the meditative mood of the *Well-Tempered Clavier*, just as the obsessive strains of Rachmaninoff's *Rhapsodie on a Theme of Paganini* infuse "Variations on a Theme" and a certain reflective whimsy colors "Quodlibet."

In each chapter, these aesthetic resonances are developed differently. Music gives "Prelude" its pace and its style and provides a literal reflection of Bach's structure. In "Fugue," polyphonic music is a metaphor and a general framework for the argument. In "Motet," the musical history of the Renaissance is used as a metonym to the legal history of the same period. In "Requiem," Mozart's music influences the form of the chapter and at the same time provides an ironic commentary on it. In "Variations," the music of Brahms and Rachmaninoff provides stylistic and analytic insight into the argument about obsession developed there. In "Quartet," the music of Messiaen and others provides historical and cultural insight into the development of legal theory. In addition, in both "Quartet" and in "Quodlibet," aesthetics is defended as a human value of intrinsic importance. The experience of musical appreciation is therefore a normative influence on the ideas about justice there advanced.

The ideas which this book crystallizes have developed over several years; parts in some of the chapters have appeared in other published sources. Part of "Motet" was originally published as "*Statuta* v. Acts: Interpretation, Music, & Early English Legislation," *Yale Journal of Law & Humanities* (1995), vol. 7, pp. 317–66, and is reproduced with their kind permission. Part of "Variations" was originally published as "Metamorphoses: Clashing Symbols in the Social Construction of Drugs," *Journal of Drug Issues* (1995), vol. 25, pp. 799–816, and is reproduced with their kind permission. Part of "Quartet" was originally published as "Beyond the Provincial: Space, Aesthetics, and Modernist Legal Theory," *Melbourne University Law Review* (1996), vol. 20, pp. 1048–71, and is reproduced with their kind permission. All were substantially rewritten for the submission of a doctoral thesis to the Institute of Comparative Law at McGill University, Montréal. The whole was then completely rewritten for the purposes of this book. None of this could have come to fruition without the constant help and support of many people, including my family and friends on three continents. I am especially grateful to the support and enthusiasm of the Law Program in the Research School of Social Sciences, Australian National University, which in 1996 gave me the perfect environment in which to finally complete this work. But the bulk of my research and writing was done in Montréal from 1991 to 1995. My study was funded, and generously so, by a Commonwealth Scholarship from the Government of Canada. The officers of the Canadian Bureau of International Education and the International Council for Canadian Studies, who at different times administered the scheme, were unstinting in their generosity and unfailing in their enthusiasm. Study under such conditions was a rare privilege.

In Montréal, my teachers, colleagues, and friends in the Faculty of Law at McGill University welcomed me into an intellectual community subtler, more sophisticated, and warmer than I could possibly have imagined. I am forever in their debt. My supervisors, Professors Margaret A. Somerville and Roderick A. Macdonald, gave me the inestimable gifts of their time and patience, their wisdom and their friendship. It is invidious to single out one over the other: both showed me an interest and engagement above and beyond the call of duty. Appropriately enough, I learned more than I can say. In return, I note that the scholar who said *tempus edax rerum* did not understand the workings of memory.

The final work on this project was completed while I worked in Australia, first at Macquarie University and then at the University of Sydney and with the great support of the University of California Press. I am especially grateful to Ed Dimenberg, who as commissioning editor took a brave punt on this book—my respect and gratitude are unbounded. And my thanks are due, too, to Professor Peter Goodrich, then at UCLA Law School and Birkbeck College, London, and now at Cardozo School of Law, New York; to Tracy Strong, the Department of Political Science at UCSD, and to Susan McClary, the Department of Musicology at UCLA. All provided invaluable comments and suggestions about the whole text. The support and friendship of Peter and Susan, in particular, is a continuing source of delight to me.

I could not even have conceived of this project without this polyphonous encouragement, for they helped me develop words out of *my* raw and unformed voice. But for the final product of these labors I am entirely culpable. The core of my argument is that aesthetics is a crucial part of how we understand the world. If this is true, then it is important not merely to talk about aesthetic meaning in law but to embody it; to exemplify aesthetics as well as to explain it. Inspired by writers such as Italo Calvino, Claude Lévi-Strauss, and Douglas Hofstadter, the use of music in this work is one way in which I attempt to communicate symbolic meaning aesthetically as well as discursively. At some point, then, we must all stop putting into imperfect words our emotions and debts, our thoughts and our feelings, and begin rather to enact them. That point, I think, is right now.

Part 1

THE METHODOLOGICAL DIMENSION

Prelude
Senses and Symbols in Aesthetic Experience

PHILOSOPHIES OF AESTHETICS

Introduction 1: A Musical Voyage. A little piece of music, the manuscript of which is reproduced above, might even now be heard as it flies through deep space aboard the Voyager spacecraft. It has been sent on a mission in search of other worlds, our frail hurtling embassy to the unknown.[1] A gesture to the galaxy, the regular pattern of sounds which these written signs denote has been chosen to represent something ineffable but eternal about our planet, about a species which happens to inhabit it, about a way in which that species expresses itself, about an aspect of its being which finds fulfillment in the expression. A pattern of pitches, unfolding with unhurried inexorability, never quite predictable, never quite surprising; hammers striking keys, a bold sound and sudden decay; the unmistakable interpretation of Glenn Gould. The composition is the merest gesture of hope amidst the sterile silence of space, and in that it is a perfect counterpoint to the spinning craft which carries it forward, and out, and away.

Introduction 2: An Aesthetic Voyage. What is it about those few bars which seems to embody the creative process? In the pages that follow I explore how our experience as aesthetic beings is an aspect of our understanding of the world and the law; how there is a way in which aesthetic discourse, and the experiences which underpin it, can enrich and make more complex our often crudely dichotomous understanding of the relationship between legal order and social conflict. Clearly, when I talk about "the aesthetic dimension" of experience, I do not mean simply a painting or a piece of music. I am trying to get at a much more pervasive part of our perception of the world, of which art and music are simply a greatly refined and concentrated aspect. What is aesthetics about and how does it contribute to our understanding?—that is my task here. This chapter is a prelude, then. It lays the groundwork and hints at future themes. My interest lies in the idea of aesthetics generally and not in its characteristics in any particular medium. But before extending it to the world at large, I wish to begin by discussing the meaning of aesthetics in the more familiar context of art and music. The first prelude of Bach's *Well-Tempered Clavier*[2] will serve as a sextant as we embark on this voyage. Its advantages are its beauty, its familiarity, and its simplicity. To be sure, it is Glenn Gould's idiosyncratic rendering of that text which traverses the galaxy and which is etched upon my mind. But let us try and move away from the specifics of a particular performance, to a consideration of the musical text.

Well-Tempered Clavier 1: Rhythm.   Here music is stripped to its most elemental form. There is no melodic line here, no change in dynamics, no rhythmic complexity or variety. With the exception of the last line, every single bar is made up of a simple unit or pattern played twice. Just eight notes, one after another, repeated. And every bar thus formed is like the one that follows it and the one that goes before. The only textual variety is therefore harmonic, and even here there is as little change as possible. The piece is in C major, the simplest of keys to play. In every bar the pattern of ascent and descent is identical—five notes form a climbing arpeggio, the last three notes repeated, thus providing an eight-note unit which is then repeated without variation.[3] The actual notes that form this pattern change in each bar—but only minimally.[4] Normally only one or two notes of the five that form the arpeggio will change from bar to bar. Each is thus only a fractionally modified version of its neighbors. The effect is of subtly changing harmonies, the aural equivalent of the gently shifting hues of a sunset.

Well-Tempered Clavier 2: Structure.   Nothing programmatic guides our thoughts away from the pure abstraction of the notes. It is simply called a "prelude," which is to say a beginning or an introduction. It has a number, not a name, and thus takes its place as the first of twenty-four, each in a different key, corresponding to the twenty-four different major and minor keys possible—the pieces again being so organized that the move from the key of one piece to that of the next is also, stepwise, as small as possible.[5] These twenty-four, along with the fugues which are their companion pieces, belong to a book. The *Well-Tempered Clavier* is made up of two such books, each arranged in the same way. There is a multiple symmetry at work here: the structure of the *Well-Tempered Clavier* as a whole is reflected in the structure of the first prelude, like an oak caught in an acorn. The unbroken regularity of note pursuing note, throughout the prelude, is paralleled by the unbroken regularity with which prelude and fugue succeeds prelude and fugue, throughout the book. At the same time, as the repetition or doubling of each unit (which forms a bar) is consumed by a gradually changing harmony (which forms the prelude), a gradually changing tonality from piece to piece (which forms the book) is consumed by the repetition or doubling of each book (which forms the whole work).[6]

Philosophy of Aesthetics 1: The Dream of Certainty.   Let us expand our discussion from a particular musical artwork to the concept of art more generally. From the standpoint of philosophy, the aesthetic appears as a problem. As a discipline traditionally based on the paramountcy of reason, philosophy has tried not to explain the power of the aesthetic but to tame it. Behind this attitude has lain philosophy's search for objective and absolute "right answers" to moral questions. The relationship of the rational and the nonrational, the faculty of reason and the realm of the aesthetic, has developed in the shadow of this quest.[7] Thus for the Greeks and those who followed, truth was "out there" in the universe and discoverable by dint of intellectual reflection.[8] In Plato, art is at best an imitation (*mimesis*) of this external truth (so too in Plotinus) and, at its worst, a kind of falsehood or surrender to "feelings and unhealthy cravings." The aesthetic was "the soul's foolish part."[9] And in St. Thomas Aquinas, for example, though objective truth has been sanctified, its existence is not in question. Aquinas defends metaphor and poetry as Plato does not. God's truth can be discerned rationally, by the literal Word, or revealed spiritually, by metaphorical words. But for Aquinas both are means of access to the same objective reality, albeit "veiled," in the latter case, by "sensible imagery."[10]

Philosophy of Aesthetics 2: The Enlightenment. The great Enlightenment trend toward scientific rationality made problematic the idea that this truth was "out there," whether in the structure of the universe or the mind of God. But later philosophers did not abandon their desire to find truth an objective and absolute home. Rather, they simply transferred the place in which it resided inward, to the newly autonomous human self and to the faculty of human reason. It was now the uniquely human discourse of reason which was treated as the window to an absolute and objective reality.[11] In this context, the danger of the aesthetic, for philosophy, still lay in its capacity to undermine the promise of reason; its legitimacy, on the contrary, was as a different and subservient mode of apprehending the same rational truths. Kant and Schiller sought to domesticate "the egoism of taste" by positing the meaning of beauty as a force through which we could learn to internalize the rational call of conscience and of duty.[12] Beauty was the inner sense by which the voice of reason came to be not only heard but felt—transforming authority to hegemony, force to free conformity, and punishment to discipline.

Beauty and Nature 1: As Truth. With the Romantics, the hegemonic function of the aesthetic remained, although its status changed from that of a servant of rationality in the quest for truth to a substitute for it. Not, of course, that this was an approach without its forebears. Long before the golden age of Greek philosophy, with its valorization of the rational, art was the traditional repository of truth claims; in many societies that remains the case.[13] How could such societies even conceive of the dichotomy of reason and beauty when art was everything and everything was art? The Romantic conception of art began again to assert its authority at the expense of reason rather than in its service, but it still did so in the search for a source of objective truth and not as a rejection of it. If truth could no longer be derived from the universe, God, or reason, the Romantics supposed it could still be discovered through feeling.[14]

Beauty and Nature 2: As Objectivity.   For Keats, and in similar terms in the Earl of Shaftesbury, "beauty" and "truth" were treated as equivalent. Bosanquet, whose *History of Aesthetics* was long influential, declared axiomatic "the objectivity and necessary historical continuity of the sense of beauty."[15] Following Rousseau, neoclassical and early Romantic texts frequently justify the aesthetic as a way of discerning the truth encoded specifically in nature. Where before, beauty was supposed to give voice and vision to the wisdom of God or the reason of man, it was now interpreted as expressing the truth of nature. But notice that art continues to be mimetic of something objectively true for all time and all people.[16] Its claims to a transcendent universal content thus shored up, the aesthetic continued to perform an ideological function, rendering power relations "natural" and therefore beyond argument.[17] After all, remarked the Earl of Shaftesbury, it was "not porters or beggars" whose nudity we would find beautiful but only "bodies . . . of the finer sort."[18]

Nietzsche 1: Relativity.   There have been voices of dissent from this tradition, in which beauty has been used as the means of communicating and legitimating one supposedly objective authority after another. Most eloquently, Nietzsche, turning orthodoxy on its head as he did so often, insisted that the time had come for philosophy to justify itself to art. Inasmuch as the philosophy of the aesthetic had so often been concerned with the regulation of feelings, the achievement of control over emotions, and the smothering of the turbulent will, Nietzsche, for one, would have none of it. Here at last was a clarion call to attack the hegemony of reason in the construction of values; an agenda which has been pursued with relentless vigor over the past century.[19] Our faith in the ability either of reason or of nature to ground objective truth must now be taken to be as shaky as our faith in the ability of God or the universe to do the job.

Nietzsche 2: Certainty.   Nietzsche, however, did not surrender his desire for certainty any more than Plato or Kant. He merely transferred the locus of the fulfillment of that desire yet again, to the sense of beauty itself.[20] In Nietzsche, the mimetic aspect of the aesthetic is finally broken: the aesthetic is no longer a mirror which reveals the truth of God or reason or nature. Rather, beauty becomes a means of access to a truth that glows within us. But there is still an assumption here that the aesthetic is not contingent, that it has something objective to tell us about the world.[21] In Nietzsche's philosophy, moreover, a mighty ego was at work.[22] When he wrote that "it is only as an *aesthetic phenomenon* that existence and the world are eternally *justified*,"[23] he was by no means speaking as a relativist. Nietzsche believed in the objective validity of his *own* perception of beauty. Ironically, Nietzsche is at one with Kant on this point, for Kant too declared that in claiming that something is beautiful we are making a judgment which demands universal assent.[24] Though their visions of the beautiful differed radically, both transformed their egotistical desire for an objective basis to their own feelings into a fundamental principle.

The Objectivity of Beauty 1: Introduction. This desire for objective truth about the world (born, perhaps, of a fear of uncertainty which often finds expression in a distrust of emotions and the subjective)[25] has constantly underpinned the philosophy of aesthetics, though the way in which it has fulfilled this desire has varied through the ages. Yet surely any attempt to reduce the aesthetic to the status of a dependent variable—a singer in the song of God, reason, or nature—must now seem contrived. To some extent this realization gave birth to the modern tradition which we find in and after Walter Pater, wherein the conjunction of aesthetics with ideas or truth has been abandoned in favor of a focus on the very experience of beauty and the phenomenology of the feelings it engenders.[26] But we are not yet home and hosed. Grant autonomy to the aesthetic as a discrete "universe of discourse,"[27] and the Voyager-like quest for certainty in that universe has not yet been extinguished. Indeed, from Aristotle on, a current of writers has attempted to establish the objectivity of aesthetics not in terms of other discourses, of logic or of ethics, but in its own terms.[28] Still we are engaged in a quest for something absolute and unchanging, although now we do not wish to know whether an aesthetic judgment is (really) true or (really) right but whether it is (really) beautiful.

The Objectivity of Beauty 2: Beardsley. Working in this tradition, Monroe Beardsley argues that a "true" judgment of aesthetic merit can be achieved by evaluating an artwork in the light of three variables: unity, complexity, and intensity. Put succinctly, the more that a work of art possesses all these qualities, according to Beardsley, the greater its intrinsic aesthetic value.[29] This is helpful; it certainly aids in our appreciation of a work of art to consider these aspects. Beardsley, however, would go further and argue that these criteria allow us to make an objective judgment of the work. Such an assertion of universally applicable "general canons" or rules is surely wrong. Unity and diversity are both, in the appropriate context, virtues, as are differing degrees of complexity and simplicity, intensity or passivity. What we mean by aesthetics cannot include reference to some objective criteria of value, since so much of our response is contingent on the particular work and its context.

A Critique of Objectivity 1: Bach.   What of the prelude? Could anything be less complex in design or realization? And yet an extra note, the introduction of another variable, would flaw the experience it creates. Beardsley would argue that its simplicity is compensated for by its great unity and intensity.[30] This grievously misdescribes the experience: its simplicity is not a defect overcome or a disadvantage outweighed—it is the very heart of its magnetic power and beauty, as it is also, perhaps, in some of the paintings of Mark Rothko. We have something of a test case in relation to the prelude, since the Romantic composer Gounod added a tune to the words of "Ave Maria" above Bach's harmonic ground, leaving the latter untouched. The unity and intensity of the original are surely unimpaired; all that has been added are various levels of complexity. But as beautiful as the Gounod is, who would suggest that it therefore betters Bach?

A Critique of Objectivity 2: Mothersill.   When we are faced with the particularity—the uniqueness—of a work of art, no principles can predict our experience or judge its effect. Beardsley's canons may provide us with a language in which we can describe why we like something, but they cannot provide us with reasons to guide our judgment beforehand. A "law" or a "principle" of aesthetics would be a proposition, whether universally applicable or only particular to an individual, which could define for us what it is about an artwork that makes it aesthetically appealing. Mary Mothersill argues, however, that "nothing I have learned from past experience gives me grounds for saying in advance of a work by Bach . . . that provided it manifests a particular feature, I will be pleased by it." The merit of a poem or a piece of music is so specific to it that nothing we could say about why we like it could help us assess or predict the merit of something else (equally specific).[31] There are no criteria that can allow us to determine as a rule whether something is aesthetically pleasing or otherwise.

THE SENSORY

The Aesthetic 1: And Art.   We must conclude, therefore, that any hope that the aesthetic is a representation of objective truth, or even that beauty itself can be defined, must be set aside. Let us move, then, from the content of the aesthetic to its process. The right question is not what the aesthetic communicates to us but *how* it does so. As Hans-Georg Gadamer and John Dewey emphasize, the aesthetic at its heart involves an experience or process of sensory perception, whether the experience is that of an artist or an audience.[32] Crucially, such a perception is not limited to things which we choose to classify as works of art, or even to things that are beautiful. Rather, we are dealing with a *way* of experiencing which always has something in common with the heightened way in which we approach "art" but is nonetheless present to some degree at every moment of our lives.[33] By examining art and the artist, as I do in the sections that follow, I intend to illuminate what aesthetic perception is about, but I do not intend to limit it.[34] In fact, John Dewey in *Art as Experience*, a tellingly named book, insists that if we wish to understand art, "we must begin with it in the raw."[35] The aesthetic aspect is central to every experience of our lives in which we become involved, through sensory perception, with the communicative power of rituals and objects. Art but heightens that quotidian experience.

The Aesthetic 2: And Creation. The idea of human intention or agency, therefore, is not a necessary element of the aesthetic. We can and do experience a jar or a textbook aesthetically, though they may have been created with nothing but functionality in mind; we hearken to the sounds of a river and gaze rapt at the colors of a sunset, though no human being was responsible for their composition. But in addressing these objects aesthetically, we treat them *as if* they were so willed. Intention is therefore important in how we look at an aesthetic object, although it may well be a hypothetical or fictional intentionality. They are treated *as if* they were created by somebody, though we may know that this assumption is purely notional or attribute it to the workings of our own mind or the mind of God. To the extent that Stanley Cavell insists on the relevance of actual intention, he is clearly defending a theory of art as opposed to one of aesthetics.[36] In the discussion that follows, in which I treat the artwork as a template for the aesthetic, the relationship of the artist to her product is to be construed as a metaphor for the nature of the aesthetic and not a literal truth.

The Sensory Aesthetic 1: Presentational. Once we reject the ideal of an objective or transhistorical content to aesthetic experience, as I have argued, with what are we left? Aesthetics is a way of knowing. We are not in the realm of the rational or the literal. This is not to say that it has no meaning for us—the question of meaning is something to which I will return in due course—but that the mode by which we apprehend this meaning is not through argument. Its meaning comes from its presentation and its form.[37] The aesthetic speaks to our senses and not our intellect; our emotions and not our logic are engaged.

The Sensory Aesthetic 2: Emotional. When we are moved by a piece of music, as grand as opera or as microcosmic as a Bach prelude, it is the sensory part of us which is addressed, although its power traverses the whole of our being. As Terry Eagleton writes, "aesthetics is born as a discourse of the body," taking its origin from the Greek *aisthesis,* "the whole region of human perception and sensation."[38] The sense of beauty, to use the title of a celebrated book by George Santayana, is as physical and emotional as the senses that inform it.[39] The effect of color and movement and sound on us, the way in which songs or smells evoke the emotional resonance of the past, the power of an image to sway us or persuade us[40]—by understanding the force of this kind of communication we begin to recognize the strength of the aesthetic in all our lives.

Senses and Culture 1: Vision. Two aspects of the particular sensory priorities of Western culture are worth noting. First, in modern Western society, vision dominates our sensory array. Other cultures set great store by the senses of hearing, of touch, and even of smell as means of access to the world. For us, "seeing is believing"; the rest of that old saw ("but touching's the truth") has been long forgotten. This is part and parcel of the linear and discursive turn of the Western mind, for vision is the most abstract and the most logical of the senses.[41] It is because of the hegemony of sight that I have deliberately chosen to begin my analysis with a piece of music.

Senses and Culture 2: Language. Second, the dominance of the ordered and the rational in our culture is further evidenced in the unprecedented authority attached to the written word. The consequences of this focus on abstract semiotics, itself further abstracted and commodified by the use of alphabetic script, have resounded through the centuries.[42] This is not to say, however, that language has in some way been stripped of its aesthetic element. Language too appeals not just to the faculty of reason but to the senses. There is an aural and rhetorical element to language, which finds expression in the pervasive use of metaphor, itself often the transposition of an image or a sound. Poetry draws our attention to the aesthetic and emotive elements of language, but they are to be found in every sentence and every document. As we shall discover, there is aesthetic in a legal text no less than in a play by Shakespeare, in the sound of a word and the look of a page and the feel of a book.[43]

The Aesthetic Object 1: Abstract or Concrete.   Aesthetics is sensational, but it is not anarchic. Our aesthetic attention is absorbed by a specific phenomenological object (whether the object in question is a piece of music or a pot).[44] As Santayana put it, beauty is value *objectified.* This is the sense in which the aesthetic is objective: not that it is universal or impartial but that it is experienced as if it were a quality to be found in a thing or object itself.[45] Aesthetics, says Thomas Munro (supporting Beardsley), brackets the thing from its surroundings: it places a frame around a picture, covers on a book, a proscenium arch on a stage.[46] In Kant, the observed object and the observant subject confront each other in a space entirely purified of function. In this theory, aesthetics is the science of the abstraction of essences, the appreciation of an object divorced from its context and valued purely for itself. But against this, we find Martin Heidegger, according to whom the aesthetic experience, whatever the object which inspires it, is based upon its "thingness," its material reality.[47] For Heidegger, the thing is not to be purified but grounded—it is not a collection of disembodied Platonic essences but rather a dweller in our midst. "Much closer to us than all sensations are the things themselves. We hear the door shut in the house and never hear acoustical sensations or even mere sounds."[48] Even abstract forms have this concrete character. Lines (the softness of a curve, the sharpness of a table edge) and colors (the green grass, the blue sky) carry with them a resonance with those objects of our experience that epitomize them for us.[49]

   The Aesthetic Object 2: Artwork or Equipment.   The art in an artwork, according to Heidegger, is not then a pure abstraction of shape or line or color devoid of context, but neither do we thus treat it as a mere piece of equipment. This is a fruitful distinction to make. In a tool, color, surface, material, and so on "disappear in usefulness"—they are treated merely as means toward a functional end—while in the work of art they remain present for contemplation.[50] It is the distinction between walking and dancing.[51] In between the utilitarian view of objects which requires form to be subservient to function and the Platonic idea expressed by Beardsley and much favored by nineteenth-century aesthetes lies a more accurate description of how we actually engage with an object aesthetically.

The Person and the Object 1: Thesis.   How can we get closer to the meaning of this paradox? Consider Kant, according to whom human beings are entitled to respect in the light of which they are to be treated purely as ends in themselves and never as means. Slavery or hostage-taking takes this respect away because people are treated precisely as if they were pieces of equipment, to be used for others' ends. Now for Hegel the free will of the person is compromised by this disrespect. Human beings have the capacity for agency and are therefore only to be treated as ends, while everything else, necessarily lacking free will, can properly be treated as means. It is, moreover, in the exercise of our will over things that our capacity for agency finds self-expression.[52] For Hegel, "things" are that with which we can do what we will and into which we place our will in every act of creation, or possession, or use. In all these ways we necessarily treat "the thing in its subservience to human preoccupations."[53]

The Person and the Object 2: Antithesis.   For Hegel, the "thing" is just a passive receptacle of human will. There is an unpleasant prejudice here, since he treats the environment, the land, and all its creatures as reducible to human needs. But Heidegger would turn Hegel on his head and interpret *every* thing in terms of its soul. Rather than seeing the thing as an extension of the will, Heidegger treats it as possessed of a self of its own. A pair of shoes, a painting, a jug, are all treated as possessing a self, which by and large we associate only with humans. As against Hegel's anthropocentrism, then, stands Heidegger's anthropomorphism. There is a clear conflict of understanding here, which seems to map in a significant way the difference between Kant's understanding of personhood and Hegel's of the object. Hegel's harsh perspective stems from the very dichotomy between person and thing which Heidegger rejects.

Attitudes to Aesthetics 1: The Drive to Create.   As contradictory as these perspectives are, there is a point of synthesis. Hegel's notion of placing your will into a thing, artificial as it sounds, is true of the experience of the artist. Yet at the same time, for the artist, the person and the thing stand together. As Heidegger saw, there is something human in the object of our creation. The potter at her wheel or the musician in whose hands mute wood or brass begins to speak—their need and their product alike are an externalization of the will. That, after all, is the meaning of "expression": a transfer of something from inside to out. The drive to create is the desire to convert ourselves and our experience of the world into a tangible metaphor.[54] And when the song is sung, the quilt made up, the building built, we say that there is "a little bit of ourselves" in every stanza, stitch, or stanchion.

Attitudes to Aesthetics 2: An Object of Respect.   In relation to the work of art, Hegel and Heidegger are both right, and perhaps a shadow of this truth pervades everything about us. After all, the relationship of artist to artwork, though marked by a unique intensity, is no different in kind from the experience of the audience.[55] Anything we experience aesthetically transcends the use or value assigned to it by others. Rather, it is treated as a function of the human (or notional or imagined) will it instantiates. But, Hegel to the contrary, a thing, considered as art, is no mere shadow of its author. A creation is indeed a child, albeit a child of the will and not the body. No more than children are they clones of the desire that gave them birth; rather, they come alive and develop a personality of their own. They become imbued with the breath of life. As Kant would say, the work of art— and, by extension, any object looked upon in this way—is entitled, through the will that we imagine having endowed it and the life that is in it, to be treated as an end in itself. Concepts such as being faithful to a play, listening to a piece of music, or treating an antique or a landscape with respect, all make sense the moment we appreciate, with Stanley Cavell, that aesthetics involves treating objects as having attained a quasi-personhood. Hegel's understanding of its production together with Heidegger's understanding of its existence combine to require its treatment with something akin to Kant's idea of respect. "They mean something to us, not just the way statements do, but the way people do."[56]

Aesthetic Distance 1: Philosophy.   There is a further objection to this argument. Attempting to preserve the idea of form without content, or design without meaning, Kant, among many others, has argued for the idea of an "aesthetic distance."[57] It was an idea which found a particular resonance in the ascetic and tubercular sensibilities of the Romantics.[58] On this understanding, aesthetic appreciation requires a certain disengagement, in which we discount as much as possible our own personal circumstances and values and meet the object of our gaze on somehow neutral turf. Schopenhauer, as scared by desire as by will, sought escape in the lustless world of "those admirable Dutch artists" whose pictures of "still life" (*natur mort*) provided him with a "peaceful, still, frame of mind . . . free from will."[59] Aesthetics, then, is disembodied, incorporeal, and conceptual.

Aesthetic Distance 2: Music.   Let us return to the world of the artist to evaluate this claim. A pianist goes through a period in which mind and body have to be focused exclusively on the mechanics of note production. But at some point this conscious decision making ceases to be necessary, and one can observe one's fingers executing the music. The music seems to play itself. There is perhaps a kind of distance here that supports Kant's notion of a purified, formal space and Schopenhauer's idea of a mind free from will. This stage of automatism, though necessary, is not, however, the end of the matter. The real experience of piano playing—the real experience of the aesthetic—has no analogy with a pianola, in which the keys move up and down apart from one's volition.[60] There is an important underlying assumption here, according to which the meaning of the aesthetic object is singular and needs only to be correctly deciphered—a sequence of specific notes, played at a certain speed, will tell you all there is to know. The theory of decipherment treats meaning as "in" the music and the performer as a dentist, skilled in the art of extraction.

Critique of Distance 1: Relationship.   Music is not a code. It is a relationship. There is a dialectic established between performer and composition (and so too between listener and performance) in which the performer (or listener) becomes joined with the music, so that the will or sensibility it expresses becomes indistinguishable from her own. When Thomas Aquinas says beauty is that which the apprehension itself (*apprehensio ipsa*) pleases, there is an engagement implied in that word *apprehensio* which should not be taken lightly.[61] Apprehension goes far beyond observation: to apprehend is to detain, to arrest; to fear, as of the unknown; as well as to understand. Perhaps these meanings are all related, and the understanding it describes involves a holding fast of the object, and a fear of its otherness, before finally grappling and overcoming that resistance. Between the work of art on the one hand and the performer or observer on the other, there is a synthesis, in which the work has been truly grasped and remade. As each speaks through and with the other, the distinction between the language of the player and the language of the music evaporates. In this relationship, the performer's perspective is not left behind but is used to inform and transform the music, as it does likewise in return.

Critique of Distance 2: Hermeneutics.   Relationship is the key word— and here we must progress beyond Heidegger's conception of the "thing" as elemental and essentially phenomenological in character.[62] Aesthetic meaning, like the meaning of language, is never given or unmediated: it is always hermeneutic, a process of translation and therefore a dynamic of participation.[63] Indeed, this is Gadamer's central insight, although it applies far beyond the aesthetic: meaning is found not in the dichotomy between subject and object, a dichotomy assumed by Kant and Schiller no less than by Heidegger and Beardsley, but in their relation. We are not beings in the world in the way that a chair is "in" the room but rather as one is in love or in motion.[64]

THE CULTURAL

Objective Interpretation 1: Bracketing the Self.   Thomas Munro explains the aesthetic as a combination of perception (the sensory phase) and apperception, the interpretive phase involving the "perception of meaning."[65] Whether playing the piano or walking in the mountains, the self is engaged, and our experiences cannot be bracketed or left at home. Now I come to the heart of what I mean by an "aesthetic dimension." Beardsley and the New Critics, like Kant, insist that when we make an assessment of the aesthetic merit of a work of art, it is improper to treat as relevant either the personal associations or memories which become attached to a piece or, on the other hand, the life experiences or politics or supposed intentions of the artist.[66] Mothersill likewise argues that the personal and the political have no place in the discourse of the beautiful. For Mothersill, as opposed to Beardsley, beauty is subjective. But she argues that it is a discourse which ought be confined to talking about the pleasures we get in contemplating "the thing itself," apart altogether from the context or personal or cultural background which envelops it. Thus for Mothersill, only certain aspects of a thing relate to its beauty—its line but not your memories, its color not its history. She does not wish to determine what in fact counts as beautiful but rather to limit the properties in relation to which a claim of beauty can properly be made.[67]

Objective Interpretation 2: A Critique.   The gravitas of the discussion in the previous section, however, is that aesthetics is our sensory engagement (giving weight to both those words) with the world. It is a way of experiencing things and not just a way of judging them, though the experience draws forth the judgment. If this is so, Beardsley's and Mothersill's distinctions alike must fall to the ground. How could we even imagine the parenthetical suspension of aspects of our self in the process of aesthetic judgment if this judgment is by definition hermeneutic and relational?[68] As Santayana has argued, the values which we find expressed in beauty come from within us, though they are experienced as if they belonged to the object itself.[69] For Mothersill and Beardsley alike there is an altogether too naive and pedantic distinction being drawn between the characteristics of "the object" and the characteristics brought to it by the person contemplating it.[70] Aesthetic experience is never neutral: it is the subjective and personal sensory engagement with an object or moment. Just as Stanley Cavell has argued, the philosophy of aesthetics' refusal to take seriously the response to the aesthetic object constitutes its most profound failure.[71]

The Personal Object 1: As Discourse.   I want to establish the relevance of, first, the personal history of the observer in this aesthetic process and, second, the cultural history of the object. First, as we have seen, Mothersill argues for an objectivity of discourse: although "associations may enhance or, on the other hand, inhibit delight,"[72] these associations are not relevant to an object's aesthetics. It is true that such personal associations are unlikely to be widely shared. My memories of the first time I heard the Bach prelude hardly constitute a reason for anybody else to appreciate it.[73] For persuasive purposes, then, we tend to talk about those aspects of a piece of music shared by a whole audience—its tone, its contours, its structure, even its unity, complexity, and intensity.[74]

The Personal Object 2: As Experience.   But yet again this confuses what we say about something—the criteria by which we claim to judge it—with how we experience it. The aesthetic, as I have argued, is to be understood as a *process* of understanding and therefore ineluctably subjective. My actual experience of the prelude is absolutely contingent on the memories which I associate with it, and while they do not provide reasons for others to feel as I do, they are nonetheless potent to me. Text, performance, and interpretation are inextricably linked. As Dewey understood so well, the object is the raw material of aesthetic experience but not its sole determinant.[75] Mothersill responds that although personal connotations are inevitable, they are not aesthetic criteria. But this is exactly how they are experienced. Personal associations are indissolubly linked to the way I hear the prelude and I cannot tell you how much the meditative mood it now creates is a product of one or the other. As the aesthetic synthesizes form and content, particular and universal, it binds subject and object together into a new and greater unity.

The Cultural Object 1: Negative Connotations.   Second, neither the cultural associations nor the history of the object itself are irrelevant to our aesthetic reaction to a work. For many Jews, the music of Wagner holds a special place of obloquy. Until recently the Israel Philharmonic refused to play any of his works. The cause of this antipathy is both historical and political, based partly on the realities of Wagner's life and music and partly on the use made of it by the Third Reich. None of this directly impinges on the feeling or beauty of his music had it been written by someone else, and someone who claimed to hate Wagner without ever listening to him could not be said to be judging by aesthetic criteria. But for many people this is not the case. When they listen to Wagner, these connotations arise unbidden and imbue the music with a symbolic meaning redolent of authoritarianism and oppression. The music is experienced as repulsive or fearsome and though the associations are cultural or political, they are experienced in aesthetic terms. They form an ineluctable part of the way in which listening takes place.

The Cultural Object 2: Positive Connotations.   And what of the opposite, where the circumstances of the production and origin of the work of art deepen our appreciation of it? We know the legend of how Mozart came to write his own Requiem,[76] the pauper's grave agape before him. Does this mythology not add a depth of feeling to our understanding of this work, a certain melancholy to be sure, but, more, a reminder to us of the human and concrete reality of death? I do not simply mean that these pieces of information about the author or his life and times add to what we get out of the work but that they are part of the work as it presents itself to our senses. Just as Mozart's experiences of life were instantiated in the music he wrote, giving it a specific shape and sound, our reception of those experiences (which will of course differ from person to person) informs how each of us listens and what we hear. We do not listen with our ears only but with our minds and with a whole cultural framework which sustains us.

The Cultural Reception of a Pair of Shoes 1: A Narrative.   Let us consider more closely the interaction of the personal meaning of an object, the cultural background which informs it, and the narratives which are told about it: the interpenetration of times, societies, and individuals in the apperceptive aesthetic experience.[77] Take two boots. They are old and encrusted with dirt. Now Van Gogh draws and paints them with a palette rich in the ruddy colors of the earth—*Old Shoes with Laces.* Heidegger sees the painting and weaves around it a narrative of particular force in the context of German culture. He writes of how they embody "the toilsome tread of the worker . . . the accumulated tenacity of her slow trudge," the earth's "quiet gift of ripening grain and its unexplained self-refusal in the fallow desolation of the wintry field."[78] Clearly the peasant poetry incited by his sensory engagement with those boots is real and moving. Yet it is perilous for him to say that "the artwork let us know what shoes are in truth."[79] His is an interpretation drawn forth by apprehension of the aesthetic object and informed by his personal experience and cultural location. The truth-claim that Heidegger makes for his interpretation is only that conceit by which the aesthetic has so often been tainted, converting a particular kind of subjective experience into a claim of objective truth.

The Cultural Reception of a Pair of Shoes 2: A Reflection. Now Meyer Schapiro joins the debate, convinced on the contrary that the shoes are the painter's own. Schapiro constructs a very different story centered on the hardship of Van Gogh's life. It is a critique written in the aftermath of World War II. The shadow of Nazi Germany has fallen over Heidegger's commentary, and indirectly over the painting itself.[80] A generation later, Jacques Derrida enters the fray, denying both their assumptions as to the origin of the work of art. Why do these shoes belong to either the artist or a peasant? Why are they a pair? Why should we assume that they even existed? Derrida uses the discourse about Van Gogh's painting as a way of demonstrating the detachable and contextual nature of meaning and the way in which truth itself is "hallucinogenic."[81] And at the far end of this discursive chain I stand and gaze at a picture in the Museum of Modern Art —*Old Shoes with Laces.* In the looking, these different and historical ways of seeing enrich my aesthetic engagement with the work. The image of the boots now presents to me all these suggestive symbols and narratives. What makes this interpretation aesthetic is the nature of the experience—a sensory response to a particular object approached with openness and respect. At the same time, however, the aesthetic is in no sense objective, and though it relates to a particular way of experiencing the object, we cannot circumscribe or prohibit the factors which give it meaning.

The Epistemological Development of Modernism 1: Renaissance. Let us place this subjective approach to the meaning of aesthetic experience within a broader cultural framework. Any aesthetic object, any idea of beauty, is embedded within such a framework.[82] Its values are themselves constructed by and against that society.[83] According to Foucault, the Classical age, at the dawn of modernism, marks a transformation in epistemology from a worldview in which knowledge is attained by the exploration of representations to one in which it is developed by processes of classification. Metaphorically speaking, there is a shift from the idea of the world as a code to that of a table or chart. During the Renaissance, every thing was seen in terms of its resemblance to everything else. The sign of a thing—its look, its shape, its sound—was nowhere treated as random or coincidental but rather as aspects of the essential connection between all things, in a world created by God to bear testimony to his truth. The practice of medicine, for example, was governed by a belief in such hints and connections. The walnut was thought to be good for the brain because the two looked somewhat alike, and this mere resemblance was treated as a sign of a deeper affinity.[84]

The Epistemological Development of Modernism 2: Classicism.   Not so for the Classicists of the eighteenth century. Here there is a double movement: first, toward distinguishing things from each other and thus charting relationships in terms of the singular and irreducible differences between them, and, second, toward finding the common building blocks or units on the basis of which these differences could be definitively measured. "This relation to *Order* is as essential to the Classical age as the relation to *Interpretation* was to the Renaissance."[85] The study of wealth, for example, moves from a direct comparison of the value of two disparate things (in the light of which the question of how to distinguish in advance the relative value of, say, wine and wheat cannot arise) to a precise ordering of their difference in terms of a base unit by which everything within the system may be measured—a currency, whether coinage or (in Ricardo) land.[86] Examples could be multiplied. Across the epistemological field, space is made uniform, identity modular, and difference measurable. Everything can be reduced to a base unit (the building blocks on which difference is built) and compared in terms of it. From a world in which knowledge is discovered through representation and interpreted analogically we approach a world in which it is learned through ordering and imposed digitally.

Foucault and Music 1: Musicology.   Foucault nowhere discusses the history of music from this perspective, but it is an intriguing possibility. It is only at the dawn of modernism that mean temperament and the incommensurable "modes" of medieval music gave way to equal temperament and a system built on major and minor scales. The scale system re-created the language of music in commodity form, repeatable and interchangeable, in much the same way as hieroglyphics were replaced by a commodified alphabetic script.[87] Equal temperament accomplished this by instituting the semitone as the base unit of musical exchange, the atom on which all Western musical difference was built.[88] The semitone is to music as the coin is to economics; and every semitone is equal to every other semitone, just as every penny is precisely equal to every other penny. It is this equality of unit which allows keys to become a currency, exchanged through transposition and measured through intervals. None of this was true before the Classical age.

Foucault and Music 2: The Well-Tempered Clavier.   Bach's *Well-Tempered Clavier*, emerging at the heart of this Classical age (in music, confusingly, the term "classicism" is used to denote a rather more specific and slightly later style), was specifically composed to proclaim, celebrate, and support these changes, its schedule of preludes and fugues rising by a uniform semitone at a time and alternating methodically between major and minor keys. The first prelude of the *Well-Tempered Clavier* captures this new epistemology. A note, uniform and modular, which serves as the unchanging structure on which every harmony is built; a bar, the one succeeding the other in steady progression, creating an order against which differences are played out and can be measured with precision. At every level of its being, Bach's first prelude and the *Well-Tempered Clavier* embody classification, calibration, the modular construction of meaning, and the interplay of identity and difference mapped onto a uniform field or grid. It is the epitome of the period of its creation; and of the period, too, of its continuing reception and appreciation. If we hear it now and marvel at its steady eloquence, it is in part the sound of the Enlightenment which it heralds that moves us. The desire for order, the search for patterns, a feeling of the world as composed of units of sameness and movements of difference: the prelude expresses, to our senses and in presentational form, an alphabetic semiology of notes,[89] a taxonomy of harmonies, an economy of tonalities. And we are products in our own way of the same modernist discipline. It has ordered and regulated us, creating contemporary human subjects both equal and well tempered.[90] The aesthetic power of the first prelude stands as both a sublime and a subliminal prophecy of the ideals of modernist order and control.

THE SYMBOLIC

The Symbolism of the Aesthetic 1: Introduction.   What we learn from such an analysis is a double refrain. First, that the creation and reception of aesthetic forms are contingent and socialized. Heidegger writes of "the thing"[91] but Foucault only of *The Order of Things* (originally, *Les Mots et les Choses*, an even more relativist statement) since for him reality emerges only in the structure and nomenclature which arises from the application of a varying and contingent epistemology.[92] The prelude grew out of Bach's culture, just as its iconic status grows out of ours. Second, it is impossible to dissociate beauty or the appreciation of form from this question of meaning both personal and cultural, subjective and intersubjective—even in art as abstract as music, even in music as abstract as Bach's, even in Bach as abstract as the prelude.[93] Aesthetics understood as a way of knowing is therefore the conjunction of two aspects: the sensory force, with which we engage something, and the symbolic meanings, which become attached to it. The heart of the process of aesthetic experience is this union of senses and symbols—of the utterly present and the necessarily absent (for a symbol, like the imagination, can work only on what is absent).[94] The object is a well of symbols which we apprehend in presentational form.[95]

The Symbolism of the Aesthetic 2: Kinds of Symbols.   This symbolism will include elements which are deeply embedded in our personal experiences and memories and others which are cultural and more or less shared. The object becomes a symbol for other symbols, an image of other imagery. As we see and live, we bring to the events around us the affinities and tone that we have come to associate with similar experiences. "The hushed reverberations of these associated feelings" construct an aesthetic reaction to the present.[96] To insist instead on the formal qualities of an object of aesthetic contemplation divorced from the symbolic meanings with which it is imbued[97] treats the aesthetic in a way which is strangely weak and placid.[98] For the power of symbols in all our lives is immense, amply demonstrated in the intensity of feeling which greets activities as diverse as the burning of flags or books or old love letters—symbolic obliterations perpetrated upon symbolic objects.

Aesthetic Communication 1: Incomplete.   The aesthetic is a mode of symbolic communication.[99] But neither is it purely semiotic.[100] This is what Cleanth Brooks so memorably termed "the heresy of paraphrase":[101] the assumption that it is possible to exhaustively decipher the symbolism of an artwork and thus to prise its meaning from its form. Cavell is surely correct to argue that a metaphor is paraphrasable to the extent that its meaning can be explained; but it cannot be fully explained, and it contains a pregnancy of meaning that cannot be predicted or defined.[102] Even more so in the work of art, the aesthetic symbol is bound up in the object or image that contains it; they arrive together and stay together.[103] Its focus is on a particular object or image and on the experience or process of apprehending that object. Cavell writes that the definition of a work of art is just that which "can only be known in sensing."[104] Thus the aesthetic appeals not to our judgment of truth or logic but to our senses. It finds expression not in a judgment of goodness or rightness but rather in a force of attraction or repulsion. Its meaning is imparted uniquely, experienced uniquely, and expressed uniquely. It is exactly because of these unique characteristics of aesthetics as a way of knowing that it touches depths of our understanding otherwise unplumbed.

Aesthetic Communication 2: Discourse.   The power and influence of the aesthetic is often greeted with dismay because of the ungrounded relativism it seems to imply. Postmodernists such as Jean-François Lyotard, on the one hand, and their critics, on the other, have both tended to see the aesthetic as based on nothing more than a kind of "transcendent" intuition, as radically given as the human body: an incorrigible feeling to whose dictates we have no choice but to succumb. The cultural and symbolic approach to the origin and function of the aesthetic which I have been advocating, however, does not treat the aesthetic as non-negotiable and does not require us to treat all aesthetic values as equal.[105] As Cavell so rightly argues, aesthetics is not simply a question of personal preference. There is relevance and irrelevance, coherency and incoherency, in their discussion. Suppose you thought that a performer's interpretation of Beethoven or Bach had no line or structure. Would you not think that my response, "Well, *I* liked it" was "a feeble rejoinder, a *retreat* to personal taste"?[106] Aesthetic values and understanding are as appropriate a subject of argument, experience, and change as everything else. To concede, as one so often hears, that there is no room for argument in matters of taste is facile counsel. The aesthetic is neither logic nor psychology but a discourse all its own.

The Pervasive Aesthetic 1: Bourdieu.　Exactly because the aesthetic is best understood as a way of knowing and of being, it envelops our lives: it affects how we view not just Van Gogh's shoes but our own. In this way, my analysis of music and of art has been intended to clarify the nature of aesthetic knowledge by focusing on a specialized intensification of it and never thus to confine its relevance. We are always undertaking aesthetic judgments of this kind, consciously or otherwise; in how we listen to the traffic as much as how we listen to Bach; in the symbols and imagery conjured up by certain words or phrases. This is Dewey's point, but even more so it is closely aligned to the work of Pierre Bourdieu, according to whom the "bodily hexis" is a kind of corporeal sense or collection of habits of the body, which predispose our thinking and reproduce power.[107] "The body," wrote Bourdieu, "is the site of incorporated history."[108] Lest this sounds too determinist, the aesthetic also offers a broad vista for accomplishing profound change. It is important to draw attention to the role of senses and symbols in our lives. But this is not purely an analytic point. People can be changed by appealing to their aesthetic values, and their aesthetic values no less than their political or ethical values can be commented on and argued about. Aesthetic experience is a way of knowing, and a way of changing, too.

The Pervasive Aesthetic 2: From Bach to Law.　In short, the aesthetic realm suffuses our engagement with everything about us. It is a union of senses and symbols—a register of seeing and of speaking and at the same time a registry of symbols. It is part of what it means to be a human being, part of our relationship to the world, part of our inner temperament.[109]

And to be well tempered is surely to be attuned to this aspect of ourselves, to think about how it affects us, to be aware of its power, and to explore how it might be harnessed as a force for good. Reason and aesthetics stand not in hostile counterpoint. Each in its own way is engaged in making of the bare bones of life a human being. Nothing remains untouched by the aesthetic temperament—not even that most ostensibly rational of human endeavors, the law. The well-tempered lawyer must reflect on how our aesthetics interprets the law, on the one hand, and influences it, on the other. And one might even ask whether the law, were it well tempered, might be changed, might engage differently with the objects and subjects beneath its gaze. These are the questions, of some perplexity and interest, which will guide me as I embark as a voyager into the aesthetic dimensions of law and justice.

Fugue

A Prospectus for the Aesthetic Dimension

THE FUGUE AS METAPHOR

For every prelude there is a fugue; for every simple theme, a complex and polyphonic development awaits.[1] If the prelude represents the leisurely unfolding of an idea, the fugue expresses a fervent layering of thought. A musician from the Netherlands once said to me that he thought a fugue was just a malfunctioning canon. Somewhat defensively, I replied that a fugue was no more a kind of malfunctioning canon than the Dutch are a species of malfunctioning Germans. In fact, the fugue is one of the most elaborate and enduring forms of counterpoint. It begins with great simplicity—a single unadulterated line of melody (a subject) which is nothing more than a fragment—and one by one adds (vocal or instrumental) voices, each in turn first declaiming and then commenting upon the fragment. The subject is tossed from part to part, from register to register, sometimes merely restated and sometimes varied, each part keeping all the while its individuality. The ideas of a fugue, its subject and those that play against it, are not blended but rather stratified. Against the prelude which precedes it, the fugue represents an intensified use of melodic and harmonic musical resources.[2] It is a more richly textured and intricately faceted articulation of musical ideas.

A fugue then is an experiment: trying out a musical idea with different voices and different tonalities—sung first in the tenor, perhaps, then in turns by alto, soprano, bass—overlapping it with other voices, doubling and halving its speed, reading it back to front or upside down.[3] But there is also something matter of fact about the fugue, which begins with such a clear statement of its subject and reiterates it so insistently. The theme is, in its variety, at all times recognizable, although, unlike the structure of a theme and variations, for example, its different aspects are developed not discursively but simultaneously in different voices. Perhaps the best way to distinguish the feeling of a prelude and a fugue is that, where the prelude is suggestive, the fugue is declaratory.

At the same time, a fugue typically uses "episodes" to break up the various voices' intense statements of the subject matter. In an episode, a particular aspect of the subject is explored in more detail. The fugue intersperses the theoretical with the concrete and the general with the particular. Its strength lies in its ability to present a subject—on the one hand to explore it and to present it in a variety of contexts and on the other hand to contrast it with other, balancing and related, ideas—while never attempting to subsume all these different aspects and contrasts into one homogeneous line.[4] This is how the aesthetic dimensions of law and justice (or "legal aesthetics") will be explored.

THE FUGAL SUBJECT

The Aesthetic Dimensions of Law

Sensory experience, beauty, and form are powerful influences in our lives, and symbolism imbues this power with meaning. A reaction to the form or beauty of something, no doubt, often arises unbidden from the depths of our being, demanding our assent. So "the aesthetic" is about how these realms of understanding come to deeply affect us. But the aesthetic also has force because of the intense web of symbols—some idiosyncratic and some firmly authorized by the cultures to which we belong—which we all carry around within us.

These elements of our aesthetic experience are crucial to our functioning. It would appear that most cases of autism, even among those with remarkable ability, involve an absence of exactly these features: there is a lack of aesthetic appreciation, a dulling of emotional affect, and an apparent inability to understand symbolic and conventional meaning. Our culture is autistic.[5] When Marcel Duchamp put a urinal or a bicycle wheel in an art gallery, the irony was surely double edged, for it brought into focus not only how we look at "works of art" but how we fail to look at everything else, how we pigeonhole and marginalize aesthetic meaning. Once one acknowledges that the aesthetic is not some thing to be known but a way of knowing, it becomes relevant to every corner of our lives.

The relationship to law is twofold. First, aesthetics affect the values of our communities, values which are in their turn given form and symbolism within the legal system. In the law, then, we find not only evidence of our beliefs but traces of the aesthetic concerns that have propeled them. But the converse also holds. The legal system is not merely the passive mirror of a worldview. The law is a kind of discourse whose outlook on the world takes its place as one (frequently privileged) way of perceiving events around us. If we look at a street march as an "exercise of first amendment rights" we may approve of it, while if we focused on the substantive issues behind the demonstration we might not.[6] But either way we think of the question in terms of "freedom of speech" in part because that is how the law approaches the problem. The gaze of the law influences all of us: it defines a situation in a certain way and encourages us all to look at it likewise.

To understand to what extent we are in the grip here of legal aesthetics—
a way of seeing and constructing the world—requires above all a sensitivity to language, for the law is built largely of words: statutes and cases, jurisprudence and articles make up the raw materials of its construction. Laws
are intended to have performative effects: they are expected to do something.[7] But their meaning as rhetoric, as a way of saying something, is also
important. The gaze of the law—its way of talking about problems and of
dividing up the world—influences our interpretation of the world, and we
find it revealed in the form and structure of laws and the metaphors and
imagery to be found in legal texts. An analysis of these aspects, therefore,
will tell us what a particular law or judgment actually means to a community and how it influences them.

Law, values, and aesthetics exist in a mutually constitutive relationship.
Aesthetics is not, therefore, an independent variable. Nonetheless, as with
all theory, the purpose of its study is to treat it as if it were independent, as
if its relations to the legal system could be isolated and evaluated. What
would an analysis which treated the aesthetic dimension as central to the
workings of the law look like? By treating as figure that which is normally
ground, new relations and influences can be determined, a new tool of analysis developed, and new understandings explored.

Precursors to Legal Aesthetics

Law about Aesthetics

Samuel Johnson remarked that in the service of John Donne's "metaphysical wit . . . the most heterogeneous ideas are yoked by violence together."[8]
Previous attempts to juxtapose ideas of law and aesthetics have been characterized, by and large, by little self-awareness and certainly by little appreciation of the complexities of aesthetic experience. This section surveys
and distinguishes some related interdisciplinary work as a necessary prepa-
ration for the outline of the aesthetic dimensions of law which follows.

In a narrow sense, many writers have dealt with both terms, in discussing, for example, the legal treatment of art and of the body. These we might
characterize as engaging in an examination of laws about aesthetic issues.
The question of damages for visible disfigurement, for example, certainly
touches on how the legal system deals with beauty.[9] Neither is this a simple
area. We might ask, what aesthetics of the body are embodied in law? How
does it look at how we look? Patriarchally, as for example in those cases in
which a woman's beauty and chances of remarriage following the death of
her husband have been coolly calculated by the court?[10] Or economically, as

for example in cases in which women plaintiffs have received greater damages for injuries to facial or bodily appearance than men?[11] Or subjectively, as a question of self-esteem? The courts' treatment of such issues reveals not only the traditional instrumental and economic biases of tort law but an aesthetic: a way of judging the appearance of another, on the one hand, and a way of valuing beauty, on the other. The legal system has developed a certain construction of the body which expresses the male gaze,[12] turning to object and commodity everything on which its eye alights.

Law has had to confront the question of beauty in other areas as well, in relation to the copyright of artistic material, for example, or in cases concerning the protection of the environment and freedom from "aesthetic nuisance."[13] Costas Douzinas, Shaun McVeigh, and Ronnie Warrington analyzed a court case about the proposed placement of a Henry Moore altar in a seventeenth-century church designed by Christopher Wren. In a case which dealt with the intersection of beauty and religion, the judges attempted to abjure any evaluation of either, scornfully remarking that "there are hardly any rights or wrongs in matters of aesthetics." Although they purported to decide instead on the solid grounds of semantics (the definition of an altar) and authority (the opinion of experts), the exile of aesthetics from the court of reason fails conspicuously, and the use of that enticing phrase "hardly any" foreshadows the apostasy which follows. The case finally becomes a battle of aesthetic values, between Wren and Moore, classicism and modernism.[14]

In all these instances, however, the question of the relationship of legal judgment to aesthetic judgment is raised because the case was about art or beauty. The specific subject matter in dispute seems to force aesthetics upon the law. Furthermore, the question relates to what the law says or thinks about the subject of aesthetics. There is no exploration of the intrinsic engagement of the discourses of law and aesthetics, of the aesthetic dimension of all law.

Law and . . . Aesthetics

One might expect such an exploration within or as an offshoot of the "law and literature" movement. But from the rich analyses of James Boyd White to the more reductive instrumentalism of Richard Posner, this has not been the case.[15] Literature has been used as a comparative model in more specific ways, focusing on the form of literature on the one hand (which helps us to think about the nature of language) and its subject matter on the other (which helps us to think about human nature).[16] The distinction between form and subject matter reflects also a difference between two distinct tiers of literary discourse. Literary theory deals with the question of form and contributes to law a depth of understanding about language and a variety of analyses of the problematic relationship of text and meaning. Works of literature themselves, on the other hand, by their very subject matter present complexities of human conflict which the bipolar interpretations of the legal system—right and wrong, good and bad, true and false—conceal or ignore at their peril.[17] At times, it is what literature specifically has to say about law that is interpreted for a lawyerly audience, as for example when Albert Camus or Franz Kafka is cited in debates on the malaise of justice.[18] But most often it is simply a work of literature's cultural status, familiar in its resonances yet profound in its implications, which justifies its use as evidence.

Ronald Dworkin is an example of the first tier. He is a writer for whom theories of art and literature have been influential. Dworkin has taken on board the literary criticism of objective meaning and adopts what could broadly be described as a hermeneutic approach to interpretation.[19] But for Dworkin, literature, as well as informing his appreciation of problems of interpretation, provides him with a useful metaphor. He sees a line of judicial precedents as a narrative: a "chain novel," each chapter of which has a different author. The role of a judge when faced with a new case in the course of this cooperative endeavor is, like that of a "literary critic teasing out the various dimensions of value in a complex play or poem," to read the previous installments in a way which makes sense of them all (or with most of them) and to write a new section in that spirit. Thus the narrative of the law goes on, from precedent to precedent, resembling, it must be said, not so much a novel as a soap opera.[20]

There is no space here to analyze a theory which is of considerable complexity and much glossed.[21] But while Dworkin uses art as a metaphor and literature as theory, he seems to have no real understanding of the role of aesthetics as a way of knowing, in either what laws mean or how they are produced. Even on his own terms, there is a striking simplicity to his approach. He argues that our role when confronting a work of art is not to criticize but to make it "the best it can be," to read it as kindly as possible, and that likewise we ought to strive to interpret our legal system in the best possible light.[22] But this misunderstands a hermeneutic approach, which, while it admittedly requires us to respect and participate in the tradition to which a work speaks, does not permit us to abandon our critical stance or to equate the "best reading" of something with seeing it in its "best light." This is sheer equivocation.[23]

If Dworkin is of the first tier, drawing on a theory of reading to understand case law, James Boyd White is of the second, drawing on the canons of literature. Reading specific literary texts with considerable subtlety, White treats literature as a way of improving our appreciation of law as a rhetoric which attempts to symbolically express and develop the values of a community. For White, law and ideas of justice are means of constructing healing narratives out of people's fractured lives. It is not literature as metaphor which interests White so much as its use as a resource of the truth and force of such narratives.

Here there is a stark contrast to Dworkin, who also describes law as a narrative but does not take the parallel seriously. The only voices in his narrative are those of judges, past, present, and mythological; their narration is nothing but a series of propositions about the law, laid out like bottles on a wall; interpretation is a question of consistency of meaning. In White, on the other hand, law's value, like that of literature, does not lie just in the decision rendered in a particular case but rather in the complexity and ambiguity of the judgment and in the ways in which judges try to give voice to the interwoven and differing narratives placed before them. Community is formed and advanced not simply by what is said but by how it is said. White insists upon law beyond rationality, language beyond denotation, and the polyphony of justice.[24]

Even here, however, "law" and "literature" are treated as two separate disciplines with certain aspects in common and certain things to teach each other. To think of literature as a metaphor for law's potential, which is what writers like James Boyd White do, is to have predetermined them as separate disciplines. There is no understanding of aesthetics as a way of knowing which colors each (and every) field, "law" as well as "literature." The separation which lies at the heart of the law and literature movement treats them as fit subjects for comparison but not of interaction. Rarely is there any suggestion that law might influence literature or literature change the law—ideas which become attractive immediately one ceases to treat aesthetics as a thing to be seen and instead look upon it as a way of seeing. One might even suggest that law and literature juxtaposes two nouns while the aesthetic dimensions of law explore the behavior of two verbs. In consequence, while law is said to be able to learn from literature, the aesthetics of law assumes that a relationship of inevitable interaction is already present. "Law and literature" means law *next to* literature, an argument by analogy or metaphor. The aesthetic dimension of law, on the other hand, implies that aesthetics is already in the law, an argument about the process by which we get legal meaning.

Postmodern legal theory has been marked by a resurgence of interest in aesthetics.[25] In Costas Douzinas, *Justice Miscarried: Ethics, Aesthetics, and the Law*, in particular, aesthetics is recognized as a distinct analytic perspective. Here, and in the work of Peter Goodrich among others, considerable use is made of artworks as texts through which to explore legal ideas. Not only poems and plays but paintings and architecture too are treated as creators of legal meaning, and this approach touches in innovative ways on the manner in which law is communicated through images, icons, and myths. The visual, the architectonic, and the performative context of the law all say something about what the law is about and to whom it is addressed.[26] Such a move toward the unspoken and iconic representation of law marks a significant development in legal thinking, away from a purely linguistic and literal understanding of how law is communicated.

This body of research critiques the role of traditional legal theory as part of the long history within Christianity of a distrust of images. Images were seen to be emotional, erotic, superficial, sensory. They were therefore opposed to those rational, essential, conceptual systems of meaning epitomized by Protestant religion and positivist law.[27] The reinvention and rediscovery of the relationship of aesthetics and emotion to law stands against such a tradition in order to reclaim the legitimacy of the passions and the senses as foundations of meaning and of value in law.

Yet the critical tradition which Douzinas and Goodrich have done so much to revitalize in recent years remains very much within the nascent field of what we might call "law and art." Such an approach continues to treat art, like literature, as a separate discipline to illuminate the law and not as an independent but intrinsic aspect of it. This is even more true of Gary Bagnall, *Law as Art*. Despite its title, Bagnall understands law "as" art only for explanatory purposes. Law on this analysis is "best understood as" a performative and creative institution like opera. Other occasional ventures into what we might call "law and music" have taken roughly the same trajectory.[28] The argument is always by analogy. "Art"—as in the law and literature movement—is in these cases still seen as a metaphor. This is an argument about how we should think about law rather than about what the law actually means to us and how it does so. It is this deeper and fuller engagement which the aesthetic, as opposed to the artistic, dimension of law proposes.

Looked at this way, the aesthetic dimension has more in common with "law and economics."[29] This theory treats economics as being actively engaged in the production of legal meaning and not just a disciplinary tool for thinking about it. The relationship between the two fields is treated as a day-to-day reality rather than as simply an intellectual comparison. In this tradition, economics is not *like* law—the argument does not proceed by metaphor; it is part of what law means and how it develops. This is the distinction I have been trying to draw. But of course if the analytical process of law and economics is in some ways similar to legal aesthetics, its content is most assuredly not. "Law and economics" assumes human beings to be fundamentally rational actors with economic desires. Such an impoverished understanding of human motivation and meaning explicitly eliminates the aesthetic dimension. While "law and literature" has at times a weak understanding of law, "law and economics" has a weak understanding of human beings.[30] We cannot look here, then, for any analysis of the role or power of the meaning of symbols in the law: law and economics is too weak a currency to offer us any purchase.

Law with Aesthetics

Central to the aesthetic dimension is the idea that the form of something is part of its meaning. Formal design or structure—whether of a poem or a statute—is not just the medium through which ideas are expressed but is itself an aspect of meaning. Form and style are not, then, just the receptacles into which abstract propositions of law are bundled but part of what the law says to us. Indeed, exactly because the form of something is often not on the conscious horizon of its authors, it provides us with a revealing glimpse into that which is accepted uncritically within a legal community. Form is evidence not of legal epistemology but of its ontology.[31]

In the work of some scholars, there is a sensitivity to this aspect of aesthetic meaning. James Boyd White, for example, argues that the form as well as the content of a legal opinion—the narrative design of the case method, the adversarial structure of contrasting voices, the requirement of final judgment—serves as a model of narrative, through which the voices of the participants are integrated into a common vocabulary, a means of reconciliation.[32] But White nevertheless treats legal form as a given, as if it were the rhyming scheme or meter of a sonnet, rather than as something possessed of its own contingent meaning. Occasionally, it is true, one finds experiments in form within legal writing: the judgment in *Fisher v. Lowe*, for example, was rendered in rhyming couplets.[33] But such cases manifest mere playfulness of purpose.

Within the academy rather than on the bench, the use of formal innovation has been pursued more self-consciously. Indeed, it could be said that one of the enduring legacies of critical legal studies, to some extent, and of feminist legal theory in particular has been their emphasis on personalizing legal writing as a means of opening up issues of subjectivity and of standpoint. Many techniques, such as the incorporation of personal anecdote, history, and confession into the text of legal articles, have served to raise these issues through the media of form and style.[34] In "Roll Over Beethoven," Duncan Kennedy and Peter Gabel rebel (they say) against the form of the elite law review by presenting their article as if it were a dialogue. Such a form suggests informality, tentativeness, and evolution, although it tends also toward pretension, self-indulgence, and that bravura disrespect which the establishment permits its prodigal sons.[35]

In a range of articles, Rod Macdonald has used the memo form to convey the conjunction of individual personality and written formality in evolving norms of institutional politics; a series of letters to imply intimacy and the importance of human interaction in the enterprise of teaching; and a structure of multiple references, somewhat akin to hypertext, to connote the nonlinear nature of thought and implication.[36] In each case, form contributes to the meaning of the subject matter. Neither is this kind of connection entirely new. In "The Soul of the Fugue," Peter Teachout convincingly argues that the essays of Lon Fuller, for example, need to be understood as more than merely concepts strung together using words. There is an integration of form and content here: of an approach that is ethical and practical with a design which often spirals away from a beginning in which rough dichotomies are introduced, toward a more refined conclusion where ideas of complementarity hold sway, and with a language which uses metaphors carefully, incrementally expanding their compass and implication.[37]

The few scholars who have written explicitly on the aesthetics of law, however, have tended either to take an uncritical approach to their subject or to focus on limited aspects of aesthetic theory.[38] In the former category we find, for example, Louis Schwartz, who equates justice and beauty without ever exploring what that might mean. Indeed his overriding concern would seem to be a critique of "flimsy" or "dubious" public policy arguments (that is, distributive justice), which he calls ugly, implemented at the cost of (corrective) justice, which he calls beautiful.[39] The aesthetics of justice remains a nice thought, but nothing more. Mark Kelman, otherwise so opposed to Schwartz, also characterizes views he dislikes as "inelegant" or "numbingly boring" without expanding on why or how this might matter. Ugliness in such hands is little more than a term of abuse.[40]

For Drucilla Cornell, "the aesthetic" appears to involve vision and faith, an appeal to a myth of beginnings and of endings.[41] It is a rhetoric which Robin West shares:

> We are not compelled to accept or reject an aesthetic vision of human nature that appears in a novel or in a legal theory. . . . Therefore we must decide not whether the worlds we envision are true or false, right or wrong. . . . We must ask whether the imaginative vision [it] presents is attractive or repulsive, whether it is "true" not to this world, but to our hopes for the world.[42]

Here, our "aesthetic" vision of the future is treated as a synonym for "taste" and assumed to be both purely subjective and beyond argument. It is therefore in stark contrast to an approach which focuses instead on the analytic potential of an evaluation of forms and symbols.

Elsewhere, West hunts the aesthetic quarry with greater vigor. In "Jurisprudence as Narrative," West adopts Northrop Frye's taxonomy of narrative paradigms, in which an author's vision of the future can be categorized as either "comic" and optimistic or "tragic" and negative and the author's method of narration either "romantic" (writing by comparison with an ideal world) or "ironic" (writing by comparison with the real world).[43] Mapping these two dimensions, one of vision and one of method, onto the modalities of legal theory, West identifies comedy with liberalism, and tragedy with those forms of statism (such as Hobbes's) which treat human conflict as inevitable and to be feared, natural law as romantic, and positivism as ironic.[44] I do not intend to undertake an explication of the insights this fruitful piece provides into the debates of legal theory. Modernist legal theory certainly needs to be understood as a conflict of aesthetic visions, a theme further developed in "Quartet for the End of Time," for law is not a matter only of logic or ethics but rather remains dependent on our hopes for the world and how we situate ourselves within it.

Nevertheless, West is still using a model extracted from one discipline —in fact, from one author—to illuminate another rather than exploring their interaction. The same can be said of Janice Toran, who adopts Beardsley for her purposes. She argues that procedural reforms are often motivated by a (subconscious) appreciation of Beardsley's canons, by a drive toward simplicity and unity detached from the functional purposes of reform. Her argument is therefore both descriptive and a warning against making beauty an end in itself:

> Yet the pervasiveness of references to simplicity, and the at least occasional discrepancy between modern procedural visions and reality, sug-

gest that these reformers sometimes tend toward simplicity and sim-
plification [just] because they find it more aesthetically pleasing.[45]

Along with Beardsley, however, Toran treats the aesthetic experience
as disinterested and objective. Toran contrasts Beardsley's canons with the
"subjectivist tradition," which, according to Toran, "makes disagreement
on aesthetics impossible."[46] As we have seen, this is a false dichotomy. On
the one hand, it has permitted subjectivists such as Schwartz to leave their
aesthetic values unquestioned altogether, while on the other hand, objec-
tivists such as West and Toran have found themselves confined to a somewhat doctrinaire, though certainly valuable, contribution based on analyses of the aesthetic developed by other writers working in other fields for
other purposes. Without expanding beyond the constraints of this dichotomy, a genuine field of legal aesthetics will not emerge.

Analogs to Legal Aesthetics

Law and Myth

The aesthetic dimension of law is not interdisciplinary but transdisciplinary.[47] It does not compare two separate disciplines but, precisely as it suggests, argues that aesthetics is a dimension of human experience which is
already to be found in many disciplines, including law. There has been a
tradition of just such an approach in the ancient common law, and here the
excavations of Peter Goodrich have been absolutely seminal. Intricate practices of style, language, dress, rhetoric, and argumentation constituted the
medieval legal community. In these respects, the arguments in sixteenth-
and seventeenth-century England with respect to law paralleled contempo-
raneous arguments over the meaning of ritual and imagery with respect to
religion. The triumph of the Reformation on the one hand and of the Enlightenment on the other concealed these venerable traditions of passion
and substituted in their stead the scientific pretensions of positivism.[48]

Pierre Legendre mounts a similar critique of post-Enlightenment law.
Here we find law understood as a species of sanctified speech, a collection of
founding myths, symbolized in the form of language, by which authority
the force of law is legitimated (Derrida makes much the same point).[49] For
Legendre, then, the essence of law lies in its status, which, through symbolism and metaphor, connotes an understanding of the self and a stabiliz-
ing myth of social order. Law takes its place along with other mythological
activities such as "art, poetry, dance, enigma, and music."[50]

From its poetry law derives its meaning and from its mysticism, its authority. This suggests that if we are to understand the meaning of law we

must analyze it aesthetically. Ironically, the fundamental problem with Legendre's analysis is that he maintains the nonlawyer's faith in the modern myth that modern law is mythless. He writes as one in mourning for a lost past of legal poesis:

> In place of paradox, poetry and mythologising of the early interpreters of law, in place of the living colour of law, its emblems and rhetoric . . . ultramodernity pushes at increasing pace towards an unruffled absolutism of certainties dressed in no more pleasing garb than the jargon of bureaucratic objectivity. . . . To remove interpretation and the figurative representation of law while leaving law itself in place is to leave it in a palace of ruins.[51]

For Legendre, the aesthetic dimension of ancient law has yielded its place to the instrumental rationality of modern law. But do we really think that modern law is without emblems or rhetoric? That there could be such a thing as law (as culture, as language, as structure) without figurative representation; as legal history without myth? As Peter Fitzpatrick argues, modern Western law has its own mythology about its origins, its destiny, and its rationality. "My seeing myth in terms of modernity," he writes, "does not fit the identification of myth with a world we have lost." It is part of what Derrida calls the "white [or transparent] mythology" of the West to characterize its law as being purely logical and without those mythic and mystic elements which exist only in more "primitive" societies.[52] But let us not believe such a fantasy. The task of aesthetics is to explore and reclaim these elements, fought against in the Reformation and the Enlightenment and thought lost by Legendre, from the interstices and margins of the law.

Law and Semiotics

In a number of effulgent books and articles, Peter Goodrich, in particular, has elaborated the countertradition of the English common law as a construction of rhetoric and community rather than of reason and doctrine. This can be seen in the practices of dress, style, and ritual in the medieval Inns of Court and through the rich variety of rhetorical manuals which were central to the development of a distinct English legal practice and education in the early modern era. He has, for example, explored the ways in which the calculated illogicality of legal forms such as the writ and subpoena and the arcane *récits* of legal language in general have a structural meaning that is to be found on their surface and not through an analysis of their concepts.[53] Thus for Goodrich, a writ, like a sacrament, is "iconic"—what matters is the constant ritual reenactment of the form and not its content or purpose. So it is with legal argument generally: it demands a particular form, rigidly controlled, which conveys above all the need for obedience in the face of authority.[54] Even the packaging of legal texts is symbolic:

> The law reports come in sizeable uniform volumes. They are bound in single and normally dull colours. . . . Each set of reports stretches with bland numerical indifference over seemingly infinite shelving. Each volume is extensive—not to say palimpsestic—in terms of its number of pages and the type of paper used: it is likely to be printed on thin India paper in smaller than average typeface. . . . There is no logic to the list of cases.[55]

On this analysis, the feel and look of the lawbooks have symbolic import. Here, aesthetics is semiotics. Indeed we could not have the one without the other. Without the ability to recognize that our understanding of a word (and therefore of a law) extends far beyond its literal meaning, to a whole realm of subtle connotations, we could not go beyond a rational and instrumentalist account of law; and without the appreciation that words and acts always symbolize other things, in a vast chain of cultural associations and resonances, we could not begin to appreciate how a legal text can have visual, metaphorical, or emotional significance. Both semiotics and aesthetics emphasize the infinite and pervasive influence of symbols in our lives.

It would be a mistake to subsume the two approaches. Legal semiotics has at times (even on occasions in Goodrich) been overtaken by a systematizing impulse in which the scientific pretensions of semiotics have held sway. The weakness of this kind of endeavor is that it attempts, in some of the work of Bernard Jackson, for example, to categorize the symbolism within legal language but not to explain the why and wherefore of its force. The same can be said of the works of Roberta Kevelson, who has attempted to apply to legal materials the semiotics of Charles Peirce, with their complex arrangement of orders and classes of signs.[56] Nevertheless, this is an interior monologue of the law: linguistic signs confront linguistic signs and explain themselves only by a description of their role. "Semiosis explains itself by itself . . . ," says Umberto Eco, echoing Peirce on this point. "This continual circularity is the normal condition of signification."[57] In this kind of semiotics, law is not treated as the creator or mediator of a wider social symbolism but rather as the repository of a purely internal system of signs.[58]

Neither Kevelson nor Peirce nor Goodrich, moreover, wishes to conflate semiotics with aesthetics. Indeed, Peirce wrote of the power of aesthetics as the normative basis of the symbolic order. If we want to understand how symbols provide us not only with the connotations of words and events but with their value, Kevelson argues, we must look to "legal aesthetics," which "concerns the set of values to which the law at any given time refers."[59] There is, then, a recognition here that aesthetics is something separate from semiotics.

In Kevelson and Peirce, the difference is that the aesthetic judges the symbols it perceives. Signs are the raw materials to which the aesthetic sense assigns value. Clearly this will not do, and for three reasons which flow one from the other. In the first place, there is a tendency here to treat the aesthetic as a given and, ironically, a reluctance to acknowledge that aesthetic values, too, have symbolic origins. Peirce would seem to place aesthetics beyond the self-referentiality of the semiotic world. The desire to find something objective and neutral in aesthetics, some escape from the circle of signs, thus rears its head where we might least have expected it.

Second, there is always a sensory element to the aesthetic, a way in which it makes itself felt in the core of our being, which the abstracted language of semiotics does not capture. Semiotics belongs to the universe of concepts, in which the sign is merely a transparent placeholder for the idea it represents. But aesthetics belongs to the universe of affect, in which the precise form and style of something is not arbitrary but rather intrinsic to what it means for us. As in aesthetics generally, there is no art without the use of a medium, a concrete and sensory object whose form the artist uses or alters and which is intrinsic to the meaning of the work. In this sense, aesthetics is not semiotic at all.

It is important to recognize the symbolic aspects of an aesthetic experience, but this must not be taken to lessen the immediacy of the sensory reaction. While semiosis develops a way of thinking about the meaning of things, aesthetics captures how we feel about them. Undoubtedly, behind a judgment of beauty, for example, there is a symbolic meaning based on cultural associations. But initially there is the sensation, which crowds in upon us, immediate and compelling. The idea of aesthetics also conveys that vital sensory power.

This argument also draws our attention to a fundamental difference in the kinds of signs with which each is concerned. Semiotics claims to look past the signs to the essences of things, the truth to which the sign points. But aesthetics is concerned precisely with the surface of things—with the truth revealed in form, look, and sound. There is nothing contingent about the surface, the image: it is itself a system of meaning and a representation of culture.[60]

Third, semiotics is an analytical technique: it suggests a way of deciphering meaning beneath meaning and of reading between the lines. From a methodological standpoint, it is of enormous value in revealing the aesthetic content hidden in the rational or the imagery of the textual. In the work of Goodrich, in particular, his emphasis on the oral and the visual, on the significance of form and presentation, and on the role of the symbolic in law demonstrates a powerful appreciation of aesthetics—of the importance of surface and of image in the construction of meaning.[61]

But there are connections which semiotics, as a technique, cannot make. The idea of aesthetics suggests a theory of human motivation—of the kinds of things which influence our thoughts and lives. It emphasizes the power of feelings, and not simply neutral signs and concepts, to drive us on. And, as Kevelson and Peirce recognize, it contains a normative element too, both because it insists on the necessity of addressing aesthetic concerns in the mediation of social conflict and because it implies that our legal systems ought to pay greater respect to recognizably aesthetic values such as empathy, difference, and singularity. We do best to recall the discussion of art in the previous chapter. In law as in art, the aesthetic is the union of senses and symbols; its realm is the knowledge about law which can be known only by sensing and by feeling.

Legal aesthetics is a method of interpretation and categorization, at which point it may find in semiotics an appropriate countersubject. But at the same time it is epistemological and normative. It stakes a claim not only about the meaning of law but about why the law has developed in certain areas as it has and what the law ought to be. This is why the aesthetic is a transdisciplinary rather than an interdisciplinary endeavor. It is exactly by bringing to the fore certain related aspects of many disciplines such as law and literature, semiotics, and deconstruction that the aesthetic dimension of the law comes into clearer focus.

The Aesthetics of Legal Institutions

A sociopsychological understanding of aesthetics accompanied by a broad comprehension of the law pays attention to their dynamics, the living nature of their interaction in the lives of human beings, and, furthermore, to the mutual nature of that relationship. Even within this framework, however, I have chosen to concentrate on law understood as a series of texts and ideas rather than as the practical process of particular institutions, although this too is undoubtedly an important aspect of law in our society. This section indicates some possible aspects of the aesthetic meaning of the legal process and legal practice, which nevertheless remain for another time.

The trial, for example, reveals the aesthetic dimension of law as an institution. As I have already mentioned, the architecture of the courthouse, lawyers' dress and language, the sound and even the smell of the court communicate meaning to those brought before it.[62] That is the environment in which a trial takes place. What of its conduct? Any experienced litigator will tell you that cases are won and lost on the presentation of evidence. On the style and structure of legal argument and the vulnerability, authority, or sympathy of witnesses hang lives and results. *Natanson v. Kline,* for example, was a breakthrough case in the development of the law of informed consent. In that case the plaintiff sued for the negligence of her doctors, not in the performance of an operation and diagnosis, but because, it was argued, they had failed to adequately inform her of the risks involved in a particular line of treatment even if performed with due care.[63] But why did this reasoning succeed in Natanson's case where others had failed? She was a young woman, suffering from breast cancer, who emerged from a partial mastectomy seriously disfigured in ways about which she had not been warned. On one level, then, the fact that she was young and female was obviously of importance to her distress at her physical condition, and to that of the jury too. More: the turning point of the case came as she gave her evidence. In open court, she undid the buttons of her blouse and displayed for the jury her bare, scarred breasts: "The ribs had been destroyed by the radiation and [all that could be done] was to have a layer of skin over the opening. I recall seeing the beat of the heart reflected in the movements of this skin flap."[64]

There are three elements to the revulsion here: first, to the shocking sight and undeniable reality of her mutilation, which words alone could never convey; second, to the humiliation which this young woman underwent, reduced first from a person to a patient, from a patient to a victim, and finally from victim to exhibit; and third, to the complicity of the jury and the court. What would one not do to remove the nausea which that image had instilled in every person present? From the visual impact of that particular body, and the more complicated aesthetics of revulsion it aroused, grew new law.

On another level, Jay Katz argues that cases expanding the liability of the medical profession in the United States, such as *Natanson*, have principally been related to areas in which there have been new and powerful techniques—such as the practice of mastectomy—placed at doctors' disposal.[65] The courts' reaction to this expresses a fear of technology which relates especially to the increased intrusiveness of medical practice and the extent of bodily violation it foreshadows. No one could doubt that the nineteenth-century surgeon with his saw was a greater terror than the scalpel-wielding physician of modern times; but through the wonders of anaesthesia the scalpel has been given a freedom which the body cannot resist. If the body will not fight invasion, then the law will. It may be that it is the imagery of the precision knife and the supine sheeted silent body beneath it which has inspired an aesthetic resistance couched in legal form.

Sensory images and symbolism convey meaning, however, not only in terms of the discourse of a particular trial, which is perhaps rather obvious, but, more generally, through the legal environment in which the trial takes place. Here we are dealing with the semiotics of forms and institutions—that is, the way in which buildings and practices themselves operate as a system of signs which, although not linguistic in nature, nonetheless impart powerful social messages.[66] Douglas Hay, for example, discussing judicial practice in England around the time of the French Revolution, emphasizes the aspects of spectacle in the way the court dressed and paraded, the solemnity of the occasion, and the formality of language, all of which buttressed the court's authority and mystery.[67]

The semiotics of the legal environment continues to be of the utmost importance. Macdonald has undertaken a microstudy of the ways in which power is interpreted and used through the allocation of institutional space.[68] Peter Goodrich among others has described in some detail the semiotics of courtroom behavior and how it instills alienation and disempowerment both visually and acoustically: through the size and space of the courtroom; through the placement of seats, the isolation of the dock, the looming height of the judges' bench, and their stage-managed entrances and exits; through the visible antiquity of modes of dress and address.[69] Just like the church in the Middle Ages, architecture, archaism, acoustics, theater, and costume are all vital ingredients in the concoction of power.[70] A grand cathedral and a cavernous court, the echoing of a Gregorian chant and the resounding clamor of a gavel; miter and wig, introit and oyez. For millennia, we have been summoned to obey through our senses.

The trial is typically treated as the heart of law and the adjudication of the instant case as the central element of its functioning. "The courts are the capitals of law's empire, and judges are its princes," writes Dworkin. It is a sentiment echoed throughout the literature, from positivists to realists to critical legal studies.[71] But by and large I have decided to leave these issues for another occasion. Law is too often understood simply as a process of decision making which occurs at a particular time and in a particular place. To resist this, we must descend the courthouse steps. Law is something which takes place outside the courtroom, as a product generated by the interplay of texts and images in the life of a community. Law is the work of many moments and many readers. It is not simply a set of institutional machineries but an ongoing reality in all our lives. For almost all of us, almost all the time, the law is a field of linguistic symbols, an expression of social values, and a species of terminology through which we try to make sense of things. It is a collection of ideas and rhetoric. This is the heart of law as an experience, and it is to those aspects which the argument for its aesthetic dimension must pay closest attention.

THE FUGUE AS ARCHITECTURE

Formal Structure

While politics asks us what we can do and ethics what we ought to do, aesthetics inquires into what we see and how we should see. In the chapters that follow, this inquiry develops along three distinct dimensions or axes. They are, perhaps, movements, for there is an argument which moves within them and which moves from one section to the next.

The Methodological Dimension

The first movement, the "Motet," deals with aesthetics as a methodology. A sensitivity to the use of rhetoric and metaphor, for example, can enrich our understanding of the meaning of law, for the style of a legal judgment contributes to both its weight as precedent and its meaning.[72] Law is not just a sequence of logical propositions or abstract rules. It is also a collection of forceful symbols and persuasive metaphors.

Through an approach to legal texts that is sensitive to their form, design, and presentation, the reader is offered new insights and a fresh interpretation. In particular, "Motet" compares changes in the form and language of English legislation from the thirteenth to the sixteenth century to similar changes in English music of the same period. This comparison reveals the changing understanding and assumptions of those societies as to the role and power of law. The purpose of aesthetics here, therefore, lies in its ability to help us discern meaning in the form and language of the law and to read it with subtlety and imagination. This approach is resolutely textual in nature, but it finds meaning in something other than the rational surface and logical structure of law's words. On the contrary, such a reading helps us to recognize what else is being said—sotto voce—in law's margins and metaphors.[73]

To sum up: aesthetics is a way of reading. It can be characterized as a methodology, its orientation interpretative, its raw materials textual, its tools of analysis linguistic, its purpose to illustrate how aesthetic meaning *forms* the substance of the law. It is an exposition of the aesthetic dimension.

The Epistemological Dimension

"Requiem" and "Variations on a Theme" continue to make use of the expository power of an aesthetic analysis, but in addition they explore the contribution of aesthetics to the wider values to which the law gives voice. Aesthetics here needs to be understood as an epistemology, by which I mean a way in which knowledge and value are created rather than interpreted. Aesthetics provides us with a way of seeing and judging the world and is therefore a powerful influence as to why particular legal principles have been developed. The law we often assume to have been the product of political or ethical values is also a product of aesthetic values.

The aesthetic dimension helps us to explain the language and values which law expresses. "Requiem," for example, provides an extended examination of the jurisprudence of capital punishment. The debate over the death penalty is fundamentally aesthetic, and this chapter explores the aesthetic means—the sounds, images, and symbols—by which that debate has been constructed in the United States. This is not an argument about legal texts but about the social context which generates them. And since we are interested in discovering the imagery and symbolism which forms the understandings to which law gives expression, there is an emphasis here on the meaning of visual and, more generally, sensory aesthetic experience. "Variations on a Theme" explores the law relating to illicit drugs. These laws reflect a widely felt reaction to a social problem. But, again, to what extent is this an aesthetic response—a reaction to the powerful images associated with "drug" use and the kind of symbolic meaning which that imagery has come to represent? Again, the union of senses and symbols finds expression in a particular legal framework. A focus on this dimension of the drug debate throws new light on an old and intractable problem.

To sum up: aesthetics is a way of seeing and a force in the construction of meaning. It is an epistemology, its orientation descriptive, its raw materials contextual, its analysis visual, its purpose to illustrate how aesthetic value *informs* the law.

The Normative Dimension

In "Quartet for the End of Time" and finally "Quodlibet," the argument is turned around. Aesthetics has a normative or prescriptive as well as a descriptive aspect. It is a force for change as much as for explanation. This normative edge comes in a number of guises. "Quartet for the End of Time" argues that legal theories themselves are marked by conflicting aesthetic values, which helps us to understand the nature of their disagreements. Yet despite their surface differences, they are all manifestations of an essentially modernist legal theory, which we need to transcend in particular by developing a vision of the role of law in society which is both critical and pluralist. This potential shift in legal thinking is illustrated with reference to the changing aesthetics of art, music, and science. There are two reasons to draw on such different fields of knowledge: first, because it demonstrates how the aesthetic dimension transcends and links very different ways of thinking about the world; second, because a paradigm shift in theory—legal or otherwise—requires not only an intellectual change but an aesthetic one too.[74] The discourses of reason or justice alone are not enough to facilitate change: the mind's eye and the heart, bound together in the experience of the aesthetic, must also be won. "Quartet for the End of Time" therefore characterizes otherwise conflicting legal theories in terms of their shared aesthetic and argues that a new aesthetic is both a natural and a necessary element of legal and social change.

"Quodlibet" turns briefly from law to justice. At the heart of an aesthetic approach lies a number of key concepts including tolerance, empathy, and a respect for difference. If we were to treat the aesthetic dimension as a genuinely important part of law (and society), would our vision of justice be different? Justice is a kind of judgment which is closely related to aesthetics. They are both processes and not objects: one cannot, therefore, teach anyone what justice or beauty "is." Their content is contingent and subjective, but one can encourage a way of looking at the world that embodies a commitment to both. Like justice, aesthetics operates as a tension and a supplement, even a diremption, within the workings of the law. Aesthetics is something we should value in our world, and in the valuing we may come closer to that elusive ideal of justice.

To sum up: aesthetics is a way of influencing the law. Here perhaps aesthetics can be viewed as a kind of value system implying strategies for accomplishing change, although not of course exclusive ones. Aesthetics is an ontology, its orientation normative, its analysis rhetorical, its purpose to illustrate how aesthetics might *reform* the law. It is an inversion of the aesthetic dimension, treating the aesthetic not as a force directed at the law from outside but as a force within it.

These three dimensions taken together, then, accomplish a movement from description to prescription, from cause to effect, from meaning to value, and from methodology to epistemology to ontology. Above all, they represent a movement outward from the law to society and then onward toward the future.

Polyphonic Texture

Episodes

This argument is developed through a series of case studies. The history of early English legislation, the jurisprudence of capital punishment, drug law and policy, and the aesthetic ideology of modern legal theories—each in turn holds center stage. These are the episodes of the fugue, which is to say the specific subject areas which the work addresses. The aesthetic is not a kind of alphabet. It is not composed of finite and discrete units which are provided with meaning only in their combination; on the contrary, the meaning of each symbol is invented anew. Symbolic meaning is not a commodity but art.[75]

Counterpoint

Polyphony, of which the fugue is perhaps the most complex example, means "many voices," and a fugue typically makes use of three or four separate melodic lines which weave in and out simultaneously. These voices each have their own characteristic range and timbre, high or low, male or female. They are the raw materials from which the subject and countersubjects are woven, by the exercise of the techniques of counterpoint. Such countersubjects are techniques or disciplines which both thicken the argument and offer a certain resistance, alternative paths of approach. Some of them have already been noted—semiotics, for example, and the approach taken by the law and literature movement—but there are many others that capture some of the facets of the aesthetic dimension. I am critical of the paradigm of law as a purely rational enterprise. Deconstruction, therefore, has been an important influence on my analysis. In the first place it is the approach par excellence attuned to dissecting the complexities and ambiguities in language. Furthermore, deconstruction is a method which insists that meaning and language can be understood only through a detailed reading attentive to the unique voice, movement, and implications of each individual text.[76] By introducing this eclectic range of techniques to serve as counterpoint to my subject, I mean to resist the claim that legal aesthetics is some supervening or grand theory. A dimension is not exclusive in this way. The purpose of counterpoint, after all—the simultaneous clash and harmony of independent thematic lines—is to explore the compatibility of multiple themes without destroying the meaning or relevance of any of them.

In neither music nor philosophy has such a view always predominated. In the nineteenth century, when melody was king, the many voices which supported it played an increasingly subservient role: they added texture to the melody, but they lost their own shape and identity in the process. The agenda of a piece of music is on this approach set by one idea, and the role of every other part is defined in its terms, bit players in the service of a sweeping melodic triumphalism.

It is for this reason that playing the great Romantic works for orchestra or choir—a Mahler symphony, Verdi's *Requiem,* or a Wagner opera—gives rise to contrasting feelings. On the one hand, much of the writing for the inner or lower parts lacks any independent interest. On the other hand, there is a feeling of participating in a mutual endeavor which can be quite exhilarating. As the century progressed, the musical resources used to achieve this end expanded enormously. In a choir of hundreds or a Brucknerian orchestra with sixteen horns and a cast of thousands, independence was increasingly exchanged for a musical corporatism and integrity replaced by unity.

Musical history, once again, was merely one indicia of the intellectual spirit of the times.[77] Romanticism in music was the aesthetic expression of a movement which affected philosophy, history, and politics alike. This was the story of modernity rendered aural: of totalizing ideologies which attempted to interpret every aspect of the world according to a master melody of truth. We see this tendency toward grand narratives—single melodic lines—in Marxism as in the ideologies of imperialism and capitalism which opposed it, in Darwin and in Spencer, Weber and Durkheim. From each perspective, one interpretative element—class or economics, race or gene—was treated as the single lens through which the workings of the world could be completely analyzed. Furthermore, there was a song about progress here—about where we came from and where we were headed—in which we were all just playing our little part.

This is the critique which postmodernity levels at the moderns: the imposition of a fictitious narrative (or melody) upon a "reality" altogether more fragmented and contradictory and the insistence on totalizing frameworks, all of which have claimed to show the world not only from a different angle but from the right one. In contrast, poststructural theories display an interpretative pluralism: a concern for detail, polyphony, ambiguity, and contingency.[78] The idea of the fugue captures much of this perspective.

On the other hand, in some extreme incarnations, it has been argued that any theoretical approach distorts the local and contingent nature of experience. For Foucault, archivist of the microstrategies of power, there is a distinct resistance to any kind of analysis which would see commonalities and patterns of oppression. There is simply nothing we can say and do about power from beyond or above its defining embrace.[79] Other postmodern writers similarly despair of the possibility of theoretical distance. From a very different perspective, Stanley Fish argues that our cultural embeddedness makes the very project of "theory" a pointless one. Talking about something and doing it are two unrelated activities.[80] The conclusion reached by many recent feminists is surprisingly similar. More for moral rather than conceptual reasons, they would argue that abstraction is a harmful activity which drains the color and meaning from life. Abstract arguments represent a patriarchal mode of reasoning, objectivist and impersonal.[81]

Let us concede the importance of grounding theory in practical and concrete experience—it is a caution well taken, as the episodic model of the fugue acknowledges. The distinction between abstraction and reality assumed by all these critiques, however, is fundamentally flawed. Abstraction is the stuff of meaning: it is language, it is art, it is ritual. A toddler's drawing is a masterpiece of abstraction. The point is therefore not to try to imagine the possibility of its absence but to acknowledge its incompleteness. We use abstraction on many different levels, and each highlights some kinds of relationships between things while concealing certain others. It is never a question of abandoning abstract thinking but of choosing a tool appropriate to specific episodes. As Paul de Man wrote, "blindness" and "insight" are correlative. It is only by our blindness to certain features of a situation that our mind is made free to fully explore the implications of other aspects.[82] It is surely the case that we need above all to expand the frameworks we use, to overcome the blindness of theory by multiplying the lenses of insight.

A theory, then, is not a monolith but a perspective. It need not obliterate its opposition but only contribute to it. And here too in the fugue we find an expression of that pluralism and a metaphor for the approach I have taken to theory in this book. Against the subject in its various guises, there is not a simple and supportive harmony but the play of countersubjects, each possessed of its own integrity, its own perspective. A fugue is far from concordant: even in the work of Bach, there is a remarkable degree of discord and clash as each part, maintaining its own internal shape and line, proceeds with considerable independence. Against the subject can be heard doubt, destabilization, and alternatives, and in this way the countersubjects (or theories) and the episodes (or case studies) of a fugue serve to question and comment on the subject. A fugue is an elaboration of a theme, but it provides, as all good writing should, for its own resistance.

Voices

One voice—one raw material of analysis, one characteristic timbre—runs throughout this book, and that is the voice of music. It serves as a metaphor, a point of historical comparison, a frame of reference, a case study, and a constant structural device. In ignoring the formal and symbolic meaning of texts, legal and otherwise, readers are missing a great deal of what they read. This is a central element of the aesthetic dimension, and the voice of music is central to how I demonstrate those points. The very distance between how we think of law and how we think of music adds force to their conjunction.

Imagine this book as a fugue in honor of the aesthetic dimensions of law and justice. Several voices, legal and musical, articulate the subject, each in a unique register and texture. These voices pursue three dimensions—the methodological, epistemological, and normative—in order to develop an argument for the importance of aesthetics in law. This then is the fugue as metaphor, as structure, as image. But finally, the idea of the fugue offers us an ideal of harmony and dissonance, richness and complexity. The fugue presents an aesthetic template for the promise of law in society. This is the gift of the aesthetic: it can inspire imagination. And it has inspired in me this insistence: that law is not removed from the realm of feeling and symbolism; and that this power in the world, which the aesthetic exercises over us all, should be exposed and explored, acknowledged, celebrated, and cultivated.

Motet

Statutes and Music —
An Aesthetic Methodology

DEFINITIONS

Act — something done; a deed; an action; a written ordinance of a
parliament or other legislative body [ME, fr. L *agere*, do]
Motet — a short usually unaccompanied sacred choral composition
[ME, fr. OF, diminutive of *mot*, word]
Polyphony — vocal music etc. in two or more relatively independent
parts; counterpoint [Gk *polyphonous, poly-*, many, and *phone*, voice]
Statute — a written law passed by a legislative body; a book or books
containing the statute law [ME, fr. LL *statutum*, set up, establish,
fr. *sta-* root of *stare*, to stand]

AN AESTHETIC METHODOLOGY

Two Perspectives on Interpretation

Look at the monumental change that has been wrought between the *Magna
Carta* and the prodigious legislation of the Tudors. In language, form, and
style, these laws seem almost unrelated: the former as impenetrable and
limited in scope as the latter are arrogant of their power and authority. Yet
one grew with the utmost gradualness from the other. Listen to the miracu-
lous changes that have been rung between the two-part *organa* and plain-
songs of the thirteenth century and the prodigious motets of Thomas Tallis,
up to forty vocal lines in mazy coalition. Here, too, there has been so much
formal and stylistic development that it is hard to imagine that one is an or-
nate variation of the other. The languages of law and of music, then, have
each been subject to dramatic changes in their purpose and normativity.
Further, the similarities between these parallel historical transformations
suggest that the change that was taking place extended far beyond the narrow confines of each discipline and implicated every aspect of the lives of
those who lived in those communities.

Modern readers—and writers too—all too often treat reading as a miner
treats the earth. They are insensitive to the environment of the text, its
play of light and shadow. In fiction or nonfiction, they search for syllogisms,
information to be extracted and stored, and discard the rest as mere impedi-
menta. Ideas, facts, and events are nuggets of meaning; everything else is
just rocks. The result of this discursive strip-mining is a wasteland in which
more has been lost than gained and much that was always there remains
buried. The aesthetic dimension of law is about developing a sensitivity to
these hidden truths and treasures, a matter of discerning meaning beneath

the literal surface of a text, and this aesthetic dimension can be seen as related to the growing field of legal scholarship which explores legal meaning through the changing metaphors it uses.[1] Furthermore, in recognizing the influence of aesthetic perceptions on legal principles that claim to be solely about reason, one can appreciate how "the law" is constructed within a framework of aesthetic influences as well as moral or political ones. In all these ways, the aesthetic dimension deepens our understanding of the law by giving readers new tools with which to interpret the meaning of legal texts.

Aesthetics is about deepening legal meaning. The aesthetic dimension enriches our harmonic resources—it gives us richer tools to assist in the act of interpretation: this is the "how" of interpretation and is the approach taken in the following chapter.[2] But it also broadens legal meaning—the kinds of things legal texts can communicate to you: this is the "what" of interpretation. This expansion, a second interpretative perspective, serves as the focus of the present chapter. The law is an imperfect mirror of the world beyond its bounds. If we study it carefully, with an eye to its structure and style, the law reflects back to us aspects of the world which gave it birth. It is no longer just a question of the meaning of legal texts but of legal contexts. Nothing could be further from a formalist or positivist interpretation of the law, which excludes from consideration and interest all but the text and the allegedly "legal" values and principles which generated it.[3]

Admittedly the information contained in a law case or a statute may be faulty or flawed or partial. It is not, however, the external information contained in a legal document which is of interest here but the way it portrays a worldview. Beyond the subject matter with which it deals and the principles it states—away from the immediate, performative, and functional aspects of legal writing—a judgment or a statute tells us about the context in which it was developed and the understanding of social relations and legal order which operated to produce it. A legal document, then, reveals what is meant by "law" and "order" in the society which gave it birth. It tells us about the role, power, authority, and responsibility attributed to and claimed by legal institutions. These are important legal questions typically assumed by a society, the set and not the foreground of legal texts.

Statutes and Motets

This chapter looks at early English statutes from the *Magna Carta*[4] (first obtained from King John in 1215 and then confirmed ten years later by Henry III) until the reign of Henry VIII (from 1509). At the dawn of the common law, a statute had not yet achieved its present authoritative status and regularity of form. It took its place alongside a whole range of other techniques of lawmaking, including the "common law" system of judicial decision making, writs, plea rolls, charters, year books, and so on. In fact, statutes were not a routine product of government until toward the end of the period I am considering, while, on the other hand, the line between statutes and less formal pronouncements remained unclear. Nevertheless, by trying to understand the meaning and role of the texts Parliament created, we will gain a view of the ways in which those with power saw the role of the law. How, I wish to ask, can we look at these particular legal documents? How do they appear to look at us? How did their authors look at the world?

I am particularly interested in changing ideas of normativity and the law. Why does law exert authority over its citizens—why, in other words, do we obey the law? For John Austin, first among English legal positivists, the answer is coercion: it is from the threat of harm that our duty to obey arises. "Being liable to evil from you if I comply not with a wish which you signify . . . I lie under a *duty* to obey it."[5] Indeed both Austin's model of the legal system and H. L. A. Hart's hypothetical discussion of the formative period of legal order seem to be based on just this understanding of "primitive" English law as a matter of force.[6] Superficially, the earliest English statutes, assembled and published together in 1786 under the title *Statutes at Large,* bear out this conception. According to the editor, Owen Ruffhead, early English statutes seem "rather to be Provisions extorted by some predominant influence, rather than laws instituted by the concurring Assent of a regular legislature."[7] To support this argument, the author cites many statutes enacted without any formal indication of whether or how they received Parliamentary assent. As late as 1400, one bill apparently became law although it was rejected by the House of Commons.[8] On this reading, Austinian in its implications, the laws of these early times demanded compliance from the community simply because of the force which backed them up and not because, as modern positivists argue, they were the formal and therefore legitimate products of a recognized procedure of legislative development.[9]

Retreating from his initial conjecture, however, Ruffhead defends the formal validity of such statutes by insisting that we cannot judge a thirteenth-century enactment according to the procedural standards of the eighteenth century. Certainly it is true that lawmaking practice, and Parliament itself, was amorphous and unsettled in the first few hundred years after the Norman invasion. But we must go much further. Not only procedure changed in all that time. We cannot assume that the meaning and power of law itself was the same then as it is now. To adopt such an assumption would be to indulge in a presentism more grievous than that condemned by Ruffhead, for it would be to judge the meaning of the thirteenth-century legal order by the experiences of the twentieth.

What was the purpose of statutes, then, and to whom were they addressed? Who was expected to obey the law, and why? In answering these questions I am attempting to recapture a radically different understanding of the province of statute and law. There is, moreover, a dramatic shift from 1200 to 1500 in a wide range of attitudes toward legal purposes and effects, which marks the movement from a medieval to a recognizably modern legal worldview. Statutes, and the word "statute" itself, underwent a sea change by the sixteenth century. This change is frequently presented in terms of the growth of political power and administrative machinery, the ambitions of the Norman invaders gradually being matched by their capacity. This politico-bureaucratic story, however, is altogether too simple. Rather, we are witnessing nothing short of a change of consciousness here, a change in the understanding of the purpose and functions of law and of the relationship of the individual to the forces of legal order.

A paradigm shift in consciousness manifests itself through all our senses. It affects how we read and how we listen. After reading Foucault, one should therefore not be surprised to find parallel structural changes in the development of this worldview across surprisingly different fields.[10] Take an alternative locus of normativity—the church—and consider one of its most significant means of expression, music. Explore one of the most complex and important forms that musical discourse took—the motet, a form as significant in the development of medieval music as was the statute in the development of medieval law. The word "motet" is used in England from the fourteenth century to describe any harmonic vocal music written for church use. It derives from the diminutive form of the French *mot*, or word, and although the early motets are quite different from the monophonic chants that preceded them, they share with Gregorian chant a commitment to the priority of the liturgical text. This commitment is honored in the simplicity of the motet's line and organization, in which the musical interest of the composition never detracts from, overwhelms, or operates independently from the words which it is its duty to convey. The sacred word is paramount.

Jacques Attali and Thomas Levenson have elsewhere argued that we can read the history of music as a history of the society that gave it birth. The distinction that Attali in particular is interested in is the political economy of music, its changing mode of production, while I propose to focus on the aesthetic economy of music, its changing mode of communication.[11] The history of Western music resonates with a progression of formal and stylistic changes very similar to those found in the development of the statute and illustrates the same emergence from a medieval to a modern perspective on the world. Motets had also undergone a sea change by the sixteenth century. By the end of our period of study the motet had begun to give effect to a complexity of polyphonic organization beyond imagining when the first motets were sung. So too, the statute had begun to give effect to a complexity of legal and social organization beyond imagining when the first statutes were enacted. The dramatic evolution in the form and style of the motet, and the remarkable parallels which are evident in the evolution of legislation, show the profundity of the changes that were taking place in ideas of normativity and the relationship of authority to subject; and, consequently, they reveal the logic of a social revolution which went far beyond purely legal or political changes. The changing sound and form of the motet demonstrate and communicate how fundamental were these shifts in the processes of social order. Musical history is not only a metaphor for the forces at work behind the development of the statute but an exemplification of them.

Further Aspects of Aesthetic Methodology

The use of music as a counterpoint to my legal analysis is one way in which this chapter develops an aesthetic methodology. But in addition, aesthetics influences both the process of this inquiry and its subject.

An Aesthetic Process

The legal meaning of a judicial opinion or a statute is influenced not only by rational ideas and legal doctrine but also by aesthetic and formal considerations. Just as we listen to a piece of music with an ear to its form and style, its structure and design, we can learn much about what a law means through a careful evaluation of these same factors. Musical and legal interpretation turn out to have something in common after all.

The use of these factors suggests a way of reading in which the text is treated as an elaborate and enlightening sign system in and by itself. Clearly this is an approach much influenced by legal semiotics.[12] As Richard Weisberg wrote, "Cardozo realized that the form of an opinion actively contributes to its correctness."[13] What are the consequences implied by this way of reading—what interpretative choices are involved in the reading of a legal document, such as a statute, which this approach might suggest?

Aesthetics is very much concerned with the words of a text. Our society is uniquely literary. Other cultures set great store by the senses of hearing, of touch, and even of smell as means of access to the "truth," but modern Western society has accorded, at least until very recently, an unparalleled and almost exclusive priority to the sense of sight.[14] Other cultures, moreover, transmit myth and social meaning by nondiscursive artistic representation or through oral tradition, while we inhabit a culture in which the alphabet, writing, and words—abstract, visual, linguistic—predominate. We are, says Marshall McLuhan, "typographic man" and woman. In such a culture, texts occupy a unique cultural position.[15] But an aesthetic approach is not simply an analysis of the "meaning" or denotation of words. Rather, it is attuned to connotation: to the implications of which words are used and which are not, with the kinds of ways in which language is used, and with the style and even the grammar of writing. In short, aesthetics involves a heightened sensitivity to the ambient, the metaphorical, and the rhetorical effects of language.[16]

Furthermore, we must develop an analysis of the law which explores not only the connotations of words but the very look of documents themselves.[17] At this point, an aesthetic interpretation is not interested in the content of a text (the legal details, for example, of an Act) but in its style and design. A painting, after all, is not simply "about" its subject matter: its structure and style also communicate. Indeed, for abstract paintings, there is no other meaning. So too, the formal and structural features of a statute, its design and layout, are likewise tools of an aesthetic analysis which will help us to understand how those who created and recorded the text saw their world and law's place within it. This focus on presentational form is an aspect which resonates with the theories of Monroe Beardsley.[18] The difference, of course, is that for Beardsley an appreciation of formal elements ought to be entirely removed from the contaminants of culture and social value, whereas here they are a mirror of and a window onto them. Far from being radically removed, the two are radically enmeshed.

There is a fundamental point to be made here. Aesthetic interpretation relies on our ability to find meaning in the very matters which its authors often took for granted—look, sound, and form.[19] By focusing on the presentation, structure, and style of legal documents rather than just on their intentional meaning, we approach the world in which they were written through variables which were in general deployed and modified subconsciously. Form and style inadvertently reveal to us the assumptions and procedures which a society does not question—its ontology. A focus on these aspects will often tell us more about the collective values of a society than that which is debated and contentious.[20] That which is self-evident is evidence of the self.

This is why an aesthetic methodology is developed here through historical example. By dealing with the formative period of English statutes, we are in a position to assess those formal and stylistic features which we might, in the context of our own legislative framework, take for granted. Undoubtedly such an approach is not without implications for contemporary practices. A semiotic and aesthetic interpretation of legislative form could be valuably carried on into the present day. But the distance of history helps. Our attention is drawn to the various specific elements of the language and structure of the modern statute as, one by one, we are privy to the processes of their birth and crystallization.

An Aesthetic Subject

The purpose of the analysis is to reclaim how a particular community at a particular time saw the world and the role of law within it. The analogy with the interpretation of a painting—encapsulated by words such as "seeing," "looking," and "perspective"—may prove helpful. Michael O'Toole, in *A Semiotics of Art*, seeks to understand art not only by considering what a work of art "represents" but by independently evaluating its "composition" and "mood." "Mood" here refers to how the painting "looks at" observers, the ways in which it tries to entice them into its world or, alternatively, exclude them. For example, are there people in the painting? How do they look at us or past us? How is perspective used? These and similar questions all relate to the mood of an artwork and the nature of its gaze.[21]

What a painting "represents" corresponds to the meaning and purpose of a statute and the painting's "composition" to a law's form and structure, on which I have already dwelt. But can a law have a "mood"? In other words, does it *gaze* at you? Through a legal text we can learn something of the gaze of its authors and, therefore, of their understanding of the purpose and power of law. We see them gazing at the world through the window of the laws they have written. Furthermore, those who are subject to the law often experience law as a gaze upon them. We speak of what "the law" demands of us and how "it" controls us. This is not merely a figure of speech but a phenomenon.

Here we are brought back to the work of Michel Foucault, for whom gaze (*regard*) was an essential aspect of his theory of power. The way in which the state observes every aspect of the lives of its citizens is a defining characteristic of the modern world. Whereas in the Middle Ages to be powerful was to be seen, it is now the case that to be powerful is to see—to see everybody, to know their every move and to subject them all to a penetrating and controlling gaze.[22] The common people, who once suffered from their relative invisibility, now suffer from a pervasive visibility in the eyes of the state. In consequence, there is an unprecedented degree of control exerted by authority over our lives, no less complete for its asserted benignancy, no less influential for its ubiquity.[23]

The subject of this study is the mood or gaze of the statute in the development of English law. First, to whom is the law addressed?—upon whom, in other words, does the law's gaze fall? Second, in what capacity?—are those "captured" in this gaze treated as agents, whose role is to carry out the law, as for example where the law is procedural or administrative in character?; as subjects who are expected to fit in with the way the law orders the world around them?; or as objects, whose behavior and attitudes the enactment of the law is intended to actually modify, as is, perhaps, our modern understanding of the purpose of the criminal law? Laws thus "look" at different groups in different ways. The gaze of the statute, the dramatic changes it underwent from the thirteenth to the sixteenth century, and the meaning of those changes in terms of law as a normative order, are the focus of this chapter.

In all this, the aesthetic dimension therefore fulfills three main functions. It mandates an interpretative process that sheds insight on the manifold meanings of a text by focusing on the structure and form of a statute —how these ancient statutes look to us. It provides an interpretative direction that concentrates on the ways in which a statute's gaze constructs its audience—how statutes' authors saw. And finally, it offers an interpretative parallel by exploring what we can learn from analogous developments in the composition and mood of the motet—how the changing world surrounding the statute was heard. The underlying message is simple. Don't take meaning for granted. Look. And listen.

STATUTES AND ACTS: POLYPHONY AND LEGISLATION FROM THE THIRTEENTH TO THE SIXTEENTH CENTURIES

The Thirteenth Century: Statutes without Norms?

The Language of Law

Statutes at Large, that great compilation of English enactments, was first published in the late eighteenth century and is the most accessible historical record of English statute law. It begins with the famous statutes of the thirteenth century, such as the *Magna Carta* and the *Statute of Westminster*, and proceeds year by year "down to the present day." But the familiar tradition and feeling of continuity with which this provides the reader is misleading. From the opening words of the *Magna Carta*, we enter a legal world very different from our own. Like all statutes prior to 1275, it is written in Latin: generally not a spoken language at the time, and understood by only a small, administrative, and of course ecclesiastical elite. The word "clerical" reflects this early duplication of roles since the adjective denotes equally the clerk (or bureaucrat) and the cleric (or priest). The Latin used, moreover, was not even classical Latin but "law Latin," verbose, difficult, and full of its own idiosyncrasies.[24] Even the word "statute," then, is a translation, and one should, strictly speaking, write of *statutum* and *statuta*.

We cannot even ask about the basis on which statute laws were obeyed, since for the vast majority of the population, they were literally incomprehensible. These statutes were not normative, if by normative we mean the handing down of principles and values to a community with the assumption that its members will or ought take heed. Indeed, the *Magna Carta* and other statutes of the period, despite the protodemocratic mythology that now surrounds them, did not speak to the community at all. Like sacred objects, these texts concealed their meaning from all but a privileged few; for the rest, their power stemmed from the very fact of their incomprehensibility.[25] Writing at this time was still close to its origin as runes, as mysteries, as a series of "hiero/glyphs"—"priestly signs" cloaked in the veil of religion. In a largely illiterate society, in particular, the power of writing derives from its cabbalistic mystery rather than from its specific content. In such a world, the secrets of the texts were not to be read but deciphered, and those who held the key had about them something of an aura of magic, of majesty. The power of the written law, then, like the power of the written word itself, was a matter of form and not meaning.

The use of Latin suggests that these statutes combined an iconic power with a lack of specific norms of conduct—they conveyed a message of obedience to someone rather than to some legal principle. The specific wording of the statutes provides further evidence. Translated from the Latin, the confirmation of the *Magna Carta* in 1225 by Henry III begins, "Henry by the grace of God, King of England . . . to all Archbishops, Bishops, Abbots, Priors, Earls, Barons, Sheriffs, Provosts, Officers, and to all Bailiffs and other our faithful subjects, which shall see this present Charter, Greeting."[26]

The gaze of the statute is directed at a very limited class of people who are addressed personally, as if in a letter. "Greeting," says the King. This is a very common beginning. "Edward, to all to whom these Presents shall come, sendeth greeting" begins the *Carta Forestæ;* "The King to his Treasurer and Barons of the Exchequer, Greeting," says another. "The King unto his Justices of the Bench, greeting" is also typical. It was the same form of words used in the various writs which gave the king's judges jurisdiction of a case.[27] This language implies that England's feudal masters were less interested in establishing norms of behavior to be followed by the population than in setting up a system of administrative allegiance to oversee legal norms generated elsewhere: the statutes, which were their special contribution to the legal system, were addressed to these supervisors rather than to the general population.

That was, of course, where the notion and power of the "common law" came from. The law, seen as a structure of norms, was filled on a case-by-case basis as the need arose. In the development of the common law, the king for a long time showed little interest; his gaze fell, rather, upon a limited class of functionaries, whom he saw as "agents" and not "subjects" of the law. Indeed, the whole structure of the common law "writ system" itself reflected this priority. The annual year books which became central legal documents by the end of the reign of Edward I were complex records of the practice of pleading in which the substantive decision of the courts was largely irrelevant. Time and again, once questions of procedure had been resolved, the year book simply noted "and so to judgment." As Plucknett concludes, "What the judgment was, nobody knew and nobody cared."[28] The subject matter of law was not important; who administered it was. This question of control was especially important because the Normans, assuming the role of a conquering feudal aristocracy in a foreign land, saw the entrenchment of their institutional power as paramount. The substantive Saxon common law was not only unimportant: its preservation was itself a strategy of successful conquest. Both the language and mood of these early statutes confirm the limited and nonnormative nature of their gaze.

The form and style of English vocal music at the time exemplified many of these nonnormative features of mood and gaze. By the beginning of the thirteenth century, the heyday of Gregorian chant was past. But the polyphonic forms which soon came to be called "motet" had not yet been fully developed. Polyphony—the interweaving of a number of independent musical lines—developed in *organum,* in which a second part paralleled the tenor line of a plainsong (or later, a freely composed *pes*) at an interval of an octave or fifth; within a few decades, the second part began to be sung in contrary motion to the tenor, that is, rising where the tenor fell and vice versa. Thus, although the two lines of an organum differed, there was in these early works no independence of parts; the second line was as yet entirely derivative of the tenor.[29]

Furthermore, there was not yet a modern system of notation of notes or rhythm. Despite the many innovations it pioneered, early English notation remained indefinite for another century or more.[30] An improvisational and informal character thus hung over the writing of music, which served as a memorial to the past rather than as a prescription for the future. We shall see the same thing in relation to statutes of the time. The writing of music —or of law—allowed a small group of performers to recall texts with which they were already familiar rather than prescribing the precise actions or performances of a larger community.

The vocal line was lacking in beat or accent, highly ornamented, melismatic rather than syllabic. Rhythmic variation was either nonexistent or else it merely consisted in repeating one of a small number of preset patterns or "modes." This limited approach to rhythm characterized English polyphony through the fifteenth century.[31] Listen to the cryptic contours of the music, whose steady undulations reflect an introspective rapture. The expression of that rapture is strangely confined: the tonal range of early polyphonic writing rarely exceeded six notes within a single line or a tenth from the lowest part to the highest.[32] There was almost no consciousness of rhythm or harmony as separate musical variables. At every turn the music was the product of a limited gaze, a secret compact between performers which seems, by its thin, meandering, regular, interwoven lines, thus to exclude nonparticipants rather than to draw them in. This is the sacral and iconic element of music, and one only needs to listen to the acoustical grandeur of plainchant in a cavernous cathedral to appreciate the force of its aesthetic. This music instilled obedience not through any direct communication of its message but by conveying a sense of space and mystery. Is not some of this character present in the statutes of the time, too—magisterial, florid, iconic, secret?

Neither statute nor chant demonstrated a normative intent: they were not concerned to communicate ideas or values to their lay audience. And unlike the secular and vernacular love motets which came to occupy French composers during the fourteenth century,[33] the motet in England (much like the statute) retained its character as the product of established institutions, using Latin texts for hierarchical purposes. Both music and law thus recorded the discussions of an elite which excluded the common man, not as yet encompassed by their gaze. But at the same time, both early forms conveyed, by the fact of the word or its sound rather than through its meaning, the salutary awe which power inspires. Authority was here, in statutum or organum alike, not communicated but made manifest.

The Content of Laws

If we turn now to the subject matter of thirteenth-century statutes, we find further evidence to demonstrate their limited purpose. The common law, as it began to regularize and refine the customary law of England, was normative but not under royal control. Statuta, although under direct royal control, were not primarily normative. They contain few provisions which could be interpreted as establishing general norms of behavior: for the most part, their purpose was either to clarify the procedure for dealing with writs before the king's courts or to regulate the conduct of the king's officials throughout the country. The mood was often that of a master bringing his unruly agents to heel. So in one 1266 statute, "bailiffs, sheriffs, and other officers" were instructed to "make account to the Treasurer." *An Ordinance for Ireland* (1288) partook of the same character and was a kind of letter patent to the Justice of Ireland, the king's administrator there, defining his personal authority.[34]

Peter Goodrich has emphasized the sacred and iconic nature of Latin texts of the Middle Ages and argued that they were not functional documents but relics of sovereignty. Statute laws served this function for the illiterate peasantry, as I have noted, but their immediate purpose as the private communication of a literate ruling elite was, on the contrary, decidedly administrative and practical. While they may have seemed to most people to be "holy mysteries . . . stored in sacred hiding places"—a characteristic we have already noted with respect to both statutes and chants—that was not the audience to which they were addressed.[35] To that specific audience, statutes were instructions.

The nonnormativity of statuta in the sense of their refusal to control *social* norms of behavior can be found, paradoxically, in both their iconic communal authority, then, and in the narrow procedural focus of their contents. *Organa* and early forms of the motet likewise did not attempt to persuade or compel belief: they were not normative agents either. A motet, recall, is "a little word," an etymology which reflected the prevailing attitude of the time that religious music ought not distract from the holy words it set. This view of the subordinate function of music dominated in the Catholic church at least until the Renaissance and, to a considerable extent, still governs Orthodox composition. Monophonic writing such as plainchant provides a clear example. For those few who understood it, the

words of the liturgy were of primary importance and music merely the vehicle for its communication. Consequently, even at its most melismatic, the
line and rhythm of the music closely parallels the words in question. Although florid at times, the composition never makes musical demands that
remove the focus from the "little words" it speaks.

What this means is that the persuasive or normative power of Christian
ritual was seen to stem from the words and not the music. Early polyphonic
writing did not attempt to convey the meaning of words in musical form:
music was the iconic channel through which the words were given voice, but
it was not yet a symbolic language of communication of its own. Rhythm,
melody, key, and harmony—music qua music—were not yet independent
variables imbued with meaning of their own. Furthermore, early English
composers made no attempt to relate the text to the music. A motet was an
abstract, formal vehicle for the delivery of words, but while it "presented"
a text or texts, it did not "project" or express their sentiment.[36] The music
itself did not convey value and meaning. For those who could understand
the Latin being sung, the musical form may perhaps have served as a channel for its transmission, but even this limited communicative aspect of the
motet must not be overstated. Many motets in the thirteenth and fourteenth centuries were polytextual as well as polyphonic: different singers
sang not only different musical lines simultaneously but different texts as
well. It is likely, then, that at this point the motet was not even an effective
transmitter of the words of the text.[37]

Now admittedly the "Dies irae" and other "sequences" of twelfth-
century Gregorian chant, for the first time and in a radical break with tradition, attempted to use music's expressive potential to convey the mood
and ideas of the words. The "day of wrath," whose sound and beat instill
the terror described in the text, is an archetype of the persuasive force of
music, then and now. But it is not until centuries later, in the part-writing
of composers such as Josquin des Prez and Thomas Tallis, that this idea of a
specific relationship between words and music became pronounced. At that
point, when music itself was designed to persuade the listener, through the
emotional force of sounds, of the truth of the words it set—of the mercy
of Jesus, the grandeur of the Lord, or the sorrowful peace of the dead—
then and only then did music qua music begin to exert a normative effect
on its listeners. Music had developed from being a medium of communication to a means thereof.

In these early days, then, neither English motets nor English statutes attempted to originate norms of right conduct applicable to the community
as a whole. On the contrary, many early statutes merely confirmed exist-

ing and customary principles of law. The *Magna Carta* and *Carta Forestæ* are typical, declaring that "the city of London shall have all the old liberties and customs, which it used to have"; that no one "shall be distrained to make Bridges and Banks, but such as of old time and of right have accustomed to make them"; that the ownership of woods in forests and the practice of the King's Rangers shall be "as it hath been accustomed at the time of the first Coronation of King Henry our Grandfather" (which itself upheld the law as it existed in the time of Edward the Confessor).[38] The reference to keeping things as they were in Henry's grandfather's day was quite common.[39]

The reduction to writing of a custom undoubtedly has some effect, for it reinforces a particular state of affairs and gives official imprimatur to a principle which might previously have existed only informally or imprecisely. Moreover, it may frequently restore principles which had fallen into disuse. It is, however, a very different and more limited kind of action than that which we now understand to be the function of legislation. In claiming that this kind of lawmaking is not normative, at least as we now tend to understand the word in relation to statutes, I mean to emphasize that the reduction to statutory form of existing customs does not itself generate or modify norms or values within a community.

This argument addresses a difference of opinion between Charles McIlwain and Thomas Plucknett. McIlwain argues that early statutes affirmed the common law and did not "make" new law, while Plucknett rejects this distinction and uses the evidence of the time, such as the year books, to assert that statutes were seen as instituting "special" or "novel" law. But Plucknett is discussing a period of lawmaking a century later than McIlwain, by which time a changing attitude to statute law was already evident, as we shall see. In fact, in discussing slightly earlier statutes dating from the reign of Edward I (1272–1307), Plucknett concedes that the line between statute and common law was weakly drawn. He suggests that statutes were received not as superior law but as part of the common law: "those charters and statutes are merely adjuncts to the unwritten common law, and . . . wholly partake of its nature." The prime function of this written portion of unwritten law was declaratory; as Plucknett writes, a statute was "a memorandum about a point of custom."[40]

What was called a statutum seems to modern eyes more like a narrative or history, intended rather to record the events of the court than to alter the law or social behavior. The statute fulfilled, in other words, a descriptive rather than a prescriptive function. The following statute on bastardy, which dates from 1235, is a good example:

> All the Bishops instanted the Lords, that they would consent, that all
> such as were born afore Matrimony should be legitimate, as well as
> they that be born after Matrimony . . . foreasmuch as the Church ac-
> cepteth such as legitimate. And all Earls and Barons with one voice an-
> swered, that they would not change the Law of the Realm, which hith-
> erto have been used and approved.[41]

Undoubtedly the rejection by the Lords of the Bishops' appeal was a way
of describing and confirming the current law. But in terms of a twentieth-
century understanding of what a statute does, nothing happened. No law
was passed: there was no change to the Law of the Realm. This "statute" was
merely the story of a political event. Law, politics, and history are hardly
distinguishable.[42]

Even "penal" laws demonstrated a nonnormative character. The *Carta
Forestæ* (1225), for example, said, "No man from henceforth shall lose either Life or Member for killing of our Deer: But if any man be taken, and
convict for taking our Venison, he shall make a grievous fine."[43] Observe
that the law did not make it an offense to kill royal venison—it nowhere
said, "No man shall kill our deer." The offense (that is, the normative principle) was assumed. The statute only dealt with—and, admittedly, substantially amended—the kind of punishment that may be imposed. This statute was typical in this respect, in the way in which it built on preexisting
principles. Another law dealt with the penalty for "the ravishment of a
ward" but again did not establish the meaning or wrongfulness of the conduct in the first place.[44] A modern statute, in contrast, invariably begins
with a comprehensive statement and definition of the offense and treats the
question of penalty as a subsidiary matter. Undoubtedly the wrongfulness
of taking venison or ravishing wards is a necessary implication of these statutes. But the normative grounds of the wrong are not found in legislation.
They are rooted instead in popular customary law.

Providing a specific penalty for an offense was almost unheard of. Reading these documents, one gets the impression that lawmakers at this time
did not conceive of the concrete application of their laws: they did not imagine the transgression of laws or the punishment of transgressors. This is a
detail left for others in their discretion to fill in, just as the improvisational
character of music allowed enormous freedom to the individual performer
of an organum or chant. For modern legislators, of course, the specific offense and the specific penalty go together: the modern judge, like the modern musician, is subject to far greater constraint. In one way, this is a consequence of the intrusiveness and detail of contemporary laws. But from
another angle it reflects how little the king and his advisers in the thirteenth

century saw the law as a means of literally enforcing their will on the lives of others. The king's perception of law, outside its application to a close circle of officials, was clouded and unspecific. It is a mistake, then, to conceive of early statutes as an expression of coercive power, when the act of coercion was not envisaged by the power.

The lack of specific penalties was partly a function of the limited reach of the king's power and of the very limited machinery through which laws could in fact be enforced. England was still over 350 years away from a standing army and almost 600 years from a regular police force. A lack of resources, however, was not the only factor that inhibited the establishment of a comprehensive system of penalties and punishment. Systems of penalties were not unknown, having existed in some detail in the codes of the Anglo-Saxon kings. Furthermore, the practical difficulty of a particular course of conduct is never a fully satisfactory explanation. The possible and the conceivable are interrelated: the former helps define the latter, and the latter propels the former.[45] What is done in a society—and what is left undone—is therefore valuable evidence of how that society thought.

Where statutes do actually intervene to "change the law," some justification was required. The *Statute de Marleberge* (1267) began as if by way of apology: "The Realm of England of late had been disquieted with manifold Troubles and Dissensions; for Reformation whereof Statutes and Law be right necessary." [46] Yet even here, about 70 percent of the various "chapters" (that is, subdivisions of the statute) were either procedural or declaratory of the existing law or provided limited exceptions to it.[47] Only in a few cases, therefore, did the statute substantively alter customary norms.

In general then, statuta are descriptive, not prescriptive: they organize a legal system but do not change the law, and in the main they are addressed to functionaries. For John Austin, at least, we are not in the province of jurisprudence at all, since laws that were declaratory, or specific rather than general in application, or to which no sanction applied, were for him "imperfect" or "improperly termed" laws.[48]

The Later Thirteenth Century: A Changing Mood

Visibility: The *Statute of Westminster*

The majority of the population were not yet illuminated in the eyes of the powerful, and the application of the law to them was therefore neither important nor even clearly imagined. Legislation was largely seen as a means of communication between the king and those physically connected to him, and the character of laws reflected this narrow and personal gaze. An important signpost of change occurs with the enactment of the first *Statute of Westminster* in 1275. Coming across it among the gray and desiccated parchment of *Statutes at Large*, one feels a sudden shock at the new tenor of the law, its passion, its determination, and its mood. After over half a century of Henry III's dusty rule, King Edward takes command, raising a new voice in the realm:

> And because the State of his Kingdom and of the Holy Church had been evil kept, and the Prelates and religious Persons of the Land grieved many ways, and the People otherwise intreated than they ought to be, and the Peace less kept, and the Laws less used, and the Offenders less punished than they ought to be . . .[49]

Here were the stirrings of a change of consciousness with profound legal effects. For the first time, a statute referred not to archbishops and bishops, sheriffs and bailiffs, not even to "freemen,"[50] but to "the People." The substantive clauses of the statute continued in the same spirit: "First the King willeth and commandeth . . . that common Right be done to all, as well Poor as rich, without respect for Persons."[51] Not only are the words different here, but so is the language in which they are expressed: the *Statute of Westminster* was the first English statute written in French rather than Latin. As Frederick Maitland noted, it is hardly now possible to write a paragraph of law without using words of French derivation: contract, tort, property, treason, crime, and misdemeanor; parliament, court, judge, juror, plaintiff, and defendant to name but a few.[52] French was, admittedly, the language of the conquering Normans and not by any means the "common tongue." Neither was "law French" the same thing as "spoken French" but rather a written language distorted by complex grammatical rules and highly technical legal terminology. It is fair to say that it only resembled spoken French, as margarine resembles butter. Nevertheless, "law French" was based on a living language; in fact, "law French" is a strange concoction exactly because, unlike Latin or English, it had no prior history of written use at all.[53] The official language of *parle-ment* became, as its French etymology implied, a spoken language.

What does this change imply? First, as Plucknett suggests, that a powerful class of lay legal specialists has developed, clerks and not clerics, "who understand Latin but are really only fluent in French." But at the same time the use of law French was an effort to communicate directly with a wider audience. This was a statute which was clearly intended to become widely known.[54] There was therefore an assumption here that a statute can change behavior and attitudes and, more, that adequate knowledge of its terms has this result. In this sense, we are witnessing the very birth of normativity in English statutes—that is, of law understood not only as an administrative tool and an icon of power but as a means of influencing what the people do and what they believe to be right.

This too was a revolutionary change with implications far beyond law. For millennia, the Latin alphabet had been used only to write Latin; the idea that it could serve equally well to represent the sounds of vernacular tongues was beyond the imagination of Europe. This radical change happens only from the twelfth century, and it transformed not just law but literature, science, love. Ivan Illich writes:

> Whatever is said, whatever is sung, and, soon, whatever is thought, can end upon the surface of a leaf. As the text is now detached from the concrete object, from this rather than that specific parchment, so the signs of the ABC have acquired their independence from Latin.[55]

We are witnessing here the abstraction and reification of thought, and in law, as in other realms of human life, it altered the relationship of people to texts. A law is no longer just a record of a speech: it is now a means of communication to a community potentially infinite in time and space. The little words of the law have begun to be seen as a mind-altering substance.

We may be cynical about whether the king's rhetoric really stemmed from a genuine concern for the welfare of "the people," but even the emergence of this language is significant. For the first time the law saw the commons and acknowledged that they were subject to the legal system and that their support for it therefore somehow mattered. They were now on the horizon of visibility. It was now possible for them to be "subjects" and "objects" of statutes: dramatis personae in the legal system and not merely its backdrop. This legal gaze, beginning to be focused ineluctably upon the whole citizenry, did not prove an unmitigated boon. Without it, however, our modern legal system and our modern understanding of law simply could not be.

Legal consciousness of a society of individuals which it could reach and control was accompanied by a dramatic shift in English people's consciousness of their own individuality. Foucault discusses the emergence of individual visibility as an instrument of social control in the context of the eighteenth century, but clearly people began to be "seen" as individuals much earlier. Philippe Ariès, for example, records that in and around the thirteenth century the European view of death began to change. We see the slow individualization of tombs, of wills, of bequests—all these material techniques designed to record the existence and guard the memory of the deceased as an individual and not simply as part of the ebb and flow of the community. In Ariès's words, we pass from an era in which death was "tame" to one in which people were acutely aware of "the death of the self": the emergence of self-awareness radicalized death.[56] So too, the concept of a *persona* changed, from that of a disguise, which was its Latin root, to that of an office or role whose performance had legal consequences, and finally to that of the character or essence which distinguishes each of us from everybody else. The person has changed from the outer mask we wear or perform to the inner self we are.

In the arts a similar revolution took place, albeit rather later in the specific case of painting. There is a world of difference between Fra Angelico's flat, introverted imagery, in the middle of the fifteenth century, and the works of Leonardo da Vinci at the end of it. The difference is, literally, a question of perspective. Perspective, given scientific form by Brunelleschi and in Alberti's *Della pittura* (1436), was not simply a technique which, once "discovered," enabled painters to reproduce what they saw more accurately than before. It was a revolution in the way painters saw. There is a famous picture of Erasmus drawing a landscape with the aid of a lattice grid set in front of his easel and constructed to train the eyes to see segments of space in a new way. A radical perceptual transformation was under way, and much new learning was required to achieve it.[57]

An awareness of the individual existence of the viewer was an important part of this new artistic approach. Perspective draws the observer of the painting into the picture, and this approach to art cannot exist unless the painter is specifically conscious of the observer in the first place. The incorporation of perspective into paintings was remarkable, not just in the way it represented the "real" world but in its awareness of an interaction with that world. Leonardo's *Mona Lisa* is as good an example as any: it looks at you. In contrast, early medieval art, like early legislation, is absorbed in its own world; you, as an individual observer, do not exist. In the gaze of the artwork, we begin to appreciate the changing gaze of its creators.

It is often said that the world of the Gregorian chant is similarly unpopulated by subjectivity and individualism—that it is two-dimensional, because only one line of music is heard at any one time. But by 1275, the date of the *Statute of Westminster,* the form of the motet had developed with surprising rapidity toward part differentiation, independent melodic lines, and greater rhythmic variety.[58] Musical notation, too, had developed with some rapidity and inventiveness in England, striving to express not only a standard corpus of rhythmic modes or relationships but also the precise value of each individual note. Franco of Cologne's important musical treatise, *Ars musica mensurabilis* (circa 1280), brought coherence to these developments, and his principles as to the accurate notation of rhythm soon spread to England.[59] In all these ways the motet shows itself to be not an improvement on plainchant but the product of a different vision entirely: a vision which recognizes the individuality of its participants, each responsible for a separate musical line. The changing style and form of a composition, like the wording of a statute, reflected the developing priorities of its authors. Earlier artists and musicians—and earlier lawmakers—were not incompetents, struggling along with techniques and powers inadequate to their tasks and desires; their intentions were different and the product of a different aesthetic.

The *Statute of Westminster* and the developing motet both reflected a newfound awareness of the wider world, and the gaze of each expressed the all-encompassing perspective of their authors. Undoubtedly the statute, lying at the very beginning of this process, signified, in legal as well as artistic terms, only the nascence of a trend. Subsequent statutes frequently reverted to Latin, the use of which did not die out altogether until 1324. And, of course, Latin continued to be used for centuries thereafter in writs, in legal jargon, and, until as late as 1731, as the official language of judicial records.[60] Many of the provisions of the *Statute of Westminster* are still administrative instructions to officials and, in particular, aim to curb their abuses and corruption. But not all provisions are of this kind. A more expansive legislative gaze can elsewhere be detected. Chapter 13 provided that, in the case of rape, the king may bring an action, and it expressly established a penalty of at least two years' imprisonment. In contrast to the earlier statute for "ravishment," enforcement and punishment were here specifically articulated. The law is beginning to be imagined as a physical presence in the lives of individuals.

Normativity: The *Statute of Winchester*

The statutes which followed the *Statute of Westminster* remained, in general, a declaration and record of the law "for a perpetual Memory thereof." [61] It marked, however, an important beginning, in which law's gaze began to widen and the purposes ascribed to it began to change. From 1050 to 1300 the number of written accounts and legal charters in England grew perhaps one hundredfold.[62] A revolution was afoot.

But a gradual one. The second *Statute of Westminster*, written ten years after the first, generally provided for remedies in situations where none previously existed. In this way, the principles of the law were clarified and their use streamlined. This facilitated the community's use of the legal system, but it did not directly operate on their attitudes. While the general population were now seen as subjects of the law, there was not yet a common belief in the capacity of the words of the law to somehow change their values or conduct. The law did not yet treat people as its objects.

Statutes relating to felonies, however, show a far greater consciousness of law's potential for effecting normative change. One chapter of the second *Statute of Westminster* is particularly interesting:

> That if a Man from henceforth do ravish a Woman married, Maid, or other, where she did not consent, neither before nor after, he shall have judgment of Life and a Member. And likewise where a man ravisheth a Woman married, Lady, Damosel, or other, with Force, although the consent after, he shall have such Judgment as before is said.[63]

This was the clearest statement so far of the felony of rape. In contrast to the earlier penal provisions discussed above, the text itself stated and defined the terms of the crime and provided a specific penalty for its breach. Rape had become a statutory offense.

In a statute thirty-four pages long and written in Latin, these eight lines are in French.[64] Of course, written "law French" was hardly well understood in semiliterate England. But lawmakers clearly saw this chapter as a different kind of law addressed to a wider public. A special effort was therefore made to render its provisions comprehensible. The idea of a statute as something which should communicate to all people rather than just to certain officials, should effect the conduct of all people, and if necessary should force their compliance by the threat of punishment was gaining ground. The system of legislation had begun to take on a recognizably modern form, reflecting an ideal of state control over every aspect of future behavior.

So too the musical notation formulated by Franco of Cologne had taken hold in England by the beginning of the fourteenth century. This was a language capable, at last, of defining with precision the absolute duration and pitch of each individual note. It was a system of musical legislation in a recognizably modern form, reflecting an ideal of authorial control over every aspect of future performance.

The *Statute of Winchester*, passed at the same time, was again wholly in French and demonstrated an even stronger commitment to the law as a prescriptive force. Here we find provisions, relating to the apprehension of felons and robbers, which required "people dwelling in the country" to assist in the attaint of offenders or to answer themselves for the damage done.[65] This law was not merely declaratory or procedural: common people were laid under new obligations purely by virtue of the statute.

Three structural features of this provision underscore its normative character. First, a date was set for its entry into force—"Easter next following." [66] This of course is a characteristic that every modern statute possesses, but the year 1285 marked its debut. The second *Statute of Westminster,* made at the same time, was still clearer: "All the said Statutes shall take Effect at the Feast of St. Michael next coming." [67] What does this mean?— that the statute was seen not just as a statement of intent or as a record but as an event with concrete effects. The contrast with the lack of direct effect of, for example, the statute on bastardy is quite striking. The provision for a statute's entry into force represented a fundamentally new attitude, in which the statute was no longer seen as an inert string of words but as a statement of intention to alter events in the future. On the one hand, such a provision represented an increased awareness of the "real world" and a desire to increase statutes' interaction with it. On the other hand, it represented a new faith in people's capacity to change their behavior as instructed. The relationship of "law" both to the possibility of "change" and the scope of the legal "world" is being reconstructed here. It is only in this context that the question of "when" arises. *When* is this law to change the world? It is the formulation of this novel question that made entry provisions necessary.

Second, the entry into force was postponed: "That [the provision] shall not incur immediately, but it shall be respited until Easter next following, within which Time the king may see how the Country will order themselves, and whether such Felonies and Robberies do cease." [68] The king evidently believed that the mere threat of the impending statute might change people's conduct. No more normative and instrumental understanding of law could be imagined. The fact of the law, and even the fact of the threat of the law, was expected to have a behavioral effect.

Third, normativity requires communication. Only if the content of a norm is adequately communicated can it influence our behavior. Accordingly, the law required "That Cries shall be solemnly made in all Counties, Hundreds, Markets, Fairs, and all other Places where great Report of People is, so that none shall excuse himself by Ignorance." [69] This would appear to be a logical extension of the change from Latin to French, from written to spoken. As the *Statute of Westminster* introduced a law that could be spoken as well as read, the *Statute of Winchester* provided for a law that was not only to be spoken but heard. This change reflected a rapidly growing faith in its capacity to enter people's minds and alter them. In the *Articuli super Cartas* of 1300, the *Magna Carta*, the *Carta Forestæ*, and the *Statute of Winchester* were all again confirmed, with the important addition that they were to be read publicly four times a year by the sheriffs. *De Tallagio non Concedendo* (1306) was to be read in cathedral churches and those who broke its terms excommunicated.[70] The public was now expected to know the law, to obey the law, and to change their lives accordingly. The law was now more than visible: it was audible. Music, on the other hand, benefiting from the development of a comprehensive system of notation, was now more than audible: it had become visible.

The requirement for law to be read out aloud reflected the nature of reading itself in the medieval world: as Illich describes it, reading was a physical act and not a purely mental exercise. "In a tradition of one and a half millennia," he writes, "the sounding pages are echoed by the resonance of the moving lips and tongue. . . . By reading, the page is literally embodied, incorporated."[71] How much more was the sound of law inherent to its authority when dealing with an illiterate population? In this, then, the legal text and the musical score resemble one another, gaining meaning and authority not just by the ideas they represent but through their performance.

The Fourteenth and Fifteenth Centuries: Validity and Normativity in the Structure of Statutes

The Form of Introduction

We are on the threshold of the jurisprudential question: subjected now to the gaze of the law, on what grounds were people expected to obey it? In rough outline, three broad answers might be given. Nineteenth-century positivists in England and the United States, of whom John Austin is the best known, characterized law as commands issued by a political superior. Austin's position is in fact more subtle than is commonly thought. Contrary to the interpretation placed upon his work by some later writers, Austin does not dismiss the relevance of morality to law.[72] Nonetheless, according to Austin, there can be no law without a sanction, from which our duty to obey arises. For Austin, and for Oliver Wendell Holmes and Hans Kelsen among later writers, legal obligation is rooted in coercion.[73]

This position has been attacked on a number of different grounds. Natural-law theory may be taken to imply that moral conclusions, no less than scientific ones, can be objectively deduced from first principles, whether these first principles are divinely ordained or (since the Enlightenment) rationally determined. If, as John Finnis argues in *Natural Law and Natural*

Rights, it is thus possible to reason from largely uncontentious first principles to the solution to moral problems, then each of us has the capacity to discover for ourselves those laws that are morally justifiable and those that are not.[74] Such an approach suggests that we are not required to obey a law which by such a process of objective reason is in fact immoral. Reason imposes a greater claim upon us than power.[75]

Somewhere between Austin's coercive legal order and the specter of untrammeled freedom evoked by the natural-law tradition, modern positivists such as H. L. A. Hart have sought to ground legal obligation in the authority of legal texts. According to Hart, the fact of a law's existence provides those subject to it with compelling reasons for compliance. Hart lays particular emphasis on the existence of "rules of recognition" that determine the validity of rules of obligation. A statute duly passed by Parliament, for example, is legal and authoritative, and citizens are thereby provided with an adequate reason for following the course of action it prescribes.[76] On this analysis, what matters is neither the "truth" of a law nor the "power" that backs it up but the "validity" of the procedure which lies behind it—its origin is what counts. Joseph Raz defends even more emphatically a "sources thesis," arguing that the legitimacy of the formal "sources" of a law, such as a properly enacted statute or an authoritative judicial interpretation, establishes a separate reason to obey the law apart from the justice of its contents.[77] This does characterize the approach of many people to the legal system in which they live; they justify their obedience to any particular law not because of its actual reasonableness but because of the "systemic validity" of the process by which laws in general are established.[78]

Although much debate may surround the merits of a particular piece of legislation (both before and after its enactment), the modern statute, on its face, presents no justification for the law but the law itself. The preambles of modern statutes have become almost irrelevant. This approach supports Joseph Raz's thesis: the fact that a piece of legislation has been passed in accordance with correct procedure is taken to provide us with a sufficient reason to obey it.

Let us return to the radically different gaze of the second *Statute of Westminster*. Why were people expected to obey it? The answer is not simple. Many of its chapters followed a two-step process. First, the injustice of the law was explicitly acknowledged: the previous law "seemed very hard," "was very hard," "was most hard," and so on. The same phrase was used in other statutes dating from this period.[79] The use of the word "hard" here is interesting. It is a tactile word; it has an immediate presence, a physicality about it in stark contrast to words relating to more abstract senses, such as sight. We see from afar, but we only experience hardness directly, the felt and brute reality of a resisting object. A "hard" law, therefore, is a law whose injustice is actually felt and not merely observed. The awareness of the legal system as something embedded in and touching the whole community thus continued to grow.

Second, the harshness of the present law having been established, the chapters of the second *Statute of Westminster* proposed solutions and improvements with the consistent declaration that this was to be the law "from henceforth."[80] In contrast to those statutes of Henry III which studiously preserved the law as it had been in his grandfather's day, this approach was oriented to the future and designed to change and correct the deficiencies of the past. This legislation, however, does not rely upon either the crown's coercive power or the validity attaching to the formal procedures for the statute's enactment, to elicit conformity to the changes that are made. By saying that the previous law was "very hard," a justification was given for the new law.

Indeed the structure of these chapters is that of an argument and not a declaration. The normativity of the law stems here at least in part from its appeal to justice and reason. The lengthy and emotive introductions to the *Statute de Marleberge* and the first *Statute of Westminster* provide further evidence for this suggestion. The more weighty a statute's ambitions, the more imposing the flourish of justification which accompanied it. The authors of these normative provisions took an approach somewhat akin to natural-law theory. Obedience and respect were sought through an appeal to reason stated in the legislation itself.[81]

During the thirteenth century, justificatory reasoning ran through the substantive provisions of a statute like a commentary, suggesting once again that the distinction between law, politics, and history remained extremely hazy. In the absence of other kinds of authoritative records, the statute combined substantive law and parliamentary debate—reasons and consequences. The style of statutes continued to change, however, gradually shifting from an emphasis on the reasons behind the law to an emphasis on the validating procedures surrounding its enactment. If we jump forward to the second half of the fourteenth century (by which time the use of law French in statutes was uniform), a change is already apparent. The introductory reasons for enactment are now less specific than those in the *Statute de Marleberge* and the *Statutes of Westminster*. Furthermore, these reasons are increasingly confined to a structurally discrete introduction to the statute. The statute passed in 1362 begins, "To the Honour and Pleasure of God, and Amendment of the outrageous Grievances and Oppressions done to the People, and in Relief of their Estate. . . ."[82] A rhetorical flourish like this could hardly serve as a reason justifying any particular part of the statute, which contains a number of unrelated substantive provisions.

In the following years, moreover, the introduction became ever more formal, referring to the way in which the statute was passed rather than to its content or purposes.[83] By 1407, the introduction was almost standardized, invariably referring to certain features, including the date of the Parliament, the presence and concurrence of both houses of Parliament, and the will of the Crown:

> Because that divers Complaints have been made . . . in the Parliament holden at Gloucester . . . the same our Lord the King, willing to remedy the said Complaints, with the Advice and Assent of the Lords Spiritual and Temporal, and at the Instance and Request of the said Commons, hath caused to be ordained and established divers Ordinances and Statutes. . . .[84]

We have traced the metamorphosis of this structural item from that of a means of establishing the reasons for the enactment of a statute to that of a means of establishing its validity or provenance. Each chapter—the substantive units into which a statute was divided—still contained some explanation of the purpose of its enactment, and at times this explanation was grandiloquent and rhetorical:

> The King remembering how the commons of this his Realm, by new and unlawful Invention, and inordinate Covetise, against the law of this Realm, hath been put to great Thraldom and importable Charges and Exactions . . . to their almost utter destruction . . .[85]

Nonetheless, the introduction to the statute as a whole had developed a significant and novel character. It now reflected the growing importance of procedure in establishing the authoritative nature of the law and therefore suggests the slow triumph of something like Raz's "sources thesis" in the minds of lawmakers: people ought obey the law because of who issued it rather than why.

The Act of Parliament

The increase of royal power, and the establishment of clear legislative procedure, reflected the increasing importance of procedural validity in grounding normativity. At the same time, as we have seen, the legislative gaze slowly encompassed the commons, while law's purpose began to change from declaratory to imperative, from "is" to "ought."

In 1461, amidst political turbulence and civil war, Edward IV came to power. It is not surprising, then, to find in the statute of that year a particularly detailed justification of Edward's claim to the Crown as against his rivals, dead and alive.[86] But there is a subtle and more telling change here. The first chapter of this statute confirms not only the "Judicial Acts" of his predecessors but their "acts and ordinances." There are several other references to "this Act" and "other Acts." Within a very few years, each chapter would come to be called an act.[87]

What does this word "Act" betoken? Despite the apparent similarity with the "Acts of the Apostles," the two senses are quite distinct. An "act" is "a thing done; a deed, a performance,"[88] and the apostles' "acts" were clearly deeds or things done: the New Testament text which we call "Acts" is therefore not an act itself but only a record of those acts done elsewhere. An "Act of Parliament" is very different. Where, one might ask, is the "act" to which the "act" refers? Undoubtedly a judgment or a court's decision is an "act" in the lay sense, for it has concrete and immediate effects. But the only act done by the legislation of a chapter in a statute is the act of writing. It could be termed a charter, a fiat, a decree, an ordinance, a missive, a treaty, a declaration, a communiqué, a proclamation, a writ. . . . What, after all, does "writ" mean but that which is written? Even the word "statute" derives from the Latin meaning "to stand"—a statute "stands written."[89] All these words convey the sense in which, above all (and unlike the acts of the Apostles), Parliament's acts are composed of words on paper.

The use of the word "Act" in the technical sense which is now commonplace, however, is confusing and ambiguous: Parliament's physical "act" or "deed done" is complete the moment the law is enacted. (To ease the confusion, I will use a capital 'A' when using the word in this legislative sense.) But to call it "an Act" suggests that the statute, although written down, is no longer thought of as something which just "stands" (still). In some way it continues to "act." The word "Act" thus translates the statute from marks on paper into energy in the world. It illustrates a worldview in which statutes are gradually being seen not only as historical records of events but as acts with continuing effects of their own, like the expanding ripples of a rock dropped in a pond. Furthermore, in contrast to the earlier understanding of legislation as a declaratory instrument, "Act" is active. An Act is not just a record of the world but a way of modifying it; it is a vector with velocity.

The Act therefore gathers to its bosom law's vigor, its claim to reality, and its determination to interact with the world. This is radically different from the passive understanding of law we have previously encountered. We have not yet, however, reached a particularly sophisticated understanding of the nature of the statute. For there is a sense in which the word "Act" carries the implication that the mere proclamation of the law can somehow by itself create the new reality it proposes. There is a faith here in some sort of magical osmosis between word and world. In the fifteenth century, this naïveté reflected a still-limited gaze which may have led lawmakers to assume (in many cases) that just the passing of an Act did the job. They failed, perhaps, to envisage the long process by which a statute comes to have some force and relevance, the human steps of application and enforcement required, and the resistance that might be faced from other people with opposing values and practices. Yet although flawed, the idea of the "Act" is important: you cannot believe in the normative power of law unless you assume that laws act in the world.

The structure of written law no less than its language reflected this trend. The earliest statutes were, as we have seen, narrations of political events. The statute, a historical record of the decisions of a particular session of Parliament, was the fundamental legislative unit, divided into "chapters" merely for the sake of clarity and convenience. By the fifteenth century, a change is noticeable. There are more chapters than ever before, many of them subdivided into sections. Statutes no longer have titles; chapters will soon gain them. At the same time, as we have seen, the introduction to the statute is becoming more formal and less important. By the time of Henry VIII, it had disappeared altogether and been replaced by a similar formula at the beginning of each chapter.[90] The chapter is now known as an "Act" of Parliament. The statute is merely an omnibus of these Acts, bound together at the end of the regnal year. What we are witnessing here is the demise of the statute as the fundamental unit of legislative structure and its replacement by the chapter or Act.

These structural changes reveal a conceptual shift as significant as the way in which twelfth-century compositors began suddenly to use the ABC for indexing purposes.[91] While statutes were organized chronologically— by time—each chapter or Act is designed to achieve a single purpose: they are organized by idea. Why was it now seen necessary to divide chapters into sections? Partly because of the increasingly detailed control with which each law was concerned but also because the conceptual unit was now the chapter. The sections all "belonged" within a particular chapter because they were all steps designed to facilitate the same purpose. Lawmaking had therefore changed from a record of past events (stated in the statute) to an act of present intention (captured by the chapter). We can see where this progress will eventually take us. In the twentieth century, the word "statute" has lost its original meaning as the collection of legislation of a particular regnal year and is treated as synonymous with "Act."[92] Each "statute," understood in this sense, is designed to change the law; it frequently includes hundreds of sections, all of which share at least to some extent a common purpose. Now, the statute is no longer parliamentary history at all. It is the instrumental expression of an idea.

We have, in fact, rung down the curtain on the medieval world and entered the Renaissance, an age of unbounded confidence in man's ability to change the world by an act of will. In fifteenth-century music, composers such as Ockeghem and, in England, Pycard and Byttering began to refine the "canon," a musical form which later reached its apotheosis in the fugue.[93] A canon, though, is by nature based more in rules: the musical statement of one part is copied by other, successive, voices, either exactly or in accordance with predetermined principles of modification. It is musical law, in truth as well as in etymology. Like an Act, a canon continues to enforce its will upon the world. It is a composition subjected to the governance of principles or themes laid down in advance, and with whose terms composer and performers alike must obediently comply. There is, for example, in the formidable *Gloria* of Pycard, a five-part double canon, a heightened clarity of line, and regulation of the form of musical expression—just as we have seen in the Acts of the period a heightened clarity of purpose and regulation of the form of legal expression.

Legal Subjects

Above all, the fifteenth century was notable for the triumph of harmony as a guiding aesthetic principle. Harmony became enriched, principally by the declining use of parallel fifths and the increased use of thirds and sixths, previously considered "imperfect intervals" and held in correspondingly low esteem.[94] The early fifteenth-century manuscripts to be found in the Old Hall collection mark with particular prominence this cultural development.[95]

Simultaneous with this harmonic thickening, the consonance of all melodic lines became a crucial task of composition. In the polyphonic music of the fifteenth century, then, each note was studied and integrated, not only in relation to its own line but in relation to all the other lines being sung at the same time. The compositional gaze was directed vertically as well as horizontally—directed toward deepening the control exercised over harmony as well as expanding the tonal range of melody. So the sound of Western music changed markedly, from spacious and hollow to something lush and thick. From the single melodic line of plainchant, or the simple structure and sound of the earliest motets, the field of the composer's gaze widened vastly in all directions: melodically, rhythmically, harmonically. There was a complexity of musical consciousness here, accompanied by an unprecedented degree of musical organization and control. It was this complexity of writing and hearing which the "motet" came to represent.

The statute likewise developed a heightened legal consciousness and a deeper, broader gaze. The notion that the purpose of the law was to reform, to act, and to provide norms was well established by the fifteenth century and was applied to a vastly wider range of people and over an increasing number of aspects of their lives. Law thus sought to harmonize the behavior of more citizens in ever more intricate ways. Still, the way in which the law strove to harmonize the conduct of the community remained limited. With England's rising mercantile power, for example, there came a barrage of laws controlling trade, import, and the economic conditions of the country: Acts about coins, loans, boats, bread, and wool.[96] By and large, these Acts attempt to change the conditions of the world—people's status, their land, their property, their trade—and only indirectly to influence their beliefs and desires. I do not mean that laws about conditions of trade and relations of production do not affect people's behavior and ideology. Clearly they do. But the idea that the law is normative, that its terms control how people think and how they choose to behave—a kind of attitude assumed by modern criminal law and much else beside—conceives of the mind as an object which the law can manipulate just as if it were a loaf of bread or a bushel of wheat. This approach, while it had begun to be expressed, had not yet triumphed.

In undertaking this enabling function so early, statutory law saw its citizens as its "subjects," whose actions were either circumscribed or facilitated by its terms. In contrast, the law's view of them as "agents" representing the king lay in the past, and its view of them as "objects," whose very desire for action could be made to conform to the rules of harmony, lay substantially in the future. This integration of each member of society into a whole community, obedient to laws which determined in advance their attitudes to and relationship with each other, constituted the triumph of the harmonic principle in law.

The Sixteenth Century: Validity and Power

The Structure of the Preamble

As the Wars of the Roses came to an end, the language of Acts seemed to reflect a greater consciousness of "the People" on whose behalf each side claimed to be murdering the other. Perhaps partly in an attempt to establish some popular legitimacy for his rule, Richard III made another decisive linguistic change at his coronation in 1483. Then and thereafter, Acts of Parliament are all written in English. The change from French to English was not as sudden as it might appear. As early as 1362 a statute required that all cases should be pleaded and debated in English, and around the same time some petitions to Parliament began to appear on the roll in English.[97] These were precursors to the dramatic change a century later.

Now some of the trends we observed in the preceding centuries began to coalesce. The shift from Latin to French to English, for example, was a slow and significant one which represented an increased openness of gaze and a more normative understanding of law. The broadness of the modern legal gaze—that is, its attempt to reach and influence everybody in the community—is directly correlated to a heightened faith in law as an instrument of social change and a heightened expectation of social conformity. The triumph of this movement is the emergence in our own day of "plain English," an ideology of writing style now adopted by virtually all legislative drafters in the English-speaking world.[98] Its attempt to make statutes more accessible to everyday understanding stems from precisely the belief that the law has a strongly normative effect: that is, that it really does provide powerful independent reasons for action among those who (are assumed to) read and know it. "Plain English" insists that the law will be effective if only it is understood and understood if only it is read. Behind this lies the assumption that the correct audience for a law is the community as a whole and not the community of lawyers. "Plain English" is in all these ways the apotheosis of the modern gaze and the antithesis of the medieval.

Another theme that we have observed gathering momentum over the preceding centuries was the importance of Acts' legal validity. The argumentative style of the introduction declined, and the formal details of and procedure surrounding its enactment grew in significance. By the time of Henry VII, whose accession in 1485 put an end to the Wars of the Roses (he being the only claimant to the throne left standing), every Act (i.e., chapter) itself stated that "It is ordained, established, and enacted by the Advice of the Lords Spiritual and Temporal, and the Commons in the said Parliament assembled, and by Authority of the same. . . ."[99] The chronological statute as a concept of importance had thus been entirely superseded by the purposive Act. During the reign of Henry VIII (1509–47), the introduction disappeared altogether from the annual statutes of the Parliament. All that remained was a preamble to each individual Act which cited the grounds of its formal validity. The emphasis on the legal validity of a law had not yet, however, entirely eliminated rhetoric. The preamble, it is true, was now structurally distinct from the "substantive" clauses of each chapter. It was, furthermore, frequently framed with quotation marks as if it were a recital or a quotation. Such structural devices served to separate rhetorical language from "real" law in a way that would hardly have made sense even a century earlier. Nevertheless, the preamble continued on occasion to provide reasons for the passage of the Act.[100] Many quote a petition submitted by a group seeking Parliament's help. The Act which incorporates the Royal College of Physicians is a well-known example.[101] An Act of 1512 likewise quotes an earlier Act relating to pewterers and concludes with their plea:

> "Please it therefore your Grace and Wisdom, inasmuch as the said Act is thought good and profitable, that it be ordained, enacted and established by the Lords Spiritual and Temporal, the Commons in this present Parliament assembled, and by the Authority of the same, that the said Act may endure for ever." [102]

But let us look closer at this Act and others like it. Strictly speaking, they enact nothing. The Act concludes with an entreaty for the Parliament to act and a plea that it be so ordained, enacted, and established, but, although we can assume as much from its place in the statute book, there is no positive statement to that effect. Although the recital of a petition demonstrates that the reasons for a law were still of some significance, there is a subtle change here which paradoxically points once more to the growing importance of law's formal validity. It is instructive to compare these petitions with the early statute on bastardy, which recorded the bishops' "petition" to the Lords.[103] In that case, the fact that the petition was recorded on the statute roll did not alter Parliament's inactivity. Raz, for example, argues that a law's authority derives from the validity of the parliamentary process, the statute itself being only evidence of that constitutive process.[104] Just because a petition is placed on the roll, therefore, does not mean that it has gone through the parliamentary procedure which entitles it to validity.

In the sixteenth century, however, things were different. For what does it mean that the mere recording of the petition apparently sufficed to create law? It means that everything that appears in the statute book is taken to be "law." Raz to the contrary, the statute book appears here to be iconic of law's validity: [105] the statute was not merely a symbol or insignia of law's authority but itself rendered authoritative and valid everything within it. If we ask, from our contemporary standpoint, the basic question, "Why do we obey laws?" one reason stems from the power which written law, and in particular statute law, exerts over many of us. The existence of words in the pages of a statute book seems to demand respect, to endow those words with a certain privileged status.[106] In this way, the pages of a statute are legal icons which convey value and demand obedience simply by being there on the page. It is this kind of validity of which we begin to catch a glimpse in the petitions of the sixteenth century.

Penalties and Power

The changing nature of the preamble in Tudor England demonstrates in these ways the growing importance of legal validity as the grounds of legal obedience. But at the same time we see the growth of coercion as a means of ensuring obedience. In marked contrast to the position even fifty years earlier, there was in the statutes of Henry VII a consciousness of the importance of penalties in giving people a reason, in an Austinian sense, to obey the law. Each Tudor Act typically provided an offense and each offense a specific penalty: no longer, if mentioned at all, just "a grievous fine" or "as the trespass requires" but, for example, 6 shillings & 8 pence for the first offense, 13 shillings & 4 pence for the second offense and 20 shillings for each subsequent offense.[107] A system of coercion operated here, enforcing obedience.

Law was no longer a series of instructions to the officers and agents of the Crown to carry out, as it had been in the twelfth century. It had become a volume of texts which spoke directly to the whole community. The growth of a literate society further intensified this idea of the law as a series of ideas whose written form transformed the values and behaviors of those who read it. This change in an understanding of law, however, required not only literacy but an ability to experience language as something which operated directly from the paper to the mind—in other words, silent reading. Here is another aspect of the reification which we have already seen in the way in which the alphabet became a tool for recording common speech through its abstraction from the Latin tongue. "The modern reader conceives of the page as a plate that inks the mind, and of the mind as a screen onto which the page is projected."[108] But the practice of reading as something which goes on in the mind, as Illich traces it, grew only from the thirteenth century: it is tied not just to the growth of literacy but to a changed comprehension of the relationship of minds to words. Without this change, the idea of law as a series of texts which operated on the minds of the community could not take hold. Once the text had been reconceived as something both vernacular and abstract, laws ceased to communicate to particular individuals and became instead the means of directly modifying the lives of people distant in time and space.

This can be characterized as the "objectification" of the community, the assumption that their very beliefs could be molded by legislative intervention. There is no inconsistency here with the "subjectification" of law for which I have contended above. Both were gaining strength in the minds of lawmakers, although not at the same rate. The statutes of the sixteenth century treat citizens more as legal subjects than as objects; but in comparison with earlier centuries, both these approaches have gained ground. So too, in our own time, law is seen both as the ultimate architect, redesigning the world according to its own blueprint, and as the ultimate evangelist, transforming our hearts and minds directly. If the latter, objectifying function of law is now more prominent, as was the former in the sixteenth century, it is not that our faith in legal architecture is waning—only that our belief in legal evangelism is especially strong.

The Gaze of the Preamble

The legal system was doing two things here: recognizing that laws would be transgressed and standardizing punishments. An awareness of the power of law, therefore, was accompanied by an awareness that law needs power if it is to be realized. We can see this developing understanding of the relationship of word to world in the changing syntax of the preamble. In the days of Henry VI, the following phraseology was typical: "The King, by the Advice and Assent of the Lords Spiritual and Temporal, and the Commons of this Realm of England, being in the said Parliament, and by Authority of the same Parliament, hath ordained. . . ." [109] The words "hath ordained" are important, for they place the king's will firmly in the past tense. The statute was thus, as we saw in other contexts, a historical record of an event (the king's decision) which was over and done with. There was no perception of the statute continuing to act in the world.

Soon after, however, we enter an ambiguous period in which the past and present merge. Phrases of the form "it is ordained and established" or "it is enacted, ordained, and established," [110] although they carry something of the past with them, are nevertheless in the present tense. As with the word "Act" itself, which first appeared around this time, there is the implication that the mere description of the king's will (in the past) is by itself enough to change the present. "It is enacted" and "It is established" mean "It is done." Just like that. Likewise, these phrases are written in the passive voice. There is, therefore, no sense of agency. The king's will "is enacted," somehow, by itself. The use of the passive voice leaves unexplained the process by which the statute is in fact to be established.

At the same time we begin to find examples securely wedded to the present: "The King . . . doth ordain, enact, and establish," says one Act of 1483; "the King ordaineth" says another from 1485.[111] This appears to be a statement of fact relating to the mind of the king: he ordains this or that to be so. The use of the active voice adds to this impression: it is not just "ordained"; the king ordains it. This was an expression of the king's will, then, but still it revealed no awareness of how that will was to be put into practice. "It is enacted" implied, as we saw in relation to the word "Act," that the world obeys the word; "The King ordains," although it identifies the person whose intent is at stake, says nothing about how the world responds. It is a document which records a present intention and says nothing about how that intention is to be carried out.

This ambiguity between past and present, word and action, soon dissipated. A petition dating from 1495 began, "Be it ordained and enacted by your Highness. . . ."[112] The words have the character of a wish and a request for someone ("your Highness") to act and for something to be done in the future. "Be it enacted" means "Let it be enacted." This form becomes standard in all Acts. The substantive clauses of Acts begin "Be it also enacted," "Be it ordained," "Wherefore be it enacted," "Be it therefore enacted, ordained, and established." By 1523 all Acts simply and uniformly declare, "Be it enacted. . . ."[113] This form has come down to the present day virtually unmodified. But what is the image or aesthetic which this phrase conjures up? Does it not still sound like a request—and if so, to whom is it addressed? Let it be enacted by whom? There is a clear image of command here: the king on his throne pronounces "Be it enacted"—and orders those around him to satisfy his wishes.

This is no longer a mere floating abstraction. The phrase "be it therefore enacted" is a command instructing others to act to fulfill the will expressed. The phrase suggests an awareness that it is only by this consequent action that the king's vision can be realized. There is a recognition here that laws must be enacted by future action. We have moved from the present tense into the future. We have also moved from a gaze that looks at the world to one that enters physically, practically, into it—applying, enforcing, punishing. An effort is being made to transform the world not just by relying on the sheer magic of words but by muddy, brutal practice. This gaze is decidedly modern in outlook.

A gradual increase in the detail of control and depth of gaze has marked the history of statutory form from the *Magna Carta* to the Tudors. The development of musical form followed a similar trajectory. In Renaissance music, there is a consciousness of effect and an attempt to use music as a species of communication quite unlike the introspective rapture of earlier times. The use of musical scene-painting typifies this communicative spirit in which sounds and not just words were used to project meaning. The "Pie Jesu" or "Agnus Dei" of the Mass writers of the sixteenth century conveyed the idea of mercy by strictly musical (stylistic) as well as linguistic (semantic) means, utilizing at last the full normative power of the medium. This exploration of normative potential came somewhat later to English music; but even in the compositions of John Taverner (1495–1545) or Robert Fayrfax (1464–1521), and still more so in the motets of Thomas Tallis (1505–85), there is a rhythmic variety, a differentiation of mood depending on the meaning of the text being set, and a focus on syllabic clarity in the vocalization of its words, in stark contrast to the approach of the old masters.[114] Medieval music, like medieval legislation, existed in its own private sphere; in the Renaissance, there is a newfound and vivid engagement with the community—a belief that music itself, like the law, can enact and ordain changes in the hearts of those who listen.

This expanded musical gaze and function influenced the composer's understanding of the resources at his disposal, too. Modern notation, effectively stabilized around 1400, allowed an infinite subdivision of the beat and therefore an infinite density and complexity of rhythm. At the same time, the tonal as well as the rhythmic range of an individual voice expanded, so that the bass, for example, which had rarely sung below a C, was now pushed down to an F. In England, long in the forefront of broadening the vocal range used in composition, the compass of polyphonic settings, from highest note to lowest, expanded between 1400 and 1500 from about two octaves to three, while the range of an individual vocal part, in the compositions of John Cuk or Walter Frye, for example, now typically extended to a tenth or an eleventh and on occasion a sixteenth.[115]

The changes that took place were not merely technical. We hear in the remarkable and prolific motets of Thomas Tallis an awareness not simply of abstract melodic lines but that he is dealing with voices, each possessed of its own range and character.[116] Consider the note as Tallis must have considered it. It has a temporal dimension, harmonic implications, timbre, and character; it is attached to a word, to emotions, to meaning as never before. Realms of opportunity previously unimagined presented themselves to the Tudor and Elizabethan ear. It was an aural gaze (if we can speak of such a thing) that offered a vast expansion in the means, aspects, and functions of musical control. How far removed in depth and complexity is Tallis's magisterial forty-part motet, *Spem in alium*, from the simple two-part organum, its far-off ancestor. Above all, there is a difference in sonority and feeling here. The beauty of the music of the Middle Ages lay in its space, its parallel movement, the simplicity and stark perfection of its harmonies, and the constancy of its rhythm. By the Renaissance, these very factors have become undesirable and even ugly. In law and in music there was a profound shift in perspective and in purpose, not primarily technological or administrative, but aesthetic.

MOTETS AND LITTLE WORDS

Ironically, the judiciary did not even see statutory interpretation as an appropriate legal function until the end of the fourteenth century. Indeed in 1336, one statute concluded by demanding that the "aforesaid ordinances and statutes" should be kept "without addition, or fraud, by covin, evasion, art, or contrivance, or by the interpretation of the words." Statutory interpretation was a species of fraud.[117]

Yet an aesthetic methodology of statutory interpretation has proven to be a vein rich in the ore of insight. I have traced marked changes in the conceptualization of law over 300 years, contrasting modern theories of validity (Raz), power (Austin), and reason (natural law), all of which may be advanced as different ways of explaining why it is that people accept an obligation to obey the law. As I have noted, all these ideas have changed, developed, and intermingled over time. Despite these interconnections, the relative importance of various elements has varied. I have discussed the decline in reason and rhetoric, its steady replacement by notions of formal validity, and the gradual rise, too, in the value placed on legal coercion. We have seen the role of legislation change from that of a document recording the past to that of an instruction to guide the future and its tone accordingly change from descriptive to prescriptive. The shift from the use of the word "statute" to the word "Act" symbolizes that steady movement.

At the same time, the related idea of legal normativity gradually gained acceptance. These assumptions, now commonly accepted even by very different jurisprudential schools, were foreign to the earliest statutes. The gradual shift from the use of Latin to French to English might be taken to embody this slow development. I have also related the growing normativity of law qua law to the growing normativity of music qua music. So persuasive is the language of music now, so ancillary to its meaning are the words it sets—so far removed are we from the original meaning of the motet—that most of those who hear a Latin setting by Tallis have little idea of the meaning of the words, and less interest.

The purpose of statute law changed along with "the gaze" of lawmakers: who was on the king's horizon of visibility, how thoroughly into their lives that gaze penetrated, and whether they were perceived as agents, subjects, or objects. In music and in law alike, a gaze which expanded in scope and in intensity was reflected in changing purposes and revealed in changing form and style. This aesthetic methodology could be extended much further. The result of such an analysis would be a new history of the statute. From our present standpoint, the form of modern legislation seems completely "natural." We expect to see "Acts" written in "plain English" (accompanied by conventions relating to short titles, formal clauses, substantive provisions, the numbering of sections and paragraphs, provisions for entry into force, and so on), forward looking, purposive, and reformist in nature, designed to change the world and change behavior. Indeed, a world without such a comprehensive faith in legal control and influence is, for us, virtually unimaginable. But for the one to be unimaginable, the other had first to be imagined. Through an aesthetic argument and an aesthetic exemplification of it—by evaluating the changing look and sounds of various expressions, musical and legal, of the social order—this chapter has attempted an exposition of some of the history and manifestations of that legal imagination.

Thomas Levenson makes similar points in drawing parallels between the history of science and music at this time:

> In the time of Gregory and the Frankish kings, there was the Word, and the words of Scripture . . . and a conception of science, any science, especially the science of music [or law], as the elaboration of truths already known. . . . The explosion of musical ideas between the time of Henry and Eleanor and the end of the Middle Ages . . . hinted at a transformation in the sense of what a science was, what a scientist did [and what a lawyer was and did]. From the study of experience to demonstrate external, eternal truths, music [and law] had become a tool of discovery, of innovation.[118]

Beyond the specific question of legal history, the purpose of this "Motet" has been to introduce the aesthetic dimension of legal texts—on the one hand as an interpretative tool or process and on the other hand as the subject matter of interpretation. To take the idea of an aesthetic subject first, then, my argument is that one cannot understand the ideas and practices of lawmakers in any era without delving into the way they saw the world. This understanding of the importance of aesthetics in the establishment of a worldview has directed my research toward particular aspects of the documents in question. But the process of my inquiry no less than its subject has been aesthetic. I have focused on various aspects of the language, form, and "gaze" of statutes rather than, for example, on an analysis of their content. My interest has been in the organization of statutes, for example, and the language of the preamble. The look, form, style, and rhetoric of law, therefore, constitute important sources through which to learn about the general attitude toward law and society, in which context specific statutes are enacted.

This chapter has been an adventure in words: their voices, their arrangement, their purpose. The motet, in its finest flowering, embodied an unparalleled depth, breadth, and sophistication and an unquenchable faith in its own force and authority. The statutory form experienced the same intoxicating expansion. We have seen, then, the power of language and form to both structure and exemplify patterns of thought—whether we are talking about the formal innovations of early modern music or the parallel developments of early modern legislation. In all these cases and in all these ways, the changing characteristics of the little words of law and of music have much to teach us about the world of its writers and that of its readers.

In this chapter aesthetics has been used to show how legal texts can help us explain a changing world. The next explores how our experience of the world as an aesthetic phenomenon can help us explain the judgments made in a legal text. I wish to show how senses and symbols govern the meaning of legal arguments and the motivations behind them. In the specific context of the death penalty, this argument moves away from an understanding of aesthetics which is linguistic and formal and toward those aspects of the aesthetic which suggest the influence of the emotional, the visual, and the corporeal on what we think and believe. From an analysis of a body of texts, we move to the text of the body.

Part 2

THE EPISTEMOLOGICAL DIMENSION

Requiem

*Green Death — Aesthetic Interpretations
and Influences in the Death Penalty*

REQUIEM ÆTERNAM

Requiem æternam dona eis, Domine;
et lux perpetua luceat eis.
> Grant them eternal rest, O Lord,
> and may light perpetual shine upon them.

Mozart's Requiem begins as it means to go on: solemn, sparse, expressive of the hollowness of spirit which follows the death of a loved one.[1] There is nothing lush about mourning here. Instead, there is an empty, shattered sound: a muffled organ, staccato violins barely touching their strings, and a hushed tune, the thin voice of the oboes and the dark tones of basset horns cutting the air. The excruciating beauty of a Mass for the dead is its combination of peace and failure, hope and resignation. But in Mozart, irony adds complexity to its meaning for us. A Requiem is an occasional piece. It is written to mourn. But who exactly is being mourned here? Mozart did not write it for the death of a friend, a colleague, or a patron. According to legend, an anonymous stranger commissioned the Requiem. A Requiem for the undead, then, it turns against itself and becomes in the popular imagination a Mass for Mozart, who died while composing it, and even for the Requiem itself, which his death left unfinished.[2] In the final extinguishment of the man and the masterpiece, we perceive a glimmer of the infinite promise of the future which death snuffs out; of the dramatic way in which the plans of the living are cut short by death.

The purpose of this chapter is to explore the failure of reason to effectively control the operation of the legal system. It applies a methodological approach grounded in aesthetics, as in "Motet," to a number of U.S. judicial opinions on the death penalty. I do not purport to present a comprehensive analysis of the current law which legitimates execution in the United States: in light of the complexity and incoherence of many hundreds of such cases which have come to the Supreme Court since 1976, such a task would be naïve, or arrogant, or both. Rather, the cases I discuss have been seminal in the modern development of the jurisprudence of death, and I have chosen them for their paradigmatic style of reasoning and because they were historically significant in making acceptable the idea of capital punishment, although in some of their details they have since been overtaken by later developments. I analyze these cases to illustrate two ideas. First, the meaning of legal texts can be enriched by considering their use of figurative language. This aspect uses aesthetics in the exegesis of legal texts—it helps us to read and understand what the law says. Second, the legal principles surrounding the death penalty, although they claim to be an exercise in "reason," are in fact profoundly influenced by the carefully constructed imagery of the death penalty. The aesthetic dimension of the death penalty is a complex interplay of the sensory imagery which surrounds the experience of execution and the symbolic meaning which attaches to it. This second aspect uses aesthetics to explore the genesis of legal texts—it helps us understand why the law has developed as it has.

The claim to rationality lies at the very heart of our legal system. It is of no more importance than in relation to the question of capital punishment, where judges claim to be able, by an exercise of reason, to determine who will live and who will die. The Requiem as a musical and religious form is also about judgment—about God's ability to separate with certainty the damned and the blessed. It is that terrible exercise of deic reason, the dies irae, which the Requiem anticipates and reflects on. There is a sense, then, in which the law of capital punishment not only parallels the emotional register of the Requiem but also mimics its faith in the justice of judgment. But those who sit on the bench are not gods. Death-penalty jurisprudence demonstrates above all the distance between human judgment and divine. Even human attempts at the representation of this divine judgment fall short—as the fragmentary Mozart testifies—let alone our attempts at its replication.

The structure of the Requiem, and its themes of death and judgment and incompletion, echo through this chapter, throwing light, in particular, on the legal reasoning of death and the death of legal reasoning. The "Requiem aeternam" accomplishes some preliminary work by exploring the myth of legal rationality. The "Dies irae" discusses, in relation to capital punishment, the failure of legal judgment to achieve its aspirations of rule-bound rationality. My approach is interpretative and methodological. I argue that the quest for a rational system of laws to govern the imposition of the death penalty is impossible to achieve. The "Agnus Dei" focuses on the way in which the death penalty has been organized in the United States, the way in which it allows the sacrificial execution of men and women by the sensory isolation of the condemned and their symbolic objectification by others. In exploring through senses and symbols why a death penalty is even possible, this section moves the argument from text to context, from meaning to cause, from methodology to epistemology, and from law's claim to rationality to the aesthetic dimensions that lie behind it. This conjunction of images and symbols has motivated and justified the maintenance of the death penalty in the United States.

Finally, the "Libera me" attempts to transcend the orthodox discourse about capital punishment. This section, therefore, touches on the normative implications of taking aesthetics seriously. I argue that the objectification and isolation which make execution imaginable are unfaithful to the real values which a respect for aesthetics would advance. There is a corrupt aesthetics here, an aesthetics of denial and deceit. On the contrary, an approach which respects aesthetics as a fundamental dimension of human understanding must show empathy for all human beings. By entering into the sensory and emotional experience of death row, we can begin to understand the irrevocable cruelty and belittlement which execution entails and move toward a world in which such practices are inconceivable.

Requiem æternam

Legal rationality—the promise of an objective, rule-bound, certain interpretation of the law—was always an illusion.[3] Ernest Weinrib, whose theory of legal formalism is grounded in just such a species of rationality, uses the image of the "empty sepulchre" to suggest that, Christlike, the body of an entirely rational legal order has escaped execution.[4] On the contrary, the empty coffin does not imply that legal rationalism has been resurrected but rather that it never existed at all.

Let us surrender a moment to the mythology of legal rationality. There is no gainsaying the beauty of reason, its geometric precision, its symmetry and hope of order.[5] Reason gives us pleasure; it promises us the hilt of a Gordian scythe. In Oliver Wendell Holmes's words, "the logical method and form flatters that longing for certainty and for repose which is in every human mind."[6] The priority accorded to reason is everywhere apparent: in the language of philosophy and the law and in our common language too. People "rise above" their emotions and "put their feelings aside"; the discussion "falls to an emotional level" and is then "raised up" again to a "rational plane." As Emily Martin concludes, "power, height, rationality and coolness go together on the one hand, and lack of power, low position, emotions and heat go together on the other."[7] But as we have seen, this priority does not correspond to our experience in the world or to the ways in which our decisions are made. Reason alone cannot provide the ground for our ethics or the source of our values; it explores consequences rather than determining axioms. Everywhere there is a complexity to human motivation which the discourse of reason excludes:

> Unlike most others who pronounce in the public domain, judges appear to offer, and to deliver, clear and definitive answers. Justice according to law is a coin which, when tossed, does not rest on the rim. It comes down head or tails; it is clear who has won and who has lost. The judge gives

his reasons, pronounces the result and withdraws to the chill and distant heights.[8]

In law, we find the paramountcy of reason in its understanding of legitimate language and of legitimate authority. Language first, for orthodox legal interpretation, assumes a series of related claims about the objective and logical nature of meaning: the claim that law is a logical structure of rules and regulations which provide determinate results to particular cases; that the words of those rules themselves have a core of unproblematic meaning in the application of which there is little role for judgment or discretion; and that judges shorn of personal prejudices and values can, should, and do apply reason to this interpretative exercise. H. L. A. Hart's *Concept of Law* will stand as the paradigm articulation of this understanding.[9]

Next, the concept of legitimate authority. The process of what is called "legal reasoning" traces a unique path using the techniques of precedent —the making of present decisions through reference to past cases. Edward Coke, defending the English legal system in the seventeenth century, wrote:

> The King said that he thought the law was founded upon reason, and that he and others had reason, as well as the Judges. . . . But His Majesty was not learned in the laws of his realm of England, and causes which concern the life, or inheritance, or goods, or fortunes of his subjects, are not to be decided by natural reason but by the artificial reason and judgment of law, which law is an act which requires long study and experience.[10]

Now undoubtedly this is a peculiar breed of reason. For on what did past decision makers base their inquiry? It would seem that only now are courts to be estopped from making value judgments while, on the contrary, their previous value judgments are to be enshrined. A game of mirrors, the very issue of subjectivity is avoided by deferring to a supposedly objective interpretation of the subjective judgments of the past.

Just like rationality, an appeal to precedent is an expression of the belief that prior decisions have a singular meaning; that this meaning can be determined as a matter of objective truth and can then be "applied" to later cases; and that the "right answer" to a legal problem is thus able to be discovered and implemented quite apart from the subjective value system of the interpreter. Precedent attempts to ensure the objectivity of the legal system not by applying persuasive logic but by instantiating an authoritative past.

Admittedly this is a caricature; but it is also something of an ideal. In the Requiem, too, there is an image of the dies irae, the terrible day of wrath in which the infallible judge will come to redeem the righteous and confound the damned, instructed by a "written book" wherein, through unambiguous and truthful language, "whatever is hidden shall be made manifest, and nothing shall remain unavenged." The judgment of the Lord, like the judgment of precedent, is written down, certainly expressed, and perfectly understood.

God's ability to read his own writing is not in doubt. But the marks of humans (even judges), left to be read by other humans, have proved less legible. The Requiem represents an ideal of legal judgment and reason impossible of human attainment, and the principle has been attacked in law by a wide variety of scholars. Legal realists insisted on the distinction between what law says and what law does; natural lawyers such as Lon Fuller have argued that the meaning of legal words is a function of the purposes we attribute to the law in question; hermeneuticists and conventionalists from Stanley Fish to Ronald Dworkin emphasize the cultural contingency of the meaning of legal texts.[11] But undoubtedly the Arian heresy in this regard has come from critical legal studies. Here we find an almost ritual insistence on the indeterminacy of law: on the subjectivity of legal decision making, on the impossibility of words ever fully determining meaning, and on the contradictory values to be found in the legal system as a whole.[12] The consequence of this for CLS is that objective interpretation can never be a question of the simple "application" of preexisting rules or standards.[13]

Et lux perpetua

On the other hand, the discursive aspects of law have been misunderstood as much by Marxist scholars and legal realists as by positivists, all of whom emphasize the performative and concrete elements of law.[14] Derrida too appears to adopt a rather simplistic understanding of law as a species of mandated force, of state-sanctioned violence. It is surprising to find in Derrida the assumption that law is made and imposed by "the state." He writes that "today the police are no longer content to enforce the law. . . . [T]hey invent it, they publish ordinances." But every act of interpretation has always been an invention, whether or not it is backed up by ordinances; legal interpretation happens in every corner of the social system, whether or not it is backed up by ordnance.[15]

From both the formalist and materialist conceptions of law, something crucial has been left out. There is a richness to judgments, in their rhetorical language and in their role as part of a complex discourse about the nature of our community, our past, and our future. We read a decision not merely to extract a logical proposition but to engage with its vision of the world.[16] No analysis can hope to capture what law is and does by trying merely to extract from it a sequence of logical propositions leading to a conclusion. Its meaning cannot be abstracted from the mode of its expression. As James Boyd White writes:

> We can never "understand" a text completely in the first place and what we do "understand" can really be said only in the original language and in the forms of the original text. . . . [We often imagine] something called the "meaning" of the text that is imagined to exist above, or beyond, or behind its language, when in truth the meaning is in the words as they are uttered in their particular context and nowhere else.[17]

Each decision or statute contains its own rhetorical devices which help us illuminate meaning and motivation. No one can read the judgments of Lord Denning, for example, without realizing that there is a particular image of beauty which grounds his interpretation of the law. Lord Denning fantasizes about the idealized past of Merrie England. This nostalgia involves a kind of beauty, rightly termed "pastoral" by Dennis Klinck; characterized by personal and peaceful relationships, by an accepted and peaceable hierarchy, and by unspoiled images of pasture and village greens.[18] An emphasis on the beauty of the countryside and a belief in the importance of its preservation are integral parts of a Denning judgment.[19] When he begins a judgment about personal psychological injury "It was bluebell time in Kent,"[20] this is no faux-ingenuous tug at the heartstrings, inserted for its calculated effect. It is, for Lord Denning, the real core of the matter, an appeal to the kind of beauty he wishes by his judgment to preserve—against the invasion, in this case, of that newfangled invention the motorcar. Undoubtedly there are ideological implications in Denning's sympathies, but his judgments are governed not by politics but by aesthetics.

At the same time, as Klinck has so well demonstrated, the legal system as a whole makes repeated use of certain kinds of metaphors: those of the boundary, on the one hand, and of weight and balance, on the other.[21] All this helps to provide us with the meaning of a text, as well as to govern our response to it. As Nietzsche wrote, "tropes are not something that can be added or subtracted from nature at will; they are its truest nature."[22] A metaphor, after all, is not simply the substitution or translation of an idea into new language. It develops thought as well as explains it.[23] Further, the full meaning and implications of a metaphor only begin to take shape after its expression. A metaphor is a proposition, then, in the sense that it proposes a relationship between two terms before the meaning of that juxtaposition is fully determined: it is a leap of faith and a gesture of hope in the future enhancement of understanding.

But metaphor relates to law in two other distinct ways. First, and self-evident, law is metaphorical because it works by analogy. Precedent uses past events—legal and social—as analogies for present ones; the principles of statutory interpretation apply past language—legislative and judicial—to present situations. In both cases, the law operates by bringing together two different terms and discovering their sameness and their differences. Second, like metaphor, law escapes the control of its author. As the meaning of the metaphor is only provisional at the moment of its writing, so too with the law. Its implications and its effects begin to take shape only after its pronouncement, and its metaphors, poetry, and allusions are part of the meaning it has for us.

The myth of legal rationality sets up an ideal of law as exclusively about reason. On the other hand, the critique of reason adopts at times an overly cynical rhetoric. Having laid bare the inconsistencies of legal argument and demonstrated the impossibility of ever grounding the process of judicial decision making in reason, CLS writing often seems to have assumed that therefore nothing underlies the decisions of the courts.[24] This approach, suggesting as it does a certain covert manipulation by the judiciary in the preservation of its own interests, has led writers such as Ronald Dworkin to respond, somewhat superficially, that "no one really believes that judges are tyrants."[25] Certainly judges do experience themselves bound by precedent, no matter how loosely. If one wishes to argue that those bonds are not really there, then one has to think a little harder about what it is that steers decision making in certain directions.

Our job, then, as legal readers, is to search for the meanings and origins which law suppresses by its insistent rhetoric of rationality. As Goodrich writes, "rhetoric is the pre-modern form of psychoanalysis . . . a methodology of symptomatic reading or of interpretation of the unconscious of law."[26] In demonstrating what lies beyond linguistic logic and precedential authority, the practices of deconstruction are a valuable analytical tool.[27] It is an approach sensitive to the ironic and rhetorical connotations of language. It seeks for hidden meanings, intended or unintended, in texts. In particular, it searches for the inherent contradictions through which the unreason of law makes its absence felt.

These techniques are therefore part of an aesthetic methodology which, by a sensitivity to the imagery of all legal writing, may help to provide us with interpretative insight into the connotations of legal texts. The aesthetic dimension of law is there all along, in the text, part of the meaning and force it has for its readers, and a clue to the values which have helped to construct it. Can law establish a rational system to determine life and death? If it cannot, two further questions arise: what governs the judgment of law, and by what forces has it been constructed?

DIES IRÆ

Dies iræ, dies illa,
Solvet sæclum in favilla . . .
> The day of wrath, that day will
> dissolve the world in ashes . . .

In many countries around the world, those that employ capital punishment as part of their legal armory and those that do not, the question of its justice and efficacy continues to be a matter of passionate argument. In *Furman v. Georgia* (1972), the U.S. Supreme Court held that the death penalty as then applied was unconstitutional because its "arbitrary" and "standardless" imposition made it a "unique penalty . . . wantonly and freakishly imposed."[28] It was this arbitrary character which made the punishment "cruel and unusual," contrary to the Eighth Amendment. The moratorium declared in *Furman* was, however, brief.[29] Four years later a series of landmark decisions authorized the use of the death penalty again.[30] The Court time and again has insisted that in this area of the law, as elsewhere, "any decision to impose the death sentence [must] be, and appear to be, based on reason rather than caprice or emotion."[31] Neither has this faith in legal rationality been abstract. Since 1976, several hundred human beings—almost all of them men, almost all of them young, almost all of them black—have gone to heaven, hell, or oblivion at the hands of U.S. legal rationality.[32] Hundreds more await their turn.

Quantus tremor est futurus

Quantus tremor est futurus,
Quando judex est venturus,
Cuncta stricte discussurus!
> How great a terror there will be
> when the Judge shall come
> who will thresh out everything thoroughly!

Academic literature on the death penalty in the United States demonstrates the ultimate failure of rationality to resolve a question as contested and as emotional as the extinguishment of human life. Stephen Nathanson, for example, insists "that we can *reason* our way through difficult moral questions. . . . I disagree that the death penalty is a matter to be decided by the gut rather than the head."[33] Nathanson, like his adversaries, clearly believes that a writer or a judge, be his *discussurus* only *stricte* enough, must arrive at the right conclusion. But in the end, he proves only that arguments from moral desert do not necessitate the conclusion that murderers deserve to die.[34] Such an argument, of course, is conclusive only because Nathanson starts from the premise that death-penalty advocates are required to prove their case. This assumption is surely based on an intuition about the intrinsic wrongfulness of the death penalty: the whole idea of a burden of proof stems from a "gut reaction," just as the notion of "beyond reasonable doubt" itself stems from a gut reaction.[35]

The debate on the death penalty is focused on the question of deterrence. This appears to be the crux of the debate on capital punishment. Put crudely, the issue is whether the existence of the death penalty deters future potential murders more effectively than would a lesser penalty. It is a question of the differential efficacy of capital punishment.[36] Here it might seem that we are in the realm of facts and evidence, logic and reason. But this is an illusion which soon evaporates. How can we evaluate the likelihood of murders that have not yet been committed? How can we guess the possible effect of different penalties when the best testimony we have, that of murderers themselves, testifies above all to the failure of deterrence?

Among a plethora of similar studies, Thorsten Sellin's comparative work on the murder rates of different contiguous states, some with and some without capital punishment, provides powerful evidence that the death penalty deters no better than long-term imprisonment.[37] And it is hard to put the psychology of the matter any better than Diodotus, whom Thucydides reported over 2000 years ago:

> Hope and desire persist throughout and cause the greatest calamities—
> one leading and the other following, one conceiving the enterprise, and
> the other suggesting that it will be successful—invisible factors, but
> more powerful than the terrors that are obvious to our eyes. . . . In a
> word it is impossible (and only the most simple-minded will deny this)
> for human nature, when once seriously set upon a certain course, to
> be prevented from following that course by the force of law or by any
> other means of intimidation whatever.[38]

Yet for all that, deterrence is a red herring. It is seminal neither for those opposed to the death penalty nor for those in favor of it. Thus Hugo Bedau and Nathanson, both indefatigable opponents of the death penalty, insist that the question is, at heart, about the impossibility of reconciling the process of execution with the idea of human dignity. For Nathanson, even if the death penalty "saved" a substantial number of lives, the unanswered question of the justice of legally killing a person would remain. We would still be faced with an "anguished choice" in order to justify its use.[39]

How then are we to explain the continuing focus on the question of deterrence when it begs the central questions of dignity and justice? How can an argument come to seem so crucial when, even were they wholly wrong about it, those opposed to capital punishment would not change their minds? Ironically, the answer must be because of the rhetorical rather than the logical role of the question of deterrence. Because deterrence is a game played with statistical tools, an attack on the validity of deterrence presents the case for abolition in a logical and unemotional light.

The question of deterrence is at least as prominent in arguments in favor of capital punishment as in those against it, but it is likewise irrelevant. That much seems evident from the logic of the argument itself. For if the death penalty is an effective deterrent for murder, why not use it for rape, or robbery, or drug trafficking, or anything at all? The evidence suggests that murder is one of the crimes least likely to be deterred, regardless of the penalty we impose. We would get much more bang for our buck if we imposed the death penalty for traffic violations.

Ernest Van den Haag's approach is revealing. Although he claims to support the use of the death penalty even in cases of drunk driving, and thus to hold to a position based purely on deterrence wherever it is found to work, he is careful to qualify his position:

> I would demand much more conclusive proof of the size of the deterrent effect on drunken driving than is now available even for the effect of the death penalty on murder . . . [because] I believe the murderer deserves it in any case. . . . A year in prison for driving while drunk . . . would reduce the drunken driving rates as much as it can be reduced.[40]

Van den Haag acknowledges that punishment above a certain severity has greater costs than benefits. Cost-benefit analysis is the heart of deterrence theory, since there is a point of diminishing return beyond which any additional punishment (such as torture), although it might deter, deters no better (or not sufficiently better) than lesser penalties. Yet while he applies this analysis to drunk driving, he does not do so when it comes to murder. The difference is that for Van den Haag, the murderer's life is already forfeit, and therefore there is no cost in killing him. The point of diminishing returns cannot be reached. Murderers, he says, "deserve it in any case." It is not the principle of deterrence, then, which justifies the death penalty.

The same applies to the argument occasionally raised that execution is cheaper than life imprisonment. Even if this were true, then it would likewise be cheaper to execute robbers and rapists.[41] The argument still does not tell us why murderers as opposed to anybody else are so dispensable. There is something instead about the relationship of the action of killing and the response of execution which is being asserted, a relationship which is both more important and anterior to the idea of deterrence which masks it. Van den Haag writes:

> I shall favor the death penalty . . . as long as there is any chance that by executions we can deter some future murders of future victims. The life of these victims is valuable to me, whereas, in my eyes, the murderer has forfeited his life by taking that of another. That much from the viewpoint of deterrence.[42]

Van den Haag does not write that much "from the viewpoint of deterrence." His argument first assumes that the murderer's life has already been forfeited. But if this is Van den Haag's assumption, what purpose does deterrence serve except a rhetorical one? It enables the writer to appear to be engaged in a rational calculation, balancing "the lives of the innocents" against "the lives of murderers,"[43] when in fact the decision has already been made to kill the murderer just in case someone is deterred.

Walter Berns also attempts to present a "rational" argument for deterrence. He relies on Isaac Ehrlich's controversial studies, which claimed that every execution saves eight "innocent lives." From this conclusion, Berns proceeds to a detailed description of a number of particularly dreadful murders and follows that up by describing the murder committed by Henry Jarrette while on leave from prison.[44] But what purpose is served by these horror stories? The deterrence argument is that the simple fact of the death of a murderer—any murderer—serves as a means to discourage future potential murders. Its purpose is to look forward, not backward: the violence or evil of the condemned man's acts is irrelevant to this calculus since it is too late to deter those particular and tragic deaths. Berns asks us rhetorically whether we value "the life of Henry Jarrette or the lives of his victims"[45]—again he is addressing actual victims and not future victims, actual murderers and not future murderers. Indeed, after some thirty pages of discussion, Berns comes to that very conclusion: "the principle of deterrence is incompatible with the principle of just deserts."[46]

Beneath the language of calculation in which arguments for the death penalty are couched lies an intrinsic belief in a special relationship between acts and consequences, between the life the felon has taken and the life which is to be taken from him. It is a relationship whose origin stretches back to the *lex talionis:*

> Life for life,
> Eye for eye, tooth for tooth, hand for hand, foot for foot,
> Burning for burning, wound for wound, stripe for stripe.[47]

This is not a rule. Treated literally, no one is likely to defend it. An eye for an eye, let alone burning for burning, could scarcely be contemplated. Treated metaphorically, as surely it must be, the lex talionis merely establishes that serious crimes should be punished with proportionate severity —it leaves completely open how severe punishment ought to be. Although it can be conceded that the punishment for a crime should reflect the relative degree of social condemnation attached to it, we are no closer to determining what form that punishment should take.[48]

Liber scriptus

Liber scriptus proferetur,
In quo totem continetur,
Unde mundus judicetur.
> A written book will be brought forth
> which contains everything
> by which the world shall be judged.

Let us turn our attention from philosophical to legal texts. The U.S. Supreme Court's resurrection of the death penalty in state legislation focused on the meaning of the Eighth Amendment, which prohibits "cruel and unusual punishment." The Supreme Court draws our attention to legal rationality—the importance of precedent and the search for rules. Both these ideas stem from the need to define in advance the circumstances in which courts can impose the death penalty and thus to remove the infliction of capital punishment from the arbitrary discretion of the judges. There is a faith here in the ability of words—of the Constitution, of prior cases, and of death-penalty statutes—to establish definite and objective criteria for decision making. On the day of judgment, we are promised a *liber scriptus,* which will "contain everything by which the world shall be judged."

Jacques Derrida argues that all language attempts to reflect two contradictory goals. We want our words to be both an accurate reflection of the unique experience of their author and at the same time a shared commodity. Any writing will find itself trapped by the conflicting demands for subjective expression and intersubjective communication: "In order to function, that is, in order to be legible, a signature must have a repeatable, iterable, imitable form; it must be able to detach itself from the present and singular intention of its production."[49] This is the paradox of the jurisprudence of death. The Court has to find a decision-making process which is on the one hand unique to the individual case before it and on the other hand repeatable and consistent. It finds itself faced with an insoluble, and unavoidable, problem. In striving to be reasonable, the law is tugged in two directions at once.[50]

Precedents

Precedent was a crucial factor in the judgments of those who dissented from the moratorium imposed by *Furman v. Georgia* in 1972 and then were in the majority which four years later declared the death penalty constitutional again in *Gregg v. Georgia*.[51] Justice Powell, for example, dissenting in *Furman*, was at pains to recite the previous cases which had held without exception that the "mere extinguishment of life . . . cannot be said to violate the constitutional concept" of cruel and unusual punishment.[52]

Nevertheless, while these judges—Burger, Powell, and Rehnquist—insisted that personal feelings ought to be subservient to the impartial application of precedent, their language gives them away. Although they would have us believe that their personal preference was beside the point, their judgments clearly manifest a belief in the value of the death penalty. Justice Rehnquist mourns that the majority in *Furman* "today strike down a penalty that our Nation's legislators have thought necessary since our country was founded." He was again in dissent in *Woodson v. North Carolina*, in which a statute providing for mandatory death penalties for certain offenses was overturned: "The plurality's glib rejection of *these* legislative decisions as having little weight . . . seems to me more an instance of its desire to save the people from themselves."[53] But of course, the Bill of Rights was designed expressly to prevent popular legislative will overriding the interests of the minority. Whenever the Court overturns a piece of legislation it acts to "save the people from themselves."

Justice Blackmun's dissent in *Furman* is more interesting:

> I yield to no-one in the depth of my distaste, antipathy, and, indeed, abhorrence, for the death penalty, with all its aspects of physical distress and fear, and of moral judgment exercised by finite minds. . . . That distaste is buttressed by a belief that capital punishment serves no useful purpose that can be demonstrated.[54]

Yet Blackmun nevertheless upheld the death penalty in *Furman* and *Gregg*. This appears then to manifest a commitment to precedent: a demonstration, perhaps, of the triumph of legal rationality over a visceral response. He would like to strike down the death penalty; but he cannot.

I am not so sure. His judgment in *Furman* concludes on a different note.

> Nevertheless, these cases are here because offenses to innocent victims were perpetrated. This fact and the terror that occasioned it, and the fear that stalks the streets of many of our cities today, perhaps deserve not to be entirely overlooked. Let us hope that, with the Court's decision, the terror imposed will be forgotten by those upon whom it has been visited, and that our society will reap the hoped-for benefits of magnanimity.[55]

There is here a glimpse of a very different worldview, a feeling that the violence of the cities brings forth the violence of the state. This paragraph is all the more revealing for its style. Note the sarcasm of Justice Blackmun's conclusion, which contrasts the real and brutal danger of the streets with the naïve aspirations of the majority that terror will be "forgotten," a quaint "magnanimity" which is only "hoped for." Note the mazy language which adds to the feeling of confusion and darkness the paragraph evokes: "offenses to innocent victims were perpetrated. This fact and the terror that occasioned it. . . ." Which fact? Occasioned by what? Against whom? When? The powerlessness of urban victims, the feeling of being encircled, is intensified by the powerlessness of readers, entrapped by language.

Note above all the passive construction, in which terror is "occasioned" and "imposed" and offenses "perpetrated." Again, this suggests a lack of agency which gives the reader a sense of ignorance and powerlessness when confronted by faceless violence; the darkness of causality parallels the darkness of the streets. The active agent in all this is not a specific individual or class of people but rather "fear" itself: it is fear personified which "stalks the streets," terror, unforgotten, which is stealing our cities. What we see in Justice Blackmun's judgment, in fact, is a conflict between emotions. There is considerable uncertainty here about the justice of his conclusion. But through the trope of prosopopoeia—the personification of a symbolic object—the face of fear finally triumphs over his visceral distaste for execution.[56] Justice Blackmun's judgment emerges as a battle, not of precedents, but of images.

Years later, in the 1994 case of *Callins v. Collins*, Justice Blackmun dramatically declared that he would in the future hold the death penalty "as it is currently administered" unconstitutional, and since then he has done so in case after case. In the light of his decision in *Furman*, and his consistent support of death-penalty legislation for twenty years thereafter, this represents a momentous transformation in his position. Later I will outline the reasons for that reversal. Suffice it to say at this stage that it was not juris-prudential arguments against the death penalty which governed his deci-sion but a significant change in his aesthetic focus, the transformation of a generalized fear of violence into a more particularized understanding of the sensory reality of capital punishment. Indeed, the failure of rationality and the importance of aesthetic knowledge forms the heart of my argument in this chapter. Justice Blackmun demonstrates that, above all through aes-thetic engagement, a change of opinion on this issue is possible.

Rules

In trying to decide whether the death penalty was in fact "cruel and un-usual," the Supreme Court in *Furman* seized on the question of arbitrari-ness. If some determinate criteria could be set to guide juries and judges in making that ultimate life-and-death decision, then the law would not be arbitrary and death would not be cruel. Thus Justice Douglas criticized the fact that "no standards govern the selection of the penalty. People live or die, dependent on the whim of one man or twelve." Likewise, Justice Bren-nan insisted that "the very words 'cruel and unusual punishments' imply condemnation of the arbitrary infliction of severe punishments." [57]

The approach of the Supreme Court demonstrates confidence in the abil-ity of rational criteria and written rules to provide objective guidelines even to such controversial questions. The 1976 cases which reinstated the death penalty sought to give content to this desire for an abstract, prescribed cer-tainty. Nevertheless, the final result of these decisions, which still form the core of the jurisprudence of the death penalty in the United States, merely demonstrated the impossibility of that rationality. Regardless of the crite-ria set down in any statute, the only real question is, Should this man die? Legislative "criteria" allow the decision makers to allocate their decision to a particular category, but they cannot change the unfettered way in which that decision is made.

Let us consider three death-penalty statutes upheld by the Supreme Court in 1976. In Georgia, the statute provides that, following the defen-dant's conviction for murder, there is a penalty phase. The jury can impose the death penalty only in certain circumstances: for example, if murder was committed in the course of a felony or for the purpose of robbery, if the victim was a "peace official," or if the murder was "outrageously and wan-tonly vile, horrible and inhuman." [58] But how does this establish "clear and objective standards"? On the one hand, the jury under this statute has complete discretion not to impose the death penalty for any reason it chooses. And on the other hand, can it be imagined that a jury, wanting to sentence a particular defendant to death, would find itself unable to do so because of the words of the statute? The reference to "outrageously and wantonly vile" murder, in particular, is bereft of determinate meaning. Admittedly, although this provision passed constitutional muster in 1976, it was later struck down; nonetheless, similar catch-all provisions remain popular in many jurisdictions.[59] Thus in Florida, the murder must have been committed in the course of a felony or by a prisoner or must have been "especially heinous, atrocious, or cruel."[60]

Neither is there any reason to believe that the words of the statute will actually form the basis of the jury's decision. The jury may decide to impose the death penalty on any grounds it chooses: because, for example, the defendant is a black man and his victim was white. As a matter of legal interpretation, the statute's "criteria" are broad enough to encompass almost any murder. As a matter of psychology, the criteria do not and cannot constrain the actual considerations relied on by the jury either in imposing or refusing to impose the death penalty. Far from forcing juries to act rationally, they merely require them to label their decisions appropriately.

The Florida statute makes a further attempt to rationalize the imposition of the death penalty. Justice White made much of this distinction:

> Under Florida law, the sentencing judge is *required* to impose the death penalty on all first-degree murderers as to whom the statutory aggravating factors outweigh the mitigating factors. There is good reason to anticipate, then, that as to certain categories of murders, the penalty will . . . [now] be imposed with regularity.[61]

But there is nothing objective about this. The "weight" to be given to the specified aggravating factors and unspecified mitigating factors is indeterminate: the sentencing court is entitled to give any weight it likes to any factor. To pretend that this amounts to some sort of constrained discretion is to mistake imagery for logic. The word "weight" is a useful metaphor which suggests an externally verifiable system of measurement, but this objectivity is an illusion.

In Texas, they do things differently. Both who may live and who will die are subject, it appears, to what appears to be determinate criteria. The death penalty there can be imposed only for murder committed in certain situations such as felony murder, murder for remuneration, and murder while escaping from lawful custody. There is no category relating to "heinous" or "atrocious" murder. The categories of murder for which the death penalty may be imposed are therefore strictly limited. Furthermore, if the jury then finds three, supposedly factual, "special issues" proven, the most important of which being that the defendant is likely to be "a continuing threat to society," the infliction of the death penalty is mandatory.[62] But this is exactly where the statute's attempt at constraint falls apart. The ability to satisfactorily predict future violent conduct is virtually impossible. Indeed, according to the American Psychiatric Association's evidence in *Barefoot v. Estelle*, it is the "unanimous conclusion of professionals in this field" that only one out of three predictions of future violence is correct.[63] "Scientific evidence" in this area does distinctly worse than a coin toss.

One might have thought that the conditions for the use of the death penalty in Texas could consequently never be satisfied, but the courts have not taken that approach.[64] Rather, in determining if the defendant is a "continuing threat to society," they have resorted to exactly those discretionary judgments ostensibly excluded by the statute. Was the crime brutal—or atrocious—or cruel? Not only do these questions inevitably color the decision as to which conflicting scientific evidence is to be believed: without hard facts, they become the only relevant questions. *Jurek*, of all the cases on capital punishment decided by the Court in 1976, was most sensitive to the facts which gave rise to it. Justice White even argues that the Texas statute limits capital murder to "a narrowly defined group of the most brutal crimes"[65]—even though the Texas statute purports to avoid just that kind of evaluation. In other cases Texas courts have relied upon evidence as disparate as the lack of a rational motive for the crime; the defendant's lack of repentance; the helplessness of the victim; or the mere brutality of the crime.[66] Absent valid scientific evidence, discretionary considerations of this sort are all that remain.

The failure of rules to constrain discretion relates to the question of mitigating as well as aggravating circumstances. In *Penry v. Lynagh*, the Supreme Court held that the jury could provide only a "reasoned moral response" as to whether the death penalty should be imposed in Texas if it were provided with jury instructions which expressly permitted the jury to "consider and give effect to [all] mitigating evidence," regardless of whether that evidence actually helped them answer one of the "special issue" questions alone before it.[67] In effect the Supreme Court has not just permitted but required a jury instruction "that allows the jury to say 'no' even when the answer 'yes' is supported by uncontradicted evidence." Even the illusion of rule-bound decision making has in this case proved unpalatable, and the Court has instead insisted that, in every capital scheme, decision makers "must not be precluded from considering, as a mitigating factor, any aspect of a defendant's character or record." [68] But a system which "simply dumps before the jury all sympathetic factors . . . so that the jury may decide without further guidance" is not based on reason or the constraints of legal rules. With the paradoxical decision in *Penry*, "the Court has come full circle." [69]

On each occasion, the Court's attempt to channel discretion into the furrows of rationality has come undone. The only way out of this dilemma might seem to be the enactment of genuinely "mandatory" death penalties. Ironically, however, the Supreme Court has expressly ruled this out. Perhaps the Court envisages a "Goldilocks approach" between the two poles of absolute discretion (*Furman*) and none (*Woodson*). In Georgia, for example, it might be argued that the list of statutory aggravating circumstances provides determinate rules which narrow the class of those eligible for the death penalty and then allow the jury to exercise a discretion which is limited and guided. Such an approach, however, would ignore what we have seen about the exercise of discretion: it cannot be limited or guided. Capital punishment cases amount to a global judgment of worth and worthlessness. And the Supreme Court, faced with the possibility of eliminating that discretion altogether, has refused to do so. Indeed, as we have seen in *Penry*, the Court seems to have insisted that there always be some moment of unguided discretion during jury deliberation. As Justice Scalia describes it, "the sentencer's discretion to impose death must be closely confined, but the sentencer's discretion not to impose death (to extend mercy) must be unlimited." [70]

The Supreme Court's jurisprudence has struggled to make the death penalty, in Justice O'Connor's words, both "reasoned" and "moral." But the tension between these two terms has proved irreconcilable. Discretion consumes guidelines. And although freedom is thus the "dangerous supplement" which undermines the aspirations of the rule of law, it is nevertheless a necessary element of justice. This, too, the Court recognized in *Woodson*. The Court there insisted that "contemporary standards of decency" require an individualized assessment of the defendant.[71] Without that flexibility, that subjectivity, capital punishment is, according to the Supreme Court, unjust and indecent.

This unalterable paradox finally led to Justice Blackmun's reversal in *Callins v. Collins.* After years of supporting the death penalty, in 1994 he declared that "from this day forward, I no longer shall tinker with the machinery of death." Justice Blackmun conceded that "both fairness and rationality cannot be achieved in the administration of the death penalty":

> Experience has taught us that the constitutional goal of eliminating arbitrariness and discrimination from the administration of death can never be achieved without compromising an equally essential component of fundamental fairness—individualized sentencing.

"It seems," he concludes, "that the decision whether a human being should live or die is so inherently subjective . . . that it inevitably defies the rationality and consistency required."[72]

The relationship of discretion and rule is archetypical of the conception of justice in general, which seeks to be both unique and iterable. The essence of discretion is its sensitivity to a unique and changeable context. The incessant rule is iterable—it functions similarly in every different case. We ask of a just legal system that it be both reliable and flexible, consistent and individualized. Indeed, as Blackmun has emphasized, "all efforts to strike a balance between the two" must fail "because there is a heightened need for both in the administration of death."[73] In this we express the hope of a fragmentary aspiration, for these two elements are unresolvable: each attracts and repulses the other. It is a paradox which gives rise to what has been termed the "impossibility of justice."[74]

Confutatis maledictis

Confutatis maledictis
Flammis acribus addictis,
Voca me cum benedictis.
> When the damned are confounded,
> And consigned to keen flames,
> Call me with the blessed.

Furman insisted that "any decision to impose the death penalty [must] be, and appear to be, based on reason rather than caprice or emotion."[75] This is a vain hope, for rationality in this instance requires the achievement of two contradictory goals. Instead, decisions about death are reduced to an aesthetic response; to the viciousness of the act, and in particular to the image it imprints upon us.

How can anyone decide whom to call with the blessed and whom to consign to keen flames—or high voltage, or acrid gas? The damned are, finally, confounded, not by a rational judge and the *liber scriptus* that rules them, but instead by the emotion of the *dies irae,* the day of wrath. This tension between language and feeling, reason and emotion, runs throughout the Requiem. Although much of its text, like the jurisprudence of the death penalty, appeals to reason, the music sounds notes of anger and horror instead. A reading of the death-penalty statutes enacted in response to *Furman*, and the cases which have sought to explain them, likewise suggests that beneath the text of reason lies aesthetic responses that govern its interpretation.

In Georgia, the death penalty may be imposed if the murder was "outrageously and wantonly vile, horrible and inhuman in that it involved torture, depravity of mind or an aggravated battery to the victim." Similar provisions apply in Florida and, by implication as we have seen, even to some extent in Texas. Section 27–2534.1(b)(7) is nothing more or less than a surfeit of imprecise and highly charged phrases whose effect is to provoke the emotions of the reader. Neither can it be said that the latter part of the clause somehow defines the former. The references to torture, and "depravity of mind," in particular, are more inflammatory than explanatory. They amplify and legitimate the passions of an enraged jury. Undoubtedly such criteria invite an emotional judgment. Yet, ironically, the statute also provides for a compulsory review of all death sentences by the Georgia Supreme Court, during which the Court must consider, inter alia, "whether the sentence of death was imposed under the influence of passion, prejudice, or any other arbitrary factor."[76] One could hardly take this safeguard seriously. Dix, reviewing the decisions of the Georgia Supreme Court, concludes that appellate review is not a meaningful constraint on the discretionary imposition of the death penalty.[77]

In *Blake v. State*, for example, the Supreme Court held that throwing a two-year-old child off a bridge constituted "torture" because death must have caused some pain. So too in *Spinkellink*, a shooting death was characterized as a capital crime because it was "unnecessarily torturous to the victim" even though the victim was actually asleep at the time.[78] As ever, the words which ought to provide guidance prove to be infinitely malleable.

AGNUS DEI

Agnus Dei qui tollis peccata mundi;
dona eis requiem.
    O Lamb of God, that takest away the sins of the world;
    grant them rest.

The attempt to create rules for the application of the death penalty implodes to reveal a core of unfettered discretion. No reasons guide that discretion;

no logic compels the choices that are made. It is instead a sensory response to images of violence and symbols of fear. The question is not, finally, how it is that some defendants come to be sentenced to death while others are sentenced to life. The question is rather how it is ever possible for a fallible human being to make the decision that another human being ought to die. Once we arrogate that right to ourselves at all, the question of what constitutes appropriate criteria is secondary. The answer lies in an investigation of the process and system of execution as it actually exists in the United States: a consideration of the sensory experience and symbolic meaning of legal death.[79] This argument moves toward an explanation of the genesis of the jurisprudence of death, the particular aesthetic perspective that makes the death penalty possible. The aesthetic dimension of law and justice is here an epistemology.

Let us begin by a comparison with torture. Torture effects and requires the denial of the humanity of the victim. The procedures of torture and the indoctrination of its practitioners and accomplices succeed in this denial by the slow process of objectification, turning the human body into a mere artifact, tool, or instrument. In the days when torture was a normal weapon in the arsenal of the state, this was accomplished publicly. The mutilated bodies of traitors were displayed as if they were statues or icons on which state power had been etched. Their wounds were symbols for which their bodies had become a canvas of dissemination.[80]

Nowadays, torture is practiced covertly. But as Elaine Scarry argues, the same processes of objectification are at work. The human being is still treated as a commodity to be dispensed with or used. The secrecy of torture itself facilitates dehumanization. Victims are isolated, devoid of support, unable even to discern if anyone knows or cares what has happened to them. The experience of pain further intensifies this loneliness. For pain is intrinsically isolating; it withdraws the sufferer into a circumscribed world where only pain truly exists and everything else is experienced as if from a gauzy distance. Stripped of all the necessary resources of identity and community, the victim's room becomes all the world. And this room is a collaborator in the torment: each wall and object itself is an instrument in the infliction of pain until, the world unmade, only pain remains. That accomplishes the complete dehumanization of the victim—and of the torturer too.[81]

The death penalty is possible just as torture is possible. The process of dehumanization in either case involves two elements which I pursue below: objectification and isolation. With isolation, we are concerned with the sensory experience of the victim and how it affects the victim's body and self. With objectification, our attention moves to the symbolic meanings appropriated by perpetrators and collaborators; how, in short, they come to see—or rather, fail to see—the violence they cause in such a way as to permit it to go on. That is exactly what objectification involves: a refusal to feel, a denial of the sensory experience of another. It is through a complex of practices of denial that the condemned man disappears from the scene of his own death, a convenient absence which allows us to think of execution as something abstract and inhuman.

This analysis is not concerned with theories of the efficacy of deterrence but with the sensory experience of death and isolation. Such an approach directly confronts the aesthetics of those who support capital punishment, since their perspective is exactly to objectify the condemned and to deny the reality of that experience. Perhaps "anaesthetic" is a more accurate word, a numbed absence of feeling. In an operation, the patient is anaesthetized in order not to feel pain; here, on the other hand, the surgeons are anaesthetized in order not to feel the pain they are inflicting.

The Aesthetics of Dying: From Being to Not Being

The process of execution is long drawn out, and every stage requires an increasingly intensified isolation. First, this turns the victim from a human being into an object. Second, it distances our knowledge of this sensory experience. In this, the death penalty is merely an extreme version of our approach to death itself. We struggle mightily to ignore death and to conceal it. In modern Western civilization in particular, the dying are shunted off and hidden from view. At the very moment when each human being most needs to feel part of a community and a family, they are at their most alone: sent to nursing homes and forgotten; sent to hospitals and processed; sent home and tiptoed past. From a society in which sudden death was abhorred, we have become transformed into a society in which it is desired.[82] Our society cauterizes death.

The death penalty brings these elements to the peak of perfection. Capital punishment denies death, as torture denies pain. The structure and environment of death row all insist that the condemned man is no longer living—on the contrary, bit by bit, they are dying. Indeed, those awaiting capital punishment are known as "dead men"; when they are moved from cell to cell the cry goes up, "Dead man coming through."[83]

Death row is an environment which alienates the condemned man step by remorseless step from the world of the living. In Alabama, a typical example, "death row" is deeply embedded within the bowels of the prison. One arrives by a tortuous route: through the gate to the prison compound, through the gate to the prison itself, through the gate that allows one into the internal areas of the prison, through the gate that leads from the main blocks to the isolation unit, through the gate to death row itself, and then finally through the gate that separates each man in his cell: each gate a barrier with its own sound and protocol; each one requiring a process of unlocking, opening, passing, closing, and locking again. "You got to go some to get in here," says one inmate.[84]

The physical isolation communicated by the design of death row is accompanied by emotional alienation.[85] The cells are stark and lacking in any amenities. All confinement is solitary. Typically, the condemned man is kept in his cell twenty-three and a half hours a day. They exercise, alone, in an outdoor cage for the other thirty minutes. Restrictions on visits are significantly more severe than with other prisoners. In Alabama, for example, the condemned man is entitled to a single one-hour contact visit per month, handcuffed and guarded. Non-contact visits are also limited: "You have to talk through little pencil holes in the glass. There's no closeness, ya know? It's not like touching. . . . I think it puts [family] in a hopeless situation. They sit there and feel like they're isolated, ya know?"[86]

There is no communication here; only observation "peculiarly reminiscent of the viewing at a wake."[87] Indeed, the condemned man is constantly watched, night and day. It is a regime reminiscent of Jeremy Bentham's Panopticon, an "ideal" prison so designed that every prisoner could be seen from a central guardroom but no prisoner could see any other. As Foucault so passionately argued, surveillance is an exercise of power which emphasizes the vulnerability of its subjects.[88] To be watched is to be made intensely aware of one's own powerlessness.

As execution day draws closer, the condemned are increasingly removed from the world.[89] Either when a date is announced for their execution, or on the day of their expected death, or both, they are moved to another cell, a "death cell" or "silent cell." The deconstruction of the world has left only one tiny room. Even more isolated than death row, the feeling of imminence which the move conveys is intensified by its location. Typically it is adjacent to and often in sight of the death chamber itself. Human beings now matter little; the move and the physical location of the cell are signs that the condemned man is now merely part of the technology of death. In the hours prior to death, this technology takes over. The dead man changes out of his own clothes and into those determined by the institution as necessary. He is shaved. For an electrocution, his whole head is shaved and also a section of his calf muscle. The diodes will be placed here, and smooth skin is preferred. He is fitted with a pair of special pants and, often enough, an anal plug to ensure that, in the final extremity, he does not behave inappropriately. Already, then, he has lost control over his body. He is stoppered, halfway embalmed. Finally, a cap is placed over his head. The dead man has lost his identity and become a faceless instrument for the more efficient conduct of electricity. Like the torture victim and with infinite slowness, he has been stripped of community and of identity, turned from a human being into an object.

Every element of the environment of death row conveys its message aesthetically, in the look and feel of a situation and in the way we react to it; in its objectification of the condemned and our own distance from them. Even color plays its role. Why is it that across the United States so many death chambers—often the gas chamber or electrocution chamber itself, sometimes the death cell—are painted a particularly bilious shade of green?[90] Biologically, green encourages passivity. T. S. Eliot writes of "the cold green light of hell," an imagery taken up with great effect in the paintings of Francis Bacon and in Wilfrid Owens's text for Benjamin Britten's *War Requiem:*

> Out there, we've walked quite friendly up to Death; . . .
> . . . We've sniffed the green thick odour of his breath.[91]

Perhaps the shade of "the little green room," the "chill green solitude of the gas chamber," is the color of nausea. Perhaps, also, the very frequency of its use in this context adds to its associations. Whatever the complex of reasons, the effect of this color is deeply disturbing. This is not the green of the trees or the sea but a green invented by human industry. For those outsiders who look at this green, artificiality alienates and overpowers, denying nature, comfort, and human warmth. And within this peaceless green, the condemned man finally dies: observed from behind plexiglass but alone.

The Anaesthetics of Watching Death: From Being to Object

Dehumanization

Let us reverse our perspective and consider the language and processes of the defenders of capital punishment. Their aesthetic experience—and ours, in tacit consent—is also controlled. In war and in torture, the enemy is transformed into something subhuman; capital punishment does the same thing. It therefore creates an image, for the purposes of denial, with an important symbolic function. With the condemned's humanness destroyed, he becomes a scapegoat for the rest of us. "Scapegoat" is hardly strong enough, since the goat chosen to symbolize evil was exiled, while the condemned man is executed.[92] A sacrificial lamb, agnus Dei, then—provided with a bestial image to ensure we are not killing one of "us," then slaughtered for the expiation of social violence: "It would be nice if we could get rid of evil by defining it out of the human species, declaring that anyone who does these horrible things is not human. But it will not work. The capacity of man to do evil, no less than good, is what defines us as human." [93] There is an ironic parallel here with crime itself, for a murderer frequently "selects a scapegoat for his own painful state of mind," finding someone to blame for his lack of control over his life and feelings. Capital punishment replicates this pattern, representing an attempt to control fear in society by "selecting for death a personification" or symbol of these problems. [94] The murderer may seek to still the rage and rising panic within by lashing out at a helpless target; society does the same.

The very labeling of the condemned man takes away his individuality. Throughout his book, Berns contrasts "the criminal" with "the law-abiding citizen," as if the two were different species. The same processes of labeling and dismissal are apparent in Van den Haag, who declares that "[t]he more I understand some people—Nazis, Communists, criminals (even some others)—the less I condone what they have done or are doing." [95] All these groups are, we may presume, discrete categories—we know one when we see one. And just as normal people could never be "Nazis" or "Communists," they could never be "criminals" either.

Deviance labeling also refashions the identity of its subject. [96] Writings on the death penalty consistently bestialize criminals. "It's genetic. They're animals," said the chief justice of the Georgia Supreme Court. [97] The turning of the criminal into a beast is in fact routine. Caryl Chessman, whose celebrated books, written while he languished for over a decade on death row, did not prevent his execution in 1961, makes the point with characteristic irony:

> On the Row at the present time we have, according to no less an authority than the newspapers:
> 1. Two "fiends" and three "monsters"
> 2. One "moon-mad killer"
> 3. One "cold-eyed, cold-blooded leader of a 'Mountain Murder Mob'" . . .
> [4.] Me
> [5.] An assortment of "vicious," "sneering," "leering," "brutal" and "kill-crazy" murderers, plus a former private-eye turned "diabolical" kidnapper.
> The weirdest factor of all is this: if chance, fate, or circumstance had acquitted or imprisoned the "monsters" presently held on the Row, & had doomed those acquitted or imprisoned, the Row still would hold the same number of monsters. [98]

This transformation of the condemned man into a beast is nonetheless paradoxical. It is only the sane who can be executed. The image of the condemned man seems to point in two directions. On the one hand, everything is done to turn him into an animal. Yet on the other hand, he must be proved to be sane and responsible for his actions. This double rhetoric reaches a peak in cases of synthetic competence, in which American courts have been called upon to decide the legality of the forced treatment of criminals suffering from mental illness. The purpose of this treatment, principally pursued by intensive drug therapy, has been to induce a state of mental balance just long enough for the execution to proceed.

What is it, we might ask, that is inhuman, bestial, yet sane? The answer is, a man possessed, a "fiend" or a demon. Their very sanity adds to their alienness: like Mephistopheles, the more human they appear the more dangerous they are. Condemned men are made into "creatures on the lam from Hell."[99] These Janus-faced images of human and animal operate together as strategies of alienation. The two techniques coexist because they operate in different emotional registers. Remove the human problem of execution by bestializing the condemned. Remove the moral problem of executing by treating them as abstract human beings. The result is a creature too mad to be human and too rational to be animal. Such a creature does not exist in biology or mythology, but the image has been constructed to fulfill the specific requirements of the death penalty.

The role of the "other," one might say, is not as an alien but rather as a distorted reflection of oneself. It is a kind of inverted narcissism, in which we gaze into the pond and see only the image of what we are not. The conversion of sameness into recognizable difference characterizes exorcism and scapegoating—the sins of the world, *peccata mundi,* taken away by the death of the other. An animal or an alien could not be the receptacle of our violent potentialities, but neither could the death of someone just like us reassure us that these traits had been effectively banished. It is precisely the double dehumanization of the condemned which allows him to undertake this sacrificial role.

The influence of racial prejudice on the implementation of the death penalty needs to be seen within this understanding of "otherness." Statistical evidence of the Baldus study established that capital punishment falls overwhelmingly upon black people in the United States. In particular, a black man found guilty of killing a white person was dramatically more likely to be sentenced to death than either a white defendant or a black man who had killed another black man. A white man found guilty of killing a black person was least likely of all these groups to be sent to death row. Despite the facile dismissal of this evidence in *McCleskey v. Kemp*,[100] later statistical studies have only confirmed these findings. The race of the victim is particularly significant in determining whether the defendant is put to death or not.[101] Race is a visible sign of difference and therefore a ready means of distancing the white middle class from the criminal, proof of his object status. Racial prejudice is not rational, but it is for many people a powerful aesthetic which determines how they see the world and whether they treat a person as "like" them or not. Once a white man or woman, judge or jury, looks at a defendant and sees not a person but a black man, the process of turning them into an objectified other is already well begun.

In *McCleskey v. Kemp*, the Supreme Court insisted on treating racial discrimination as if it were a possible instance of the "wanton and freakishly imposed" or "arbitrary and capricious" sentencing prohibited by *Furman*, which declared unconstitutional any system of capital punishment in which being sentenced to die was as random as "being struck by lightning." [102] This was treated as the touchstone of the decision in *McCleskey*, as if the color of a person's skin is as meaningless as the color of their hair. It is not; in our society, it continually affects how that person is treated. As the Baldus study so clearly showed, there is nothing arbitrary about discrimination—the words are opposite in meaning. Racism is a consistent practice of dehumanization based on visible difference. So it comes as no surprise that black people should be chosen as fodder for the death chamber. It is, on the contrary, exactly what one would expect from a society in which so many people are objectified on the basis of their color, and from a system the operation of which relies on a process of objectification.

Technology

The invisible death of an objectified other constitutes therefore a necessary isolation of the victim and a necessary denial by the collaborators. The technology of execution serves similar purposes. It is a complex symbolic experience which manufactures death not to protect the dignity of the condemned but to shelter the imagination of the rest of us.

FROM PUBLIC TO PRIVATE   Execution is carried out away from the public gaze. It was not always so, of course. Foucault describes in graphic detail the torture and execution of Damiens the regicide and argues that the public inscription of power on his poor body reflected a specific way in which early modern European states visibly manifested their authority. The presence of the mutilated corpses of criminals instilled and demonstrated the potency of the state.[103] Up until the mid-nineteenth century, public execution was the norm. Huge crowds gathered, tempted by the spectacle, drawn by the horror. Public sites of punishment were landmarks as unexceptional as a church or a bridge:

> By the Gallows and Three Windmills enter the suburbs of York. . . . You pass through Hare Street . . . [and] part for Epping Forest, with the gallows to the left. . . . You pass Penmeris Hall, and . . . Hilldraught Mill, both on the left, and ascend a small hill with a gibbet on the right. . . . You leave Frampton, Wilberton, and Sherbeck, all on the right, and by a gibbet on the left, over a stone bridge.[104]

The last public hanging in England was in 1868, although in the United States, Roscoe Jackson was hanged before a crowd in 1937.[105] The covert death has replaced it. Execution normally takes place in the dead of night or by dawn's early light.[106] It takes place in front of a few chosen witnesses. It takes place in a special room given over to the purpose. And above all it takes place away from the prying eyes of the public.

Steven Wilf has argued that the change from public to private execution reflected a changing aesthetic, a shift from "a spectacle designed to bombard the visual senses to one that sought to influence the imagination."[107] We have moved from visible to invisible power. But while invisibility may add to our nightmares of execution—that was certainly the expectation of late eighteenth-century reformers—at the same time it removes any proper understanding of the real event. This change is always seen as progress, but it is not so simple. In England, the real concern with public execution had nothing to do with the dignity of the condemned man. On the contrary, the fear of the rabble-rousing behavior of crowds motivated reformers. Charles Dickens, and before him Samuel Pepys, both witnessed public executions and were disgusted at the spectacle—of the crowds.[108] The lack of respect for death, the crowd's appropriation of execution day as an occasion for expressions of exuberant life, reflects an old attitude to death, perhaps morbid but also vigorous and earthy, which was itself becoming increasingly marginalized at that time. The condemned man, dragged by cart to Tyburn's Tree, could be the subject of continual abuse. But he could also be made a hero, cheered onto the scaffold, which was also a podium. The dead man's last words, intended to be an occasion for remorse, could also incite anger or pity. And death itself, intended to instill respect for the law, could and did sometimes seem merely an instrument of oppression.[109]

The theatrical stage (itself a scaffold) evolved in much the same way. Plays in medieval and Renaissance times were normally performed in the round or on the street. These were occasions, not merely of silent observation, but of vocal participation, and the stage managers of this pageantry were not fully in control of what happened: meaning took place not just within the framework of the play but in the larger context of an event in which the audience were full and active players. Unlike the mummers, they were by no means silent. The emergence of the proscenium arch changed all that, creating a public which was passive and physically distanced. So too the elimination of the public procession to Tyburn's Tree in London and the institution of hangings on a stage erected for the purpose outside the gates of Newgate prison—and later still the end of public executions altogether—created a context which was much more closely controlled.[110]

The visibility of public execution was a two-edged sword. The aesthetics of death aroused by such close proximity are complex and unpredictable, and the anaesthetic of death which replaced it made empathy less likely. The individual and public death was replaced by death made routine and, as Foucault suggests, the "theatre of power" in which public execution and torture took place replaced by a secret power.[111]

FROM THE AXE TO THE NEEDLE   The history of execution over the past hundred years represents the perfection of this invisibility. The observer's perspective, and not that of the condemned, has been of paramount concern. For example, since the nineteenth century, it has become almost invariable for the executioner and the condemned man alike to be covered in a robe and hood.[112] If this procedure had any virtue in the case of death by firing squad, it has none in the case of the gas chamber or the electric chair. There is nothing to see here, and so nothing from which to shield the eyes of the condemned man. For the condemned man, the hood only increases discomfort, loneliness, and terror.[113] But the hooding of the victim is very helpful for those who are required to watch him die. It protects them first from seeing the pain of his death and second from acknowledging his identity. The Romans put clown masks on those they threw to the lions.

From decapitation to hanging to electrocution to the gas chamber to lethal injection, the developing technology of capital punishment is often presented as progressing toward a painless death.[114] Yet there is in fact very little evidence that hanging—or, for that matter, beheading—is any more painful than gas or electricity, while at the same time any method of execution is frequently neither as instant nor as painless as it is often made out to be. In fact, the courts have shown little interest in the experience and pain of the death penalty. In the 1947 case of *Francis v. Resweber*, Willie Francis, "a colored citizen of Louisiana," had been placed in the "official electric chair of the State of Louisiana." The switch was thrown and a current passed through his body. "At that very moment, Willie Francis's lips puffed out and his body squirmed and tensed and he jumped so that the chair rocked on the floor. Then the condemned man said: 'Take [the hood] off. Let me breath[e].' Then the switch was turned off."[115] The Court held, however, that the reexecution of this man would not constitute cruel and unusual punishment.[116] No one at any stage sought to ask the "victim" of this "accident" about his experiences.

If no one cares much about the pain of dying, they do care about the discomfort of seeing it. It is not the painless death which we seek but the bloodless, markless death. Beheading is clearly unacceptable on these grounds. Hanging also stretches the neck and disfigures the body; debates on the change to electrocution in some states emphasized that point. Electrocution, initiated with the celebrated execution of William Kemmler in 1890, was undoubtedly seen as an improvement in that regard, although here too the process leaves temporary distortion and the odor of charred flesh. But the gas chamber, first used in Nevada in 1924, leaves no mark[117] and therefore leaves no physical sign of the suffering that preceded it or the institutions that perpetrated it. It is the very opposite of the psychology of punishment which in anciens régimes visibly inscribed state power on the body of the victim. Now, death just seems to have happened, on such and such a day at such and such a place—no cause, no trace.

Lethal injection is the natural next step. First used by Oklahoma in 1977, it is now practiced in all but two of the twenty-one states of the United States in which there has been an execution since *Gregg*.[118] Lethal injection, silent and markless, perfectly safeguards the sensibilities of its perpetrators. Furthermore, since it is performed by the medical profession, what I have termed the "anaesthesia" of death coalesces with a more familiar anaesthesia.[119] The condemned man is not being killed but put to sleep.[119] It is common practice for doctors injecting the mixture of drugs which will paralyze and kill the condemned man to first swab his arm with alcohol. This is what doctors always do when giving an injection: it prevents infection.[120]

Not only doctors but the imagery of the medical profession has been coopted to mask an act of violence. The reality of state power has been camouflaged by the image of medical authority. Return to the color of the death chamber: bilious green—also known as "hospital green." The color of hospital walls, of nurses' uniforms, or of starched sheets on the sick bed. It is the color of clinical efficiency and of the routine but justified infliction of discomfort on the one hand and of medical legitimacy on the other. This is not death, it is science. This is not politics, it is medicine.

Therefore what makes execution still possible is the absence of the body of the condemned man from the visible process. Berns writes, ironically attempting to justify the secrecy of the death penalty, "Men cannot witness the lopping off of heads or the breaking or stretching of necks without becoming less human as a result." [121] For Berns, therefore, doing these acts is humane, but seeing them is not. In this deception the condemned are made collaborators.

> Don't nobody want to sit in that chair. They are saying the reason they don't want to sit in the chair is because it messes the body up terrible. I say that too, out loud. But deep down inside, the real reason is because I am afraid that I might break down before I get to the chair. You've got to walk to that chair. [122]

Why do you have to walk to that chair? The answer is of course how much easier it makes it on everybody, for it denies the reality of what is going on. This does not always happen. In 1923, Mrs. Thompson went to her death in panic and despair. So brutal was the manner of her dying and the force required to subdue her that the executioner attempted suicide shortly afterward and the prison governor became severely mentally disturbed. [123] Such nightmarish scenes have a profound effect on all who experience them because they break through the barriers of isolation and objectification which the system has so carefully manufactured.

Why do we demand the sanity of those we execute? Ritualistic behavior requires either drugged indifference or mental acuity. Like the fool of old, an insane man may express the truth of the event. But a sane man may do likewise; his body may betray him. Accordingly, as I have noted, the anus of the executed man is plugged. Like the question of sanity, what is being suppressed here is any evidence of how our senses react to being killed. The body and the emotions of the condemned man must be restrained. Otherwise he may turn out to be more human than we want.

LIBERA ME

Libera me, Domine, de morte æterna in die illa tremenda . . .
Requiem æternam dona eis, Domine, et lux perpetua luceat eis.
Deliver me, O Lord, from eternal death in that awful day . . .
Rest eternal grant them, O Lord, and may perpetual light shine
upon them.

Empathetic Meaning

The purpose of this argument has been twofold. First, the rationality of the laws of capital punishment cannot stand scrutiny. Second, it is rather the way in which the condemned man and execution itself have been con-structed—their imagery and symbolism—that has motivated and justified the death penalty. Quite contrary to the conception of power which the tor-ture of Damiens exemplified, what now makes the death penalty possible at all is the multitude of ways in which the condemned's body is concealed, rendered absent and inhuman. The lack of awareness of what is actually happening to a human being makes the death penalty tolerable in our soci-ety: we have anaestheticized ourselves.

I move from an aesthetic analysis of why capital punishment is accept-able to an argument for the different ways in which aesthetics might suggest deliverance from the pseudo-rationality of the debate: moving from the in-terpretative insights of aesthetics, let us briefly consider its normative im-plications. My opposition to the death penalty stems not just from the ster-ility of the arguments mounted in its defense but from a respect for the experience and horror of death. In this approach, aesthetics has a moral point to make: aesthetic interpretation is built on empathy. In *Francis v. Resweber,* the U.S. Supreme Court ruled that the reexecution of Willie Francis would not be cruel, although his first electrocution was hideously botched, and in *Gregg v. Georgia* the Court confirmed that capital punish-ment was not inherently cruel.[124] The Court seemed to think that, except when the amount of pain inflicted is objectively excessive such as to offend "the basic concept of human decency," cruelty comes from the intentional infliction of suffering. Intention here means not only an intent to do the act which inflicts the suffering but also a conscious intent to cause suffering.[125] In Willie Francis's case, on the other hand, the state did not intend to do more than "extinguish [his] life humanely." The additional suffering he had to endure was merely "the unfortunate and unintended consequence of an intended act."[126]

Imagine a typical case of cruelty: a child pulling the wings off butterflies or tying firecrackers to a cat. Children are often cruel because they live in a solipsistic universe in which nothing is real outside their own experience. It is exactly this lack of awareness that constitutes cruelty. The question has not entered their calculations, as a cat "playing" with a mouse does not stop to ask the mouse if it wants to play. Their cruelty is a literal indifference to the feeling of another living thing. Only their curiosity matters, as only their pain is real. We are born into a world conjugated entirely in the first person; we learn the difference between self and other, learn to appreciate how others suffer from our actions. If we do not, if we remain as children, we become cruel—a product not of intention but insensitivity. So it is with a character such as Iago, in *Othello,* who wrought utter havoc all about him, all the while demonstrating a clinical and dismaying disinterest to the harm his actions caused. Cruelty, in short, is the opposite of empathy.

Now the judgment of the Supreme Court in *Francis v. Resweber* takes on a different complexion. The plurality did not care about Willie Francis's pain. They showed no interest in the narration of his experience at all. Instead they concentrated on the intent of the state. The attitude of the self and not the suffering of the other was the focus of the Court's concern. Everywhere they manifest a failure of empathy and imagination. Their interpretation of "cruel and unusual punishment" is itself an act of cruelty. Like a small boy, the U.S. Supreme Court says that it does not mean to cause Willie Francis any unnecessary suffering. It only wants to rip his wings off . . . twice.

Sensory Meaning

The aesthetic imagination does not demand of us forgiveness or even love. It may not even change our mind. But it offers the possibility of a way forward much more promising and powerful than endless disputes over statistics. It is not an easy task, especially when faced with a violent murderer, for it demands of us that we try to understand, from the inside, the particular experiences and life history of the condemned man. It is a perspective which even committed abolitionists have shied away from.[127] But Sister Helen Prejean's remarkable book *Dead Man Walking*, for example, narrates her experiences as the spiritual adviser to condemned men in Louisiana.[128] Prejean portrays her charges without distortion, bluntly acknowledging their horrible crimes, their cruelty, selfishness, and weaknesses. All the same, they come across as human beings, needing love and afraid of death. Such an approach finds, even under the most aberrant of conditions, familiar patterns of human behavior on the one hand, while on the other hand it seeks to understand those unique circumstances of each individual's history which have led him to such a crossroads.

An aesthetic approach seems to demand that we imagine the unimaginable. What is it to die? we might ask, and shrug our shoulders. Supporters of the death penalty and its critics alike have tended to concentrate on these issues of pain, death, and the void thereafter. They have defended or decried, in other words, the fact of death. Echoing the words of Sir Walter Raleigh, who is said to have remarked on the way to the executioner's block that his was "a sharp medicine," capital punishment is treated as "a few moments of violent pain followed by total oblivion."[129] Justice Scalia, for example, focuses on the moment of death, for the victims of murder, brutal, and for the condemned man, apparently peaceful. In *Callins v. Collins*, for example, Callins's victim was "ripped by a bullet suddenly and unexpectedly . . . and left to bleed to death on the floor of a tavern. The death-by-injection . . . looks pretty desirable next to that."[130]

But this shows a poverty of imagination. Ask not what it is to die but rather "what is it to wait for death?" The death penalty is not a moment but a process, and very dull medicine indeed. While the system of capital punishment may cease to be painful, it cannot avoid the infliction of suffering caused by a system which "warehouses for death."[131] Imagining the sensory experience of the death penalty does not center on the fact of death, then, but rather on the consciousness of the imminence of death. This is an experience everyone shares; we are all "before" death and living in the face of it.[132] Through the exercise of imagination, the anaesthetic of death, on which justification for the death penalty has been built, might be replaced by the aesthetics of dying—dying institutionalized and made routine, marked not by violence and oblivion but by lengthy waits, gradually intensified isolation, and the slow death of hope.

Hear the gates being opened and shut, feel the damp, close spaces of the row, see the green of the death chamber. These touches bring reality home to us. Even the emptiness of death may be approached in this way. Here is Caryl Chessman, writing shortly before his own execution: "The floor officer will go to the dead man's cell, accompanied by the prisoner who does clean-up work on the Row, remove the dead man's personal effects and bedding, place these on a rubber-tired utility cart."[133] What does it matter if the trolley is "rubber-tired"? It does not, but actual experience is always a riot of meaningless details, fixed upon randomly by the senses. To adequately enter into a situation, we require the accumulation of details, unimportant as well as vital. This is what it means to understand something aesthetically; and this is what it means, too, to begin to truly empathize. Both require an engagement of the senses within the infinite particularity of a situation.

We can see the importance of the aesthetic imagination as a force for change by considering again the judgment of Justice Blackmun in *Callins v. Collins*. The change in tone from his dissent in *Furman* is quite remarkable. There, he wrote about "fear" that "stalks the streets" and that, personified, the death penalty aims to extirpate. But the beginning of *Callins* is very much more specific and radically changed in perspective:

> On February 23, 1994, at approximately 1:00 A.M., Bruce Edwin Callins will be executed by the State of Texas. Intravenous tubes attached to his

arms will carry the instrument of death, a toxic fluid designed specifically for the purpose of killing human beings. The witnesses, standing
a few feet away, will behold Callins, no longer a defendant, an appellant,
or a petitioner, but a man, strapped to a gurney, and seconds away from
extinction.[134]

This important transformation has been wrought by Blackmun's newfound consciousness of the sensory reality of capital punishment. The language here is utterly different from that of *Furman*. The faceless fear of terror has been replaced by a "man," with a face, undergoing a very real and
slow experience: "the machinery of death" with which Justice Blackmun
declares he will no longer "tinker." It is not the "lethal injection" of Justice
Scalia but the experience of "intravenous tubes" which concern Blackmun;
not a "sharp medicine" and oblivion but the experience of being "strapped
to a gurney." This is how it actually happens, says Justice Blackmun: at a
particular time ("From this day forward . . . "), in a particular way ("the instruments of death"; "the machinery of death"), to a particular person ("no
longer a defendant, an appellant, or a petitioner, but a man").[135]

From *Furman* to *Callins* was for Justice Blackmun a journey from personified evil to a real person, from an abstract solution to a concrete experience, and from death to dying. I have no doubt that Justice Blackmun's
years of sitting on the bench, hearing petitioner after petitioner only a desperate appeal away from extinction, gave him this knowledge of what institutionalized death really feels like. In contrast to this sensory and imag-
inative understanding which has so transfigured his understanding of the
death penalty, Blackmun sees only "verbal formulas." He uses the phrase
twice and it sticks in his craw, for it connotes everything which is wrong
with the failed attempt to subjugate the discretion of judgment to the exercise of reason: rules which cannot be applied, generalizations which cannot be sustained, and laws which cannot deliver justice.

There is, as I have suggested, an unavoidable incommensurability between justice and law, rule and emotion, universal and particular. Yet we
need both. The Requiem, already imperfect in Mozart's fragmentary realization, recognizes this. *Kyrie eleison, Christe eleison, Kyrie eleison:* Lord
have mercy, Christ have mercy, Lord have mercy. In the Latin Mass, a text
of reason and power and judgment, these few words are the only ones spoken in Greek, and the only reference to mercy. The bracketing of the "Kyrie" in this way singles it out for special treatment. The section stands apart
from the words around it, prominent and alien. There is a different register
here, a register which cannot be absorbed into a rational system but is nevertheless intrinsic to our understanding and our humanity. Law and mercy

are different languages, necessary yet incommensurable, and one cannot be spoken in the voice of the other.

Kyrie eleison: perhaps even the use of Greek to make this appeal is appropriate. The aesthetic dimension, which captures the insurrectionary force of justice and mercy, is not literal and functional like Latin but metaphorical and expressive like ancient Greek; it is not the language of lawyers and administrators (like the Romans) but of philosophers and poets (like the Athenians). It is not as modern as reason but as old as our engagement with the world. This sensibility stands apart from the law and yet is part of it as it is part of us, inviting, perhaps, a way of seeing and a way of feeling which may help deliver us from the modern curse of institutionalized, rationalized killing.

Dona eis requiem

Variations on a Theme

Metaphors of the Boundary
and the Boundaries of Metaphor

THEMES AND VARIATIONS

Variation I (Precedent)

What musical form expresses the idea of meaning through resemblance? What is the musical form of metaphor? It is surely the theme and variations.[1] Life itself is a theme with perpetual variations, twisting ribbons of DNA giving birth to the myriad forms of living matter around us. Repeated everywhere on a scale as vast as the galaxies and as small as an amoeba, the variation form derives from the tumult of nature and, in return, gives it voice. Perhaps because of this organic character, it is a form which has proved of unsurpassed resilience throughout the history of music.[2] From the Bach Chaconne and the *Goldberg Variations*, to the symphonies and late piano sonatas of Beethoven,[3] to a great part of the jazz tradition,[4] the theme and variations has proved a fundamental form in the history of music, at once accessible to a wide range of listeners while at the same time enabling the most searing exploration of musical and emotional resources.

The very simplicity of the form permits this depth. A theme is chosen, something melodically and harmonically straightforward, and short enough to be able to be held in the listener's head. This theme, this law, is then developed through a series of interpretations, each of which elaborates one aspect of the theme: typically keeping the harmonic progression constant while changing the rhythm of the parts, exploring this or that little motif, or breathing into it a variety of different characters, by turns tranquil, melancholy, strident, impassioned, or laconic. The variations are not exhaustive in any sense; terse, epigrammatic, they provide only enough detail to encapsulate a concept. They are sketches. In the finest examples of the genre, there is, moreover, a gradual resolution at work, until at last we come to understand the theme anew, as containing within it all those disparate forces and elements which the variations have slowly unraveled. The repose comes from having seen, in that simple shard of a theme, a mirror of the world.

Each variation, taking a point of resemblance as a point of departure, reveals a different aspect of the theme. By thus rendering explicit that which was previously only implicit, our understanding of the theme is enriched beyond measure. A similiar enrichment is the hallmark of metaphor. It too treats a point of resemblance as a point of departure and, by creating a conflict between sameness and difference, improves our understanding of both.

There is a distinction. A metaphor is a stranger in a foreign land, and its strength comes from the shock of the new. All metaphors started life with the element of surprise, a striking conjunction of images.[5] The metaphor, then, is literally a "transference across" or translation from one realm to another. It is a boundary violation, an immigrant—an adoption. The variation, on the other hand, is always nascent in the theme—a chrysalis. Variations on a theme are a particular subspecies of metaphor, because they find their tension and novelty within the belly of the theme itself and thus disclose its innate problematics. They are begotten, not made.[6]

Niccolò Paganini's famous theme and variations for solo violin—the twenty-fourth and last caprice of those published together as his opus 1— is a quintessential example, not just for the ardor of the theme but for the fecundity of its progeny. Paganini wrote a theme—simple, rhythmic, repetitive—and composed twelve variations on it. Brahms rewrote the theme and fourteen variations on it. And then another fourteen variations. Then Rachmaninoff, with twenty-four variations, not to mention Schumann, Liszt, Lutoslawski, and so on.[7] Rachmaninoff claims to be writing a *Rapsodie sur un thème de Paganini,* which is undoubtedly true. But is it not Brahms' variations which serve as his guide here? Who is the dialogue between? And what of Lutoslawski?—is it really the Paganini which has influenced him or the Rachmaninoff? Variations on variations on variations. We are in the midst of a culture here, a tradition of composition in which succeeding generations have found it necessary to go back to the *Urtext* and stake their own claims to cultural competence by contributing to a tradition—"an argument through time."[8] The debate is ongoing and collective. Each composer is engaged in a dialogue not just with Paganini but with all those who have elaborated the theme and all those who will come after. The complexity of the metaphoric elaborations of the original theme is therefore further enriched by the plurality of their authors, each contributing a unique language or palette.

Theme

Aesthetics is a methodology, a way of enriching our interpretation. If we approach legal texts with an aesthetic eye, there is much we can learn about their meaning and that of the world around them; "Motet" was, accordingly, largely textual in its approach. "Requiem" marks a transition in this argument, for it traces a movement from text to context, from figure to background, and from methodology to epistemology. If we approach legal arguments with an aesthetic eye, there is much we can learn about their motivation and the deeper concerns that generate them. This approach can be applied to other areas of legal discourse. The law relating to illegal drugs, for example, is likewise explained not in terms of its logical coherence but rather by the aesthetic horror, the instinctive reactions which the imagery of "drugs" brings forth. This argument incorporates ideas about aesthetics into an epistemology of law: how, in other words, we as a community, or parts of it, come to have the values and knowledge which law, however imperfectly, expresses. Aesthetics helps explain not only the "what" of legal meaning but the "why."

The theme of these variations is that aesthetics forms as well as reveals the law. Aesthetics exercises this influence over our beliefs in two interrelated ways. First, we must recognize the persuasive force of our sensory reactions and instincts, acknowledge the relevance of this voice to our lives. Second, our aesthetic reactions are not given, unmediated, or absolute. They are a response to images and experiences which are culturally or personally imbued with symbolic and metaphoric significance. Aesthetics, then, is in part a felt judgment in reaction to an image. But it is also about the way those images operate through and draw upon a kind of symbolic grammar.

As a case study, this chapter examines the relationship of sensory experience to symbolic meaning in the legal construction of drugs—I use the word in its popular sense, referring in particular to "illegal substances" such as opium and heroin. The kind of legal framework we have in almost all Western societies is characterized by a complete prohibition of these substances and severe penalties aimed at eradicating their use. Again, there is no rational explanation for this remarkable absolutism. We must look instead to the role of our sensory imagination in how we understand drugs and its complex and ambiguous symbolism within our society. The first section, comprising the theme and first two variations, introduces the argument and in particular emphasizes the important role of the idea of the boundary in our society and the way in which this concept is expressed symbolically through images such as pollution. The boundary is a place of danger, a place of great significance, skirted with totems and taboos. It is a representation of belonging and not belonging, and the social fear of its destabilization finds many forms: "At borders, as at death and in dreams, no amount of prior planning will necessarily avail. The law of boundaries applies; in the nature of things, control is not in the hands of the traveller." [9]

Under the rubric "Metaphors of the Boundary," the next three variations look at the ways in which the fear of boundary violation has been given symbolic expression and sensory power in relation to "drugs." Through history and in the contemporary world, drugs have been constructed as a "problem" because of what they symbolize and not because of what they do. As Lacan wrote, if the symptom is a metaphor, it is not a metaphor to say so.

The third and final group of variations, "The Boundaries of Metaphor," argues in two ways for a more sophisticated recognition of the meaning and power of symbols. Symbols are by their nature ambiguous: the fearful imagery of drug use, for example, has another side, a seductive symbolism which helps us understand why the violation of boundaries can and always will seem attractive to some people. To appreciate the symbolic power of drugs—from both sides—may help us recognize that drug use will never be eliminated, for its urges lie deep within us all. This argument suggests not only the power of the aesthetic realm but its perils. A metaphor or a symbol adds a new dimension to our understanding of a particular circumstance or problem, but it cannot simply substitute for it. We can treat symbolic meaning too literally; if we forget what something is a metaphor for, it becomes a metastasis. As J. Hillis Miller writes, using Ovid's *Metamorphoses* as his text, "tropes tend to materialize in the real world in ways that are ethical, social, and political." [10] Throughout the world we treat metaphors as if they were the literal truth; as if they were in fact the things they only symbolize. [11] As metaphor or metonymy, this is the very power of aesthetics, to transform symbols into icons and tropes into sacred relics. [12]

The real problem here is that drug law, like the drug user, has literalized the symbolic. We have treated drug laws as laws about drugs. They are not. A failure to appreciate that drugs really matter in our society because they are a metaphor for the fear of transgression has led to a legal fixation on substances—on the purely literal manifestation of symbolic meaning. The failure to recognize the aesthetic and metaphorical dimensions of these legal norms has had the most alarming social and medical consequences.

Variation II: Health

The power of sensory experience and symbolic meaning in the construction of social values is nowhere more apparent than in relation to health. After all, health is not simply a fact or an idea. It is also a compound of images, ranging from the socialized ideals of beauty about the human body to the ugly and unsettling images that manufacture our approach to sickness and death. [13] Consider, as Susan Sontag has suggested, how the symbolic meaning of AIDS in relation to disease and sexuality, as of tuberculosis in the nineteenth century, has determined the depth of our fear and the nature of our response. Health and the imagery of health have always been powerful rhetorical weapons in the battle over social values, and illness, as Sontag says, is a way "to impute guilt, to prescribe punishment." [14]

This conjunction, however, frequently remains covert. Aesthetics, though an important influence on how we think and feel, often lurks as the silent minor premise behind social syllogisms couched in discourses of justification. "Health," like "law," is such a justificatory discourse, ostensibly rational and socially authoritative. The implicit discourses of aesthetics, the symbols and metaphors that guide our understanding, are therefore to be found legitimated by the language of health. If we are to illuminate the power of aesthetics in the construction of social values, we must learn to distinguish the two.

Immigration provides an excellent illustration of the use of aesthetics in the expression of social conflict and its sublimation within a discourse of health. In particular, the rhetoric of "dirt" and "dirty immigrants" appropriated the idea of health to express, in symbolic terms, a fear of difference. Hardly surprising. Immigration, after all, directly confronts expectations of conformity in people's appearance and behavior. Moreover, as Mary Douglas argued in *Purity and Danger*, dirt is "matter out of place." The law of nuisance provides a legal illustration. Many cases, especially in the nineteenth century, focused on the question of pollution, of the smell of a factory or stable, and the invasion of personal space it implied. But it was always the relationship of "matter" to "place" which determined whether pollution was truly a nuisance. A Montréal stable or factory was not by itself dirty, but only in relation to particular—inappropriate—urban contexts. It was the social construction of "dirt" which formed the basis of legal doctrine.[15]

In its place, dirt is "soil" or "earth" or "the land": health, strength, and nationhood. But in the wrong place it is filthy, even taboo. It is problematic, at least in part, because it is a breach of boundaries: the "outside" world trampled "inside," or our own insides made outwardly visible. Dirt represents a crucial breach in the ramparts we have built between the public and private spheres.[16]

But in a homogeneous and introverted society, immigration is itself a threat to the boundary between self and other. It exposes the rock pool of a culture to the oceans of humankind. The result is perhaps a feeling of being swamped, in which the migrant community itself is perceived as "matter out of place." Given this feeling, the suitability of the metaphor of disease to the expression of horror becomes apparent. That is why terms such as cultural "pollution" or "invasion" are so common. The rhetoric of immigration is an example of prosopopoeia, in which a metaphor is treated as if it were literally true. From a symbolic understanding, in which immigrants are taken to represent pollution, we move quickly to a situation in which they are treated as if they were actually polluted.[17] Throughout the nineteenth century, well-publicized cases of plague and smallpox carried by migrants served only to underscore this connection.[18]

The rhetoric of dirt demonstrates the importance of understanding the symbolic basis of these attitudes, for the absence of such an understanding has had the most tragic consequences. The history of the Chinese in nineteenth-century Australia, to which I now turn, is by no means the most egregious example of our failure to be aware of the power and role of metaphor in the construction of social policy. How was the Holocaust possible except in part through prosopopoeia?—the deliberate insistence through images and language that Jews were a plague, parasites, pests to be sent to "disinfectant centers" and "exterminated" with Zyklon B, a gas developed from common household insecticides. Metaphors of pestilence encouraged a certain way of thinking. More, as we have already seen with respect to the death penalty, it made the inconceivable possible.[19]

METAPHORS OF THE BOUNDARY

Variation III: Dirt — From Defilement to Disease

In white Australia's long history of racism, the treatment of the Chinese merits a special place of ignominy.[20] Fear of the "yellow peril" dated back as far as the early gold-rush years of the 1850s, when sizable Chinese emigration to Australia began. Places such as Canada and the United States underwent similar experiences, where railroad building and the Pacific gold rushes attracted large numbers of Chinese. From the 1860s law after law of the colonial legislatures attempted to limit or outlaw Chinese immigration, a policy finally enshrined in one of the first Acts passed by the newly federated Australian government in 1901.[21] Nonetheless, until the turn of the century, there were large Chinese communities on the goldfields and in Australia's major cities. Seventeen thousand Chinese were working the Palmer River goldfields of North Queensland in 1877 and only 1,400 Europeans; by 1887, the Northern Territory had a population of 7,000 Chinese and only 1,000 Europeans.[22]

For some protagonists, the racism directed against the Chinese seemed an economic imperative, part of an ongoing debate in Australia between capitalism and the unions, protectionism and free trade.[23] The *Bulletin*, Australia's premier weekly, insisted that "the badness of the Chinaman, socially and morally, is the outcome of his low wages"; they were, apparently, "jaundice-coloured apostles of unlimited competition."[24] But this was not just a debate about economics. The Chinese were vilified in language striking for its visceral hatred and excess. A pamphlet written by "Humanity" was by no means unusual: "The Chinese [live] amidst their evil surroundings, and their filthy and sinful abodes of sin and swinish devilry. . . . It would never be believed that our Saxon and Norman girls could have sunk so low in crime as to consort with such a herd of Gorilla Devils."[25]

The Chinese were not only portrayed as evil but as "filthy" and "swinish." Indeed, the imagery of the "dirty Chinese" was a constant refrain. Here once more is the *Bulletin*, writing in typically purple prose for an 1886 special edition on "The Chinese in Australia":

> Disease, defilement, depravity . . . these are the indispensable adjuncts which make the Chinese camps and quarters loathsome to the senses and faculties of civilised nations. Whatever neighbourhood the Chinese choose for the curse of their presence forthwith begins to reek with the abominations which are forever associated with their vile habitations.[26]

This is an evocation to make our senses reel. Undoubtedly ideas about health —about the dangers of "disease"—were intended to legitimize the invective, but if we look closer it is apparent that health is here understood overwhelmingly in aesthetic terms. It is not in fact the health of the Chinese (or of the wider community) which concerns the *Bulletin* but its impact on our senses. "Disease and defilement" nicely sums up this dichotomy: you may be diseased, but I am defiled by it.

The same conflation was made by the Sydney City and Suburban Sewage and Health Board, for whose 1876 report five members inspected the living quarters of some of the poorest parts of Sydney, touring day and night for fifty-one consecutive days.[27] Yet although the inspectors did not particularly concentrate on Chinatown, the board treated the squalor they encountered there as a trait of the community in general. "If these people ever wash themselves, they do it by stealth," reported Alderman Chapman and Dr. Read, going on to recount in lurid detail their experiences: "For the next forty-eight hours . . . the horrible sickly smell of opium smoking which pervades all the Chinese quarters seemed to adhere to us, to say nothing of the fear of infection, which is not a pleasant sensation."[28] The observers' experience was of prime concern here and not the inhabitants' health: the smell, after all, adhered "to us." In a world in which disease was understood to be transmitted through miasmas in the atmosphere, the defilement of the air was, of course, of no small importance. But it was not the spread of infection that concerned the board. Rather it was the fear of infection about which they expressed anxiety. This fear affected them and not the Chinese at all.

Why did the ideas of "disease" and "defilement" congeal in this manner? It was surely the difference of the Chinese, in their appearance and manner, their customs, and their sequestration in separate communities, which provoked such a powerful need to label and condemn.[29] As a response to immigration, the metaphors of pollution and defilement were literalized and translated into the language of health. Dirt, then, was a rhetorical miasma for the transmission of sensory and symbolic meaning.

At times, more specific health allegations were leveled against the Chinese. With anti-Chinese sentiment at its height early in 1888, the *Afghan* and three other ships arrived in Australia from Hong Kong, bearing a total of nearly 600 Chinese passengers. Those on board tried to disembark in Melbourne and were denied permission to do so. They sailed on to Sydney, and again they were denied. There they waited, hoping vainly for a change of heart, while angry crowds lined the shore and demonstrated against their presence, and the New South Wales Parliament debated new legislation to ensure their exclusion. Finally, defeated, the *Afghan* set sail, eventually returning in failure to Hong Kong.[30]

The actions of the governments of Victoria and New South Wales were illegal, even under the suggestively named *Influx of Chinese Restriction Act.*[31] But Sir Henry Parkes, the great New South Wales premier and "founding father" of the Australian Federation, appealed to a "higher law" "to terminate a moral and social pestilence and to preserve to ourselves and our children, unaltered and unspotted, to preserve the soil of Australia that we may plant upon it the nucleus of a future nation stamped with a pure British type."[32] Note the contrast between purity and pestilence, soil and dirt. In this rhetoric, the question of disease was crucial.[33] The *Afghan* was declared infected with smallpox and flew the flag of quarantine. The refusal to land its passengers seemed then sound health policy. But the *Afghan* had not been to an infected port. Furthermore, non-Chinese and, following an order of the Supreme Court of Victoria, fifty Chinese, too, were finally allowed to come ashore.[34] A strange disease, this, that exercised discrimination in contagion.

Smallpox was a disease closely associated with the Chinese. Phil May's infamous 1886 cartoon, "The Mongolian Octopus-Grip on Australia," depicted the Chinese as a giant octopus, "every one of [whose] arms, each of [whose] sensile suckers has its own class of victims or special mission of iniquity." Alongside gambling, opium, and "immorality" among others are the tentacles of "smallpox" and "typhoid" squeezing the life out of two white children.[35] The fear was undoubtedly real, but it was a fear of Chinese immigration as well as of disease. In the public mind, the two were inextricably linked. Even the phrase "yellow peril" suggests these connections, for yellow connotes contagion, fever, jaundice, pus, and poison. It is no coincidence that a disease like smallpox served the rhetorical and justificatory purposes it did. Smallpox is visible and extremely contagious. It was therefore a perfect metaphor for the pollution and violation which immigration itself was seen to represent.

Variation IV: Opium — From Disease to Depravity

The disgust these associations engendered became part of a whole racist folklore based on the image of the Chinese as squalid and infected. There was nothing accidental about this. The anti-Chinese rhetoric of dirt and pollution, typical in places such as Australia and the United States, was a powerful sensory expression of the metaphor of boundary violation, treated as if it were a literal truth. Tropes materialize "in the real world in ways that are ethical, social, and political" [36]—and, one might add, in ways that are medical. Nothing better illustrates these imbrications than the question of the Chinese use of opium. Here we can see most clearly both the importance of our senses in the very construction of social values and legal responses and the symbolic grammar which imbues those sensory reactions with particular meaning.

Of all the things that served to set the Chinese apart, their use of opium was the most horrifying to white Australians. From small beginnings in 1857, the importation of "prepared opium" increased dramatically through the century, catering to an almost exclusively Chinese market. Best evidence suggests that somewhere between 50 and 90 percent of the Chinese population in Australia regularly smoked opium.[37] Australia, of course, was not a temperate society. Per capita, Australians were the world's greatest consumers of patent medicines, the active ingredient of which was frequently opium.[38] But the Chinese did not drink their opium or take it in tablets; it was their custom to smoke it, specially prepared in pipes and frequently in "dens" fitted out for the purpose. There were occasional users and addicts; houses in which the smoking of an opium pipe was regarded merely as a courtesy, and others in which it was serious business.

The opium smoker in his den was a sign of visible and constant difference. White Australia's hostility to Chinese opium use, though again typically framed in the language of health, betrays once more an aesthetic basis. What are we to make of this description of the dangers of opium uttered in 1893 by Dr. Scott, the Victorian minister for health?: "Who has not seen the slave of opium—a creature tottering down the street, with sunken yellow eyes, closely contracted pupils, and his skin hanging over his bones like dirty yellow paper?"[39] We do not learn from Dr. Scott what "opium slav-ery" feels like but rather what it looks like. The slave of opium was not a man but a "creature," "dirty" and "yellow." Here again was the image of the Chinese, dehumanized, polluted, and discolored.

The pollution of being Chinese and the odor of opium smoking com-mingled. Here is the beginning of the *Bulletin* article "The Chinese in Australia":

> Down from the fan-tan dens are stairs leading to lower and dirtier abodes: rooms darker and more greasy than anything on the ground floor: rooms where the legions of aggressive stinks peculiar to China-men seems ever to linger. . . . Yet the rooms are not naturally repulsive, nor would they be so when occupied by other tenants; but the China-man has defiled their walls with his filthy touch; he has vitiated what was once a reasonably pure atmosphere with his presence, and he has polluted the premises with his disgusting habits. . . . The very air of the alley is impregnated with the heavy odour of the drug.[40]

In the alien environment of the crowded opium den, everything impinges upon the senses at once, strange and disordered, until only the sensation of dirtiness remains.

The sensory objection to opium, and it ran and still runs very deep, can-not be separated from its symbolic association with the Chinese. Indeed, opium is best understood as a metonym for Chinese immigration. Meton-ymy, as distinct from metaphor, uses an evident or paradigmatic fragment or adjunct to represent something much greater than itself. The opium dens of Sydney or Melbourne were the highly visible face and pungent symbol of the Chinese "invasion." Opium was the tentacle that came to stand for the whole octopus.

We need to go further in our analysis of the role of the aesthetic di-mension in the construction of these social values. Why did opium come to play this role? What about opium smoking in particular transformed it into a symbol of such overwhelming negativity, in fact, that between 1891 and 1908 every colony and state of Australia outlawed its use and possession in language of unique and Draconian severity?[41]

First, certain aspects of the aesthetic experience of the drug, the sensory strangeness of opium itself, made it particularly well suited as a symbol. It is not surprising that the smoking of opium should elicit this deeply hos-tile reaction. The imagery of the *Bulletin* was to some extent visual, using the familiar language of dirt and filth, of darkness and descent. But the smell of opium in particular highlighted the difference of the Chinese and stimulated revulsion. The "pure" atmosphere of the room was polluted by the lingering "aggressive stink" of opium; there was an odor, clammy and overpowering, which seemed to impregnate "the very air," just as the "horrible sickly smell of opium smoking" clung to the inspectors of the Sydney City and Suburban Sewage and Health Board.[42]

The olfactory system is directly connected to our emotions and serves as a powerful trigger of feelings. Smoking, moreover, is the mode of drug consumption which most involves the observer. We experience others' smoke as we do not experience their taste or sight. Smells physically challenge our sense of boundary: they escape, they are shared, they envelop—they cling. The liminal and communal nature of the sense of smell is in itself a violation of autonomy.[43] Even more so, an unfamiliar odor violates the normal. A strange smell peculiarly associated with the Chinese was uniquely placed to become an important symbol of pollution and danger.

The second reason for the symbolic importance of opium lay in the mythology which surrounded it, conflating dirtiness not only with disease but with depravity. Consider "Mr. Sin Fat," a fictional opium trader whose story appeared in the *Bulletin* in 1888.[44] Mr. Sin is the wealthy owner of dens "reeking with the nauseating odour of opium and pollution and Chinamen, and always clouded with smoke." Already the boundaries between metaphor and reality, disease and defilement, have been violated by a series of conflations: smell and the senses; invasion and pollution; and the Chinese. Mr. Sin Fat's particular pleasure is to entice innocent young girls into his lair, turning them there into hopeless addicts and sexual slaves. The story ends when one new victim turns out, unbeknownst to Sin Fat, to be the daughter of his wife: she finds out and in a fit of rage stabs him to death with a pig-sticker.[45] For the *Bulletin*, no symbolism was too heavy-handed.

"Mr. Sin Fat" is an image of evil, and his name says it all—"Fat" implies bodily unhealthiness and "Sin," moral unhealthiness. The *Bulletin*'s main purpose was to link the two conditions. As Sin Fat flourishes and becomes more and more sinful, so too he gets fatter until at last, "he was fatter than fat, his obesity was phenomenal. . . . Layers of blubber bulged about his eyes . . . and his mighty neck rolled almost on to his shoulders, and vibrated like jelly with every movement." [46] Fatness, although suggestive of prosperity and power, is portrayed as ugly just as the smell of opium is ugly, and that ugliness was treated as if it were not merely a symbol or metaphor of sin but evidence of it.

Just as "defilement" was translated into the scientific correlative of "disease," then, "disease" became the visible correlative of "depravity"—from ugliness to dirtiness, and uncleanliness next to ungodliness. The ugliness of opium use came to stand for sin, just as we saw the ugliness of dirt coming to stand for disease. In both cases, metaphors have been literalized: defilement construed as if it really were a symptom of disease and disease as if it were the stigmata of depravity.

In urban legend, opium was alleged to encourage a specific form of depravity. The defining myth of opium use in Australia last century was that (white) women who consumed it either lost all sexual control or became so addicted that they were unable to resist (Chinese) seduction. The *Bulletin*, to give only one example, argued that there was "only one possible result when a lustful and unscrupulous Chinaman is one of the parties and an unsuspecting, though perhaps instinctively cautious girl, the other." The effect of opium was, it was said, to enable "criminal and sensual Chinese" to have their way with white women.[47]

> "I went to —— place when I was only about 16 because he used to give me presents. He then wanted me to smoke, but I never would, because the pipes looked so dirty. But one day he put a new pipe before me, and made it ready, and after the first whiff from it, he or any other man ————. I was completely at their mercy, but so help me God I was a good girl before that."[48]

Despite the repeated denial of this fantasy,[49] the attribution of near-magical powers to a drug found in no less potent form in any number of commonly available patent medicines continued to have a powerful hold over the minds and imaginations of Australians. To understand the reason that opium exerted this power, we must return to its role as a metaphor for deeper fears. Miscegenation—interracial or intertribal coupling—has always been a key question of social organization, girt round by rules and regulations relating to its prohibition or authorization. What greater violation of the community's boundaries could there be; what more disturbing affront to the sensibilities of a homogeneous and prudish society?

Unsurprisingly, the fear of cultural and social change which Chinese immigration raised was most intently concerned with sexual relations between Chinese men and "white women." And in looking for symbols through which to express this fear, "prepared opium" was uniquely well qualified, a drug (that is, already a metaphor of violation and loss of control) identified solely with the Chinese. Opium was in fact the ideal metaphor through which to express those fears of invasion, boundary violation, and pollution which Chinese immigration raised, which the specter of miscegenation epitomized, and which opium had come to symbolize. The result was a potent amalgam of fear, the symbolic forms of its representation, and the sensory forms in which it was expressed.

Variation V: Drugs — From Objects to Symbols

The strength of this complex interplay of reference and reverberation created a value system about the use of "drugs" which continues to be enormously significant. In Australia, as in Canada, the United States, and elsewhere, the association of the Chinese with opium was the beginning of the modern legal prohibition of "drug" use.[50] Let us move, then, from history to the present.

There is something to explain here. Around the world, there is an awful sameness to the offenses and penalties which control the use of substances such as cocaine, marijuana, and the opiates (including opium and derivatives such as morphine and heroin)—a sameness not of content but of character. In the Philippines and Jamaica, in Malaysia and Singapore, drug trafficking is an offense punishable by death. In the several states of Australia, the trafficking of a "commercial quantity" of a drug may typically lead to a penalty of twenty-five years' imprisonment and in addition a fine of up to $250,000. In some jurisdictions the guilty are liable to $500,000 fines and to life imprisonment.[51] In Canada likewise, and in the United Kingdom, trafficking in a narcotic drug or even possession for that purpose is each punishable by life imprisonment. As Bob Solomon and S. J. Usprich have argued, the *Narcotic Control Act* (Can.) and its many analogs are extraordinary, not simply due to the severity of particular provisions but through the fact that so many exceptional devices have been harnessed together.[52] Other laws also provide for harsh penalties; for mandatory sentencing; for a reverse onus of proof, requiring defendants to prove their innocence; for expanded police powers of search and seizure. Only in drug laws, however, do all these measures coalesce. The result is that modern drug laws are an expression of fury in legislative form.

The smoking of opium, as I have noted, symbolized the transgression of boundaries. The same is true of the odor of marijuana: we can close our eyes but not our noses.[53] Smoke connotes contagion and invasion. What of the needle? No other image so pervades the field of drugs. From lurid airport paperbacks to gray and scholarly monographs; incorporated into the logos of a hundred organizations and conferences, and undoubtedly in the mind of the public, the needle is the very icon of illegal drug taking. But injection is neither necessary for the consumption of any substance nor even the most common means. The image of the needle exerts a fascination out of all proportion to its significance. A syringe, made of plastic; a tapering tube, hollow at one end, at the other a plunger. Into this is placed a very thin tube of metal, sharp yet hollow, which can be inserted under the skin. Now it will work; it will act as a medium between the outside world and the inside of our bodies.

Most people have an aversion to needles. They do not look at it puncturing their arm. They look away or close their eyes in discomfort. What accounts for this aversion? Surely not the pain itself, which is, after all, not that great. Rather, the fact of bodily violation itself disturbs us. This unnatural invasion governs our understanding of the injection of drugs, and, although in certain well-defined medical contexts we are prepared to ignore our revulsion, there is no such charity for the illegal drug user. The hypodermic syringe is the ultimate boundary violation. It is, to misquote Mary Douglas, "metal out of place" and the drug user, by definition, polluted.[54]

The olfactory violation of smoking, the visual and tactile violation of injection, or the violation of normality, all generate a powerful sensory reaction due to the challenge to boundaries which they symbolically represent. To carry further this idea of the boundary, consider the question of ritual, in which illicit drug use is embedded. In this case, it is not the dismantling of boundaries but their unwanted construction which provokes hostility. There is always a certain discomfort occasioned by alien rituals. The nonbeliever sits in church, shifting self-consciously in his pew. The guest at dinner worries about which fork to use. Traditional behavior and rituals of all kinds bind a community together—but simultaneously they create boundaries against outsiders.

The strangeness of others' rituals alienates us, and often particular objects used in those rituals become metonymic of that alienation. The photographs and illustrations which accompanied the 1980 Australian Royal Commission into Drugs provide a good example.[55] The pictures are disturbing: full of unusual objects or objects in unusual contexts. A radio next to a bag of heroin; a collection of bloated condoms. But there is no effort at explanation or contextualization here. In fact, there are no people in these pictures at all, only objects: agents of corruption and places of secretion. This photo essay draws attention to the mystery of these objects, the uses of which remain perplexing and alien.

Drug paraphernalia may generate the same feelings of disgust in us, which is perhaps one reason there are often specific statutory provisions which allow for their confiscation and make their possession an offense.[56] In the U.S. Supreme Court case of *Harmelin v. Michigan*, Justice Kennedy wrote that the petitioner was found with the "trappings of a drug trafficker," "including marijuana cigarettes, four brass cocaine straws, a cocaine spoon, 12 Percodan tablets, 25 tablets of Phendimetrazine Tartrate, a Motorola beeper, plastic bags containing cocaine, a coded address book, and $3500 in cash." [57] Seen in isolation, these objects are not exclusively the trappings of the trafficker, but they build an intimidating portrait of their owner through their juxtaposition. There is an aesthetic reaction here to the mere conjunction of items whose use is mysteriously specialized ("four brass cocaine straws"—the brass suggesting a hidden culture of drug use whose very refinement is contemptible, just as the Puritans found so offensive the ornate and intricate artistry of Catholic icons) and a perversion of the normal (tablets of Percodan and Phendimetrazine, a "coded" address book, "a Motorola beeper").

A needle and a rubber coil; a collection of brightly colored pills; a rolled-up dollar bill and a mirror. These powerful images seem to outsiders a strange and even random assortment of objects. The peculiarity of their association emphasizes the existence of rituals to which we are not privy. Our hostility to such mysteries is as emotional and potent as that which the Incas and the Aztecs must have felt at the arrival of men carrying incense and crosses—objects whose symbolic power they could sense but whose meaning they could not fathom.

THE BOUNDARIES OF METAPHOR

Variation VI: From One Side to the Other

The social hatred of "illegal drugs" to which the legal system gives dramatic expression is born of a reaction to images, senses, and objects associated with the metaphor of the boundary. "Drugs" have come to symbolize belonging and not belonging.

But this alone is inadequate to explain the hostility which laws about illegal drugs reflect. It is the ambiguity of these symbols, the multiple and contradictory meanings which in fact they encompass, which makes them so problematic and requires their meaning to be policed. A symbol never just means one thing to everybody: its richness comes from its flexibility, its many possibilities, and its lack of denotative precision. Symbols are, in fact, "potential bearers of meaning." This is the other side of the symbol, and it is important to understand it in order to get to the heart of those social battles which are "contests fought in metaphors." [58]

As Elaine Scarry argues, the same is true of real battles. War, like law, is not merely an exercise in brute force but rather a series of symbolic acts. Death and mayhem have great symbolic power, but for each side the meaning of these sacrifices is different—the loss suffered for the sake of "freedom" or "anticommunism" by one side represents "ethnic community" or "anticolonialism" for the other. The intensity and violence of war is to be understood not simply as an exercise in power but as a dispute over contested symbols.[59]

Political battles are no different, the prize "the capture of a core of accepted implications which will support further metaphorical elaboration, and may, at length, become part of what we mean when we talk about the primary subject of these metaphors."[60] Behind "the war on drugs" lies precisely this symbolic dispute centered on the metaphorical field of the boundary. The drug war is a battle about what these things are to symbolize in our communities. Boundaries, after all, have at least two sides, although we often wish to keep one hidden from view. So much is immediately evident with respect to the question of ritual. Inherent in any ritual is its doubleness, which serves to define insiders who know what to do and outsiders who don't. The needle is also invested with double meaning, depending on whether one is an insider or not. Illicit injection might appear to symbolize death, pain, and danger. But from the tain of the mirror, within the community of heroin users in particular, the symbolic meaning of the act of injection is different.

The very aspects of discomfort and violation which account for the negative connotations of intravenous injection have been appropriated by users. As with rituals involving the commingling of blood, the very difficulty and unpleasantness of the procedure becomes a boundary and a rite of passage.[61] This is why there are many different levels of heroin users: some do not inject, some inject subcutaneously but not intravenously, and still others do not inject themselves but get a partner to do it for them.[62] Each is a step along a gradual course toward self-identification as a heroin user.

Further, the image of injection has been radically reinterpreted within the culture of the needle. From the outside, it looks like death and harm. From within, it connotes sexuality. The phallic needle, the act of penetration, the orgasmic rush—this much is obvious: undoubtedly a stereotypical and heterosexist view but very commonly expressed among users. But rather than being mere analogies which one might observe, these notions are central to users' understanding of their experience. For many users, the act of injection has the same memorable and life-changing quality about it as a first sexual experience: "I fell in love with heroin that night in my good friend's house. I felt very secure. Like I wasn't alone any more. I realized that things wouldn't be the same for me, now that I've used the needle."[63] Injection is an invasion, certainly. So is intercourse, and equally compelling for some.

The sexual nature of injection is particularly marked in relation to the sharing of needles. Some writers have emphasized that there are pragmatic reasons for this: the availability of the drug rather than the availability of needles governs the behavior of many users.[64] Whatever the functional needs which may have given rise to needle sharing, however, it has become a cultural practice of some significance. The neophyte is almost always injected by somebody else, a more experienced user, with their equipment.[65] For many users, sharing and submission remain the normal mode of proceeding long after. Here the symbolism of penetration and rush is most persuasive, the feeling of sharing and intimacy most compelling, and the power differential in the relationship most marked. Accordingly, needle sharing tends to be gendered in a fairly stereotypical way. Most women never shoot up alone, and a majority always share; about half of all women users, but only 5 percent of men, are tied off and injected by somebody else.[66]

The intimacy of needle sharing is not simply sexual. Injection by a partner may become a substitute for sexual activity, not only metaphorically but physically.[67] But more than this, "running partners," who seek out, purchase, and consume heroin together, develop an alternative intimacy. The blood brotherhood of needle use is further strengthened by the experience of heroin use itself, through which partners begin to develop a shared physical rhythm of life, getting high together, suffering withdrawal together.[68] This is the double-sidedness of the injection: what seems to be horrific from one perspective is seductive from another. Just as the power of drug imagery to conjure up revulsion and horror explains the deep-rooted hostility to those who transgress the boundary between medical and nonmedical use, so too the alternative imagery and symbolism of the drug user explains the dogged continuance of transgression.

It is not enough to draw attention to conflicting interpretations of the needle by mainstream and mainline culture. The needle holds an ambiguous place within mainstream society, too. Although the needle connotes bodily violation, it also symbolizes the promise of modern medicine. You submit to the needle as you submit to doctors, and in return science cures you. As Scarry and Douglas would both emphasize, the internal contradiction here, the very fragility of the boundary between good and bad, makes it vital to guard its frontiers. But the use of the hypodermic syringe in illegal drug use undermines that boundary. And that is why the border is policed so jealously.

Variation VII: From Other to Self

What revolts us is not simply ugly or hateful. Horror movies, pornography, and drug use may all be "revolting," but all have their adherents. Revulsion arises from fascination, at times appalling, but perhaps at other times quite compelling. We are not aloof from the culture of the needle, from its enticement, its secrecy, and its violation of social order. Revulsion against the images of drug use betrays, I have no doubt, a certain allure: the experience of being caught looking, of seeing in the object of your revulsion aspects of your own character or shared humanness which you would rather deny. There is, after all, nothing so vociferous as denial.

The central thing to understand in this conflict over symbols is that it is not simply a conflict between "our" interpretation and "theirs," self and other, but a conflict between two alternative ways of looking at the boundary, and indeed at the meaning of drug use, which are inherent within our own way of looking at the world. The prohibition of drugs, therefore, is the exile of part of ourselves. What boundaries do drugs seem to violate? One answer to this question is that drug use is feared as a challenge to the boundaries we have erected between mind and body, reason and emotion, self and other. The modernist Western concept of the mind entails a number of related themes: a dichotomy between the mind and body and the greater importance attached to the former in our self-identity; the mind as an individual and abstract faculty; the equation of its "natural" and "proper" state with clarity and rationality. Any deviation from this norm constitutes a deterioration in condition. Drug use challenges exactly these assumptions.[69]

The common revulsion or fear of drug use arises because of the importance we attach to maintaining inviolate our control over the self and the mind. But this boundary is also double-sided. We do not always yearn for self-control and autonomy; we are more complicated than that. As Friedrich Nietzsche put it, Western culture since the time of the ancient Greeks has struggled to accommodate both Dionysus, representing the irrational and the ecstatic, and Apollo, god of order, rationality, and discipline.[70] Both appeal to desires deep within us. Above all, the dominant aesthetic of the mind is based on a selective view of what constitutes normality—a model of conformity which denies much that is human. Andrew Weil, in his ironically titled *The Natural Mind*, argues that altered states of consciousness are a natural human desire and experience.[71] Sleep, dreams, daydreaming, meditation, and trances are all manifestations of changed consciousness; the child who spins and spins until the world spins with her is experimenting with her mind as much as the drunk or the religious ecstatic.

In most cultures, these desires are channeled into carefully organized rituals in which there is often extensive drug use by some persons or on some occasions as part of the spiritual and emotional life of the community. Often these drug-induced experiences, which may last days or weeks, have poetic significance.[72] In our culture, however, the Cartesian model of mind has overborne all that. The contradictory messages which the symbols of boundary and transgression therefore evoke are not simply challenges to the social order from "outside," from deviants or social pariahs. The same conflict is to be found within us, in our shared values, in a culture which, like all cultures, is by its very nature contradictory.

Toward the end of Rachmaninoff's *Rapsodie sur un thème de Paganini,* there is an epiphany. Suddenly, the intensity and agitation of Paganini's original theme evaporates and a new theme emerges out of the cocoon of the old, harmonically clarified, transparent, and with breathtaking calm.[73] This variation sounds fundamentally different and unrelated to its predecessors, but it is in fact an inversion of the original theme. Where the original theme rises a certain interval, the inversion descends by the same amount, and so on. This is the transubstantiation by which the new variation is developed: the world turned upside down. It is the revelation of a hidden truth. After waiting for over a century, buried deep within Paganini's theme yet always there for those who cared to listen, a tranquillity and introspection that serve to contrast and in fact to resolve the original are revealed by Rachmaninoff. This is the paradox and the gift of the *Rapsodie:* by embracing its opposite, it makes of its theme something greater than it ever was before.

The fear of boundary violation, which generates the aesthetic reaction to drugs we have seen, seeks to deny something which is buried deep within us. Drug use violates the demarcation between mind and body, rational and irrational, self and other. The symbolic war on drugs is fought against that unsettling instability of boundaries. But there is an alternative to this war. In both its organic nature and its ability to reconcile the contradictory, the *Rapsodie* argues for an approach which is ethical no less than musical. It tells us, and the idea of the Jungian "shadow" is close to the surface here, that our opposite, the "other," is not an alien but an aspect hidden within all of us.[74] Our inversion is within us, not beyond us.

Variation VIII: From Symbols to Fetishes

We cannot prohibit drug use because we cannot prevent the expression, by many people, of a natural human desire, though for many of us it exists as the denial of a shadow. What stops us, therefore, from recognizing the metaphorical nature of social attitudes to drugs? What prevents us, furthermore, from giving to drug users the respect and tolerance which they are owed?

The problem lies in the literalization of metaphor. The life of the addicted user is completely absorbed by the discovery, procurement, and consumption of the drug—it is a full-time occupation that, often enough, leaves little room for other thoughts.[75] Indeed, the drug experience itself becomes so focused on the apparatus that surrounds it that this equipment and not the substance itself comes to actually cause the physical high.[76] Ironically, for heroin users in particular, the needle and not the drug is the sine qua non for the rush they seek. In this limited gaze, even the human body becomes an object to be understood in relation to the needle and the drug. Longtime users stare with envy at those whose veins are fresh and new.[77] This is the culture of the needle and indeed the culture of the vein.

Desire is intensified into obsession and fixation, leaving in its wake a trail of illness and death. One way of describing this is as a fetish, the all-consuming passion for a symbolic object realized in material form:

> Irreducible materiality; a fixed power to repeat an original event of similar synthesis or ordering; the institutional construction of consciousness of the social value of things; and the material fetish as an object established in an intense relation to and with power over desires, actions, health, and self-identity of individuals whose personhood is conceived as inseparable from their bodies.[78]

The fetishist comes to associate some bodily pleasure with an object and eventually cannot find satisfaction without it—it alone has the power "to repeat an original event." The same is often true of the drug user. But this is merely another example of the literalization of metaphor. The real desires and problems which drug use expresses are concealed because the user treats a symbol of pleasure as if it were the sole cause of it. In this process, the drug object—a metaphor and a means—becomes the fetish of his or her desire until eventually no satisfaction can be achieved without it. Drugs, says Weil, "have the capacity to trigger highs; they do not contain highs."[79] The fetishist forgets this truth.

How does the law see drugs? As we have seen evinced in the severity and detail of legislative provisions, the law is fixated by certain drugs. Neither is it the use or harmful consequences of these substances which occupies the law. Simply their possession or sale brings about the intervention of the legal system. In other words, the law is focused not on problematic behavior but on the drugs and equipment themselves. The gaze of the law is directed not on people but on things; not consciousness but needles and powders mark out the scope of its vision.

The law sees the world the way the addict sees the world. They share a worldview which literalizes the metaphoric. The legal system, much like the drug user, has succumbed to a fetish, believing in its magical potency and thinking that the only answer is to prohibit it absolutely—to outlaw high heels, or leather . . . or dried weeds. Prohibitionist legislation, like the addict, thus treats the symbols of bodily, mental, and social boundary-violation as a reality and fixates upon them. Would our concerns about the traversal of boundaries disappear if drugs vanished from our lives? Of course not. Yet law's drug fetish prevents us from seeing where our fears really lie, which is to say, it prevents us from seeing ourselves.

To take sides in this ritual conflict between the law and the drug user is to miss their deeper parallels. Just as we have already seen in relation to the internal contradictions of the needle, and of the mind, it is a mistake to see the law and the user as opposites. If the legal system expresses a revulsion of illegal drug use, this is exactly because of the hidden similarities of their position. One is an organic inversion of the other. Indeed, the institutional and legal construction of deviancy creates identity.[80] We understand a person who uses drugs as "an addict" or "a drug abuser" and focus on one aspect of their life as the explanandum for any and all supposed behavior patterns. "The drug abuser" does this or that: the anthropological approach entitles the observer to ascribe difference without ever having to explain it or put it in context. The effect is that, in and around that one aspect of the person's life, an identity is created for "the addict" which they, no less than the rest of the community, adopt. It is not only true, then, that the addict and the law share a fixation. By fixating on the specific objects of that addiction, the legal system perpetuates it.

Contemporary drug legislation fuels the fetish it wants to destroy. It constructs a literalized image of drug users. It ignores the natural desires which drug use expresses, whether for intimacy, community, liberation, discovery, or transcendence. It ignores the serious problems which drug use may express, whether of poverty or oppression, and there too sees only secondary manifestations of those problems—needles, powders, and weeds. While the abuse of drugs therefore stems from the belief that certain desires can be satisfied only chemically, the law itself actively promotes that belief, ignoring both the real desires and the real problems and fixating instead only on the chemicals which have come to symbolize them. This concerted imagery has a normative effect: the statute's fetish becomes our fetish, its metaphors our metaphors.

Literalization is a corruption of metaphor which arises from ignorance of its use. On the one hand, drug use is frequently a symptom of poverty, alienation, and abuse: it does not cause any of those things. On the other hand, addiction likewise resides in the mind and personality of the user and not in the substance.[81] In both cases, we do ourselves no favors by focusing on the chemical substance as if it were the problem. The reality of social change and conflict has been displaced by literalized metaphors.

Variation IX

Variations are not simply repetitions—they are not fetishes. But one may easily elide into the other. What is a series of variations but a structure of obsession? A theme and variations requires an unremitting focus on slight thematic material. It focuses on a single musical object to the exclusion of all distractions. Play it again. Play it again. Play it again. There is a fine line between continuation and repetition, interest and fixation.

The Paganini, for example. Why have so many composers found it necessary to return to a theme which has little but energy to recommend it? Why this itch that so many composers have found an urge to scratch? The answer is that the fury and magnetism of the theme makes it a perfect partner to the form. The theme goes around in your head incessantly, demanding repetition. After an hour or so of this, an hour of twelve or twenty variations, nothing but the feeling of being in the music remains. This is as close as music comes to an altered state.

Obsession, which is the variation form's temptation, is perfectly matched to the obsessive character of Paganini's theme, simple and rhythmic, but for that very reason nagging and mesmeric. The theme and variations, then, is a metaphor for metaphor and Paganini's caprice its paradigm. But it is also a metaphor for and a musical articulation of the dark side of compulsion and caprice. In the progression of a symbol or metaphor into an idée fixe[82] lies the danger of addiction: we find ourselves absorbed by a single symbol, focusing on one object of desire, to the exclusion of all else, around and around until all other reality is excluded and one theme, constantly reiterated, takes over our lives. Metaphor is an invaluable tool in the creation of meaning, but the peril of literalization also awaits us there, awaits the drug user and the drug lawyer alike.

The fact that the aesthetic dimension is a force in our lives makes it both creative and perilous, a source of metaphors and the origin of fixations. This raises the central question of judgment. For finally, how can we tell the difference between the literal and the metaphoric, the variation and the fetish? When does symbolic meaning and sensory power stop being an important part of how we understand the world and become a rhetorical ploy or a way of exploiting emotions?

These are difficult questions. The aesthetic dimension, I have argued, is a way of seeing, a way of reading, and a way of knowing. Whether this methodology and epistemology is used to advance good values or bad ones is a different question. So far, then, the aesthetic dimension has told how to recognize but not how to choose between aesthetic values. Is there a normative element to the aesthetic? Does it not only tell us how we judge and what we judge but also guide us toward the content of that judgment? The final two chapters address these issues and argue toward a normative approach which takes aesthetic values seriously.

Part 3

THE NORMATIVE DIMENSION

Quartet for the End of Time
Legal Theory Against the Law

Conceived and written in captivity, my *Quartet for the End of Time* was given its first performance in the Stalag VIII A, January 15, 1941, in Görlitz, Silesia, in atrociously cold weather. The Stalag was shrouded in snow. We were 30,000 prisoners . . .

—Olivier Messiaen, *Quartet for the End of Time*

VOCALIZE, FOR THE ANGEL ANNOUNCING
THE END OF TIME: THEMES AND STRUCTURES

"The first part [of my *Quartet*] . . . evoke[s] the power of this
strong angel, crowned with a rainbow and clothed in clouds, one
foot on the sea and the other on land. The [second] section deals
with the impalpable harmonies of heaven, the piano playing soft
cascades of chord."[1]

Space, Time, and Modernism

Olivier Messiaen's contemplation of the "end of time" has an apocalyptic
quality which stems not only from the millenarianism that has influenced
it—the day of judgment and the Book of Revelation—but from the human
conditions of its creation. Written amidst the ravages of war and the moral
and physical desolation of Europe, in the very heart of darkness, in the very
depths of winter, Messiaen's music is steeped in despair. In the snows of
1941, the world looked as if time itself had come to a stop, as if the Thousand Year Reich was eternal, and as if only the end of time and the intervention of the divine could save the world from ruin.[2]

So much may be heard in the woody clarinet's "Abyss of the Birds." But
Messiaen sees something more here, the promise of a new beginning. Time
is something to be survived in order to proceed beyond it. So the "end of
time" is met with "A Tangle of Rainbows," dense and rapturous clusters of
notes. Thus belaureled, the angel ushers in a new era beyond the torments
of temporal existence.[3] Messiaen is inspired by the songs of birds and the
visions of angels.

Devastation makes us think of chaos, but when Messiaen looked around
him, he saw not chaos but an excess of order. The catastrophe of totalitari-
anism represents the apotheosis of modernism, of system building, both
physical and ideological: the triumph of the single and totalizing perspective which modernism adopted. Max Horkheimer and Theodor Adorno, also
writing in the middle of World War II, declared that "Enlightenment is to-
talitarian." There is nothing incoherent about Stalinism or fascism; indeed
it expresses an inexorable logic.[4] It was a logic which destroyed Europe with
exhaustive efficiency. Chaos could hardly be worse.

When Messiaen alludes, therefore, to the "end of time," I read him as
heralding the end of "modern time": the end of modernism and the end of
the modernist conception of time.[5] From Isaac Newton to Richard Dawkins,
one of the most enduring images of modernism has been that of the universe as a clock, a mechanical instrument for the regulation of time.[6] The

clock enforces, as Bergson argued, a spatialized image of time: linear and precise, able to be mapped out, subdivided and pinned down. Clockwork converts an idea of some mystery into an image of manufactured and predictable parts. It represents the attempt to define and thereby conquer time. In short, clockwork is the epitome of modern time. It converts rhythm to regulation and art to technology.[7]

Our understanding of time has been governed by modernism—carved up into discrete units in a process which Michel Foucault sees as paradigmatic of the era, to be saved and spent like a currency, measured and defined like an object.[8] Norbert Elias says that time was built as a functional human tool, a product of our capacity for synthesis and memory; but it has been treated as an abstraction, external to us, and therefore experienced as a powerful instrument of social discipline. This is the heart of the matter, for these factors conceal each other—the reification of time and space into a thing which rules us legitimates its regulatory operation.[9]

Boaventura de Sousa Santos, following Chaim Perelman, argues that, since modernism has privileged temporal metaphors, postmodernism ought to "resort to spatial metaphors."[10] To be sure, modernism has been obsessed by temporal ideas of progress and advance—"time's arrow," a clockwork universe, and the theory of evolution. But this is a particular understanding of time as something constant, linear, and objective, which Santos adopts as if it were what "time" really is.

In fact, time and space in modernism are subject to the same pressures: both are treated as things which exist aside from our human construction and interpretation of them, as abstractions in which we happen to find ourselves rather than as regulatory constructions devised by human minds to serve specific social purposes. To distinguish them or to express a preference misses the point. They exist together.

> In brief, every change in "space" is a change in "time"; every change in "time" a change in "space." Do not be misled by the assumption that you can stand still in "space" while time is passing: it is you who are growing older. . . . The change may be slow, but you are continuously changing in "space" and "time"—on your own, while growing and growing older, as part of your changing society, as inhabitant of the ceaselessly moving earth.[11]

Indeed, the modernist understanding of "time" and "space" emerged together. Leon Battista Alberti and Filippo Brunelleschi were central figures in the development of theories of perspective which exemplified, in art, that movement toward the subjective individual located in an objective and reified space. Galileo's experiments on the acceleration of falling bodies, a century later, used for the first time techniques of "time" to measure phenomena in the "objective" and "natural" world. Time and nature are conceived as external and regular sources of order and we as individuals in it but apart from it. We see here the beginnings of the reification of time: its conversion into something God-given like the oceans rather than human invention like the boats that sail upon them.

Four Movements, Four Instruments, and a Fifth Dimension

Reification, the conversion of a human concept into an external thing, is therefore one of the central features of modernist thought. In modernist legal theory, "the law" also is an example of a concept which has been reified, of a human invention which has come to be seen as a "system," objective and abstract. There is a normative element to this chapter, since it uses ideas about aesthetics and aesthetic change to advance a pluralist understanding of law and legal theory. Let me foreshadow some of the steps in the argument.

The "Abyss of the Birds," the title of the next movement, is Messiaen's somber reflection on the ravages wrought by the modernist reification of space and time. Legal theory at the present time finds itself in an abyss of its own, caused by the disjunction between its changing intellectual focus and the continuing modernism of its aesthetic—an aesthetic governed by ideas of coherence and the reification of space. Different legal theories, despite their internecine squabbles, in fact share these problems and this modernist perspective. The aesthetic dimension, particularly as it has affected the conception of space in legal theory, illuminates important aspects of what is at stake in these different theories, as well as revealing the imagery and vision of the world which has generated them.

In the following movement, "A Tangle of Rainbows," the discussion moves from the effect of modernism in legal theory to changes that have taken place in recent years. The "Abyss" is an aesthetic analysis of legal theory, while the "Tangle" proposes a new vision for law—a vision which is critical and pluralist. The last movement, "Crystal Liturgy," looks at the changing epistemology and aesthetics of the world around us. Legal theory is always influenced by currents of vision and desire. In the "liturgy" I focus on the aesthetic paradigm shift which has taken place in science and in music and call on these trends in support of a new aesthetic and new metaphors to understand it. A movement beyond modern times in thinking about law must be accompanied by an aesthetic no less than an intellectual shift in paradigms. Critical pluralism appeals to the changing perspectives of both.

Taken as a whole, this chapter draws together the modernist intellectual and aesthetic legacies that legal theories share, at the same time as it looks at the trends that are moving us in different directions. The analysis is framed with four interactive variables: music; legal theory; the epistemology of science and philosophy; and aesthetics. I could have chosen others, but these four instruments will suffice: a quartet of separate but interactive voices.[12]

This "Quartet for the End of Time" stands opposed to the reification of "time," "space," and "law." We do not live in four passive dimensions, but rather we are constitutive of five or more. What is a dimension? It is a structurally distinct variable, and the number of dimensions corresponds to the number of coordinates it takes to specifically define any point within it. A dimension, then, is a "degree of freedom." To conceive of time and space in four dimensions is to present them as objective things removed from human interpretation. The fifth dimension is the human dimension, which emphasizes the power of human ideas and symbols to effect our understanding of the world. Interpretation is a degree of freedom. This human and symbolic dimension renders "the law"—it sounds just like a four-dimensional thing which exists apart from us—actually multiple, indeterminate, and interpretive. Legal meaning is therefore human, not objective; contested, not determined.[13]

A three-dimensional object appears to throw a two-dimensional shadow.[14] A four-dimensional object, mathematicians tell us, throws three-dimensional shadows. So it is that, in our own lives, we observe the passage of time—the fourth dimension—through the shadows it throws in three-dimensional space. A monument, a graveyard, or a Constitution: these are the shadows time leaves behind. What of the fifth dimension? We would expect it to leave a four-dimensional shadow. And do not ideas, for their part, leave traces in time? Each era is subject to the workings of a certain framework of ideas and concepts, whose substance we cannot directly observe though its shadow is everywhere to be seen.[15]

We have lived in the shadow of modernism for many years. One of its effects has been the effacement of its own fifth-dimensionality—the human and subjective nature of its symbolism—and the presentation of its shadow as something unavoidable and objective. The reification of time and space is thus both an aspect and a technique of modernism: an aspect of how it orders the world and a technique for the totalization of that order. Messiaen's music invites despair at the collapse of the modernist system yet the possibility of proceeding beyond it. It represents the potential for a new aesthetic, an invitation to imagine the end of modern space/time as a new beginning.

THE ABYSS OF THE BIRDS:
LEGAL THEORIES IN MODERNISM

"The abyss is time, in its sorrows and lassitudes. The birds offer a contrast, symbolizing our yearning for light. . . . The piece begins in sadness. . . . The return to desolation is manifested in the dark timbre of the clarinet's lower register."[16]

Denial: Space and Geometry

Legal theorists have responded to the precipitous changes in their social and intellectual world by denial, despair, or accommodation.[17] Each embodies an aesthetic temperament as well as an ideology. Further, since they have arisen from the same cultural moment, these aesthetics have much in common and share a similar approach to space/time.[18]

As Saul Levinson and Jack Balkin argue, there are close parallels here between legal theory and music theory. This is hardly surprising, since the cultural moment of which law is one expression is itself constructed through every aspect of our lives in which symbols are given meaning.[19] These parallels center on time in modernism. The denial of change, in the first place, may manifest itself as an attempt to reclaim a wholly mythical past.[20] Tradition is here understood as something frozen in time, not to be developed but rather thawed out.[21]

In music, for example, the "original instruments" school sometimes naïvely judges musical performance according to how closely it is said to replicate the "authentic" performance style and standards of the time of composition. One does not need to rehearse the many arguments why this approach is doomed to failure.[22] And what of the case of Olivier Messiaen's *Quartet* itself, "conceived and written in captivity"? "The four instrumentalists played on broken instruments: Etienne Pasquier's cello had only three strings, the keys of my piano would stick. Our clothes were unbelievable; they had given me a green coat all torn, and I was wearing wooden shoes."[23] Even if we could determine it, is this the kind of authenticity we want?

"Original instruments" are to music as "original intent" is to law: both attempt to preserve historical meaning in aspic. As Levinson and Balkin note, the obsession with "authenticity" captures not past meaning but present anxiety and reflects the denial of the distance of the past which is one response to that anxiety.[24] The attraction of this originalism has nothing to do with the ultimate authority of the past and everything to do with the sensibilities of the present. In law as in music. On the one hand, originalism in law offers us a coherence with the past for which we yearn; on the other, it offers us a certainty of meaning, in which we can no longer happily believe, by locating that certainty safely in the past. We no longer know what is true now, but we can still know what was true then.

Originalism is one face of the denial of the uncertainty and multiplicity of contemporary legal relations. Coherence is another. A vast literature argues that law is indeterminate and incoherent, plural, disorderly, and ambiguous. But a belief in the internal coherence of law denies our experience of these aspects of law. This is not simply an intellectual position but an aesthetic desire, a passionate belief in the beauty of the modernist commitment to order, consistency, and system. Lon Fuller recognized the strength of the desire for order in law:

> All theories of law have this in common, that they attribute "law" to one source. . . . But even when one does not subscribe to any particular theory of the "nature of law," one is apt, consciously or unconsciously, to embrace . . . the "fiction of the unity of law." We talk constantly as if there were a unified body of rules proceeding from somewhere which constitute "the law."[25]

There is an aesthetic of organization here, of austere and unbending lines, which is admired for its own sake and not merely as a means to an end. There must be in law, says Karl Llewellyn, something "aesthetically satisfying" of itself, something which appeals to our desire for "sense" and "balance." "Is it not fair to conclude, then," asks Llewellyn, that "there can be no part of our institution of law which may not yield fresh light, if one knocks at it asking, there also, after Beauty?"[26]

John Austin and, in different ways, modern positivists including H. L. A. Hart and Joseph Raz share a definition of law which requires a linear pedigree recognized by singular state paternity. Law is thus a closed structure which establishes rules of recognition by which every law can be determined and related.[27] Part of the motivation for this approach comes from its promise of certainty. Still more so is this apparent in Hans Kelsen, whose *General Theory of Law and State* describes law as a complex hierarchy of norms finally traceable to a *Grundnorm* from which everything else is derived. For Kelsen, anything less than this closed and determinate system does not count as law at all.[28]

Formalists such as Ernest Weinrib were born under the star of this linear aesthetic. Formalism dismisses the relevance of other disciplines — sociology, or economics, or literature — in explaining the structure and doctrine of "law." Law is to be understood in its own terms, as a product of purely internal logic and morality. For Weinrib, therefore, we can understand the basic structure of tort law, for example, not by reference to the efficacy of deterrence or compensation (external and functional principles), but because it recognizes a particular moral relationship between the parties, a relationship based on abstract principles of agency. The very structure of tort law is meant to reflect this understanding of social relationships.[29] To Weinrib, striving for anything less than a hermetically sealed explanation of law seems a "shortening of ambition."[30]

Weinrib claims for law an "immanent intelligibility" answerable only in its own terms.[31] Yet, like Hans Kelsen before him, Weinrib ultimately grounds law in (an idiosyncratic reading of) Aristotle, Hegel, and Kant.[32] Why law ought to be a species of philosophy and not a species of politics, literature, or aesthetics is unclear.[33] More important, Weinrib justifies his approach solely in terms of coherence. He aims to find in legal rules "an internally coherent whole . . . a single justification that coherently pervades the entire relationship . . . the most abstract and comprehensive patterning of justificatory coherence [possible]." He continues: "Coherence . . . is the interlocking into a single integrated justification of all the justificatory considerations that pertain to a legal relationship. . . . Coherence thus denotes unity."[34]

The more abstract and coherent the explanation for laws or for conduct, the better. But what exactly, in the context of an explanation of legal phenomena, does "better" mean? Not "better" in the sense of describing the complexities of people's conduct or the inconsistencies of their actual motivations. Not "better" in the sense of providing the community with a richer set of moral principles to which it might aspire. Not "better" in the sense of capturing the jumble of intentions and processes by which laws are actually developed.[35] Rather, "better" amounts to an aesthetic criterion. It is an appeal to the beauty of an internally regulated system in which each part is related to each other part in set proportions such that there is a "harmonious interrelationship among the constituents."[36]

Weinrib's style parallels this image of law — it too is abstract and densely argued. The Homeric reiteration of talismanic phrases such as "immanently intelligible," "justificatory coherence," and "law's aspiration" serves a rhetorical purpose, because it creates exactly the image of coherence which he values. But this coherence, too, is purely formal, since his usage is so elusive that its meaning is difficult to fathom.[37] One is left with the image of coherence unanchored to meaning, words without referents.

The idea of coherence runs through much modern legal theory like a refrain. Ronald Dworkin, too, urges a kind of coherence that in his case goes under the name of "integrity." Although Dworkin's approach is hermeneutic where Weinrib's is hermetic, each treats coherence as a model for the proper functioning of the legal system. Dworkin argues that integrity is a separate value in our legal system, and we ought therefore strive to make that system as consistent as possible in the application of political principles.[38] Whether "integrity is a virtue" is arguable.[39] But for Dworkin, the virtue lies not just in whether integrity exists in law or society but whether it is seen to exist:

> Here, then, is our case for integrity, our reason for striving to see, so far as we can, both its legislative and adjudicative principles vivid in our political life. . . . If we can understand our practices as appropriate to the model of principle, we can support the legitimacy of our institutions. . . . [Integrity's] standing as part of an overall successful interpretation of these practices hinges on whether interpreting them in this way helps show them in a better light.[40]

Dworkin wants to see integrity "vivid in our life" so we "can support the legitimacy of our institutions." This is not a descriptive model, then, but neither is it simply normative. There is an aesthetic appreciation of a chain of laws stretching from the past into the future as a coherent narrative. This is why he vents his spleen against writers in critical legal studies who deny that law is or ever could be consistent: "Nothing is easier or more pointless than demonstrating that a flawed and contradictory account fits as well as a smoother and more attractive one."[41] Dworkin justifies his theoretical preference for an account rooted in the consistency of legal principles by an appeal to "smoothness" and "attractiveness" as criteria of judgment.

Perhaps there is nothing wrong with seeing beauty in order and coherence. The problem lies in the superhuman efforts of formalists to avoid all trace of dissonance and incoherence in the model of the law they present as "real." The desire for a particular aesthetic works to erase all evidence to the contrary. One is struck, for instance, by the absence of human beings from the austere aesthetic of formalism. Weinrib treats human actors as nothing but abstract free agents bereft of context and personality. The reality of human conditions or specific problems is completely irrelevant to this equation. Law is envisaged as a system which functions for its own benefit, "indifferent" and anterior to the "goodness" or "desirability" of particular human purposes or well-being.[42] His landscape is unpeopled.

Weinrib is at pains to remove from his equation real live lawyers think-ing about real live law; since coherence is only an aspiration, it can be criti-cized for falling short. Lawyers who think that law has certain instrumen-tal goals "are simply making a mistake."[43] "The point is not that the positive law . . . necessarily embodies justificatory coherence, but that such coher-ence is possible, and that positive law is intelligible to the extent that it is achieved and defective to the extent that it is not."[44] Law, then, is thrice ab-stracted from reality: first from the human beings that act and suffer un-der it (but are no part of it); second from the legal community that actually gives it whatever meaning or effect it possesses (but are no part of it); and third from any actual instantiations of law (that are no part of it).[45]

Instead of people, there is the most remarkable reification of the law it-self. Weinrib claims, for example, that "law's most abiding aspiration [is to be] immanently intelligible"; that legal systems "striv[e] . . . toward their own justificatory coherence"; that "implicit in the law's conceptual and in-stitutional apparatus . . . is the claim to be a justificatory enterprise." The claim to speak for "law's own aspirations" is particularly prevalent.[46] But what is this "law" that aspires and strives, and how does it do so? To this question there is no answer. People do not think and act and realize in this world; only law does.

Roberto Unger argues that idealists run the risk of idolatry and utopian-ism. "Idolatry consists in mistaking the present situation of the state for the accomplishment of the ideal. . . . [I]dolatry is the form taken by a politi-cal imagination surrendered to pure immanence."[47] I would go further: an idol is the reification of an abstraction, and it is by constant reification and abstraction that Weinrib comes to believe in the immanence of his idolatry.

Dworkin, despite his differences, also makes law reified and spatial. He too believes in "law's empire," in "law's ambitions for itself," and even in "law's dreams."[48] Admittedly, while Weinrib sees law as an entity to be de-clared and thus discovered, Dworkin sees it as an entity to be interpreted and thus developed. This interpretative turn peoples the landscape in a way quite different from the empty planes of Weinrib, though often enough one finds myths and archetypes rather than human beings.[49] But in both cases, "law" is understood as a thing, a tangible and finite reality that can be mapped with some precision. It is in this sense that the yearning for co-herence is an aesthetic based on the desire for order in reified space.

The guiding image is of linear geometry, a field that has always had an association with ideas of social ordering and with the image of truth as ab-straction. What, after all, is geometry but the abstraction of spatial form, land without people and shape without context? Geometry is the paradigm of pure abstract reasoning. Early modern "legal science" in particular used geometry as a point of reference and of inspiration. The comparison of Euclid to the great scholars of Roman law was something of a commonplace in the eighteenth and nineteenth centuries. It was by no means unusual to see mathematicians engaged in legal thought. Leibniz, to give only the most celebrated example, perceived of the ideal legal system as a moral derivative of his calculus.[50]

Weinrib takes the metaphor further, referring approvingly to "shapes" of moral experience. Law, on this account, is a distinct "form" or "shape" which, to be adequately realized, must be kept "internally coherent."[51] The intrusion of external values would constitute a violation of geometry — an attempt, as he says, "at squaring the circle."[52] The circle, the corral, encloses all within it and excludes all those beyond its pale. Any pluralism of forms or multiplicity of justifications would constitute a deterioration in condition.[53]

An interest in coherent time (history) as well as coherent space (geometry) marks out the terrain of Dworkin's jurisprudential project. But it is modernist time, unidirectional and linear. He wishes to show that, despite the undoubted ambiguity of meaning in legal texts, there is a coherence in the history of the common law which provides it with legitimacy. History has always served this legitimating function, a belief in the authority of the past which distinguishes English tradition from Continental reason. Thus Blackstone treated lex non scripta as the building blocks of law, and Coke appealed to the power of "immemorial usage."[54]

The high point of this tradition came in 1898, when the House of Lords proclaimed that it was bound by its own decisions.[55] It is no surprise that that case should have emerged when and as it did. The conjunction of a system based on tradition and hierarchy with the high modernist desire for consistency and truth logically required that the decisions of the final arbiter of the system be irrefutable. A system which had evolved on the basis of earlier values of power and stability could thus be reconciled with modernist ideals of progress and truth simply by insisting that the holders of ultimate power were the repositories of ultimate truth. That other great medieval institution, the Catholic church, faced with the same pressures at the same time, responded in like fashion by transforming supremacy into infallibility and authority into immutability.[56]

The rigors of infallibility have long since passed, in the common law if not in the Catholic church, but the doctrine of precedent remains central.[57] This is what concerns Dworkin, who wants to legitimate the legal tradition by demonstrating its coherence through time. "The chain novel" vivifies his understanding of interpretation, which is committed to the authority of legal texts written in the past, though not to a particular meaning of those texts. A judge interpreting a case, for example, must show maximal consistency with earlier cases: they must render previous decisions coherent with present ones.[58] Dworkin does not respect the past as an authoritative guide to its own meaning, as the doctrine of original intent does, or as a time of special wisdom, as rhetoric about the U.S. Constitution often implies, or as the purveyors of a tradition which we as its trustees are duty bound to protect, which one often finds in English decisions. Neither is he interested in the purposes and forces which have in fact shaped the past.[59] For very different reasons, all these approaches value the pastness of the past. Not so Dworkin, who treats the past as present, as if all the relevant precedents had been decided just yesterday. It is an approach which renders precedent ahistorical, time flattened and without dimension.

Despair

Critical legal studies on the contrary has insisted on the incoherence of legal texts and the indeterminacy of legal judgment. It is hardly surprising that these arguments have provoked visceral hostility. For someone devoted to law as a beautiful story or a beautiful shape, CLS seems perverse. Why would you want to see law in anything other than "its best light," as anything other than a "systematically intelligible" enterprise?[60] This is a criticism not against their arguments but against their lack of desire to find system in law.

Late modernity is characterized by an overwhelming anxiety, about losing the past, about the incoherence of the present with respect to it. As the other side of anxiety is alienation, so the other side of denial is despair. In much contemporary musical composition, Levinson and Balkin argue, we find a relentless search for novelty. There is no connection with a living tradition here, either, but rather a detachment from it. Though reference may be made to past styles, the past is treated as raw material to be plundered: a process of appropriation which exactly highlights our distance from its spirit. There is alienation and despair here borne of anxiety that our past has been irretrievably lost.

These authors argue that the same can be said of CLS.[61] Here too an eclectic attitude toward the past accompanies a restless search for the future. In CLS, there is a distance from the past—the coherent, innocent past— tinged with yearning. Formalism is not nostalgic for lost certainty (one can hardly be nostalgic for the immanent). Critical legal studies is. Nostalgia is just this sense of impossible contrast, a disjunction between our aesthetic vision (a continuing desire for coherence) and our philosophy (a cynical contemplation of its contemporary impossibility).

One senses this despair in CLS's nihilism and in its so-called trashing of the existing conceptual order.[62] Yet beneath such efforts at obliteration, traces of desire remain. The substitution of "new" rights for old, or "new" hypotheses about human nature and human society for old, does nothing to transcend the indeterminacy of rights or the vacuity of abstraction:[63] it merely replicates them.

Sometimes the desire for certainty suggests little more than a sneaking suspicion, as when Arthur Leff confesses, sotto voce, "And yet: some things *are* evil."[64] Sometimes the whole intellectual edifice comes tumbling down. Unger, at the end of his seminal book *Knowledge and Politics*, turns to the question of "the imperfections of knowledge and politics." He mourns this lack of perfection; he yearns for "a complete and perfect understanding of reality."[65] But only God can achieve this; only God can "complete the change of the world" which humanity by itself cannot accomplish. Unger ends with despair: "But our days pass, and still we do not know you fully. Why then do you remain silent? Speak, God."[66] Demand? Entreaty? Chastisement? This appeal to a higher reality assumes all that it has been the earnest ambition of critical legal studies, among a host of other movements, to abolish once and for all.

The aesthetic of transcendence and unity has survived despite the most earnest attempts at its exorcism. Having been so vigorously swept out the front door, the hope of right answers, of determinacy, and of objective truth somehow sneaks in through the back. It is an aesthetic envisioned as union and order. But it is an aesthetic experienced as despair and nihilism, because it is everywhere observable only by its absence.

Critical legal studies therefore shares with its brethren an aesthetic ideal but differs as to its perception of reality. Robin West comes to a similar conclusion in her "aesthetic analysis of modern legal theory."[67] For those opposed to the "dangerous and limiting cynicism" which the "tragic" disjunction between reality and idealism provokes, this perspective can appear, as Roscoe Pound said of legal realism, "a cult of the ugly"—a critique which foreshadows precisely the distaste which some find in CLS.[68]

Accommodation: Space and Geography

Legal pluralism provides a striking contrast in temperament. If CLS diverges from formalism on the question of the "reality" of the legal system, CLS and pluralism diverge on the question of their ideals. Pluralism welcomes incoherence. Conventional accounts of the legal system argue that particular products of the state alone count as "law." Legal pluralism says otherwise. John Griffiths declares, "Legal pluralism is the fact. Legal centralism is a myth, an ideal, a claim, an illusion." In a similar vein, Marc Galanter attacks centralism as an "ideology" attempting to delegitimate alternative sources of normativity.[69] But ideology always affects our understanding of the world.[70] What if the "myth," the "illusion," of a single normative order were universally believed? Would not any alternative norms thus have lost their power to guide conduct and affect behavior? Would they not, in other words, have ceased to be norms for that society? All law is in fact "a claim" to normative authority, more or less effective.

Legal pluralists therefore resist the claim not just because it is untrue but because they do not wish it to be true. It is desire again, in this case the desire for incoherence, which governs their interpretation. There is a trust in disorder here and an attraction to the small-scale, contingent, and even contradictory workings of what Clifford Geertz called "local knowledge."[71] Accordingly, legal pluralism matches its philosophical critique of "the big system" with its aesthetic vision. Unlike in CLS, in legal pluralism desire and thought are, to some extent at least, companionable.

The denial of incoherence is legal geometry—abstraction and reification; the accommodation of incoherence is legal geography—specificity and contextualization.[72] Legal pluralism acknowledges the indeterminacy of the way law claims to control space. Nevertheless, the priority of the spatial in an analysis of law is never questioned. Consequently, there are significant limits to the degree to which legal pluralism analyzes this incoherence. Pluralism therefore accommodates indeterminacy and conflict within a modernist framework.

The connections between space and pluralism are immediately evident. In its simplest form, pluralism posits that more than one legal order inhabits the same physical territory. In this, it stands directly against both the explicit construction of legal space in formalism and that implicit in ideas of the "province" of law, or "law's empire." On any such construction, "law" is understood to be the monopolization by a state, within a discrete physical territory, of a particular species of norm creation. It is just this exclusivity which pluralism rejects.

Multiplicity in legal space is pluralism's organizing image. Law on this analysis is not an empire but a contested terrain. This is not just metaphor. Modern legal pluralism originated in a far more literal argument over questions of empire and terrain. It emerged out of the colonial experience: out of the attempt to impose imperial legal order onto the existing, and sometimes resilient, indigenous legal system of a colony.[73] Pluralism connoted the complex interaction of native legal systems with the imposed law of the metropolis. Until recently, the *Journal of Legal Pluralism* bore everywhere the marks of this history.[74] Its articles are empirical and anthropological in perspective, and they are spatial in orientation because they see the problem of law as the clash between "indigenous" and "state" laws within the same space.

When later scholars began to explore the plurality of law within developed societies themselves, therefore, they brought with them a framework forged in the colonial experience.[75] Peter Fitzpatrick and Leopold Pospisil in Papua New Guinea, Boaventura de Sousa Santos in Brazil, and others are scholars who began by chronicling the interaction of indigenous and imposed law and only later translated their perspective to include developed or "core" societies themselves.[76] Furthermore, in what we might call a first stage of "modern pluralism," a clear political agenda reified the legal order. Whether in colonial societies, Brazil, or the inner city, "pluralism" stood for resistance to the established legal order. Consequently, the analysis was driven by totalizing power asserted by that order in the first place. The monopoly of legal space, according to this political pluralism, was both the problem and the solution.

The metaphors of pluralism have accordingly been spatial: "spheres of justice," "legal levels," "competing, overlapping, constantly fluid . . . associations," and "semiautonomous social fields."[77] The image of reified legal space recurs, whether in Marc Galanter's reference to "the legal order" or "indigenous ordering" as preexistent and independent entities or in Sally Engle Merry's definition of legal pluralism as "two or more legal systems [which] coexist in the same social field."[78] The world is here imagined as overlapping objects in space. "Law"—whichever law is meant—is understood as an object with a definite and determined content. It is not the meaning of law but its sources, its claim to authority, which is questioned. The very language that suggests that alternative processes of norm creation exist in or as the "shadow" of law reveals this.[79] Legal pluralism multiplies legal systems, but it does not doubt their objective and defined meaning in their own terms. On this analysis, we can know what a particular "legal order" demands of us, although there may be several such orders in competition or engagement.

A second phase of pluralist writing, including that of Sally Falk Moore and Pospisil, for example, managed to disanchor pluralism from the politics of resistance.[80] Now it was not just a case of a state legal order against a subjugated group but rather of the conflict between varying orders claiming normative authority—unions, businesses, syndicates, communities, churches. But when faced with the need to explain what made these orders "legal," pluralism fell back on precisely the criteria of authority and certain meaning claimed by legal centralism. Legal pluralism presented alternative legal orders as mirrors of the state, thereby replicating its conceptual apparatus. It is certainly true that Moore, for one, rejects the positivistic conception that law passes from lawmaker to individual without being transfigured. The social space between legislator and subject is not a vacuum. Yet even here Moore conceives of law as the interaction of semiautonomous fields and not of semiautonomous individuals. In other words, the individuals who are subject to law are understood as the inhabitants of interacting social fields and not their authors.

The third phase of pluralism includes the literature on "law and geography." Santos, who has done more than most to radicalize pluralism in recent years, also continues to conceive of pluralism as a problem of overlapping space, of multiple "maps" of the law—each, to belabor the point, independent and objective. Although his latest work discusses "the timespaces of law," the examples he gives of plurality—"local," "national," and "transnational" law—remain resolutely spatial and reified in orientation.[81]

This modernist conception of law as composed of determinate fields is not unavoidable. Notably in the work of Nicholas Blomley, space and law are both treated as indeterminate and mutually engaged. Blomley attempts to move from a model of "law" and "space" as two separate variables affecting each other toward an understanding of their mutual construction.[82] Nevertheless, this sensitivity to the relativity of space remains an exception. Even among pluralist theories, law has been reified. Whether "state law," "local law," or "people's law," legal systems are typically understood as separate and determinate objects in contention.

TANGLE OF RAINBOWS, FOR THE ANGEL ANNOUNCING THE END OF TIME — AGAINST REIFICATION: LEGAL THEORIES IN POSTMODERNISM

"In my colored dreams I become dizzy, bathed in the gyration of sound and color, combinations of blue-red, blue-orange, or gold-green, these daggers of fire, these shooting stars, and here lies the tangle, here are the rainbows."[83]

Two critiques emerge from this discussion of the abyss of legal theory. The first is aesthetic, because it addresses the imagery through which we experience the world. Legal theories, whether of geometry or geography, remain governed by the reification of law which we have seen in both formalism and pluralism. Its rejuvenation requires a more sophisticated recognition of the indeterminacy of "the law" and of legal systems.

The second is a question of aesthetics, because it addresses vision and desire. Legal theories, whether of denial or despair, remain governed by the desire for order and coherence. The rejuvenation of legal theory requires a new aesthetics, which appreciates the value of disorder by developing alternative metaphors for legal ideals. This question of vision is by no means secondary. A paradigm shift is marked by an aesthetic no less than an epistemological shift. The shift from the premodern to the modern was marked by a change in music and art no less than in science and technology. We are going through such a change now, and clues to the metaphors which we will need in order to make sense of it lie all around us.

To combine these two critiques requires an integration of CLS and legal pluralism. This integration has two aspects. On the one hand, pluralism must take from CLS an indeterminacy of meaning to accompany its familiar insistence on an indeterminacy of sources. Such a project serves to undermine the reification of legal space: this is the first critique, which I address in this movement. On the other hand, CLS must take from pluralism its celebration of disorder and multiplicity. Such a project serves to advance a new aesthetic ideal in tune with the tenor of the age: this is the second critique, which I address in the movement which follows.

Dimensions of Indeterminacy

On the indeterminacy of legal meaning, CLS has been exceedingly vigorous. On the other hand, as we have seen, pluralism has tended to reify a particular "legal system," of whatever kind, as if its internal principles and meaning—"the law of the state" or "customary law," "the tax laws of a local Mafia," or the law of England or of a tribe in Papua—could be determined with precision. This then has been the strength of CLS and the weakness of legal pluralism. But when it comes to the multiplicity of legal sources, CLS has yet to incorporate the insights of pluralism. There is still, in much "critical" writing, an overweening faith in the exclusive authority of "mandarin materials" to determine legal ordering.

To avoid the reification of law, we need therefore to combine these aspects. The sources of law no less than the content of laws are indeterminate and multiple. Moreover, these elements of indeterminacy are mutually interactive. Law does not just exist in four dimensions but as a human intellectual creation: a product of five dimensions. We are not located "in" law any more than we are located "in" time and space but rather consistently reinventing them through acts of symbolism and interpretation. This can be understood on three different levels.

First, indeterminacy is a function of the multiple entities, formal and informal, responsible for the interpretation of legal texts. Let us not imagine that there is a magical osmosis been word and world, between what "the king ordaineth" and what his citizens experience. Not only legislators and judges decide what a law "means"; academics and lawyers, journalists and politicians, policemen and bureaucrats also do. As Robert Gordon writes, "We'll never understand the power that legal form holds over our minds unless we see them at work up close, in the most ordinary settings[,] . . . the field levels of lower-order officials, practitioners, or private law-makers." [84] At each step along the way, there are acts of legal interpretation. For example, perhaps the single most important development in the history of Western law was the reception of Roman law into medieval Europe, a process accomplished above all by academics in a movement distinct from either the political or the narrowly "legal" professions.[85] Academic influence on the meaning of law today exists not through the articles scholars write but simply by misleading generations of trainee lawyers.

To take as another example the question of bureaucracy, let me turn once more to drug policy. One central issue that arose throughout the world in the administration of new drug laws in and after the 1920s was whether it was legal for doctors to prescribe "dangerous drugs" simply to "maintain" addicts on a controlled dose of their drug of addiction. Australian regulations in several jurisdictions expressly prevented this.[86] Despite the clear words of the statute, the maintenance of a sizable number of middle-class addicts continued for over thirty years as a settled policy requiring the connivance not only of state law-enforcement agencies and health departments but of the Commonwealth government. Provided the addicted user was being prescribed the drug by a medical practitioner and being supplied by only one chemist, the government authorized an additional amount of the drug needed to fulfill their requirements.

What was "the law" in this case? Was the Department of Health "wrong"? This mischaracterizes the situation. Law is a matter of authoritative interpretation, and in a world of conflicting interpretations the question of meaning resolves itself into the question of who decides.[87] The situation might be different if there is no genuine belief in the legitimacy of the interpretation being acted upon, for in that case the "internal aspect" of law, the belief that the legal obligation in question "ought" to be followed, might be absent.[88] But that is not the case here. Law does not exist without legal interpretation, exercised by a raft of institutions, all of which refract and influence what is experienced as law.

Second, not only institutions, but communities, serve an interpretative role. This is Bob Ellickson's argument, in bringing R. H. Coase's simplistic but celebrated story of the rancher and the farmer out of the realm of fable and into the "real" world. According to Ellickson, questions of cattle trespass, fencing rules, and so on are not resolved "in the shadow of the law," as Coase had argued, but in fact through the application of norms constituted by a variety of social mechanisms. Ellickson argues that the community of Shasta County, his case study, continually "got the law wrong" in the principles it applied, but the cattlemen, despite all evidence to the contrary, believed that it was the insurance companies and the courts who were making the mistake.[89]

Here, I think, Ellickson misses the point. The practice of cattlemen and farmers demonstrated a consistent understanding of "the law," and, although it might have been different from the principles applied in the courts from time to time, their understanding had a shared and binding meaning for them. The legal texts of judicial decisions may be an important aspect of what counts as "law," but social practices are also interpretive. In this context, it is not helpful to try to contrast "official" with "unofficial" law or "law" with "nonlaw." There was no such conflict, by and large, in the consciousness of the Shasta County community.

Third, the proposition that law involves both a multiplicity of interpretations and a multiplicity of norms applies to individuals as well as to groups. Law involves the interpretation of norms and the mediation of concepts in a way which is experienced differently for each of us. For the most part, I do not experience "law" as saying one thing and "informal norms" as urging another. On the contrary, the two come together in my mind and influence each other. The result is that law means something to me which is different from what it means to you, just as does a piece of music or a book. This psychological and personal dimension of legal meaning most actively undermines the reification of "the legal system" as an entity which could ever be capable of objective definition.

As Marc Galanter said, law is to be found in the courtroom no more than health is to be found in hospitals.[90] From time to time law is an external authority which may arrest us or fine us. In these cases, or even in the face of the threat of such action, we might characterize law as a code marked by the dyad legal/illegal or as principles marked by specific procedures of justiciability.[91] From the legal realists to postmodernists such as Dragan Milovanovic, from CLS's hermeneutics of suspicion to Ronald Dworkin's hermeneutics of credulity, law is treated almost exclusively in its juridical, not to mention juridogenic, dress.[92] But for most of us most of the time, law wears mufti. Undoubtedly, in the process of the social construction of law which marks our most typical experience of it, we are all gravely affected by legal texts and judicial decisions—either because we read them or hear about them—and by the pronouncements of law made by judges, lawyers, or academics. But these influences are at the same time intermingled with our other normative beliefs, cultural, religious, literary, or personal; and with myths, archetypal and urban alike, about legal obligation.[93] All these influences affect our individual understanding of what we believe the law requires of us.

How we think about law is relevant to its character as law. The attitudinal aspect of law was, in fact, one of Hart's most important insights. In drawing attention to the "internal aspect" of law he acknowledged that law is a question of self-regulation as well as of the imposition of order by an external power. But Hart never pursued these ideas as an aspect of meaning rather than simply of legitimacy.[94] Just as our ethics are created by the complex interaction of authoritative texts (such as the Bible or Aristotle) and significant interpretations (such as those of priests or philosophers) with social norms and personal values, so too the law is subject to interpretation on all these levels. The result is that law is a psychological phenomenon in which we all interpret its claims upon us in a slightly different way or form.

The human dimension is necessary to any genuine pluralism, for it rejects the reification of "system," "society," or "community" as a thing which can think or read. Law is not manufactured by "a multiplicity of closed discourses"[95] because it is only realized in the actions of particular human beings who exist simultaneously in several discourses and who are, therefore, themselves plural. We must go beyond understanding law as a system, a clash of systems, or even as the interaction of subsystems if we are to take full account of the lessons of indeterminacy.

In these ways, therefore, it is evident that the insights of pluralism must be extended to combine a pluralism of sources with a pluralism of meaning. Legal pluralism in its original incarnation operated according to a spatial understanding of "law's empire." It saw informal norms as operating first "under the law" and then in the "shadow of the law."[96] Later writers have suggested that norm creation is a process which goes on "without the law."[97] We need to take another step and recognize that pluralism in fact operates "within the law" and indeed within the law within ourselves.[98]

We see some glimmers of this more radical pluralism within rather than between social systems in a variety of recent scholarship. Peter Fitzpatrick, for example, has recently turned his attention to the inherent problems of legal interpretation. The notion of "integrative pluralism" suggests that ultimately the interpretation of law's meaning is a question for each of us to resolve, integrating in our minds a whole variety of normative demands.[99] The need to extend ideas of indeterminacy to legal pluralism has perhaps been most suggestively explored by Santos, who moves toward an idea of "interlegality" according to which codes and norms are mixed in reality and in the contents of our minds.[100]

> [W]e see at work not one legality, but a network of different and sometimes conflicting legalities: local informal legality, state legality, transnational human rights legality, "natural" law legality, insurgent and revolutionary legality, and top-down terrorizing legality.[101]

In the *favela* of Rio, for example, state law, the law of the shanty, and moral and procedural principles are all interconnected and form a complete and different whole. There is no conflict between the demands of one system of law and another here, only an interplay which finally resolves itself as "the law": a manifestation in response to a particular conflict.[102]

Reimagination: Space and Chaotics

The map is an appropriate metaphor for the reimagination of legal theory by critical legal pluralism. It is a metaphor about how we understand space and therefore in keeping with one of the main themes of this chapter. Formalism, I have suggested, is legal geometry and pluralism is legal geography: they are each ways of mapping space. But the spatial metaphor best suited to this reimagination is legal chaotics. Now chaos is a grand and multifaceted idea. Chaos theory itself is a collection of perspectives in a wide variety of disciplines rather than a single body of knowledge.[103] The science that emerged through and out of the rubble left over from the cataclysmic clash of modernist ideologies—capitalist, fascist, socialist—had many aspects: indeterminacy, uncertainty, and quantum theory come to mind. But, to overgeneralize, chaotics displays an interest in space relativized rather than reified, nonlinear rather than linear, complex rather than simplified.

Take the fractal.[104] A fractal is a way of measuring the degree of roughness or irregularity in an object; a fractal maintains that complexity regardless of the scale of analysis adopted. A coastline is a good example. If you look at a map, say of a country, it has a certain irregularity to it: you see tangled lines that represent rugged cliffs or meandering rivers.[105] If you enlarge the scale, this tangled quality does not disappear. Bays and inlets turn out, on closer inspection, to have bays and inlets of their own. At every level, there is a certain degree of complexity—a fractal dimension—which does not change. No matter how detailed the map, the fractal dimension remains the same. The measurement of the length of a coast depends entirely on the scale of measurement adopted, which determines those irregularities which get noticed and measured and those which do not. There is no final answer. The map of a coast is an infinite line nested in a finite space.

In the humanities, the image of the fractal bears a striking similarity to the approach of Foucault. He too is concerned to draw our attention to similarities in contour between different disciplines; he too insists that the degree and character of the implementation of strategies of power of a certain time remain constant regardless of the level of analysis.[106] The "disciplinary society" surveys and controls its members at every level from the most intimate to the most general.[107] There is a seamless constancy to this process which is, perhaps, fractal in nature.

In law, legal chaotics adds complexity to the geometry and the geography of the map.[108] All maps—all theories of law or the legal "system"—are metaphors whose worth varies depending on their function. For some purposes, it is useful to focus on law as a system of rules, or as a series of judgments, or as a species of practice. For some purposes we need generality and for others, specificity.

Santos develops the metaphor in just this way. Each of us carries many maps around with us, varying in scale, projection, and symbolism. One need only recall the elaborate symbolism and ornamentation of medieval maps, their interlaced portrayal of spaces physical, relational, and mythological, to appreciate how various, political, and deceptive is the work of map making.[109] The different symbolism of modern maps, the equality of perspective they attempt to achieve in their efforts to capture a part of the world as seen from beyond its boundaries—from some all-seeing and external point—all this does not suggest that maps are now any less selective than they were but only that the contours of that partiality have changed.[110]

So it is with law: there are many maps, each of which draws attention to various features, scales, relationships, and values to the utter exclusion of others. At times it is relevant to think about law as an emanation of the state, and at other times the customs of a small community are what concerns us.[111] The only perfect map, as any cartographer will tell you, is drawn on the scale 1:1. To ask "what is law?" is like asking what map to use; it depends utterly on why we want to know:

The large-scale legality is rich in details and features; describes behaviour and attitudes vividly; contextualizes them in their immediate surroundings; is sensitive to distinctions and complex relations between inside and outside, high and low, just and unjust. . . . On the contrary, small-scale legality is poor in details and features, skeletonizes behaviour and attitudes, reducing them to general types of action. But, on the other hand, it determines with accuracy the relativity of positions (the angles between people and between people and things), provides sense of direction and schemes for short-cuts and finally it is sensitive to distinctions (and complex relations) between part and whole, past and present, functional and non-functional.[112]

Further, to concentrate on the statewide—or the supranational—emanations of law is to ignore the differences in how different communities, for example, understand and receive law. To focus on the "community" as a homogeneous group of perceptions is to ignore the divisions without that community. Even to focus on subgroups is to ignore the differences between individuals' own understandings of law. It is a problem which feminist legal theorists, in particular, have been forced to face in recent years, confronted from within by critics who resist the essentializing project of making generalities about what it is to be a "woman" in the world.[113] In resisting the reification of law, pluralism no less than chaotics must appreciate that the process of segmentation is never ending. The law is a network of interactions characterized by a high fractal complexity. This suggests not only a purposive approach to theory but a humble one. Law is an infinite line nested in a finite space.

A second aspect moves the discussion from theory to praxis and from the present to the future. Chaos develops because many biological systems are dynamic: the rules which govern their operation interact with each other. It is this interaction which makes the function they describe nonlinear. Most typically, interaction occurs because the output from applying the rules which operate in the system becomes an input in the next operation of the system, thus creating a vast feedback loop.[114]

Let us think of law as a series of actors in a web of influential communities: judges and lawyers, bureaucrats and police.[115] Each of these "variables" has its own responses to a legal question, and these responses influence the responses of other actors in a never-ending cycle of intensifying perturbation. It serves us well to understand that this process is itself a dynamic one and its results therefore nonlinear. For law is generated by the constant iteration and reiteration of rules and understandings, a feedback loop as inherently unpredictable as Chinese whispers.

The legal regulation of "drugs" again provides an example. Drug laws were enacted to lessen use. Yet this legislative framework has instead been responsible for the impoverishment of inner cities, the sickness and death of drug users, a vast drug market, and in many places a hopelessly corrupted political and judicial system.[116] From its beginnings in a few countries such as the United States, the ramifications of this legislation have encompassed the globe in an ever-expanding sequence of unintended consequences, unforeseen alliances, and the perturbation of good intentions.[117] It is a story that evidences the ultimate failure of the modernist ideal of law as control.

To accept the limits of predictability in law is perhaps to recommend a certain caution in the implementation of legal regulation. It contrasts the modernist dream of order with the significance of the practical limits to human knowledge.[118] The natural world—and a fortiori the human world—is not a giant clock, nor are we but cogs within it.[119] This approach, then, is not quietism; on the contrary, it is the standard model which encourages passivity. Modernism assumes almost without exception that "systems" are normally linear in function. Imagine a diagonal line on a graph, the end product of a linear equation: the implication of this model of the world is that the scale of action corresponds to the scale of transformation.[120] A small input will have a proportionately small output. But nonlinearity turns that on its head. Small variables have disproportionate results as they magnify and feed back through the system. The model of chaos implies the importance, and indeed the imperative, of "local knowledge" and local action.[121] Its message is, in part, the interdependence of every scale of human interaction. There is an endemic overstating of the power of law on a macrolevel in our society. But as pluralism and chaotics alike attest, social change does not take place by legislative pronouncement.

CRYSTAL LITURGY — TOWARD AESTHETICS: NEW METAPHORS FOR LEGAL THEORY

"Around five o'clock in the morning, a lone bird improvises, surrounded by fine fragments of sound, by a halo of harmony lost high in the trees. Transposing that to a religious level, you have the harmonious silence of heaven."[122]

From Newton to Mandelbrot

We are all products and producers of our era; as legal theory by and large has matched the beliefs and anxieties of modernism, so this emphasis on illusion and metaphor, indeterminacy and incoherence, pluralism and subjectivity, is part of the new spirit of the times.[123] We are living through a paradigm shift in the epistemological foundations of society. A shift in intellectual paradigms requires a shift in aesthetics, which will not deny, despair, or merely accommodate change but will rather embrace and develop it.[124] Legal theory always embodies an aesthetic element, as we have seen, and to date this aesthetic has been resolutely modernist in character. The transition to a critical legal pluralism, therefore, requires new metaphors and a new way of seeing.

The change from linear to nonlinear aesthetics has been a fundamental element of both the intellectual appeal of chaos and of its intellectual trajectory.[125] Benoit Mandelbrot and Heinz-Otto Peitgen, for example, have both intentionally contrasted the image of the fractal with the "geometric straight-line approaches" of modern art and have thus defended the new sciences on aesthetic grounds.[126] John Briggs similarly insists that "art has always been fractal. The science of chaos is helping to newly define an aesthetic that has always lain beneath . . . changing artistic ideas."[127]

The aesthetics of modernity—in legal and political theory as in science and music—spoke to the necessity of order and coherence. It was the beauty of clockwork time and geometric space. This paradigm of beauty, Hobbesian and Newtonian,[128] established a dichotomy between anarchy and order as it did between tradition and reason. Here Arnold Schoenberg, in some senses the herald of modernism in music, proves himself to be a complex figure. A system builder, certainly, but at the same time he believed his compositional structures created order not of the human kind but rather (like the order within chaos) one that could not be deciphered or predicted. It was rather a subterranean order, beyond the powers of the analytic mind, felt but not perceived. Schoenberg set his face against the static and the beautiful and advocated instead a new aesthetic built on change, dynamism, and responsiveness.[129]

In this new aesthetics, which has been emergent through the century, the dichotomy of anarchy and order has been shattered. "Is this the face of chaos?" asked the front cover of *Scientific American*, somewhat astonished at the gorgeous technicolor mathematical models of fractals it had published. Chaos, it turns out, is beautiful and colorful; in architecture, art, and human life, we value the nonlinear and the fractal and find, on the contrary, linearity to be deeply alienating.[130] Chaos, then, is not to be feared and not to be confused with anarchy. It is above all an appeal to complexity and to the surprise it promises. These elements of unpredictability— our expulsion from the divine and unchanging order of Paradise—asks us to abandon the relentless and arrogant system building of modernity and direct our attention instead to the poetry and power of the local and the particular.[131] In this sense, chaos theory is ultimately empowering. Butterflies matter.

The aesthetic dimension provides a valuable tool for understanding law, as I have argued. But it is also an essential element of what the normative means and an essential element in how that normative vision gains acceptance. If the "abyss" into which legal theory has plunged has been its yearning for coherence, it is on the other hand only by an embrace of complexity that we will truly have come to the "end of modern time" and the beginning of something else.

The aesthetic of pluralism, in keeping with the aesthetic spirit of the time, celebrates multiplicity in stark contradiction to the legal trinity of coherence, order, and control. Uncertainty, indeterminacy, unpredictability, particularity: these are not failures of analysis if we abandon the equation of order with beauty and chaos with ugliness. Pluralism is local knowledge and local action, a recognition of the cultural, communal, and individual construction of legality.

Though modernist liberal theory claims to value pluralism, it does so as a kind of safety valve: unprepared to decide which "good life" is objectively to be preferred, we allow people and communities to make their own choices with a minimum of interference—not because these differences are themselves desirable but because liberalism has no way of arbitrating between them. Pluralism is valued as a necessity and as a process, because it allows *us* to live the kind of life we want.[132]

Social communities often seem to be expected to position themselves in one of two characteristic ways: by assimilating or through the creation of kinds of ghettos. Both are static conceptions which limit social change either by expecting one tradition to absorb another or by isolating one from another. The assimilation valued by modernist monism is in denial. It conceives of a single community as a product of homogeneous space and linear time. The ghettoization of modernist pluralism is in despair, for it conceives of multiple communities as a product of reified space and frozen time—as unchanging and impermeable. The so-called pluralism of the Internet or of niche marketing, for example, every person connected to a "virtual community" of interests in the privacy of their own home, is not a critical pluralism at all. There is no interaction here; it is the multiplication of monisms, the ghettoization of the mind. It limits and controls our interaction with difference and encourages a retreat into stasis and solipsism. The nightmare of this image can be well imagined, a city of a million unconnected lights, each of us alone and typing silently in the half-light of a computer screen which reflects back only ourselves.[133]

The aesthetics of critical pluralism must go further. It is not about preserving intact the hermetic integrity of any particular community. On the contrary, beauty lies in their conjunction, in the way tiny perturbations may have unpredictable results. The result is a vibrancy and anticipation which is worth celebrating not just in spite of but because there is no predicting where it will end up. Unger and Santos have written in utopian vein on the creative and spiritual benefits to be obtained by living on the margins and the frontiers, by living a life governed by reinvention and destabilization.[134] The study of chaos and its marvelous complexity is a study of the wonderful things that happen when the going gets turbulent.

The connection is clear: both chaos theory and pluralism aim to multiply and to weaken boundaries.[135] Even more generally, "chaos is a science of process rather than [of] state."[136] If capitalism celebrates "having" and communitarianism celebrates "being," then pluralism celebrates "becoming." Instead of denying the loss of control or despairing at it, we can welcome the question marks it brings.[137] Within the aesthetic of modernism, diversity and nonlinear change have always been seen as threatening. Modernism encourages fear at the thought of unpredictable movement, and we see this fear all around us: in the fear of social change, the fear of drugs, the hatred of immigration. The new aesthetic, on the contrary, sees the beauty of turbulence and, in our own lives as in our societies, appreciates the whorls and eddies of everyday life. As Messiaen and Schoenberg in their own ways recognized, there is a beauty to dissonance and an order to change, though it is not an order that can ever be predicted or subjected to human control.

From Bach to Messiaen

These ideas are not just descriptive: no legal theory ever is. It is a normative vision which gains strength from its aesthetic vision. Aural metaphors in particular express in aesthetic language the aspirations of pluralism. Plato warned that "when modes of music change, the fundamental laws of the State always change with them."[138] Jacques Attali said something similar: "For twenty-five centuries, Western knowledge has tried to look upon the world. It has failed to understand that the world is not for beholding. It is for hearing. It is not legible, but audible."[139]

"Sight isolates, sound incorporates," wrote Walter Ong.[140] Sight is the most specific and the least diverse sense. It provides a single perspective, a unitary point of view, and a sense of distance. On the other hand, we hear from every direction at once. To see is to see one thing at a time. To hear is to be enveloped by diversity. So too, colors, like smells, commingle when mixed and amalgamate to form something completely new. Sounds do not operate like that. They do not, in fact, blend at all but maintain instead their integrity.[141]

The Middle Ages were tactile and aural, but dramatic technological developments such as printing, and spectacles, for example, heralded the birth of an intensely visual culture.[142] Philosophy has laid great store in the centrality of sight and the eye at least since the Enlightenment: for its rationality, for its distance, for its monism. For Foucault in particular, but by no means exclusively, sight has been central in the development of power relations in modernity. The gaze is an act of objectification, distancing, and surveillance; the ideal instrument of modern discipline is the Panopticon, a structure which enables all within it constantly to be seen by unseen authority.[143] Modernity is the condition of the tyranny of the eye and Luis Buñuel's razor-sharp assault upon it a sacrilege.[144]

Marshall McLuhan argues that we are becoming again a culture of hearing, and Bernard Hibbitts emphasizes the changing metaphorical nature of American law, the growing use of metaphors of "hearing" and of "voices" in legal doctrine and legal theory.[145] The changing paradigms of our age involve a movement from the visual to the aural, which is itself a movement from monism to pluralism.[146] But the character of music itself is changing. When we try to think about "time" or "space," our understanding is initially overborne by our modernist interpretation of it. So it is with music. How then has the paradigm shift away from this intellectual framework affected music? And what might this change tell us about a new pluralism?

Let us go back, from World War II to World War I and from the conflagration of modernity to the first intimations of its flammability. Vladimir Nabokov writes about *Sounds*. It is 1914; the sounds of change knell Romanticism's doom: "An instant passed. During that instant, much happened in the world: somewhere a giant steamship went to the bottom, a war was declared, a genius was born. The instant was gone."[147] That was the year that Alban Berg began his revolutionary opera *Wozzeck*. The development of atonality, though still shocking to the ear, does not mark the death of modernity any more than trench warfare or Guernica, Auschwitz or the gulags.[148] On the contrary, they each manifest the inexorable unfolding of its rationality. In the case of the twelve-tone system, that is particularly evident. Arnold Schoenberg is insistent that his work, far from undermining

Beethoven and Brahms, is their natural heir and successor: here the democracy and finitude of the musical staff—the impossibility of any sound other than the twelve semitones which it depicts, and the radical equality and independence of these notes—is pursued relentlessly.[149] But as Theodor Adorno wrote, Schoenberg marks the turning of modernity against itself, "the suppressing moment in the domination of nature, which suddenly turns against subjective autonomy and freedom itself."[150] Modernist politics and music—and legal theory, too—share an aesthetic love of the reified, the abstract, the individualized, the austere, the systematic.

For Nabokov, the anticipation of those acoustic traumas, let alone the demise of modernism that was to follow its excesses, fills him with intimations of loss. He looks instead to the past for comfort.

> You were playing Bach. . . .
>   I had a feeling of enraptured equilibrium as I sensed the musical relationship between the silvery spectres of rain and your inclined shoulders, which would give a shudder when you pressed your fingers into the rippling lustre. And when I withdrew deep into myself the whole world seemed like that—homogeneous, congruent, bound by the laws of harmony. I myself, you, the carnations—at that instant all became vertical chords on musical staves. I realized that everything in the world was an interplay of identical particles comprising different kinds of consonance: the trees, the water, you. . . . All was unified, equivalent, divine.[151]

Nabokov's view is predicated on the assumption that harmony is a question of the configuration of "vertical chords on musical staves." That is, each note is married to those that sound at the same time (vertical chords), according to predetermined principles of order (musical staves).

I want to interrogate that phrase "vertical chords" first. Nabokov's understanding is Romantic. For him, one starts with the melody—only one at a time allowed. From the melody derives the harmony which supports it. And the harmony having been decided upon, the other musical parts are simply slotted in to their relevant supporting roles. Each part is but a servant of the harmony determined by the melodic line. Nothing could be more monist, more modernist, than the melody, whose supremacy throughout the nineteenth century relegated every other voice to the role of a vertical —a pillar—in its support. And though the number of "voices" to be heard at one time grew and grew, the independence and clarity of each individual voice was accordingly lessened.

Nabokov listens to Bach, then, with the ears of a late-Romantic Russian.

He listens to polyphony, but he hears vertical harmony; hearing harmony, he understands it to mean vertical unity. On the contrary, the polyphony of a Bach fugue grants to each part a radical independence and equality. Each line develops according to its own internal dynamics, and there is therefore a pluralist and horizontal rather more than a monist and vertical imperative. Of course, there is a harmonic coordination at work, but we must be careful not to misstate it. In polyphony, the many voices come together at the same time as they remain apart. Harmony is not alchemy.

The message of polyphony is far more complicated than a mere "vertical chord," and it is a message with which the contemporary world finds itself much more in tune than the modernists and Romantics ever were. That is why Bach had such a mixed reputation until Felix Mendelssohn began the process of rehabilitation almost a century after his death and why Bach's canonization has never been so secure as now. It will not do to say that we were right and the past was wrong; we have experienced a shift in aesthetic paradigms and find ourselves, in some ways, closer in ear to the eighteenth century than to the nineteenth.

The strength of the metaphor of polyphony is that it provides a model for the diversity and fragmentation of the contemporary legal order which currently provokes much disquiet. A fugue is, literally, flight, parts tumbling one upon the other in independent and turbulent conversation. Listen to Bach, and let its infinite complexity astonish you, its whorls and eddies, subplots, new directions, and sudden reunions.

Polyphony has on occasion been cited as a model for law, though often without much understanding of how it actually works.[152] The very word polyphony—"plural voices" in interrelationship—is a key to understanding legal pluralism: it tolerates difference and conflict as a melodic model does not. It would see the interaction of different social groups and individuals as mutually constitutive, as the notes in a chord are, in a quite physical sense, mutually constitutive. It would celebrate diversity and independence rather than coherence and unity. Above all, the image of "voice" is about harmony, not silence and "peace."[153] The image of voice is a noisy one, and it connotes sounds constantly in contention.

What of the "musical staves" which ground Nabokov's harmony? Here, on the contrary, we find ourselves much more distant from Bach than from the modernists. A staff is a kind of a grid which marks the parameters of the possible in music. It establishes norms and limits, customary and shared expectations within which the composer functions. From the development of modern notation codified by Franco of Cologne, which I discussed in

"Motet," to the very recent past, composers despite their radically different sensibilities have worked within a common framework, a common law.

For Nabokov, the existence of these staves is assumed—in music, and in society. They are the common norms of which we are all part. When he writes of our basic consonance, an "interplay of identical particles," he sees us all taking our place against a shared field. We are all notes on the same staff of life. It is this shared background which configures his empathy. This reflects Foucault's characterization of the modernist mentality, in which everything—the species, the coin, the alphabet, the atom, and the human subject—is understood as unitary, equal, individual, modular, regular.[154]

We live in a world in which those staves have faded away to nothingness. Compositional techniques have burst the bounds set down by Franco of Cologne: new sounds are now possible, but at the same time the reinvention, by every composer, of tonality, sonority, and notation has led to a radical individualization of musical language, an interiority of meaning. With the death of the shared reality which those musical staves represented, inevitably the author has become alienated from the audience. Much music now expresses but does not communicate. Here we are faced with the paradox which Derrida has done so much to expose. In inventing a language which is unique, cleansed of the ambiguity which pollutes any vocabulary shared among others, we create a purely personal and therefore ultimately incomprehensible symbolism.[155] The insularity of Western "classical" music, caused by its loss of a shared language, may eventually lead to silence. But on the other hand there remains a creative possibility opened up by the constant reinvention of communicative codes, of musical syntax as well as musical semantics.[156] This possibility is essentially a pluralist and chaotic one. It requires reinvention on an entirely localized and specific basis, through "individuals and small groups [who] dare to reclaim the right to develop their own procedures, their own networks."[157]

Nabokov's "musical staves" have been lost in law as in music. As Franco's notation and the totalizing ambitions of state law arose together, so also are they in decline. Speaking literally, we have lost the common law, a sense of widely shared and understood values: pluralism exists in the subjective comprehension of legal meaning as in the multiple sites of legality. This then is the preeminent task of law in the postmodern era: to provide the facilitation and freedom of polyphony, understood as more than obediently vertical chords, through a world in which the musical staves on which we build our life are invented by each of us anew. The beauty of any legal system built on these principles will not be homogeneous, congruent, unified.

It will not even be coherent. Rather, it will resemble chaos in its unpredictability and its interactive complexity. But there is more to harmony than peace and more to beauty than coherence.

The end of modern time is neither a moment of despair nor a retreat into silence. It is the promise of something different, something disorganized but liberating. We hear a glimpse of that vision of the future in Messiaen where a surprising beauty shrouds his work. First, there is the value he places on an individual note, a single note or repeated note going on almost eternally, it seems, loaded with a weight of emotion which seems only to intensify the longer it continues.[158]

Second, the piano in particular often has "tangles" of notes thick with dissonance. Not one, but crowds of notes compete for attention under the hand of the pianist. Yet Messiaen makes of this cluster of discord something lustrous: "Tangles of rainbows." There is something spiritual in these dissonances which makes me wonder whether the most beautiful sound might not be the most various, the most discordant. Dissonance here is not experienced as rivalry or irresolution but as an infinite and all-inclusive unity. The "harmony of heaven" might not be silence but on the contrary the capacity—and the willingness—to hear every note, to the fullness of its truth, at once. Again, there is a strong sense in which reading Schoenberg only as the creator of an authoritarian order, a musical fascist, does an injustice to his role in developing this new aesthetic. For Schoenberg, long before Messiaen, claimed to be involved in the "emancipation of dissonance" and the destruction of the old order of human certainty. In its place he founded a vast new palette of expressive possibilities on which composers such as Messiaen have been able to build with imagination and freedom. As Schoenberg wrote, "here, liberated dissonance became anew harmony, psychological chaos, a meta-sensuous order."[159] Releasing the potential of dissonance from the shackles of Romantic harmony is emblematic of what amounts to an ultimate pluralism.[160]

Finally, Messiaen always focuses intently on the symbolic and emotional meaning of rhythm. Rhythmic forms are charged with extraordinary significance throughout his work: "As a musician, I have worked on rhythm. Rhythm, by its very essence, is change and division. To study change and division is to study Time."[161]

Modern time is one thing: linear, absolute, objective, and reified. It divides the world into isolated and equal parcels, symbolized by clockwork, the metronome, and serial composition. But for Messiaen, time is rhythm, changeable and subjective. It exhibits a care for relationship for it exists only in combination. As one becomes absorbed in rhythm, one can learn the lesson of our interdependence and mutual constitution. Here then is a final contemporary metaphor for critical pluralism: a theory which does not conceive of human beings as equal and abstract but instead as related, interdependent, and context-specific. Exemplified in the work of Messiaen, the "end of time" may also be the beginning of rhythm.

Quodlibet

Just Aesthetics and the Aesthetics of Justice

Quodlibet [a. L. *quodlibet* (f. *quod* what + *libet* it pleases (one)) . . .]
    1. Any question in philosophy or theology proposed as an exercise in argument or disputation, hence, a scholastic debate, thesis or exercise on a question of this kind. . . .
    2. A fanciful combination of several airs; fantasia, medley.

—*Oxford English Dictionary*

Variatio 30. Quodlibet. a 1 Clav.

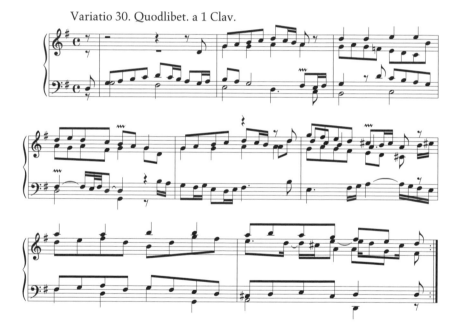

Music is not just noise: it has rhythm, harmony, tone, and so forth. But an important difference between the two is form, which is always a system for the channeling and control of power.[1] Noise without form is a weapon.[2] This is why the relationship of form to content, and the speaking of each through the other, has been such an integral aspect of these *Songs without Music*. Formally, I have attempted to communicate my understanding of the meaning of law, the forces which influence it, and the nature of interpretation precisely through the structures I have developed and the metaphors I have adopted. Substantively, and in light of the understanding of the aesthetics of change outlined in the "Quartet for the End of Time," I have urged a broad pluralism, a joy in difference for its own sake, a restraint on legislative social control and regulation, and a focus on local knowledge. But none of this is to say that there is no place for "law" in society. Law is one of the ways in which form is developed in society, and law expresses itself through form and structure and style and ritual. Form and content are bound together. To abandon form altogether is to abandon creative tension, for it is through the constraint of form that content forms. Peter Brooks puts it this way:

> The realm of the aesthetic needs to be respected, by an imperative that is nearly ethical. . . . [P]ersonality must be tempered by the discipline of the impersonal that comes in the creation of form. "Form" in this sense is really an extension of language, which is itself impersonal in the same way. . . . To understand that [language] possesses and defines us—that it is a formal system in which and through which we speak— is a necessary condition of subjectivity.[3]

We come now to an exercise in disputation. If aesthetics is about lessening and pluralizing laws, what does it say about justice? Is aesthetics silent as to the contours and meaning of justice? Is aesthetics, ultimately, of analytic but not of normative significance? Does it describe but not choose among different values? On the contrary, the aesthetic suggests very strongly a particular normative dimension in the pursuit of justice. This is the argument I will pursue in the fantasia which follows. A quodlibet was frequently used as the short, concluding section of a set of variations, intended to play on the themes of the rest of the piece, but in a more liberal and reflective style. The same is true here.

Justice is inevitably connected with aesthetics. We might begin by noting that they share a history of contention. The literature on both is vast, yet there is no agreement as to their meaning. The philosophy of aesthetics seems to be a series of false starts and new beginnings. So too with justice, which is described according to a wide variety of different frameworks —as procedure or as content, as desert or as fairness—while the adherents of one have little to say to the advocates of another.[4] One begins to suspect that "justice" is nothing but a rhetorical spice used to mask the stench of festering prejudices.

The meaning of justice and of aesthetics is not, then, a matter for agreement. It seems to encompass a variety of contradictory impulses, and we can concede, with Plato, that the good is never entirely knowable, "for it does not admit of verbal expression like other branches of knowledge."[5] Yet the history of aesthetics is replete with dogmatic assertions as to the "inherent" nature or necessary shape of beauty. Now, undoubtedly both justice and aesthetics are felt to be unarguable in our lives. Beauty, says Kant, is experienced as something so compelling that we take it to be universal:

> Since the judgment of beauty or of taste must be universally and necessarily valid for all men, its ground must be something identical in all men. . . . For the fact of which everyone is conscious, that the satisfaction [in the judgment of beauty] is for him quite disinterested, implies in his judgment a ground of satisfaction for all men. . . . For it has this similarity to a logical judgment that we can presuppose its validity for all men.[6]

The same feeling of "oughtness" overwhelms us in the face of justice. An appeal to justice, like an appeal to beauty, is hard to explain exactly because it is felt to be bedrock and self-evident. Justice or beauty admit of assertion but not of definition because they are felt to be axiomatic in our lives. Kant's error, however, lay in confusing the experience of universal truth with its reality. There is nothing absolute or acultural in what counts as beauty or justice—though it feels as if there is.

It is this absolutism which accounts for the questionable lineage of those who have sought to incorporate aesthetic arguments into the ethical and political realm. For Friedrich Nietzsche, the idea of aesthetics was a way of approaching a world "beyond good and evil." Through aesthetic arguments, Nietzsche glorified the beauty of power, the triumph of will over morality, and those "artists of violence . . . who build states."[7] Yet although Nietzsche's aesthetic values are very different from Kant's, he is equally guilty of universalizing his preferences. For Nietzsche the "will to power" which guided his life was never questioned.

Nazism likewise treated a love of power and force as somehow intrinsic to the idea of beauty. Joseph Goebbels used the power of aesthetics to quell resistance, inspire conformity, and subjugate the individual to the state. "The aestheticization of politics"—Walter Benjamin's devastating indictment—sums up, on the one hand, the chilling immorality of treating the state as a work of art and, on the other, the victory of spectacle over meaning, "providing imaginary reconciliations to contradictions that remained unresolved in the real world."[8]

Nazism demonstrates the power of aesthetics but also its corruption. In fact, what we see in Nazism is above all the manipulation of the modernist spirit in art. Benjamin argues that "reproducibility" is the essence of modernism, manifested in the cult of the signature as a guarantor of value and in the importance of the artist reproducing some trademark style from canvas to canvas. Baudrillard likewise declares that the "serial character of modern art [is] precisely that which assigns value to the singular object." Not uniqueness but rather constancy of "gesture and signature" has been the hallmark of modernism.[9]

It is this characteristic which was played upon with such success by the Nazis, gaining emotional force precisely by the massification of gestures —of salutes and swastikas and blue-eyed blonde youths multiplied division upon division. Ironically, the Nazi suppression of modernism in art was wholesale and vicious. But "degenerate art," as the famous Munich exhibition of 1937 called it, included everything generative in the artworld. All that was left was "art" and rituals which, for the most part, had been rendered deracinated and static.[10] Although Nazism was able to successfully appropriate some of the symbolism and emotional techniques of modernism, it saw only danger in the process of artistic creation itself.

"Process" is the key. To see what aesthetics and justice share, one must move to a higher dimension of analysis, away from the deeply contingent claims as to what beauty or fairness "really is" and toward the common process by which they structure a discourse.[11] We can draw conclusions about how aesthetics and justice are experienced and exercised rather than about what they are said to require. Both are modes of apprehension and expression: a way of seeing, and not a thing to be seen.[12]

There are two ways in which the aesthetic process relates to our ideas of justice and can help to inform it. First, the aesthetic dimension is part of our best understanding of the nature of justice in our society. This is the aesthetic nature of justice. Second, the aesthetic is, in itself, a liberatory process which aims "to retrieve the totality and harmony of the human personality."[13] Appreciating aesthetics is part of the work of making a better society. This is the just nature of aesthetics.

The aesthetic nature of justice is suggested by several different perspectives. Both are kinds of judgments. They weigh up the merit of a thing or a person. Kant's discussion of aesthetics, for example, is to be found in his *Critique of Judgment*. The postmodern "return" to aesthetics, therefore, particularly in relation to law, far from constituting an abandonment of ethics, is a recognition of their intimate alliance.[14]

Such judgments are in fact closely connected. Let us focus on justice as a way of knowing. Kurt Gödel may provide a useful insight. Roger Penrose puts it helpfully: "Human mathematicians are not using a knowably sound algorithm in order to ascertain mathematical truth."[15] Gödel's theorem proves, from within the logic of the mathematical system, that certain things which are true according to its premises nevertheless cannot be logically derived from it. All systems have "metamathematical properties" which cannot be observed from within.[16]

Our knowledge of these truths, then, stems from some understanding of the system of rules and axioms which the system does not itself replicate and cannot either manufacture or comprehend. It relates to an awareness of the "why" of the system to which the system itself—mute sequence of rule-following algorithms—has no access, just as a computer can carry out rules but cannot display a consciousness of what it is doing.[17] The most rigorous and analytic theory or system requires a supplement which is both necessary to its functioning and yet cannot be admitted by its structure.[18]

This supplement is an awareness of the "purposes" which motivate the system, an argument most closely associated with Lon Fuller. Fuller's point is nothing but an analogous case of Gödel's theorem and vice versa. Positivism conceives of specific rules or a whole legal system as an algorithm and nothing but an algorithm: "some system of formalized procedures for which it is possible to check, entirely computationally, in any particular case, whether or not the rules have been correctly applied."[19] But well before CLS, Fuller insisted that the process of interpretation always requires an understanding of the reasons we are engaged in interpretation. For Gödel and Fuller alike, the "is" and the "ought," the how and the why, of legal interpretation are inextricably linked:[20] "Human lawyers are not using a knowably sound legal rule in order to ascertain legal truth."

Gödel's theorem demonstrates that legal meaning exceeds rule following. Even from the point of view of law as a system of rules itself, legal meaning requires another element which, by definition, cannot be defined in terms of those rules and systems and remains an indigestible supplement or remainder to them. Justice is one name for this supplement, something both utterly apart from and yet embodied in the operation of law. It is a mistake (nonetheless frequently made) to conflate the two, as if an exacerbated quantity of the latter could somehow accelerate the former.[21] Neither the rote application of law nor the random exercise of mercy constitutes justice.

Justice can never be found through the application of an abstract rule. It is understood as the application of general principles, but at the same time —and especially within the common-law system—it demands an acknowledgment of the "irreducible singularity" of each individual context:[22]

> This other—insofar as we can apprehend it at all—*is* the familiar, strangely lit, refracted, self-distanced. . . . It is, in each text, a *singular* process; otherness cannot be generalized—which would mean that it could be coded, carried away, replicated—but must be staged *as* uniqueness, as untranscendable contingency.[23]

A just decision, therefore, is not an act of rule following but of the rediscovery, as an act of free will, of the appropriateness of a general principle in the particular case:

> In short, for a decision to be just and responsible it must in its proper moment, if there is one, be both regulated and without regulation: it must conserve the law and also destroy it or suspend it enough to have to reinvent it in each case, remystify it, at least reinvent it in the reaffirmation and the new and free confirmation of its principle.[24]

The same is true of the work of art. The judgment of aesthetics, as I argued in the "Prelude," sees the object on which it is focused as a statement of the universal and as an incommensurable singularity. But it is not a treatise. The universal nature of its content must be fused with and arise organically out of the singularity of its form. For the grounds of beauty, like the grounds of justice, may be felt, but the specifics of what is being articulated lie always fractionally out of reach. The meaning of justice and the meaning of the aesthetic may both be sensed, but they can never be codified or entirely understood. They lack an essence, or a definition; they exist in specific performances rather than as general propositions.[25] The aesthetic and the just alike deny the application of a priori models or abstract understandings and instead focus on the tangible and unrepeatable experience of singular events. The artwork and the moment of judgment come each time differently. Reproduction is forgery.

Above all, the idea of aesthetic value provides us with an important clue as to what people mean when they demand "justice." On the one hand "justice" sounds an appeal to sympathy or fairness, whether formal or substantive. But justice has a hard edge that ought not be dulled by politeness. The "revolutionary justice" that supposedly legitimated the terrors of the French or Russian revolutions found expression in secret executions and public massacres. The language and practice of "popular justice" implies peremptory and violent retribution. It is a term which scarcely invites either formality or compassion.[26] But it would seem that this "rough justice" is genuinely understood to be a kind of justice, however arrogant and merciless its practitioners.

This is what we need to explain: not what you or I believe justice demands in any case but rather what those who use the language of justice share despite their substantive differences. The answer, I suspect, is that the process of justice appeals to aesthetic values. One of those values is the idea of proportion or balance. This is to say no more than Montesquieu: "justice is a relationship of fitness."[27] Justice is never understood as being about pragmatism; it focuses exactly on establishing, in a universe devoid of other considerations, a "fit" between the individual subject (a criminal, for example) and the social response. To return to the "Requiem," supporters of the death penalty, for example, resort to the rhetoric of justice, specifically in terms of the lex (or lexicon) talionis. "An eye for an eye, a tooth for a tooth" proclaims the importance not only of enforcing responsibility for acts committed but of enacting that responsibility in a way which balances the two. The act of execution is seen to balance the act of murder. The promise of closure derives from an appeal to symmetry. Opponents of capital punishment differ on just this point. State-sanctioned murder is for them not seen to balance the act of murder but on the contrary to compound it. Far from being symmetrical, the second death merely multiplies the imbalance and disproportion.[28]

The question of balance is but one aspect of a broader point. Justice is in fact a kind of aesthetics because it operates by a language of symbolic meaning expressed in sensory form. To say that "justice is done" is therefore not simply to say that the right result has been achieved but also that it has been done in the right way—a question of form and imagery. In *Othello*, the Moor and Iago plot Desdemona's murder:

> IAGO: Do it not with poison, strangle her in her bed, even the bed she hath contaminated.
>
> OTHELLO: Good, good; the justice of it pleases; very good.[29]

At times, and especially in periods of revolution or turbulence, the symbolic aspect of punishment becomes even more significant. The "popular justice" of the poor in eighteenth-century England typically took symbolic form.[30] Look at the burning of wealthy farmers in their silos during the rural terror of revolutionary France. Neither do such acts live only in the distant past. Here is a case of so-called popular justice during the Vietnamese revolution, a young man whose eyeglasses raised in his interrogator the hackles of suspicion and enmity: "'Are you trying to act blind? We are the people; we are the justice. We know you so well, traitor. Why don't you come and get them?' . . . [He] dropped the glasses into the dirt, lifted his foot, then brought it down, grinding glass into the dust."[31]

I am not for a moment suggesting that this was a just or a justified act. But it was an act which was believed to be "justice." In this case, the rhetoric was extremely complicated and stemmed from the accuser's belief that the victim was an "intellectual." His glasses thus represented both the knowledge which alienated him from the peasantry and his blindness, therefore, to their plight. The act of destroying the glasses was therefore intensely symbolic, and it is precisely because of its symbolic dimension that it was claimed to be an act of justice and not of law or of vengeance.

It is, I think, the symbolism of the act which is most horrific. At the same time, when I think about what I want when demanding of others "justice," they are the ones who genuinely confront the nature of their actions. This internal reckoning is not accomplished simply by external acts of confession or punishment.[32] It is more likely to be accomplished by the way in which symbolism speaks to the heart; that is, by the power which aesthetics has to reach us as nothing else can. The aesthetic element of justice therefore has two aspects. For the claimant, the combination of the sensory experience of punishment and its symbolic meaning promises fit and some kind of symmetry. And for the recipient, it is meant to induce a jarring and personal recognition of a truth. Even a trial, with its enactment of the rituals of presence and its statement of public values, involves important elements of symbol and memory. The public process of a trial is an aspect of the cry for justice and not just law, or retribution, or administration.

Justice and aesthetics share important characteristics as processes of symbolic judgment. Now we can consider the way in which aesthetic judgment is exercised as a model for the exercise of justice. First, as I argued in "Variations on a Theme," the central characteristic of a symbol is that it is double-sided and ambiguous. This uncertainty is part of the strength of the artwork, for it creates its own resistance.[33] In a work of art there is potential for alternative interpretations which goes beyond intention and beyond convention. The symbolic and the nondiscursive invite a freedom which cannot be stamped out. So it was even with an event as stage managed as a public execution; the aesthetic meaning of the scaffold threatened to foment such countercultural acts of defiance that it had, finally, to be abandoned altogether.[34] The symbolic realm stands, at least potentially, outside the pedantry of social control.

Justice should provide a space for resistance too. It ought to listen to the voices which express alternative concepts of right and wrong. That is the value of a dissenting judgment or an open-ended one. There is a long history of lawmaking as a revolutionary mode of radical transformation, although it is a tradition now subjugated by the ideology of law as order.[35] I do not say that this should be the sole concern of the idea of justice, but it is an aspect which is too often ignored in the headlong rush toward a blind and reductive faith in the meaning of rules. Justice is a species of symbolism and of aesthetic judgment. A radical resistance to univocal meaning is the heart of the value that the aesthetic has for us, so too it ought to be the heart of the value we place on justice.

Second, aesthetic judgment is empathetic. There is an "otherness" to a work of art, a painting, a poem, or a quartet, an otherness that begins with the work's very artifice and its formal quality, which continues in its symbolic depth and refusal to spell out what it means and which is intensified by the way it is set apart for special contemplation.[36] Yet in striving to understand it, we are invited to engage with it on its own terms, to appreciate its worth despite that difference. It requires us, as observers or as creators, to treat the object of contemplation not simply as something of utilitarian value for us but as a thing of worth itself. Justice too must be construed as a recognition of the individuality and difference of others. Justice is not instrumental; it does not treat people as means; it does not demand conformity. On the contrary, it attempts to understand people and communities precisely on their own terms, no matter how hard that might be. This is not to say, of course, that the requirement of justice always results in forgiveness, but it must begin with an effort at comprehension. A refusal to understand is never under any circumstances just.

Third, the aesthetic is part of the task of community building in society. Art creates a shared discourse, a compendium of cultural references which bind together a community or even a collection of otherwise disparate communities. One can see this in the reception of Shakespeare or Bach. Their works have become a common currency—a shared vocabulary that allows a vast range of ideas and experiences to be understood, exchanged, and valued.[37] Even if we just go and see a concert, the mutual experience of the audience creates a shared field for discussion and thus mediates communication. At the same time, the very act of witnessing creates among the audience a sense of belonging. The presence of the symbols binds together those in its gaze, even as their interpretations differ. In this way, the aesthetic media "both compose and reflect community."[38] Justice likewise can be understood as an effort to create community through symbolic performance. A trial is a field in which different visions of the right and the good are, again, translated into a common currency—a shared vocabulary that allows those visions to be understood, exchanged, and valued.[39] For the participants and for the broader community, the performance of justice, if successful, provides us with a canvas for communication and with a sense of belonging through witnessing.

"Justice" is always "poetic," always expressive and symbolic. To propose the aesthetic nature of justice is not therefore a surrender to emotion and feeling. As Schiller made clear, the aesthetic constitutes a way of understanding and not a denial of thinking. It is a question of what the aesthetic can teach us rather than what it forces us to abandon, for "if man is ever to solve the problem of politics in practice he will have to approach it through the problem of the aesthetic."[40]

Now to the just nature of aesthetics. A society which values aesthetics will itself be progressing toward justice. Consider the question of empathy. According to Schiller, the lesson of learning to appreciate natural beauty is transferable to intersubjective relations. In both cases, individuals come to respect the otherness of different objects and subjects rather than dominate them.[41] The approach we adopt to color and sound, to beauty and ornament, affect us throughout our lives, encouraging a habit of apperception and appreciation, a way of looking which becomes a capacity of understanding. Aesthetic appreciation, moreover, is a way of looking which is inherently about empathy, simply because it operates on the level of representation. What is representation but the attempt to portray something by way of something else? The experience of aesthetic observation is always an experience of distance and therefore is intrinsically about the communication of otherness.

Art requires effort to accomplish and to understand; it exemplifies the difficulty of intersubjective communication and the leap of understanding; it suggests the complexity of meaning and the possibility of alternatives. These elements of complexity and resistance lie at the very heart of Western art, whose canonical works continue to resist the attempt to define what they "really" mean. But these elements are also to be found in new art and symbolization. The beauty and meaning of the Messiaen *Quartet* lies in its difficulty, in the very opacity which demands the engaged participation of the listener, and in the rich variety of interpretations it offers as reward.

The symbolism and resistance inherent in the artwork have a social effect. A work of art requires the art of work. It is an act of revolt against the generic and the complacent. This bodily habit of perception and recognition influences our lives. It has nothing to do with what is being perceived but with the process by which perception comes about. The more we listen to music, the more we listen; the more we look at art, the more we look; the more we are accustomed to engagement, the more we are prepared to engage in the transformation of the structures around us. There is a further, and still more elemental, level to this relationship. Aesthetics does not just talk about these things: it does them. And the doing is a becoming, in which we are also participants. Aesthetics does not just reflect justice, it exemplifies it; it does not just exemplify justice, it realizes it.

Why do the aesthetic dimensions of law and justice matter? Robin West emphasizes that legal theory, because it is a narrative, is an exercise in world making. The theories we adopt will depend on our aesthetic values and on the images of beauty through which we feel and understand and judge the world:

> We are not compelled to accept or reject an aesthetic vision of human nature that appears in a novel or in a legal theory. . . . [W]e must ask whether the imaginative vision [it] presents is attractive or repulsive, whether it is "true" not to this world, but to our hopes for the world. To the extent that legal theory is narrative, however, it is also art. Therefore we must decide not whether the worlds we envision are true or false, right or wrong. Rather, we must decide whether they are attractive or repulsive, beautiful or ugly.[42]

More than this, a recognition of the relevance of aesthetics is of normative as well as analytical significance because if we value the aesthetic in the life-world, we ought to value certain features of the legal world, too. Respect for aesthetics demands a certain kind of theory of law which I have summed up as critical and pluralist. Respect for aesthetics demands a certain kind of approach to justice which I have summed up as symbolic and empathetic. To take aesthetics seriously demands that we respect the particular, the diverse, the local. Aesthetics is a process, a realm of apprehension, but it is not neutral as to values. It is a way of engaging with the world to which we should aspire.

The preceding chapters attempted to unfold some of the dimensions of that idea. If you want to understand what "the law" means and where it is to be found, you have to explore the aesthetic—formal and stylistic—elements of law's meaning. That is a methodology which explores the depth of legal meaning. If you want to understand what people believe and why, you have to explore the aesthetic influences which are central to their values. That is an epistemology which explains human motivations and values. And aesthetics is also a normative framework which mandates of people a certain stance to law and to each other. Nietzsche, on the genealogy of morals, mutatis mutandis: "[aesthetics] as consequence, as symptom, as mask, as tartufferie, as illness, as misunderstanding; but also [aesthetics] as cause, as remedy, as stimulant, as restraint, as poison. . . ."[43]

These are difficult tasks because the aesthetic, although of visceral power, is a submerged discourse in modern society, and one sees its operations indirectly, sideways, or through a looking glass. Yet this is also the advantage of such an analysis. For the sudden glimpse of a concealed discourse comes as a revelation. The aesthetic, inadvertent and habitual, has much to teach us. Such an approach has something, therefore, in common with the psychoanalysis of law, in which the symbolic meaning of sensory experience is understood as the discursive manifestation of deep desires.[44]

Above all, and uniting all these aspects, the aesthetic dimension is of great force: something about the particular moment, the concrete case, and the symbolism it connotes shakes us to the depths of our being. The aesthetic makes ideas tangible, and in giving them form it gives them meaning and power. Whether a metaphor or a painting or a piece of music, the aesthetic creates meaning through concrete sensation and belief through feeling.

Aesthetics helps us apprehend the meaning of form, style, and metaphor. It is a discovery of the significance of these ways of understanding. Aesthetic judgment satisfies the desire for expression, enriching sensory experience with symbolic meaning. Where is the aesthetic in law? The answer is, everywhere. Law is a cultural medium of expressive form, through which senses and symbols are combined, communicated, and interpreted. In the multiple levels of that expression are to be found the aesthetic dimensions of law and justice.

Notes

1. See "Voyager," in François Girard, *Thirty-two Short Films about Glenn Gould* (Montréal: National Film Board of Canada, 1993).

2. J. S. Bach, *Das wohltemperierte Klavier*, Tiel 1, BWV 822 (1722).

3. We can describe this pattern of climbing intervals and repetition, performed throughout with rhythmic invariance, in the following mathematical form:

$$[A < B \{<(C < D < E) \times 2\}] \times 2.$$

4. Thus: the change from bar 1 to 2 is of a semitone (the top note alone moving), and from 2 to 3 also a semitone (the bass note alone moving); from 3 to 4 there is a change of a tone, each outer part accounting for a semitone; then, from 4 to 5 the top note rises a fourth and in the next bar falls a fifth, while from 6 to 7 there is a change of a diminished fifth (the top note rising a fourth again while the bass note falls a semitone, changing the interval from a ninth to a thirteenth or a flat thirteenth).

5. Thus: C major, C minor, C-sharp major, C-sharp minor, D major, D minor. . . . Compare this intellectual conception of tonal distance (based on major keys arranged in chromatic order and parallel minors), which served a necessary function in relation to the specific musical and, one might almost say, political agenda of *The Well-Tempered Clavier*, with the distinctly aural and harmonic understanding of juxtaposition expressed in the design of Chopin's *Twenty-four Preludes*, op. 28, and Shostakovitch's *Twenty-four Preludes and Fugues*, op. 87 (1950–51), both of which are based on the cycle of fifths and relative minors: C major, A minor, G major, E minor. . . . Both of these cycles of compositions are, nevertheless, specifically modeled on Bach.

6. It might be objected here that only the first book of these preludes and fugues is correctly entitled *The Well-Tempered Clavier*, the second being written over twenty years later, BWV 846–869 (1744). The question of Bach's intention need not concern us. The two books together do form a unity and are

universally perceived in that light. We do not properly call them *The Well-Tempered Clavier*, but we do speak of "the 48" as a whole. Undoubtedly Bach did not write Prelude I with the second book in mind, but the meaning it has for us is colored by the structure which has grown up around it.

7. For a recent survey of the problematic of moral objectivity, see Bernard Williams, *Ethics and the Limits of Philosophy* (Cambridge, Mass.: Harvard University Press, 1985).

8. See Plato, *Republic*, trans. B. Jowett (Oxford: Clarendon, 1921), e.g., the analogies of the sun, the cave, and the line: 306–25. The imagery of an external, abstract, and discoverable Truth pervades all Plato's work.

9. Ibid., 439d, 442.

10. St. Thomas Aquinas, "The Nature and Domain of Sacred Doctrine," in Hazard Adams, ed., *Critical Theory since Plato* (New York: Harcourt Brace Jovanovich, 1971), 118; see St. Thomas Aquinas, *Summa Theologiae*, vol. 1 (London: Eyre & Spottiswoode, 1963), 18. See also the extracts from St. Augustine and Marsilio Ficino in Albert Hofstadter and R. Kuhns, eds., *Philosophies of Art and Beauty: Selected Readings from Plato to Heidegger* (Chicago: University of Chicago Press, 1964). We are far from the idea of metaphor as a means of generating new and not otherwise discernible truths. See for example the understanding of metaphor in Paul Ricoeur, *The Rule of Metaphor: Multidisciplinary Studies of the Creation of Meaning in Language*, trans. Robert Czerny (Toronto: University of Toronto Press, 1977); José Ortega y Gasset, *Phenomenology and Art*, trans. P. Silver (New York: W. W. Norton, 1975); Hans-Georg Gadamer, *The Relevance of the Beautiful and Other Essays*, trans. N. Walker (Cambridge: Cambridge University Press, 1986).

11. See Immanuel Kant, *Critique of Judgment*, trans. W. Pluhar (Indianapolis: Hackett, 1987); Hofstadter and Kuhns, eds., *Philosophies of Art*, 283ff. See also the discussion of Alexander Baumgarten's *Reflections on Poetry* in Terry Eagleton, *The Ideology of the Aesthetic* (Oxford: Blackwell, 1990), 13–28; and David Wellbery, *Lessing's Laocoön: Semiotics and Aesthetics in the Age of Reason* (Cambridge: Cambridge University Press, 1984).

12. Eagleton, *Ideology of the Aesthetic*, 15ff.; Friedrich Schiller, *On the Aesthetic Education of Man*, trans. E. Wilkinson (Oxford: Clarendon Press, 1967), 141–47, 197–215, for example, envisages the "play-drive" as a freely chosen "real and active determinability" (XX.4), in which the rational in humanity is not cast aside but experienced as an inner voice rather than an external compulsion (XXVII.3). In the aesthetic, Schiller sees a *harmonization* of the sensuous with the rational and of desire with necessity (IX.7). In aesthetics, wrote Schiller, "universally valid judgments and universally valid actions" become a product of will and "an object of the heart's desire" (XXIII.5, IX.7); see also Eagleton, *Ideology of the Aesthetic*, 102–19.

There are interesting parallels here with the internalization of state controls through regimes of surveillance, a process of self-disciplining explored in Michel Foucault, *Discipline and Punish*, trans. A. M. Sheridan Smith (New York: Vintage Books, 1979); and even with the idea of "the call of conscience" in Heidegger: see A. Ronell, *The Telephone Book: Technology, Schizophrenia, Electric Speech* (Lincoln: University of Nebraska Press, 1989). In Kant, of course, the final transcendence of reason and duty over the senses finds expression in the development of the idea of the "sublime" over and above the idea of "beauty": Eagleton, *Ideology of the Aesthetic,* 70–100.

13. Hans-Georg Gadamer, "The Relevance of the Beautiful," in *Relevance of the Beautiful,* 3; the work of Giambattista Vico (1668–1744) in Adams, ed., *Critical Theory,* provides an early exploration of this insight. See also the discussion of art and civilization in John Dewey, *Art as Experience* (New York: Milton, Balch & Co., 1934), 326ff.

14. John Keats, Percy Bysshe Shelley, Thomas Carlyle, and Ralph Waldo Emerson provide a few examples.

15. John Keats, "Ode on a Grecian Urn"; Earl of Shaftesbury, *Freedom of Wit and Humour,* in Hofstadter and Kuhns, eds., *Philosophies of Art,* 241; Bernard Bosanquet, *History of Aesthetics* (London: Allen & Unwin, 1922), 333, discussed in Thomas Munro, *The Arts and Their Interrelations* (New York: Liberal Arts Press, 1949), 170–73.

16. For an early example, see Alexander Pope (1688–1744), *An Essay on Criticism,* in Adams, ed., *Critical Theory.* In *An Essay on Man* (Cambridge: Cambridge University Press, 1913), he likewise sees the connection between aesthetics and the natural world as a continuation of a mimetic understanding: in Plato, art is mimetic of ideas, in Aquinas of God, and in the neoclassicists of nature.

17. See the discussion of the Earl of Shaftesbury and Edmund Burke in Eagleton, *Ideology of the Aesthetic,* 40–61. The question of the ideological functions and utility of aesthetic discourse is, of course, the central theme of Eagleton's book.

18. Earl of Shaftesbury, quoted in Hofstadter and Kuhns, eds., *Philosophies of Art,* 274.

19. See, for aspects of the vast project of the critique of rationalism with a particular bearing on the aesthetic, Jacques Derrida, *The Truth in Painting,* trans. G. Bennington and I. McLeod (Chicago: University of Chicago Press, 1987); Martin Heidegger, *Poetry, Language, Thought,* trans. A. Hofstadter (New York: Harper & Row, 1971); Friedrich Nietzsche, *The Birth of Tragedy/The Case of Wagner,* trans. Walter Kaufmann (New York: Vintage Books, 1967); idem, *Beyond Good and Evil,* trans. R. Hollingdale (London: Penguin, 1990); idem, *Thus Spake Zarathustra;* Jacques Derrida, *Of Grammatology* (Baltimore: Johns Hopkins University Press, 1976); Michel Foucault, *The Order of Things: An Archaeology of the Human Sciences* (New York: Vintage Books, 1973).

20. Much can be explained if we understand philosophy itself as a battle between contrasting aesthetics: Kant saw beauty in order and the purity of reason, while Nietzsche saw it in power and force. In Marx there is a remarkably similar understanding of the world as a play of conflicting forces; the difference here, too, is aesthetic. For Marx, the masses have a nobility and beauty, but Nietzsche sees them only as slavelike and impoverished; in Marx class conflict

is a stage on the journey toward a utopia of peace and plenty, while for Nietzsche struggle is the life-force itself. It is not their approach but their sympathies which differ: see the discussion of Nietzsche and Marx in Eagleton, *Ideology of the Aesthetic*, 240–44.

21. Thus for Arthur Schopenhauer, for example, "the impetuous and blind striving of will" and the "eternal, free, serene subject of pure knowing" are located at opposite poles (see Hofstadter and Kuhns, eds., *Philosophies of Art*, 463; see also p. 457). Nietzsche would not reject this polarity, only the hierarchy it implies.

22. See the marvelously self-centered *Ecce Homo* in Friedrich Nietzsche, *On the Genealogy of Morals and Ecce Homo*, trans. Walter Kaufmann (New York: Vintage Books, 1989), replete with chapter headings such as "Why I Am So Wise," "Why I Am So Clever," and "Why I Write Such Good Books."

23. Nietzsche, *Birth of Tragedy*. Italics in original.

24. Compare Samuel Taylor Coleridge: "We *declare* an object beautiful, and feel an inward right to *expect* that others should coincide with us. But we feel no right to *demand* it" (Adams, ed., *Critical Theory*, 467).

25. See George Santayana, *The Sense of Beauty* (New York: Dover, 1955), 3–5.

26. "With this sense of the splendour of our experience and of its awful brevity, gathering all we are into one desperate effort to see and touch, we shall hardly have time to make theories about the things we see and touch" (Walter Pater [1839–94], *Studies in the History of the Renaissance*, in Adams, ed., *Critical Theory*, 645). Cf. Santayana, *Sense of Beauty*; Rudolf Arnheim, *The Phenomenology of Aesthetic Experience* (Evanston, Ill.: Northwestern University Press, 1973). This approach, with its emphasis on aesthetics as an expression or invocation of feeling, so typical of the late Romantic spirit, has not of course been without its critics. Anti-Romantics such as Irving Babbitt have seen this approach as a flatulent sentimentality, a mawkish self-indulgence and (along the lines of Plato) even a threat to the search for truth.

27. Cassirer, *Essay on Man*, in Adams, ed., *Critical Theory*, 994, 998, 1007.

28. See for example the discussion of Pierre Corneille and John Dennis in Adams, ed., *Critical Theory*. In the work of Nelson Goodman there is the same systematizing and taxonomic instinct, although without the normative implications for value claimed by Beardsley (see n. 29). In Goodman most of all the aesthetic becomes reduced to a question of definition: Nelson Goodman, *Languages of Art* (Indianapolis: Hackett Publishing, 1976).

29. Monroe Beardsley, *Aesthetics: Problems in the Philosophy of Criticism* (New York: Harcourt, Brace, & World, 1958), discusses these criteria at 190–209 and 328–29; Beardsley claims a canonical status for them at 456–64.

30. Ibid., 456–70, where similar arguments are made.

31. Mary Mothersill, *Beauty Restored* (Oxford: Clarendon Press, 1984), 96, 108–9, 119–22; see generally "The First Thesis," 100–122.

32. Gadamer, *Relevance of the Beautiful*; Dewey, *Art as Experience*; and see Victor Kestenbaum, *The Phenomenological Sense of John Dewey: Habit and*

Meaning (Atlantic Highlands, N.J.: Humanities Press, 1977). For more on the primacy of experience as the preconceptual fountain of meaning, see also Maurice Merleau-Ponty, *The Phenomenology of Perception*, trans. C. Smith (London: Routledge & Kegan Paul, 1962). We find antecedents to what appears to be thus an almost phenomenological approach to the sensory experience of life in Kierkegaard, discussed in Eagleton, *Ideology of the Aesthetic*, 173–95.

33. See the introduction to Gadamer, *Relevance of the Beautiful;* see also Pierre Bourdieu, *Language and Symbolic Power* (Cambridge, Mass.: Harvard University Press, 1991), discussed at greater length below.

34. See the discussion of the relationship of art to aesthetics in Stanley Cavell, "Music Decomposed," in *Must We Mean What We Say?* (Cambridge: Cambridge University Press, 1969), 180–212.

35. Dewey, *Art as Experience*, 3–15.

36. See Stanley Cavell, "A Matter of Meaning It," in *Must We Mean?*, 213–37. See also Monroe Beardsley and Wim Wimsatt, "The Intentional Fallacy," in Wim Wimsatt, *The Verbal Icon* (Lexington: University of Kentucky Press, 1969).

37. For more on the presentational meaning of art, see in particular Susanne K. Langer, *Philosophy in a New Key* (Cambridge, Mass.: Harvard University Press, 1942); Goodman, *Languages of Art.*

38. Eagleton, *Ideology of the Aesthetic.* As Thomas Munro puts it, "*Aesthetic* experience is directed, more or less continuously, by a group or series of outside sensory stimuli," although this emphasis on the sensory initiation of the aesthetic does not deny the relevance of "association, understanding, imagination, conation, and emotion" (*Form and Style in the Arts: An Introduction to Aesthetic Morphology* [Cleveland: Case Western Reserve University, 1970], 12).

39. Santayana, *Sense of Beauty*, is imbued with this emphasis.

40. For more on the differential force of the senses in various cultures, see David Howes, ed., *The Varieties of Sensory Experience: A Sourcebook in the Anthropology of the Senses* (Toronto: University of Toronto Press, 1991); David Howes, "Odour in the Court," *Border/Lines* (Winter 1989–90): 28.

41. Howes, ed., *Sensory Experience;* Marshall McLuhan, *The Gutenberg Galaxy: The Making of Typographic Man* (New York: Signet, 1969); David Howes and M. Lalonde, "The History of Sensibilities: Of the Standard of Taste in Mid-Eighteenth Century England and the Circulation of Smells in Post-Revolutionary France," *Dialectical Anthropology* 16 (1991): 125.

42. See Jack Goody, *The Logic of Writing and the Organization of Society* (Cambridge: Cambridge University Press, 1986); Ivan Illich and Barry Sanders, *ABC: The Alphabetization of the Popular Mind* (London: Penguin, 1988); McLuhan, *Gutenberg;* Stephen Pinker, *The Language Instinct: How the Mind Creates Language* (New York: William Morrow & Co., 1994). On the paradoxical status and hierarchy of writing and speech in the Western philosophical tradition, see Derrida, *Of Grammatology;* Jacques Derrida, *The Post Card*, trans. A. Bass (Chicago: University of Chicago Press, 1987); and extracted in Peggy

Kamuf, ed., *A Derrida Reader: Between the Blinds* (New York: Columbia University Press, 1991), 486–516.

43. See the discussion of Gadamer's aesthetics of language, as sound and as metaphor, in J. Weinsheimer, *Gadamer's Hermeneutics* (New Haven: Yale University Press, 1985), e.g., 68, 238. Pinker (*Language Instinct*, 167–68) also discusses the "phonetic Symbolism" of words, the way in which, for example, the compressed physical space made by the tongue in forming the short 'i' or 'ee' sound leads to its association with words connoting littleness—mice *squeak* while elephants *roar* (although, of course, they don't, they trumpet).

44. See Arthur Schopenhauer, *The World as Will and Idea*, trans. R. Haldane (London: K. Paul, Trench, Tubner & Co., 1927), extracted in Hofstadter and Kuhns, eds., *Philosophies of Art*, and see the discussion of his work in Eagleton, *Ideology of the Aesthetic*, 153–72. But note that Schopenhauer was equally disturbed by the notion of desire in aesthetic experience and accordingly insisted upon aesthetics as a distanced and neutral phenomenon—see further, below. Schopenhauer understands "Will" as an objective phenomenon and is afraid of its subjective power in a way which differs markedly from the emphasis on the will as a human characteristic in Hegel.

45. Santayana, *Sense of Beauty*, 28–31.

46. Munro, *Form and Style*, 15.

47. Martin Heidegger, "The Origin of the Work of Art" in *Poetry, Language, Thought*, 69.

48. Ibid., 26. Gadamer makes the same point about sound: see Weinsheimer, *Gadamer*, 94. I am indebted to Nicholas Horn for pointing out to me the interesting parallels to this in the poetry of Gerard Manley Hopkins, who writes of the "inscape" of things as a discovery of their essence:

> . . . Each mortal thing does one thing and the same;
> Deals out that being indoors each one dwells;
> Selves—goes itself; *myself* it speaks and spells,
> Crying, *"What I do is me: for that I came . . . "*
> "As Kingfishers Catch Fire"

49. Dewey, *Art as Experience*, 27ff., 100–101.

50. Heidegger, "Origin of the Work of Art," 65.

51. A contrast made by the French symbolist poet Valéry in Adams, ed., *Critical Theory*, 921.

52. Charles Taylor, *Hegel* (Cambridge: Cambridge University Press, 1975); G. W. F. Hegel, *Lectures on Aesthetics*, in Hofstadter and Kuhns, eds., *Philosophies of Art*, 379ff. See also the discussion and expansion of these points in Robert Nozick, *Anarchy, State, and Utopia* (Totowa, N.J.: Rowman, 1974); Ernest Weinrib, "Causation and Wrongdoing," *Chicago-Kent Law Review* 63 (1987): 407; idem, "'Legal Formalism': On the Immanent Rationality of Law," *Yale Law Journal* 97 (1988): 984; idem, "Right and Advantage in Private Law," *Cardozo Law Review* 10 (1989): 1283; idem, "The Jurisprudence of Legal Formalism," *Harvard Journal of Law and Public Policy* 16 (1993): 583; and see Terry Eagleton, "The World as Artefact" in *Ideology of the Aesthetic*, 120–52.

53. Hegel quoted in Albert Hofstadter, "Introduction," in Heidegger, *Poetry, Language, and Thought,* xvii. The consequences of this kind of approach have come under considerable attack in recent years in relation to the implications such an anthropocentric view has for the treatment of animals and the environment.

54. While I have emphasized the broad range over which Hegel's understanding of the thing in this way extends, it is nonetheless true that he particularly had in mind an understanding of art as essentially creative self-expression: Hegel, *Lectures on Aesthetics,* in Hofstadter and Kuhns, eds., *Philosophies of Art,* 79.

55. Mothersill too makes this mistake, treating the artist's knowledge as if it were merely technical and the appreciation of the connoisseur as of a higher order: Mothersill, *Beauty Restored,* 287–93. In contrast, see Tolstoy's "What Is Art," discussed in Munro, *Arts and Their Interrelations,* 64ff.

56. Cavell, *Must We Mean?,* 198.

57. Immanuel Kant, *Critique of Judgment,* "First Division, Analytic of the Aesthetical Judgment," is extracted in Hofstadter and Kuhns, eds., *Philosophies of Art,* 283ff. Eagleton (*Ideology of the Aesthetic,* e.g., 31–40, 70–100) discusses not only Kant but Hegel and David Hume in this light and emphasizes the relationship of the idea of distance to the universalization of the aesthetic which I have already elaborated. See also the somewhat glib but perspicacious critique of aesthetic distance in Goodman, *Languages of Art,* 241; G. Dickie, "The Myth of the Aesthetic Attitude," *American Philosophical Quarterly* (1964): 1; Mothersill, *Beauty Restored,* 320–22.

58. For more on the way in which tuberculosis—consumption—was given an aesthetic, even glamorous, gloss in the nineteenth century, especially among women, see Susan Sontag, *Illness as Metaphor/AIDS and Its Metaphors* (New York: Anchor Books, 1990).

59. Schopenhauer, *World as Will,* quoted in Hofstadter and Kuhns, eds., *Philosophies of Art,* 458. We see here a fear of personal will and an objectification of cosmic "Will" which provides an interesting parallel with the thought of Hegel: see Munro, *Arts and Their Interrelations,* 177. Clive Bell likewise declares that "to appreciate a work of art, we need bring with us nothing from life, no knowledge of its ideas and affairs, no familiarity with its emotions" (quoted in Mothersill, *Beauty Restored,* 223)—this seems to me near enough to a *reductio ad absurdum* as makes no difference.

60. Gadamer, *Relevance of the Beautiful,* xv.

61. Discussed in Mothersill, *Beauty Restored,* 323–24. For Munro (*Form and Style,* 69), "Attention is always a focusing of conscious awareness," an approach which clearly connects the idea of addressing the aesthetic object with that of respect.

62. At the same time, we must guard against a too trite "perception of phenomenology." Even Merleau-Ponty insists that "the relationship to the other enters into the very essence of the conscious act," in which "self and world are mutually and reciprocally determinative" (quoted in Kestenbaum, *Dewey,* 25, 91).

63. Gadamer, *Relevance of the Beautiful;* see also George Steiner, *After Babel: Aspects of Language and Translation* (Oxford: Oxford University Press, 1992). Gadamer makes the hermeneutic point in relation to aesthetics specifically in *Truth and Method;* see Weinsheimer, *Gadamer,* 6. Further, the notion of a "fusion of horizons" is key to Gadamer's understanding of the hermeneutic process.

64. From Gadamer, *Truth and Method,* discussed in Weinsheimer, *Gadamer,* 159–61. The collapse of the subject–object dichotomy in the closely analogous context of game playing is discussed in Weinsheimer, *Gadamer,* 103.

65. Munro, *Form and Style,* 20.

66. Beardsley, *Aesthetics,* 52; see also 534–35.

67. Mothersill, *Beauty Restored,* 145–76, 323–66. Thus for Mothersill an appreciation of the color or line of something can lead to a claim of beauty— although not everyone will agree that the line is in fact beautiful—but an appreciation of the context in which you first saw it cannot be. Hers is thus an argument which seeks to define the discourse of beauty and not to defend a particular vision of the beautiful.

68. See especially the phenomenological perspective: José Ortega y Gasset, "On the Concept of Sensation," in *Phenomenology and Art,* 106.

69. Santayana, *Sense of Beauty,* 30–31.

70. Thus see Beardsley, *Aesthetics,* 52–53. Kant also, according to Dewey, treated perception as a one-sided phenomenon, as if beauty had only to be recognized and not constructed. It was his quest for the objective and the rational in beauty which led him to this passive understanding of aesthetic experience: Dewey, *Art as Experience,* 252.

71. Cavell, *Must We Mean?,* 185–86.

72. Mothersill, *Beauty Restored,* 400.

73. Even this is of course not always the case. There are many pieces of music that I immediately associate with those memories and ideas of it which other people have shared with me. These second-hand images have sometimes transformed profoundly my understanding of the piece and greatly enhanced my feeling for it.

74. Here again I overstate the point for the purpose of the argument. The "aesthetic properties" of an artwork are not inherently shared by everyone who listens, though they are more likely to be. Even among experienced listeners, there may be very different understandings of the tone or structure of a piece, and of course an assessment of the virtue of such aspects is entirely subjective.

75. Dewey, *Art as Experience,* 53–67. "It takes the wine press as well as grapes to express juice, and it takes environing and resisting objects as well as internal emotion and impulse to constitute an *expression* of emotion" (64).

76. W. A. Mozart, *Requiem Mass,* K. 626 (1791).

77. See Munro, *Form and Style,* 66–67, for whom the "apperceptive process will tend to spread out along paths of associations," some the result of "previous intense, emotional experience," others from "repetition, learning,

and habit" or from the "socially established meanings" of symbols and ideas entrenched in a culture.

78. Heidegger, "Origin of the Work of Art," 33–34.

79. Ibid., 35.

80. See Jacques Derrida, "Restitutions of the Truth in Painting," in Kamuf, ed., *Derrida Reader*, 277–307.

81. Ibid. Interestingly, in the context of language, Pinker also suggests that if understanding were also governed by listener expectations rather than sound perception, it would be a "barely controlled hallucination"; he argues for the objectivity of words (though not necessarily of meaning), although even on this limited point he is not entirely convincing: see Pinker, *Language Instinct,* 185–88.

82. The same is surely true of our aesthetic appreciation of nature. It does not simply appear to us as beautiful; rather, when we look at the natural world aesthetically, we impose certain forms and ideas upon it. Far from finding in nature the aspects in art we value, we impose those values upon nature by looking at it with an artist's eye. Thus it is that, as our values have changed, the aspects and features of the natural world which we have chosen to value have also changed, at times radically. Nature is an artistic construction and not vice-versa. Our approach to the idea of "wilderness" stands as a case in point: see Cassirer in Adams, ed., *Critical Theory*, 1002; Gadamer, *Relevance of the Beautiful,* 30–31; see also the discussion of Nietzsche in Eagleton, *Ideology of the Aesthetic,* 250.

83. See in particular the introduction to Eagleton, *Ideology of the Aesthetic.*

84. Foucault, *Order of Things*, 27; generally, see 3–45. Michel Foucault, *The Birth of the Clinic: An Archaeology of Medical Perception*, trans. A. M. Sheridan Smith (New York: Vintage Books, 1975).

85. Foucault, *Order of Things*, 57.

86. See ibid., 166–211. The idea of money as an abstract tool of conversion, whose intrinsic value (its gold or silver content, for example) is unrelated to its value in exchange, awaits this conceptual shift.

87. See Goody, *Logic of Writing;* Illich, *ABC;* McLuhan, *Gutenberg.*

88. See Stanley Sadie, ed., *Grove's Dictionary of Music and Musicians*, 5th ed. (London: St. Martin's Press, 1952); Llewellyn Lloyd, *Intervals, Scales, and Temperaments* (London: Macdonald & Jane's, 1978); James Barbour, *Tuning and Temperament: A Historical Survey* (New York: Da Capo Press, 1972).

89. See Foucault, *Order of Things*, 78–120.

90. Toby Miller, *The Well Tempered Self: Citizenship, Culture, and the Postmodern Subject* (Baltimore: Johns Hopkins University Press, 1993).

91. Martin Heidegger, "The Thing," in *Poetry, Language, and Thought,* 165–86.

92. Thus Heidegger (*Poetry, Language, and Thought*, 69) writes of "the thing's thingness" and says that "the thing things"; Foucault insists that, on the contrary, it is *we* who give whatever thingly character they possess and create

an order of knowing in which the verb itself is possible. It is only humans which have *be-ing* (*Order of Things*, 92–110).

93. This we see in particular in Santayana, *Sense of Beauty*, who distinguishes between different aspects of beauty, of which the beauty of form is only one. He goes on to speak of "beauty in expression," emphasizing the symbolic effects of the aesthetic, and thus makes an argument similar to the one I am developing here.

94. Julia Kristeva, *Proust and the Meaning of Time*, trans. Stephen Bann (New York: Columbia University Press, 1993), 53–67.

95. See Langer, *Philosophy in a New Key;* idem, *Feeling and Form: A Theory of Art* (London: Routledge & Kegan Paul, 1953); Goodman, *Languages of Art.* In Goodman, the symbolic nature of art is particularly explored and its parameters defined. Goodman emphasizes a kind of symbol which he calls "exemplification," by which he means symbols which do not merely denote their referents but in fact possess them: thus a painting of a blue bird denotes (is a symbol of) a bird (and, we may go on, connotes happiness) but exemplifies blueness. The symbolic force of art, for Goodman, arises especially in the ways in which it exemplifies qualities (such as color, shape, speed, and so on), although he concedes that any symbol which is taken to be possessed by or intrinsic to the artwork becomes "metaphorically exemplified" by it. It would seem, therefore, that, although useful from the point of view of definition, these distinctions are not crucial to the argument I make here: see Goodman, *Languages of Art*, 53–86, 252–53 (arguing that there is a tendency toward exemplification in art but that this is not a "crisp criterion").

96. Santayana, *Sense of Beauty*, 119.

97. Beardsley, *Aesthetics*, appears particularly confused on this point. He concedes the symbolic meaning inherent in art (see, e.g., 289–90) and then proceeds to radically cauterize both the symbolic and the subjective reasons for a work's appeal from the question of aesthetic merit. But if, as he concedes, the lasting effects of, for example, literature "take place through the formation of *beliefs*" (568), how then is it possible to try to distinguish this force from aesthetic appreciation? Clearly, for spectator or reader, the two are bound together so that in our experience we cannot distinguish between its "pure aesthetic value" (570) and its effect on our lives.

Again, let us consider the question from the point of view of the artist. Surely she is not capable of distinguishing what she means by something from the form in which that meaning is expressed. Can we imagine the creator subjugating her symbolic meaning to an interest in unity or complexity? Not at all: for the artist as for the audience, symbolism and form are bound together. She says what she says in the way that she says it. To speak of the meaning of the artwork, its symbolism, and its effects on our "beliefs" as merely "the side effects of aesthetic objects" (570) is nonsensical, for the "magnitude" of the aesthetic experience lies not in its formal qualities alone but in the emotional and life-changing—and therefore meaning-ridden—force it exerts.

98. I say this in implied critique of the thin view of the formative and meta-

phorical capacities of language expressed in Noam Chomsky, *Syntactic Structures* (The Hague: Mouton, 1957), and Pinker, *Language Instinct*, 88, 93–94. The power of the metaphor is indeed shown here in its ability to *generate* thought and transform nonsense into new meaning—"what occurs is a transfer of schema, a migration of concepts. . . . Indeed, a metaphor might be regarded as a calculated category-mistake" (Goodman, *Languages of Art*, 73).

99. See Dewey, *Art as Experience*, e.g., 290; the paradox inherent in the idea of communication—that is its embodiment of the possibility of the failure of communication and the necessity of the imperfection of communication—is explored *inter alia* in Derrida, *Of Grammatology;* Jacques Derrida, "Scribble (Writing-Power)," *Yale French Studies* 58 (1979): 117; Derrida, *Post Card.*

Tolstoy in particular has argued for the communicative power of art: but at the same time we need to be cautious inasmuch as this word might imply an overemphasis on the intent of the artist. When dealing with the aesthetic generally, we are better to say that an object means something (for us) rather than that it communicates (to us). "In that way, we would not be assuming that the picture is an actual putting out of the artist's own state of mind" (see Munro, *Arts and Their Interrelationship*, 79–85).

100. See the critique of Goodman, *Languages of Art*, in Mothersill, *Beauty Restored*, 7–11.

101. See Cleanth Brooks, *The Well Wrought Urn* (New York: Harcourt, Brace & Co., 1947), 179ff.; Stanley Cavell, "Aesthetic Problems in Modern Philosophy," in *Must We Mean?*, 73–96; Adams, ed., *Critical Theory*, 1032, 1036.

102. Cavell, *Must We Mean?*, 78–79.

103. Santayana, *Sense of Beauty*, 31.

104. Cavell, *Must We Mean?*, 191–92.

105. Martin Jay, "'The Aesthetic Ideology' as Ideology," *Cultural Critique* 21 (1992): 41, presents a more nuanced approach to postmodern aesthetics than that of the critique mounted by Eagleton; and see Josef Chytry, *The Aesthetic State* (Berkeley: University of California Press, 1989).

106. Cavell, *Must We Mean?*, 91.

107. See also the somewhat parallel approach to "habit" in the work of John Dewey discussed in Kestenbaum, *Dewey;* Dewey, *Art as Experience.*

108. Bourdieu, *Language and Symbolic Power*, 13.

109. It is in Schiller, *Sentimental Education*, XXIII.5, that we first find reference to "the aesthetically tempered man." See also Miller, *Well Tempered Self.*

FUGUE

1. As Wallace emphasizes in discussing the comparison between musical and literary forms, the use of a fugue metaphor is often claimed but rarely explored seriously: Robert Wallace, *Jane Austen and Mozart: Classical Equilibrium in Fiction and Music* (Athens: University of Georgia Press, 1983), 19. In this chapter, as throughout this work, I intend to develop the musical metaphor with some deliberation.

2. This is true of the preludes and fugues of Johann Sebastian Bach, *Das wohltemperierte Klavier*, BWV 822–845 (1722) and its companion book, BWV 846–869 (1744), such as that in C major from book 1, which is extracted above. But it is equally true of those written by Dmitri Shostakovitch, op. 87 (1950–51), or indeed of the magisterial fugues in the late piano sonatas of Ludwig van Beethoven, which to some extent serve a similar structural role of development and expansion of musical themes. I write of an "intensified use of musical resources" with some care since most often a fugue uses thematic material different from that of its prelude. The feeling of expansiveness, intensity, and growth it conveys is nonetheless unmistakable.

3. Exposition, stretto, diminution, and augmentation are standard devices of the fuguist's art. The "Crab Fugue" from *The Art of Fugue* uses its theme in reverse, and there are fine examples of inversion in several of the toccatas.

4. See Peter Read Teachout, "The Soul of the Fugue: An Essay on Reading Fuller," *Minnesota Law Review* 70 (1986): 1073, e.g., 1128.

5. Autism is by no means always accompanied by a lack of creativity, and at times there is an extraordinary degree of artistic ability, but this is always intensely focused, as if the whole aesthetic energy of the person were being tightly controlled and directed toward a single point. See certain parts of Oliver Sacks, *The Man Who Mistook His Wife for a Hat* (London: Picador, 1985), and especially Oliver Sacks, "An Anthropologist on Mars," *New Yorker* 69 (27 December 1993/3 January 1994): 106.

6. Mark Tushnet, "An Essay on Rights," *Texas Law Review* 62 (1984): 1363.

7. J. L. Austin, *How to Do Things with Words* (Cambridge, Mass.: Harvard University Press, 1962), and John Searle, *Speech Acts: An Essay in the Philosophy of Language* (London: Cambridge University Press, 1969).

8. Samuel Johnson, quoted in Wallace, *Austen and Mozart*, 9. "More than one reckless soul has embarked upon an extended inter-art comparison only to founder on the Scylla of dilettantism or the Charybdis of over-specialization" (1).

9. See, for example, Leslie Bender, "A Lawyer's Primer on Feminist Theory and Tort," *Journal of Legal Education* 38 (1988): 3; Lucy M. Finley, "A Break in the Silence: Including Women's Issues in a Torts Course," *Yale Journal of Law and Feminism* 1 (1990): 41; Judith Grbich, "The Body in Legal Theory," *University of Tasmania Law Review* 11 (1992): 26.

10. See *Nguyen v. Nguyen* (1990), 91 ALR 161; *Young v. Woodlands Glenelg* (1979), 85 LSJS 15.

11. See *Del Ponte v. Del Ponte*, New South Wales Court of Appeal, 6 November 1987; Finley, "Break in the Silence," 65: but see Grbich, "Body in Legal Theory," 56.

12. Grbich, "Body in Legal Theory," esp. 50–51. Grbich bears no responsibility for the heavy-handed metaphor.

13. See, for example, David Saunders, "Approaches to the Historical Relations of the Legal and the Aesthetic," *New Literary History* 23 (1992): 505; perhaps the richest of these, which uses the analysis of *Rogers v. Koon*, 960 F.2d 301 (2d Cir., 1992) to meditate on the conceptual and experiential differ-

ence between the mere look and form of art, and its inner strength and meaning, is Louise Harmon, "Law, Art, and the Killing Jar," *Iowa Law Review* 79 (1994): 367.

In relation to the aesthetics of the environment, see James Carter, "They Know It When They See It: Copyright and Aesthetics in the Second Circuit," *St. John's Law Review* (1991): 773; Deborah Krieger, "The Broad Sweep of Aesthetic Functionality: A Threat to Trademark Protection of Aesthetic Product Features," *Fordham Law Review* 50 (1982): 345; John Costonis, *Icons and Aliens: Law, Aesthetics, and Environmental Change* (Urbana: University of Illinois Press, 1989); James Charles Smith, "Review Essay: Law, Beauty, and Human Stability: A Rose Is a Rose Is a Rose," *California Law Review* 78 (1990): 787.

14. *In Re St. Stephen Walbrook* discussed in Costas Douzinas, Shaun McVeigh, and Ronnie Warrington, "The Alta(e)rs of Law: The Judgment of Legal Aesthetics," *Theory, Culture, and Society* 9 (1992): 93; Costas Douzinas and Ronnie Warrington, *Postmodern Jurisprudence* (London: Routledge, 1991).

15. See James Boyd White, *Heracles' Bow: Essays on the Rhetoric and Poetics of Law* (Madison: University of Wisconsin Press, 1985); idem, *The Legal Imagination* (Boston: Little, Brown, & Co., 1973); Richard Posner, "Law as Literature: A Relation Reargued," *Virginia Law Review* 72 (1986): 1351; idem, *Law and Literature: A Misunderstood Relation* (Cambridge, Mass.: Harvard University Press, 1988). For various critiques of Posner, see James Boyd White, "What Can Lawyers Learn from Literature?" *Harvard Law Review* 102 (1989): 2014; Daniela Pacher, "Aesthetics v. Ideology: The Motives behind 'Law and Literature,'" *Columbia-VLA Journal of Law and the Arts* 14 (1990): 587; Robin West, "Authority, Autonomy, and Choice: The Role of Consent in the Moral and Political Visions of Franz Kafka and Richard Posner," *Harvard Law Review* 99 (1986): 384; and see R. Weisberg, "The Law–Literature Enterprise," *Yale Journal of Law and the Humanities* 1 (1988): 1.

16. See the taxonomy of law and literature in Pacher, "Aesthetics v. Ideology." We find a similiar distinction in Thomas C. Grey, *The Case of Wallace Stevens: Law and the Practice of Poetry* (Cambridge, Mass.: Harvard University Press, 1991), 22, where he speaks of the justifications of law and literature as either "psychological" (i.e., related, as I explain it, to what literature shows us about human beings and empathy) or "linguistic" (i.e., related to how literature illuminates the use and nature of language).

17. Naturally, the distinction is itself a problematic one, and the writings of Derrida and de Man in particular have been dedicated to questioning and crossing the boundaries which delineate literary theory (in the case of de Man) and philosophy (in the case of Derrida) on the one hand from literature on the other. This is indeed the heart of the contribution of "literary theory" to law: all genres of writing share the same fundamental problems and concerns; all are creative and re-creative; all involve an ambiguous collusion between authors and readers; writing is always rhetorical and meaning always ambiguous: see for example Jacques Derrida, "Scribble (Writing-Power)," *Yale French Studies* 58 (1979): 117; idem, *Of Grammatology* (Baltimore: Johns Hopkins University

Press, 1976); Paul de Man, *Blindness and Insight: Essays in the Rhetoric of Contemporary Criticism* (New York: Oxford University Press, 1971).

18. Albert Camus, *The Plague* (New York: Knopf, 1948); Franz Kafka, *The Trial* (New York: Schocken Press, 1956); see the review of the debate between Posner and West on the meaning of *The Trial*, discussed in Pacher, "Aesthetics v. Ideology," 604–6.

19. Ronald Dworkin, *Law's Empire* (Cambridge, Mass.: Belknap Press, 1986), e.g. 45–86. For further on the question of hermeneutics, see Hans-Georg Gadamer, *Truth and Method* (New York: Crossroads, 1988); and see also David Couzens Hoy, "Interpreting the Law: Hermeneutical and Poststructuralist Perspectives," *Southern California Law Review* 58 (1985): 136.

20. Dworkin, *Law's Empire*, 228–29, and generally 228–38.

21. See, for example, Larry Alexander, "Striking Back at the Empire: A Brief Survey of Problems in Dworkin's Theory of Law," *Journal of Law and Philosophy* 6 (1987): 419; Anne Bottomley, Susie Gibson, and Belinda Meteyard, "Dworkin; Which Dworkin? Taking Feminism Seriously," *Journal of Law and Society* 14 (1987): 47; David Couzens Hoy, "Dworkin's Constructive Optimism v. Deconstructive Legal Nihilism," *Journal of Law and Philosophy* 6 (1987): 321; Alan Hunt, ed., *Reading Dworkin Critically* (New York: Berg, 1992); Allan Hutchinson, *Dwelling on the Threshold: Critical Essays in Modern Legal Thought* (Toronto: Caswell, 1988); Joseph Raz, "Dworkin: A New Link in the Chain," *California Law Review* 74 (1986): 1103; Denise Réaume, "Is Integrity a Virtue?: Dworkin's Theory of Legal Obligation," *University of Toronto Law Journal* 39 (1989): 38; C. Silver, "Elmer's Case: A Legal Positivist Replies to Dworkin," *Journal of Law and Philosophy* 6 (1987): 381.

22. Dworkin, *Law's Empire*, at several places, for example 229; and see generally 228–38.

23. See also Hoy, "Dworkin's Constructive Optimism," 344–46. Dworkin responds to the harshness of the judicial criticism leveled by critical legal studies in just this way, insisting that a skeptical analysis of law can only hold if "the flawed and contradictory account is the *only one* available" (italics added). For Dworkin then, it is enough to say of an interpretation that it "may want to show law in its worst rather than its best light," to invalidate it (Dworkin, *Law's Empire*, 274–75).

24. See James Boyd White, *Justice as Translation* (Chicago: University of Chicago Press, 1990), 235–67, and esp. *Legal Imagination*, 56–76, *Heracles' Bow*, 116–32.

25. For general or introductory material in a large and growing literature, see Alan Hunt, "The Big Fear: Law Confronts Postmodernism," *McGill Law Journal* 35 (1990): 507; Anthony Cook, "Reflections on Postmodernism," *New England Law Review* 26 (1992): 751; "Postmodernism and Law: A Symposium," *Colorado Law Review* 62 (1991): 433–598; Gary Minda, *Postmodern Legal Movements: Law and Jurisprudence at Century's End* (New York: New York University Press, 1995); Douzinas and Warrington, *Postmodern Jurisprudence*; Costas Douzinas, Peter Goodrich, and Yifat Hachamovitch, eds., *Politics, Post-*

modernity, and Critical Legal Studies: The Legality of the Contingent (London: Routledge, 1994).

26. Costas Douzinas, *Justice Miscarried: Ethics, Aesthetics, and the Law* (Hemel Hempstead: Harvester Wheatsheaf, 1994). See also Peter Goodrich, *Oedipus Lex: Psychoanalysis, History, Law* (Berkeley: University of California Press, 1995); Piyel Haldar, "In and Out of Court: On Topographies of Law and the Architecture of Court Buildings," *International Journal for the Semiotics of Law* 7 (1994): 185–200; Jonathan Ribner, *Broken Tablets: The Cult of Law in French Art from David to Delacroix* (Berkeley: University of California Press, 1993).

27. For a recent discussion, see Peter Goodrich, "Signs Taken for Wonders," *Law and Social Inquiry* 23 (1998): 707; Alan Hunt, *Governance of the Consuming Passions* (New York: St Martin's Press, 1996).

28. Saul Levinson and Jack M. Balkin, "Law, Music, and Other Performing Arts," *University of Pennsylvania Law Review* 139 (1991): 1597–1658; Jerome Frank, "Words and Music: Some Remarks on Statutory Interpretation," *Columbia Law Review* 47 (1947): 1259.

29. For celebrated examples, see Richard Posner, *Economic Analysis of Law* (Boston: Little, Brown, 1972); idem, "A Theory of Negligence," *Journal of Legal Studies* 1 (1972): 29; Guido Calabresi, *The Costs of Accidents: A Legal and Economic Analysis* (New Haven: Yale University Press, 1970); idem, "Concerning Cause and the Law of Torts," *University of Chicago Law Review* 43 (1975): 69; R. H. Coase, "The Problem of Social Cost," *Journal of Law and Economics* 3 (1960): 1.

30. See C. Edwin Baker, "The Ideology of the Economic Analysis of Law," *Journal of Philosophy and Public Affairs* 5 (1975): 3; Morton Horwitz, "Law and Economics: Science or Politics?" *Hofstra Law Review* 8 (1980): 905; Arthur Leff, "Unspeakable Ethics, Unnatural Law," *Duke Law Journal* (1979): 1229.

31. One finds this idea of metaphysics as the pre-understandings of a community in Heidegger: see "The Undermining of Western Rationalism through the Critique of Metaphysics: Martin Heidegger," in Jürgen Habermas, *The Philosophical Discourse of Modernity,* trans. F. Lawrence (Cambridge, Mass.: MIT Press, 1991), 131–34.

32. White, *Legal Imagination,* 762–73; *Heracles' Bow, passim* and 32–53.

33. *Fisher v. Lowe,* No. 60732 (Mich.), *Journal of American Bar Association* 69 (1983): 436, in Christopher Stone, *Earth and Other Ethics* (New York: Harper & Row, 1987), 5.

34. See for celebrated examples Carol Gilligan, *In a Different Voice* (Cambridge, Mass.: Harvard University Press, 1982); Sandra Harding, ed., *Feminism and Methodology* (Bloomington: Indiana University Press, 1987); Patricia Williams, "Alchemical Notes," *Harvard Civil Rights–Civil Liberties Review* 22 (1987): 1401; idem, *The Alchemy of Race and Rights* (Cambridge, Mass.: Harvard University Press, 1991).

35. Duncan Kennedy and Peter Gabel, "Roll Over Beethoven," *Stanford Law Review* 36 (1984): 1.

36. R. Macdonald, "Office Politics," *University of Toronto Law Journal* 40 (1990): 419; idem, "Academic Questions," *Legal Education Review* 3 (1992): 61; "Theses on Access to Justice," *Canadian Journal of Law and Society* 7, no. 2 (1992): 23.

37. Teachout, "Soul of the Fugue."

38. For a different overview of the same material, see Janice Toran, "'Tis a Gift to Be Simple: Aesthetics and Procedural Reform," *Michigan Law Review* 89 (1990): 352, 364ff.

39. Louis Schwartz, "Justice, Expediency, and Beauty," *University of Pennsylvania Law Review* 136 (1987): 141; see also 149, 152–53, 154, 156.

40. For further ideas of ugliness in law, see Toran, "'Tis a Gift," 364–66.

41. Drucilla Cornell, "Toward a Modern/Postmodern Reconstruction of Ethics," *University of Pennsylvania Law Review* 133 (1985): 291, 380. There is a clear connection here with what Pacher ("Aesthetics v. Ideology," 598–99) has characterized as the "utopian" stream of law and literature, an approach which mines literature for the vistas of the future it opens up.

42. Robin West, "Jurisprudence as Narrative: An Aesthetic Analysis of Modern Legal Theory," *New York University Law Review* 60 (1985): 145, 209–10.

43. Ibid., 148–51. See Northrop Frye, *Anatomy of Criticism: Four Essays* (Princeton: Princeton University Press, 1957).

44. West, "Jurisprudence as Narrative," 151–58.

45. Toran, "'Tis a Gift," 393, and generally, 375ff.

46. Ibid., 360, and generally, 357ff.

47. Robert Hodge, "Monstrous Knowledge: Doing PhDs in the New Humanities," *Australian Universities Review* 2 (1995): 35–39.

48. Goodrich, "Signs."

49. Pierre Legendre, "The Other Dimension of Law," *Cardozo Law Review* 16 (1995): 943–61; Peter Goodrich, "Law's Emotional Body: Image and Aesthetic in the Work of Pierre Legendre," in *Languages of Law: From Logics of Memory to Nomadic Masks* (London: Weidenfeld & Nicholson, 1990), 293; see also 271–72 and *passim* 260–96. See also Pierre Legendre, *Écrits juridiques du moyen age occidental* (London: Variorum, 1988); Jacques Derrida, "Force of Law: The Mystical Foundation of Authority," *Cardozo Law Review* 11 (1990): 919.

50. Pierre Legendre, quoted in Goodrich, "Signs," 294.

51. Pierre Legendre, quoted in ibid., 295; see also 276.

52. Peter Fitzpatrick, *The Mythology of Modern Law* (London: Routledge, 1992), 11–12. See also Robert Young, *White Mythologies: Writing History and the West* (London: Routledge, 1990); Jacques Derrida, "White Mythology," in *Margins of Philosophy*, trans. Alan Bass (Chicago: University of Chicago Press, 1982); Edward Said, *Orientalism* (London: Routledge & Kegan Paul, 1978).

53. In general, see Peter Goodrich, *Reading the Law* (Oxford: Blackwell, 1986); idem, *Legal Discourse: Studies in Linguistics, Rhetoric, and Legal Analy-*

sis (Basingstoke, Hampshire: Macmillan, 1987); idem, *Languages of Law;* idem, *Oedipus Lex.*

54. See, for example, "Eucharist and Law," "Grammatology," and "The Enchanted Past: A Semiotics of Common Law," all in Goodrich, *Languages of Law.*

55. Goodrich, *Languages of Law,* 233.

56. Bernard S. Jackson, *Semiotics and Legal Theory* (London: Routledge & Kegan Paul, 1985); Roberta Kevelson, "Semiotics and Methods of Legal Inquiry," *Indiana Law Journal* 61 (1985): 355; idem, *The Law as a System of Signs* (New York: Plenum Press, 1988).

57. Umberto Eco, quoted in Robert Benson, "The Semiotic Web of the Law," in Roberta Kevelson, ed., *Law and Semiotics,* vol. 1 (New York: Plenum Press, 1987), 42–43; and in R. Benson, "How Judges Fool Themselves," in Roberta Kevelson, ed., *Law and Semiotics,* vol. 2 (New York: Plenum Press, 1988), 39; and see Umberto Eco, *Semiotics and the Philosophy of Language* (Bloomington: Indiana University Press, 1984).

58. See the critique of legal semiotics in Douzinas and Warrington, *Postmodern Jurisprudence,* 99–100.

59. Charles Peirce, quoted in Kevelson, *The Law as a System of Signs;* Kevelson, ed., *Law and Semiotics,* 2:206.

60. Goodrich, "Signs," *passim.*

61. Thus Goodrich emphasizes the importance of law not just as an instrumental text but as something spoken, listened to, and lived: "This is a question of mnemonics and of the aesthetics of law, a question of the oral and of the visual quite as much as it is of the text" (*Languages of Law,* 2).

62. Haldar, "In and Out of Court"; Douglas Hay, "Property, Authority, and the Criminal Law," in D. Hay, P. Linebaugh, and E. P. Thompson, eds., *Albion's Fatal Tree: Crime and Society in Eighteenth-Century England* (London: Allen Lane, 1977); Goodrich, *Reading the Law;* idem, *Languages of Law;* idem, *Oedipus Lex;* David Howes, "Odour in the Court," *Border/Lines* (Winter 1989–90): 28.

63. *Natanson v. Kline* (1960), 350 P. 2d 1093 (Cal.); see also *Canterbury v. Spence* (1972), 464 F. 2d. 772; *Reibl v. Hughes* (1980), 114 D.L.R. 3d 1; Desmond Manderson, "Following Doctor's Orders: Informed Consent in Australia," *Australian Law Journal* 62 (1988): 430.

64. Jay Katz, *The Silent World of Doctor and Patient* (New York: Free Press, 1984), 66.

65. Ibid., 62–67.

66. Donald Preziosi, *The Semiotics of the Built Environment* (Indianapolis: Indiana University Press, 1979).

67. Hay, "Property, Authority"; E. P. Thompson, *Whigs and Hunters* (London: Allen Lane, 1975); Wilf Stevens, "Imagining Justice: Aesthetics and Public Executions in Late Eighteenth-Century England," *Yale Journal of Law and the Humanities* 5 (1993): 51.

68. Macdonald, "Office Politics."

69. Peter Goodrich, "Modalities of Annunciation," in Kevelson, ed., *Law and Semiotics*, vol. 2; and see also in Goodrich, *Languages of Law*, 184ff.; Haldar, "In and Out of Court."

70. See also "Eucharist and Law," in Goodrich, *Languages of Law*, 53.

71. Dworkin, *Law's Empire*, 407 and *passim*; see Oliver Wendell Holmes, "The Path of the Law," *Harvard Law Review* 10 (1897): 457; H. L. A. Hart, *The Concept of Law* (Oxford: Clarendon Press, 1961); Karl Llewellyn, *Jurisprudence: Realism in Theory and Practice* (Chicago: University of Chicago Press, 1962); Alvin Ruvin, "Does Law Matter? A Judge's Response to the Critical Legal Studies Movement," *Journal of Legal Education* 37 (1987): 307. Dworkin, of course, goes on to say, "but not its seers and prophets," a role he sees played by philosopher kings such as himself.

72. Peter Gay, *Style in History* (New York: W. W. Norton, 1974), makes cogent arguments for the meaning of style, in a related discipline.

73. See "Eucharist and Law," "Grammatology," "The Enchanted Past: A Semiotics of Common Law," all in Goodrich, *Languages of Law*; see also the exploration of the idea of "presentational meaning" in Susanne K. Langer, *Philosophy in a New Key* (Cambridge, Mass.: Harvard University Press, 1942); idem, *Feeling and Form: A Theory of Art* (London: Routledge & Kegan Paul, 1953).

74. Cornell, "Modern/Postmodern Reconstruction," *passim*; West, "Jurisprudence as Narrative," 209–10.

75. See Ivan Illich and Barry Sanders, *ABC: The Alphabetization of the Popular Mind* (London: Penguin, 1988); Marshall McLuhan, *The Gutenberg Galaxy: The Making of Typographic Man* (New York: Signet, 1969).

76. Jacques Derrida in particular has been at pains to emphasize that deconstruction is to be understood as a practice which unfolds a text from within rather than a method or theory imposed from without: see his "Letter to a Japanese Friend," in Peggy Kamuf, ed., *A Derrida Reader: Between the Blinds* (New York: Columbia University Press, 1991), 270–76. See also Matthew H. Kramer, *Legal Theory, Political Theory, and Deconstruction* (Bloomington: Indiana University Press, 1991), 35–36; Christopher Norris, "Law, Deconstruction, and the Resistance to Theory," *Journal of Law and Society* 15 (1988): 169.

77. See in particular Jacques Attali, *Noise: The Political Economy of Music*, trans. Brian Massumi (Minneapolis: University of Minnesota Press, 1985).

78. See Jean-François Lyotard, *The Postmodern Condition: A Report on Knowledge*, trans. Geoff Bennington and Brian Massumi (Minneapolis: University of Minnesota Press, 1984).

79. See Michel Foucault, *The Order of Things: An Archaeology of the Human Sciences* (New York: Vintage Books, 1973); idem, *Discipline and Punish*, trans. A. M. Sheridan Smith (New York: Vintage Books, 1979); idem, *Power/Knowledge: Selected Interviews and Other Writings 1972–1977* (New York: Pantheon Books, 1980); David Couzens Hoy, ed., *Foucault: A Critical Reader* (Oxford: Basil Blackwell, 1986).

80. Stanley Fish, "Dennis Martinez and the Use of Theory," *Yale Law Journal* 96 (1987): 1773, 1782–83, 1785, and *passim*.

81. This argument may be broadly said to include both postmodernist feminists and that critique of essentialist feminism in which questions of race and other differences among women has been explored: see Mary Belenky, *Women's Ways of Knowing* (New York: Basic Books, 1986); Sandra Harding, ed., *Feminism and Methodology*; Linda Nicholson, ed., *Feminism/Postmodernism* (London: Routledge, 1990); Brenda Crossman, "The Precarious Unity of Feminist Theory and Practice: The Praxis of Abortion," *University of Toronto Faculty Law Review* 44 (1986): 86; Angela Harris, "Race and Essentialism in Feminist Legal Theory," *Stanford Law Review* 42 (1990): 581; Martha Minow, "Learning to Live with the Dilemma of Difference," *Law and Contemporary Problems* (1985); Linda Alcoff, "Cultural Feminism v. Post-structuralism," *Signs* 13 (1988): 405; Sandra Harding and Merrill Hintikka, eds., *Discovering Reality: Feminist Perspectives on Epistemology, Metaphysics, and Philosophy of Science* (Dordrecht: D. Reidel, 1983); M. Hawkesworth, "Knowers, Knowing, Known: Feminist Theory and Claims of Truth," *Signs* 14 (1989): 533.

82. De Man, *Blindness and Insight*. See also the critique of postmodern localism in Hunt, "Big Fear," 532–39. So also Grey (*Case of Wallace Stevens*, 74), who writes that "impassioned prophets turn . . . a more intense light on certain aspects of experience than will ever be provided by more tolerant and catholic thinkers."

MOTET

1. For a comprehensive overview of this literature, see Bernard J. Hibbitts, "Making Sense of Metaphors: Visuality, Aurality, and the Reconfiguration of American Legal Discourse," *Cardozo Law Review* 16 (1994): 229–356. See also H. Bosmajian, *Metaphor and Reason in Judicial Opinions* (Carbondale: Southern Illinois University Press, 1992).

2. A process of multidimensional enlargement which, as I mention further below, has been under way in Western music for the past 700 years or more.

3. See in particular the work and discussions relating to Ernest Weinrib: E. Weinrib, "'Legal Formalism': On the Immanent Rationality of Law," *Yale Law Journal* 97 (1988): 984; idem, "The Jurisprudence of Legal Formalism," *Harvard Journal of Law and Public Policy* 16 (1993): 583 (and responses published therein); idem, "Corrective Justice," *Iowa Law Review* 77 (1992): 403.

4. 9 HEN. III (1225); 20 EDW. I (1292). These materials are readily available in the original and translated in various editions of the *Statutes at Large*. Christopher Runnington, ed., *Ruffhead's Statutes at Large*, vols. 1–10 (London: Eyre & Strahan, 1786), and Thomas Thomlins, ed., *Statutes at Large*, vols. 1–10 (London: Eyre & Strahan, 1811), provide different editions and different commentaries. On early translations of the Latin and French statutes, see H. Graham, "'Our Tong Maternall Maruellously Amendyd and Augmentyd':

The First Englishing and Printing of the Medieval Statutes at Large, 1530–1533," *University of California Los Angeles Law Review* 13 (1965): 58.

5. Admittedly Austin argues that "where there is the *smallest* chance of incurring the *smallest* evil, the expression of a wish amounts to a command." This might suggest that, for Austin, coercion is an analytical and not a sociological necessity of the legal system. In considering the problem that arises when one's understanding of the obligations of "divine law" contradicts the commands of positive law, however, Austin concludes that our duty is to obey whichever provides the greater sanction: "if human commands conflict with the Divine Law, we ought to disobey the command which is enforced by the less powerful sanction." The dictates of morality are of no regard. The duty to obey any law—divine *or* positive—arises from the power that affirms it; the greater the power, the greater the duty, for "it is our interest to choose the smaller and more uncertain evil" (John Austin, *The Province of Jurisprudence Determined* [1834; London: Weidenfeld & Nicholson, 1971], 91, 90, 215). Further evidence for Austin's understanding of law as a system of power relations is to be found in Lecture I, *passim*, esp. 99.

6. H. L. A. Hart, *The Concept of Law* (Oxford: Clarendon Press, 1961), 50–55.

7. Runnington, ed., *Ruffhead's Statutes*, v.

8. Ibid., v–xiv; 2 Hen. IV, c. 15 (1400).

9. See Hart, *Concept of Law*. On this analysis, it is neither "truth" nor "power" that grounds obedience to the law but the "validity" of its social sources. Joseph Raz argues even more emphatically for a "sources thesis," namely that the legitimacy of the formal "sources" of a law, such as a properly enacted statute or an authoritative judicial interpretation, establish a separate reason to obey the law quite apart from the justice or otherwise of its contents. The laws found in such sources are not just opinions about what constitutes reasonable behavior. Raz argues that laws, although informed by those various opinions, are intended to act as a definitive arbitration between them and, accordingly, to supersede them within the community. Raz therefore suggests that, according to the logic of the legal system, the existence of laws constitutes a separate reason for obedience to the matters contained therein (J. Raz, *Authority of Law* [Oxford: Clarendon Press, 1979], 47–50, 150–53, 233–61; see also idem, "Authority, Law, and Morality," *The Monist* 68 [1985]: 295).

10. See, for example, Michel Foucault, *The Order of Things: An Archaeology of the Human Sciences* (New York: Vintage Books, 1973).

11. Jacques Attali, *Noise: The Political Economy of Music*, trans. Brian Massumi (Minneapolis: University of Minnesota Press, 1985); Thomas Levenson, *Measure for Measure: A Musical History of Science* (New York: Touchstone Books, 1995).

12. For example, Roberta Kevelson, ed., *Law and Semiotics*, vols. 1–3 (New York: Plenum Press, 1987–89); Roberta Kevelson, "Semiotics and Methods of Legal Inquiry," *Indiana Law Journal* 61 (1985): 355; Bernard S. Jackson, *Semi-*

otics and Legal Theory (London: Routledge & Kegan Paul, 1985); Peter Goodrich, *Languages of Law: From Logics of Memory to Nomadic Masks* (London: Weidenfeld & Nicholson, 1990).

13. Richard Weisberg, "The Law–Literature Enterprise," *Yale Journal of Law and the Humanities* 1 (1988): 13–17.

14. See especially Hibbitts, "Making Sense of Metaphors."

15. For more on the prioritization and acuteness of the senses in different societies, and on the origins, meaning, and implications of Western visuality and the dominance of written language, see David Howes, ed., *The Varieties of Sensory Experience: A Sourcebook in the Anthropology of the Senses* (Toronto: University of Toronto Press, 1991); Jack Goody, *The Logic of Writing and the Organization of Society* (Cambridge: Cambridge University Press, 1986); Marshall McLuhan, *The Gutenberg Galaxy: The Making of Typographic Man* (New York: Signet, 1969).

16. The distinction between denotation and connotation is discussed in relation to the work of Roland Barthes in Jackson, *Semiotics*, 22–24.

17. See the discussion of the shape and form of law reports in Goodrich, *Languages of Law*, 233.

18. Monroe Beardsley, *Aesthetics: Problems in the Philosophy of Criticism* (New York: Harcourt, Brace, & World, 1958).

19. I am greatly influenced by Peter Gay, *Style in History* (New York: W. W. Norton, 1974).

20. See Hibbitts, "Making Sense of Metaphors," 236.

21. Michael O'Toole, *The Language of Displayed Art* (Leicester: Leicester University Press, 1994).

22. It is certainly true that the power of the mass media has in some respects led to a greater visibility amongst the "powerful" than ever before, to the extent where democratic elections in developed countries are fought almost exclusively through orchestrated images and appearances. This is a different issue; however visible politicians need to be in order to be elected, their power (and *a fortiori* that of bureaucrats, corporate executives, and so on) is exercised thereafter, in secret, and through the gaze they bring to bear. It is a mistake to confuse the visibility by which people are granted access to power with the visibility of powerlessness.

23. See, for example, Foucault, *Order of Things;* idem, *Discipline and Punish*, trans. A. M. Sheridan Smith (New York: Vintage Books, 1979); idem, *The Birth of the Clinic: An Archaeology of Medical Perception*, trans. A. M. Sheridan Smith (New York: Vintage Books, 1975). In *The Birth of the Clinic*, Foucault explores the notion of gaze, this time as an exercise of medical and not political power, but this book more than any of his others explains the power, intrusiveness, and political implications of ways of seeing. As the first sentence explains, "This book is about space, about language, and about death; it is about the act of seeing, the gaze" (ix).

24. The question of language is an important aspect of this chapter. Any

further clarification as to the original language of statutes quoted in the text is given in the footnotes. The translations are in all cases those of *Statutes at Large*.

25. See Peter Goodrich, "Literacy and the Languages of the Early Common Law," *Journal of Law and Society* 14 (1987): 422, 424–30, and idem, *Legal Discourse: Studies in Linguistics, Rhetoric, and Legal Analysis* (Basingstoke, Hampshire: Macmillan, 1987), 21–27.

26. 9 HEN. III (1225); 20 EDW. I (1292). The original of this statute, and all statutes quoted in the text from now on until otherwise indicated, is in Latin.

27. 9 HEN. III (1225); 28 EDW. I (1300); *Statute of Rutland*, 10 EDW. I (1282); *Statute de Anno et die bissextili*, 21 HEN. III (1236). For other examples of the type "The King to the Justices of his Bench sendeth greeting," see 7 EDW. I Stat. 1 & 2, 13 EDW. I Stat. 4. I have noted the form as late as 7 EDW. II (1313). The distinction between legislative and judicial functions was not clearly distinguished in these early years: see the work of the great thirteenth-century legal writer Henry Bracton, *On the Laws and Customs of England*, vols. 1–4, ed. G. Woodbine, trans. S. Thorpe (Cambridge, Mass: Belknap Press, 1968), and Frederick Maitland, ed., *Bracton's Note Books*, vol. 1 (London: C. J. Clay, 1889).

28. Thomas F. T. Plucknett, *Legislation of Edward I* (Oxford: Clarendon Press, 1949), 103–4; see also idem, *Early English Legal Literature* (Cambridge: Cambridge University Press, 1958); and idem, *Statutes and Their Interpretation in the First Half of the Fourteenth Century* (Cambridge: Cambridge University Press, 1922).

29. Donald Jay Grout, *A History of Western Music*, 2d ed. (New York: W. W. Norton, 1960), 75–95; David Fenwick Wilson, *Music of the Middle Ages: Style and Structure* (New York: Schirmer Books, 1990), 119–29.

30. Grout, *History of Western Music*, 198; Peter Lefferts, *The Motet in England in the Fourteenth Century*, Studies in Musicology No. 94, ed. George Buelow (Ann Arbor, Mich.: UMI Research Press, 1986), 117–20.

31. Lefferts, *Motet*, 142; Wilson, *Music of the Middle Ages*, 275.

32. Wilson, *Music of the Middle Ages*, 240, 284.

33. Ibid., 236; for further on aesthetics and law in medieval France, see Peter Goodrich, "Law in the Courts of Love," *Stanford Law Review* 48 (1996): 633.

34. *Statute de Scaccario*, 51 HEN. III Stat. 5 (1266); *An Ordinance for Ireland*, 17 EDW. I, cc. 1–8 (1289). See also *Statute of Westminster the First*, 3 EDW. I, cc. 24, 26–31 (1275).

35. See Goodrich, "Literacy," 430.

36. Lefferts, *Motet*, 155, 187–89; Wilson, *Music of the Middle Ages*, 285, 320, 344.

37. Frank L. Harrison, *Music in Medieval Britain* (London: Routledge & Kegan Paul, 1958), 126; Lefferts, *Motet*, 155.

38. *Magna Carta*, 9 HEN. III, cc. 9 & 15 (1225); *Carta Forestæ*, 9 HEN. III c. 4 & 5 (1225).

39. For another example, see *Statute de Marleberge*, 52 HEN. III, c. 10 (1267): "the Turn shall be kept as it hath been used in the Times of the King's

noble Progenitors." Almost a century later this same phrase was used to confirm the validity of those statutes and, in particular, charters made in the past: see 36 EDW. III, c. 1 (1362).

40. Charles H. McIlwain, *The High Court of Parliament and Its Supremacy* (New Haven: Yale University Press, 1934), and idem, *Magna Carta and the Common Law* (1917), discussed in Plucknett, *Statutes*, 26–31; idem, *Legislation*, 13–14. See also the similar point made in Frederick Pollock and F. W. Maitland, *The History of English Law*, vol. 1 (Cambridge: Cambridge University Press, 1895), 178–80.

41. 20 HEN. III, c. 9 (1235).

42. Plucknett, *Statutes*, 20, says, "parliament, this time meant an event rather than an institution."

43. 9 HEN. III (1225); 28 EDW. I (1299).

44. 20 HEN. III, c. 6 (1235).

45. So too one might argue that the improvisational character of Gregorian chant and early polyphony was a function of the inadequacy of musical notation of the time. But this demonstrates the point, for the technology of notation, while it enhanced the creative control of the composer, was also a response to the felt need for that control. In music, clearly, technological breakthrough propelled Western music (until the twentieth century) down a path already well begun.

46. 52 HEN. III (1267).

47. Ibid., cc. 3, 5–11, 13–16, 18, 20, 23–24, 26–29. The word "chapter" has changed its meaning over the years, a matter which is discussed below. In the period under consideration, the word "statute" was generally used to describe the document which records all the enactments of a parliamentary session (normally one a year); it is divided into chapters, each of which covers a particular issue or problem. A statute therefore is a historical unit and a chapter a purposive subdivision of it. It is with this distinction in mind that I have used these words in this chapter, although it must be conceded that, as with most things, the distinction was nowhere near as clear or systematized in the period about which I am writing. The use of the word "chapter" to divide each statute perhaps hints at a narrative quality to our modern ears. But this is anachronistic, for the association of "chapter" with a literary structure is relatively modern. A chapter originally connoted merely a division or heading (from *caput*, head); we still refer to organizations or religions having chapters, meaning branches.

48. Austin, *Province of Jurisprudence*, 97–98, 102–3.

49. *Statute of Westminster the First*, 3 EDW. I (1275). The original of this statute, and all statutes quoted in the text from now on unless otherwise indicated, is in French.

50. See *Magna Carta*, 9 HEN. III, cc. 9 & 15.

51. *Statute of Westminster the First*, 3 EDW. I, c. 1 (1275).

52. Pollock and Maitland, *History of English Law*, 1:80–81.

53. Ibid., 82; Goodrich, "Literacy," 433–36.

54. Plucknett, *Legislation*, 81. See also idem, *Statutes*, 11.

55. Ivan Illich, *In the Vineyard of the Text* (Chicago: University of Chicago Press, 1993), 73.

56. Philippe Ariès, *The Hour of Our Death*, trans. Helen Weaver (New York: Oxford University Press, 1981), 5–202. See also Charles Taylor, *Sources of the Self: The Making of the Modern Identity* (Cambridge, Mass.: Harvard University Press, 1989).

57. Hibbitts, "Making Sense of Metaphors," 249–51.

58. See Grout, *History of Western Music*, 52, 109. Indeed, these display a more complete independence of line than later writing, since there is still little awareness of harmony. Consequently, the melodic lines of the motets of this period are surprisingly dissonant. The emphasis, this time on individuality in part-writing, is also reflected in the use of polytextuality, in which each line sings a different text. The motet is still, then, centered on words and not music.

59. Wilson, *Music of the Middle Ages*, 255.

60. See 4 EDW. I, Stats. 1–3 (1276); 4 GEO. II, c. 26 (1731); Pollock and Maitland, *History of English Law*, 1:83.

61. *De officio cornatoris*, 4 EDW. I Stat. 2 (1276); *Statute of Bigamy*, 4 EDW. I Stat. 3 (1276).

62. M. T. Clanchy, *From Memory to Written Record* (Oxford: Blackwell, 1993); Illich, *Vineyard*, 97.

63. *Statute of Westminster the Second*, 13 EDW. I Stat. 1, c. 34 (1285).

64. Ibid. The rest of c. 34 is in Latin and concerns the lands of women who abscond and the abduction of nuns. Chapter 49, which prohibits the king's servants from taking land, church, or tenement which is the subject of a legal dispute, is also in French. Lord Coke suggests that this is because the chapter relates to an earlier statute written in French; it has also been suggested that c. 49 belongs to a later statute and was recorded here by mistake: see the footnotes to this statute in Thomlins, ed., *Statutes at Large*, xx.

65. *Statutum Wynton* (i.e., Winchester), 13 EDW. I, Stat. 2, cc. 1–2 (1285).

66. Ibid. c. 3.

67. *Statute of Westminster the Second*, 13 EDW. I, Stat. 1, c. 50. Original in Latin.

68. *Statutum Wynton*, 13 EDW. I, Stat. 2, c. 3.

69. Ibid., c. 1.

70. *Articuli super Cartas*, 28 EDW. I, cc. 1 & 17 (1300); *De Tallagio non Concedendo*, 34 EDW. I, c. 6 (1306); see also, for example, 7 EDW. I, Stat. 1 (1278): "We command you, that ye cause these Things to be read afore you in the said Bench, and there to be enrolled." Originals in Latin.

71. Illich, *Vineyard*, 54.

72. See in particular Robert Moles, *Definition and Rule in Legal Theory* (Oxford: Blackwell, 1987), which attempts a resurrection of the work of John Austin, especially from Hart's interpretation of him in Hart, *Concept of Law*, chaps. 2–4.

73. Hart, *Concept of Law*, esp., 90–93; Oliver Wendell Holmes, "The Path of the Law," *Harvard Law Review* 10 (1897): 457; Hans Kelsen, *General Theory of Law and State*, trans. Anders Wedberg (New York: Russell & Russell, 1961). See also the discussion of Austin in Roger Cotterrell, *The Politics of Jurisprudence* (London: Butterworths, 1989), 59–67.

74. John Finnis, *Natural Law and Natural Rights* (Oxford: Clarendon Press, 1980), 34–125; see also Michael Moore, "A Natural Law Theory of Interpretation," *Southern California Law Review* 58 (1985): 277.

75. Finnis (*Natural Law*, 319) tries to subvert this implication, arguing that the obligation to obey the law is itself a "relatively weighty" moral obligation.

> Such an ambitious attempt as the law's can only succeed in creating and maintaining order, and a fair order, inasmuch as individuals drastically restrict the occasions on which they trade off their legal obligations against their . . . conceptions of social good.

At best we can say, however, that this argument stems from Finnis's own desire to safeguard the "Rule of Law" (quaintly capitalized) and his assumption that the legal system basically does nothing more contentious than solve "communities' co-ordination problems"—such as which side of the road to drive on. This complacency is reflected in his assumption that in "normal times . . . the legal system is by and large just" (ibid., 270–74, 357). Even in his own terms, however, the mere existence of the legal system cannot deny us our freedom to examine whether the laws under which we live are "by and large just," for the "relatively weighty" moral obligation he proposes is dependent upon that premise. To this extent and arguably far beyond it, a theory of natural law expects citizens to inquire into not only what the law is but what justifications support it.

76. Hart, *Concept of Law*, 99–120.

77. Raz, *Authority of Law*.

78. Ibid., 150–53, 233, and see generally 233–61. Certainly, Raz does attempt to place a further limit on this argument. He argues that:

> No blind obedience to authority is here implied. . . . This brings into play the dependent reasons, for only if the authority's compliance with them is likely to be better than that of its subjects is its claim to legitimacy justified. (299)

The extent of this caveat is unclear. If we are to believe the statements of lawmakers, they are invariably in a better position than the rest of us to weigh up conflicting arguments concerning legal questions. In practice, however, one would have cause to doubt whether this is in fact the case. Moreover, Raz also insists that "all authoritative directives should be based, among other factors, on reasons which apply to the subjects of those directives" (ibid.). Again, it does not take more than a wholesome and average cynicism to argue that many laws have been passed where the actual reasons for enactment have not borne much relation to the purported reasons put forward to justify them. Are we to investigate the machinations behind every bill and act before pronouncing upon its authority? This opens up the possibility of a kind of Kantian approach in which not the justice of the law itself but the motivations of the lawmaker would be decisive. It is doubtful whether this was Raz's intent.

79. 13 EDW. I, Stat. 1, cc. 1, 3, 9 (1285) (original in Latin). Similarly but less judgmentally, several provisions simply present the law "hitherto": "hitherto it hath been used in the Realm," "by the law and custom of the Realm hitherto," etc. (ibid., cc. 5, 6, and see also cc. 9 and 14). For another example, see *Quia Emptores*, 18 EDW. I (1290).

80. 13 EDW. I, Stat. 1, as in cc. 7, 10, 18, 19, 23 (thrice), 24, 26, 28–30, 40, 45–47.

81. Much the same argument is made by Plucknett in evaluating judicial interpretation of both the common law and statutes in the reigns of the first three Edwards; judges' willingness to ignore or modify statutes also reflected an assumption that the enacted law was subject to reason and the *ius naturale:* Plucknett, *Statutes, passim,* and esp. 25, 49–81; see also the preface (by H. D. Hazeltine), xxiii.

82. 36 EDW. III (1362).

83. 1 RIC. II (1377) is typical and by no means the first of this kind:

Know thou, that to the Honour of God and Reverence of Holy Church, for to nourish Peace, Unity, and Concord in all the parts within our Realm of England ... with the Assent of the Prelates, Dukes, Earls, and Barons of this our Realm, the Instance and especial Request of the Commons of our Realm aforesaid, assembled, our Parliament ...

84. 9 HEN. IV (1407).

85. 1 RIC. III, c. 2 (1483).

86. 1 EDW. IV, c. 1 (1461).

87. Ibid., c. 1 (xvii), (xii), (xxii), (xxiv). *Statutes at Large* refers to 3 EDW. IV, c. 2 (1263) as the first statute to use the word "act" in its title, but this title and others of this period were added during the reign of Henry VIII, by which time the use of the word "act" to describe a chapter of a statute was indeed conventional. Although less immediately apparent, 1 EDW. IV, c. 1, is an earlier and genuine reference to "act" in this sense.

It is not the earliest reference: 29 HEN. VI, c. 2 (1450), and 33 HEN. VI, c. 2 (1454), both say "this Act"; but 1 EDW. IV, c. 1, uses the phrase more clearly and frequently. In particular, while the introductory portion of these earlier statutes declare that "Our Sovereign Lord King ... hath ordained and established divers *Ordinances and Statutes,*" the 1461 statute uses the phrase *"acts and ordinances"* (italics added). This is the significant change.

88. *The Oxford Encyclopedic English Dictionary,* s.v. "Act."

89. See Hans-Georg Gadamer, "On the Contribution of Poetry to the Search for Truth," in *The Relevance of the Beautiful and Other Essays,* trans. N. Walker (Cambridge: Cambridge University Press, 1986), 110.

90. The first statute not to have a form of introduction was 7 HEN. VII

(1491), but this was exceptional, because it was a plague year. In 1492 the introduction reappears and remains until 1509.

91. Illich, *Vineyard*, 103. For more on the changing layout of twelfth-century texts, see 97–105.

92. While the argument as to the meaning of the changing arrangement of statutes and Acts holds, it must be noted that there is some evidence that in the earlier period, chapters were sometimes in fact called statutes themselves—the last chapter of the *Statute of Westminster the Second* is one example, referring to "omnia predicta statuta." Inconsistency of terminology is hardly surprising, this time, but it is submitted that the conceptual and structural points I am making as to the way in which the organizing principles of legislation changed is not undermined. See Plucknett, *Statutes*, 11–12.

93. Harrison, *Music in Medieval Britain*, 236–40.

94. Interestingly, English composers used these harmonies significantly earlier than their European counterparts.

95. The "faburden" (faux Bourdon), basically an ornamented part in parallel sixths, became an almost routine aspect of three-part writing in fifteenth-century England. It was one of the fundamental techniques of musical education of the time: Harrison, *Music in Medieval Britain*, 247–49; Lefferts, *Motet*, 90.

96. See for example 3 EDW. IV, cc. 1–5; 4. EDW. IV, cc. 1–10; 7 EDW. IV, cc. 1–3; 8 EDW. IV, cc. 1–2. In these years, typical of the years before and after, over 80 percent of the Acts fall into this character. These are certainly not the first Acts dealing with such matters: see, for example, *Assisa Panis et Cervisiæ*, 51 HEN. III, Stat. 1 (1266), or the *Statute of Money*, 20 EDW. I, Stat. 4 (1291). But in comparison with the administrative nature of the preponderance of thirteenth-century statutes, there is a different emphasis here.

97. 36 EDW. III, Stat. 1, c. 15 (1362); see Pollock and Maitland, *History of English Law*, 85–86. See also Graham, "'Our Tong Maternall,'" 12.

98. See Ian Turnbull, "Clear Legislative Drafting: New Approaches in Australia," *Statute Law Review* 11 (1991): 161; David Murphy, "Plain English: Principles and Practice," paper presented at the Conference on Legislative Drafting, Canberra, 1992. It is ironic that this trend among drafters nonetheless remains arcane and customary rather than written down and defined.

99. As in 1 HEN. VII, c. 1 (1485). The original of this is in English, as are all statutes quoted in the text from now on.

100. Although some argue that the use of declaratory or hortatory text in legislation, of which the preamble is one species, is currently experiencing a rejuvenation: see Vernon Palmer, "The Style of Legislation in the United States: Narrative Norms and Constraining Norms," *American Journal of Comparative Law* (1994): 15.

101. 14 & 15 HEN. VIII, c. 5 (1522); see also 3 HEN. VIII, cc. 11 & 14 (1511).

102. 4 HEN. VIII, c. 7 (1512) (refers to 19 HEN. VII, c. 6 [1503]); a similar approach in a different circumstance is taken in the case of Richard Strode,

4 HEN. VIII, c. 8 (1512); see also the petition permitting the marriage of the six clerks of the High Court of Chancery, 14 & 15 HEN. VIII, c. 8 (1522).

103. 20 HEN. III, c. 9 (1235).

104. See Raz, *Authority.*

105. Goodrich, "Literacy," 428, contends that statutes were sacred icons, symbols of authority, and not practical documents in the period after the Norman conquest. But I have argued in this chapter that, in relation to statutes anyway, this is not so. The power of the statute as icon arises along with normativity and not prior to it.

106. Thus see the distinction made by William Blackstone between statute law, *lex scripta,* and the common law, *lex non scripta* (*Commentaries on the Laws of England* [Chicago: University of Chicago Press, 1979], 63).

107. 11 HEN. VII, c. 4 (1495). Of the twenty-seven chapters of this statute, fourteen establish offenses for which fifteen penalties are detailed. Only in two cases, cc. 11 and 19, is no penalty set, although the penalty for the infringement of c. 7, concerning riots, is said to be "such a sum of money as shall seem meet."

108. Illich, *Vineyard,* 54.

109. 27 HEN. VI (1449).

110. 28 HEN. VI (1450), 1 HEN. VII (1485–86).

111. 22 EDW. IV, c. 7 (1483), 1 HEN. VII, c. 7 (1485–86).

112. 11 HEN. VII, c. 12 (1495).

113. 11 HEN. VII, cc. 4 (iv), 12, 14, 15 (1495). "Be it therefore enacted, ordained, and established" was the standard form from 19 HEN. VII (1503); 14 & 15 HEN. VIII, c. 2 (1523).

114. Harrison, *Music in Medieval Britain,* 257–63.

115. Ibid., 261–63; Lefferts, *Motet,* 15; Wilson, *Music of the Middle Ages,* 284.

116. See Grout, *History of Western Music,* 182–221.

117. 10 EDW. III, Stat. 3 (1336); see Plucknett, *Statutes,* 164–67.

118. Levenson, *Measure for Measure,* 68–69.

REQUIEM

1. W. A. Mozart, *Requiem Mass,* K. 626 (1791), bars 1–8.

2. There are a number of extant completions which flesh out those movements Mozart only sketched and add in some cases a number of other sections, such as the Sanctus and Benedictus. By far the most commonly performed of these reconstructions is that of Süssmayr.

3. See the discussion of Legendre in Peter Goodrich, *Languages of Law: From Logics of Memory to Nomadic Masks* (London: Weidenfeld & Nicholson, 1990), 295.

4. Ernest Weinrib, "The Jurisprudence of Legal Formalism," *Harvard Journal of Law and Public Policy* 16 (1993): 583; Stephen Perry, "Professor Weinrib's Formalism: The Not-So-Empty Sepulchre," *Harvard Journal of Law and Public Policy* 16 (1993): 597.

5. See Thomas C. Grey, *The Case of Wallace Stevens: Law and the Practice of Poetry* (Cambridge, Mass.: Harvard University Press, 1991), 90–96.

6. Oliver Wendell Holmes, "The Path of the Law," *Harvard Law Review* 10 (1897): 457, 466. But as he continues, "certainty generally is illusion, and repose is not the destiny of men."

7. Emily Martin, *The Woman in the Body: A Cultural Analysis of Reproduction* (Boston: Beacon Press, 1987), 171–72.

8. Lord McCluskey, *Law, Justice, and Democracy: The Reith Lectures* (London: Sweet & Maxwell, 1986), 2.

9. H. L. A. Hart, *The Concept of Law* (Oxford: Clarendon Press, 1961).

10. *Prohibitions del Roy,* 12 Co. Rep. 63 (1607).

11. See Karl Llewellyn, *Jurisprudence: Realism in Theory and Practice* (Chicago: University of Chicago Press, 1962); idem, "Some Realism about Realism," *Harvard Law Review* 44 (1944): 1222; Lon Fuller, "Positivism and Fidelity to Law—A Reply to Professor Hart," *Harvard Law Review* 71 (1958): 630; idem, *The Morality of Law* (New Haven: Yale University Press, 1969); Stanley Fish, "Dennis Martinez and the Use of Theory," *Yale Law Journal* 96 (1987): 1773; idem, *Doing What Comes Naturally: Change, Rhetoric, and the Practice of Theory in Literary and Legal Studies* (Durham, N.C.: Duke University Press, 1989); Ronald Dworkin, "Hard Cases," *Harvard Law Review* 88 (1975): 105; idem, *Law's Empire* (Cambridge, Mass.: Belknap Press, 1986); idem, "Law as Interpretation," *Texas Law Review* 60 (1982): 527.

12. In a vast literature, see for example "A Bibliography of Critical Legal Studies," *Yale Law Journal* 94 (1984): 461; Peter Fitzgerald and Allan Hunt, "Critical Legal Studies: An Introduction," *Journal of Law and Society* 14 (1987): 5; Allan Hutchinson and Patrick Monahan, "Law, Politics, and Critical Legal Studies," *Stanford Law Review* 36 (1984): 199; Allan Hutchinson, ed., *Critical Legal Studies* (Totowa, N.J.: Rowman & Littlefield, 1989); Mark Kelman, "Trashing," *Stanford Law Review* 36 (1984): 293; idem, *A Guide to Critical Legal Studies* (Cambridge, Mass.: Harvard University Press, 1987); Duncan Kennedy, "Legal Formality," *Journal of Legal Studies* 2 (1973): 351; Frances Olsen, "The Family and the Market: A Study of Ideology and Legal Reform," *Harvard Law Review* 96 (1983): 1497; Joseph Singer, "The Player and the Cards: Nihilism and Legal Theory," *Yale Law Journal* 94 (1984): 1; Mark Tushnet, *Red, White, and Blue* (Cambridge, Mass.: Harvard University Press, 1988); idem, "The Critical Legal Studies Movement," *Stanford Law Review* 36 (1984): 623; Duncan Kennedy, "Form and Substance in Private Law Adjudication," *Harvard Law Review* 89 (1976): 1685; idem, "The Structure of Blackstone's Commentaries," *Buffalo Law Review* 28 (1979): 205; Roberto Mangabeira Unger, *Knowledge and Politics* (New York: Free Press, 1975).

13. See esp. Kelman, *Guide to Critical Legal Studies,* 15–63.

14. Thus see Hart, *Concept of Law;* Philippe Nonet, "What Is Positive Law?" *Yale Law Journal* 100 (1990): 667; and see generally Roger Cotterrell, *The Politics of Jurisprudence* (London: Butterworths, 1989).

15. Jacques Derrida, "Force of Law: The Mystical Foundation of Author-

ity," *Cardozo Law Review* 11 (1990): 919, 1007; see also 927, 937, 993, 995 for similiar demonstrations of a naïve legal centralism. To treat this "force of law" as fundamentally external and violent leads one reluctantly to think that, here at least, Derrida would gain from reading Hart on the oughtness of law.

16. James Boyd White, "The Reading of Precedent," in *Justice as Translation* (Chicago: University of Chicago Press, 1990), 160–75.

17. Ibid., 246–47.

18. See Dennis Klinck, "'This Other Eden': Lord Denning's Pastoral Vision," *Oxford Journal of Legal Studies* 14 (1994): 25, whose discussion includes, for example, *New Windsor Corporation v. Mellor*, [1975] 1 Ch 380 ("Today we look back far in time. To a town or village green ... "); *Miller v. Jackson*, [1977] 1 QB 976 ("In summertime village cricket is the delight of everyone ... "); *Hinz v. Berry*, [1970] 2 QB 40 ("It was bluebell time in Kent ... ").

19. Thus see Lord Denning, *The Family Story*; and constant reference in case after case to "a lovely village," "natural beauty," "prettiest [village]," "pleasing villages," "the lovely Cotswold country": all discussed in Klinck, "'This Other Eden,'" 29–31.

20. *Hinz v. Berry*, [1970] 2 QB 40.

21. Klinck, "'This Other Eden,'" 335–60.

22. Friedrich Nietzsche, quoted in Klinck, "'This Other Eden,'" 336.

23. Ibid., 342–43; see also Hans-Georg Gadamer, *The Relevance of the Beautiful and Other Essays*, trans. N. Walker (Cambridge: Cambridge University Press, 1986); Paul Ricoeur, *The Rule of Metaphor: Multi-disciplinary Studies of the Creation of Meaning in Language*, trans. Robert Czerny (Toronto: University of Toronto Press, 1977).

24. Thus see, for example, Allan Hutchinson, *Dwelling on the Threshold: Critical Essays in Modern Legal Thought* (Toronto: Caswell, 1988); Kelman, "Trashing"; Tushnet, *Red, White, and Blue*. See in particular the neo-Marxist analysis of common-law developments in American law, in Morton Horwitz, *The Transformation of American Law, 1780–1860* (Cambridge, Mass.: Harvard University Press, 1977); idem, *The Transformation of American Law, 1870–1960: The Crisis in Legal Orthodoxy* (New York: Oxford University Press, 1992).

25. Dworkin, *Law's Empire*, 111. He makes a similiar response later, when he suggests that CLS simply "want[s] to show law in its worst rather than its best light" (275). See the same defensive posturing in, for example, A. Ruvin, "Does Law Matter? A Judge's Response to the Critical Legal Studies Movement," *Journal of Legal Education* 37 (1987): 307; Louis Schwartz, "Darkest CLS-Land," *Stanford Law Review* 36 (1984): 413. As Kelman (*Guide to Critical Legal Studies*, 355) puts it so succinctly, "one can rely on Louis Schwartz to express what might otherwise be thought to be the 'straw man's' position."

26. Peter Goodrich, "*Jani anglorum*: Signs, Symptoms, Slips, and Interpretation in Law," in Costas Douzinas, Peter Goodrich, and Yifat Hachamovitch, eds., *Politics, Postmodernity, and Critical Legal Studies: The Legality of the Contingent* (London: Routledge, 1994), 107.

27. Jacques Derrida, *Positions*, trans. Alan Bass (Chicago: University of Chicago Press, 1981); Peggy Kamuf, ed., *A Derrida Reader: Between the Blinds* (New York: Columbia University Pres, 1991); Christopher Norris, *Deconstruction: Theory and Practice* (London: Routledge, 1982). For particularly useful discussions of the work which has been done on applying deconstructionist theory to legal issues, see Peter Fitzpatrick, ed., *Dangerous Supplements: Resistance and Renewal in Jurisprudence* (London: Pluto Press, 1991); Drucilla Cornell, Mark Rosenfeld, and David Gray Carlson, eds., *Deconstruction and the Possibility of Justice* (New York: Routledge, 1992); "Roundtable—The Call to the Ethical: Deconstruction, Justice, and the Ethical Relationship," *Cardozo Law Review* 13 (1992): 1219; Jack M. Balkin, "Deconstructive Practice and Legal Theory," *Yale Law Journal* 96 (1987): 743; Matthew H. Kramer, *Legal Theory, Political Theory, and Deconstruction* (Bloomington: Indiana University Press, 1991), 5–36.

28. *Furman v. Georgia* (1972), 408 U.S. 238, for example, 250 per Justice Douglas, 310 per Justice Stewart. It was the rather magical transformation of a Fourteenth Amendment issue, under which the death penalty had been upheld the previous year in *McGautha v. California* (1971), 402 U.S. 183, into an Eighth Amendment issue, which accounts for the Court's turnaround.

29. Despite the somewhat triumphalist legalism affected in some quarters: see for example Michael Meltsner, *Cruel and Unusual* (New York: Random House, 1973).

30. See *Gregg v. Georgia* (1976), 428 U.S. 153; *Jurek v. Texas* (1976), 428 U.S. 262; *Proffitt v. Florida* (1976), 428 U.S. 242; *Woodson v. North Carolina* (1976), 428 U.S. 280.

31. *Gardner v. Florida* (1977), 430 U.S. 349, 358, is oft-quoted.

32. S. H. Verhovek, "With Practice, Texas Is the Execution Leader," *New York Times*, 5 September 1993, p. E6.

33. Stephen Nathanson, *An Eye for An Eye?: The Morality of Punishing by Death* (Totowa, N.J.: Rowman & Littlefield, 1987), ix–x. Italics added.

34. Ibid., 86–87, 109.

35. The classic exposition of this principle in *Woolmington v. D.P.P.*, [1956] A.C., with its reflections on the "golden thread of English justice," are clear evidence of the emotional and rhetorical basis of the concept.

36. See for example Nathanson, *Eye for an Eye*, 16. This would hardly seem to need stressing, but writers in support of capital punishment often consume considerable space arguing that punishments (of any sort) do deter (to some degree): see for example Walter Berns, *For Capital Punishment: Crime and the Morality of Punishment* (New York: Basic Books, 1979), 104–24, 143–45. It is thus important to emphasize that this is both undeniable and irrelevant.

37. Thorsten Sellin, *The Death Penalty* (Philadelphia: American Law Institute, 1959), 79–94; and the articles collected in Hugo Bedau, ed., *The Death Penalty in America* (Chicago: Aldine Publishing, 1964), 258ff.; see in particular Sellin, *Death Penalty*, 274–84 ("Death and Imprisonment as Deterrents to Murder"), and 284–301 ("Does the Death Penalty Protect Municipal Police?").

38. Thucydides, *The Peloponnesian War,* trans. Rex Warner (Harmondsworth: Penguin, 1972), 220–21.

39. Hugo Bedau, *Death Is Different* (Boston: Northeastern University Press, 1987), 27–28; Nathanson, *Eye for an Eye,* 122–29.

40. Ernest Van den Haag and John Conrad, *The Death Penalty: A Debate* (New York: Plenum Press, 1983), 116.

41. Nathanson, *Eye for an Eye,* 34–36.

42. Van den Haag and Conrad, *Death Penalty,* 129; see also many similar comments, for example, 190, 215–16, 300.

43. Ibid., 300.

44. Berns, *For Capital Punishment,* 102–3.

45. Ibid., 103. There is another complication here, which is that the reference to Jarrette evokes, without explicitly stating, the "specific deterrence" benefits of capital punishment; that is, the argument that we should kill murderers to prevent *them* from killing again. Undoubtedly, capital punishment is 100 percent effective from that point of view. Nevertheless, I leave that issue aside for two reasons. First, although the fact that Jarrette had already been convicted for murder adds to the horror of the story, Berns never actually defends the specific deterrence thesis. Second, the evidence is overwhelming that murderers rarely kill again and indeed have a below average recidivism rate. The number of murders prevented through the specific-deterrence effects of executing convicted murderers is generally agreed not to be significant: see Bedau, ed., *Death Penalty in America,* 399.

46. Berns, *For Capital Punishment,* 137.

47. Exodus 21:23–25.

48. Bedau, ed., *Death Penalty in America,* 61; Nathanson, *Eye for an Eye,* 73–76.

49. Jacques Derrida, "Signature Event Context," in *Margins of Philosophy,* trans. Alan Bass (Chicago: University of Chicago Press, 1982), 82–111, 107.

50. See Derrida, "Force of Law," 949 et seq., 1023.

51. See *Furman v. Georgia* (1972), 408 U.S. 238; *Gregg v. Georgia* (1976), 428 U.S. 153; *McGautha v. California* (1971), 402 U.S. 183. For a useful general summary of the different positions of the justices, see Margaret Radin, "The Jurisprudence of Death: Evolving Standards for the Cruel and Unusual Punishment Clause," *University of Pennsylvania Law Review* 126 (1978): 989, 1003–1011.

52. *Furman v. Georgia* (1972), 408 U.S. 238, 423 per Justice Powell, quoting *In re Kemmler v.* (1888), 136 U.S. 436 at 447; quoting *Trop v. Dulles* (1958), 356 U.S. 86 at 99. See also 468 per Justice Rehnquist. The position of Justice Blackmun is even firmer: see *Furman v. Georgia* (1972), 408 U.S. 238, 407–14:

> The several concurring opinions acknowledge, as they must, that until today capital punishment was accepted and assumed as not unconstitutional *per se.* . . . Suddenly, however, the course of decision is now the opposite way. . . . The Court has just decided that it is time to strike down the death penalty. . . . I fear the Court has overstepped. It has sought and has achieved an end.

53. *Furman v. Georgia* (1972), 408 U.S. 238, 468, 465; *Woodson v. North Carolina* (1976), 428 U.S. 280, 313 per Justice Rehnquist.

54. *Furman v. Georgia* (1972), 408 U.S. 238, 405 per Justice Blackmun.

55. Ibid., 414 per Justice Blackmun.

56. See J. Hillis Miller, *Versions of Pygmalion* (Cambridge, Mass.: Harvard University Press, 1990), 1–3.

57. *Furman v. Georgia* (1972), 408 U.S. 238, 253 per Justice Douglas; 274 per Justice Brennan.

58. *Georgia Criminal Code,* §27–2534.1(b); *Gregg v. Georgia* (1976), 428 U.S. 153.

59. See Richard Rosen, "The 'Especially Heinous' Aggravating Circumstance in Capital Cases: The Standardless Standard," *North Carolina Law Review* (1986): 941; Shelley Clarke, "Note: A Reasoned Moral Response: Rethinking Texas's Capital Sentencing after *Penry v. Lynagh*," *Texas Law Review* 68 (1990): 407, 428–29; see the Court's decisions striking down these provisions in *Maynard v. Cartwright* (1988), 486 U.S. 356, and *Godfrey v. Georgia* (1980), 446 U.S. 420.

60. *Florida Statutes Annotated* §782.04 (1); *Proffitt v. Florida* (1976), 428 U.S. 242.

61. *Proffitt v. Florida* (1976), 428 U.S. 242, 260 per Justice White.

62. *Texas Penal Code,* Art. 1257 (b); *Jurek v. Texas* (1976), 428 U.S. 262. The other two "special issues" are largely devoid of meaningful content: see Clarke, "Note: A Reasoned Moral Response," 438–48.

63. *Barefoot v. Estelle, Director, Texas Dept. of Corrections* (1983), 463 U.S. 880, 920–21.

64. The Court's response to this problem of expert evidence was breathtaking in its superficiality: see for example ibid., 899–901. See also Peggy Davis, "Texas Capital Sentencing Procedures: The Role of the Jury and the Restraining Hand of the Expert," *Journal of Criminal Law and Criminology* 69 (1978): 300; George Dix, "Administration of the Texas Death Penalty Statutes: Constitutional Infirmities Related to the Prediction of Dangerousness," *Texas Law Review* 55 (1977): 1343; Charles Black, "Due Process for Death: *Jurek v. Texas* and Companion Cases," *Catholic University Law Review* (1976): 1.

65. *Jurek v. Texas* (1976), 428 U.S. 262, 279 per Justice White.

66. See *Adams v. State,* 577 SW 2d. 717; *Smith v. State,* 540 SW 2d. 693; *Felder v. State,* 564 SW 2d. 776; *Shippy v. State,* 556 SW 2d. 246: see the review of these cases in George Dix, "Appellate Review of the Decision to Impose Death," *Georgetown Law Journal* 68 (1979): 97, 143–49. He concludes, "Rather than openly acknowledge its apparent reliance on the offensiveness of the defendants' conduct the court tends to hide this reliance under the label of dangerousness" (149).

67. *Penry v. Lynagh* (1989), 109 S. Ct. 2934, 2952 per Justice O'Connor.

68. *Lockett v. Ohio* (1978), 438 U.S. 586, 604; see also *Eddings v. Oklahoma* (1982), 455 U.S. 105.

69. *Penry v. Lynagh* (1989), 492 U.S., 359–60 per Justice Scalia.

70. *Callins v. Collins* (1994), 114 S. Ct., 1127 per Justice Scalia.

71. Ibid., 295–96 per Justices Stewart, Powell, and Stevens.

72. *Callins v. Collins* (1994), 114 S. Ct., 1127 per Justice Blackmun (citations omitted).

73. Ibid.

74. Derrida, "Force of Law," 947; see generally, 947ff. For further on the "impossibility of justice," see Cornell, Rosenfeld, and Carlson, eds., *Deconstruction and the Possibility of Justice;* and especially chapters by Butler, Cornell, Keenan, and LaCapra therein. Dix, "Appellate Review," 160–61, makes a similar point with respect to the evident inability of appellate review of death-penalty decisions to supervise the discretion exercised at first instance.

75. *Gardner v. Florida,* 430 U.S. 349, 358.

76. *Georgia Criminal Code,* §27–2534.1(b)(7) and 2534.2; *Gregg v. Georgia* (1976), 428 U.S., 153

77. Dix, "Appellate Review," 111–13. Courts are frequently required to evaluate whether individual death sentences fall within a pattern of similar decisions in order to determine if the sentence in question has been imposed arbitrarily or capriciously. This creates another moment of indeterminacy, since the open-ended nature of what counts as "similar" allows any conceivable decision to be placed in an appropriate "category." Thus, reviewing the decision in *Blake v. State,* 239 Ga. 292, the Georgia Supreme Court concluded that dropping a small child from a bridge could be described as a "not-for-profit execution style murder" for which the death penalty had been imposed consistently: see Dix, "Appellate Review," 114.

78. *Blake v. State,* 239 Ga. 292; *State v. Dixon,* 283 So. 2d. 1, 9; *Spinkellink v. State* (1975), 313 So. 2d. 666, implicitly approved by the U.S. Supreme Court in *Proffitt v. Florida* (1976), 428 U.S. 242, 255–56, footnote 12. For a more careful examination of the jurisprudence of this section, see Dix, "Appellate Review," 107ff.

79. For two excellent studies of the reality of capital punishment in the United States, see Helen Prejean, *Dead Man Walking: An Eyewitness Account of the Death Penalty in the United States* (New York: Random House, 1993); Wendy Lesser, *Pictures at an Execution: An Inquiry into the Subject of Murder* (Cambridge, Mass.: Harvard University Press, 1993).

80. Part I of M. Foucault, *Discipline and Punish,* trans. A. M. Sheridan Smith (New York: Vintage Books, 1979), is a rich and disturbing account of the meanings and uses of torture in the anciens régimes of Europe.

81. Elaine Scarry, *The Body in Pain: The Making and Unmaking of the World* (New York: Oxford University Press, 1985). Further, see Herbert Kelman, "Violence without Moral Restraint: Reflections on the Dehumanization of Victims and Victimizers," *Journal of Social Issues* 29, no. 4 (1973): 25.

82. The literature on the historiography and sociology of death is fascinating and complex. See Philippe Ariès, *The Hour of Our Death,* trans. H. Weaver (New York: Oxford University Press, 1981), for a remarkable history of Western attitudes to death over the past thousand years: In particular I rely on

Ariès's contrast between "the tame death" and "the invisible death" (5ff., 559ff.). For more on the denial of death in Western culture, see Edward Becker, *The Denial of Death* (New York: Free Press, 1973); Margaret Somerville, "'The Song of Death': The Lyrics of Euthanasia," *Journal of Contemporary Health Law and Policy* 9 (1993): 801–74.

83. Thus the title of Prejean, *Dead Man Walking*.

84. Robert Johnson, *Condemned to Die: Life under Sentence of Death* (New York: Elsevier, 1981), 43–44.

85. "They realize, well, this person on death row, he's not getting out. They slowly cut you off.": ibid., 102.

86. Ibid., 52.

87. Ibid., 52; see also 50, 115.

88. Foucault, *Discipline and Punish;* see also John Baehre, "Origins of the Penitentiary System," *Ontario History* 69 (1977): 182.

89. See also Michael Kroll, "The Fraternity of Death," in Michael Radelet, ed., *Facing the Death Penalty: Essays on a Cruel and Unusual Punishment* (Philadelphia: Temple University Press, 1989).

90. In New York, the world's first legal electrocution took place in 1889: *In re Kemmler v.* (1888), 136 U.S. 436. Sing Sing had a green door as early as that, and there the New York *Herald Tribune* reported the death of Caryl Chessman in "the little green room" in 1960. In Louisiana, it is the death cell, in Alabama the electrocution chamber. In other states we find reference to the "chill green solitude of the gas chamber": John Laurence, *A History of Capital Punishment* (New York: Citadel Press, 1960), xxv–vi, 64. See also Prejean, *Dead Man Walking*.

91. From a war poem by Wilfrid Owen, in the "Dies irae," Benjamin Britten, *War Requiem*, op. 66 (1942).

92. Leviticus 16. Nonetheless, the Supreme Court held that exile was "cruel and unusual punishment" while capital punishment was not: *Trop v. Dulles* (1958), 356 U.S. 86; *Furman v. Georgia* (1972), 408 U.S. 238, 423 per Justice Powell, quoting *In re Kemmler v.* (1888), 136 U.S. 436 at 447; *McGautha v. California* (1971), 402 U.S. 183.

93. Stephen Gettinger quoted in Johnson, *Condemned to Die*, 1.

94. Stephen Levine, ed., *Death Row: An Affirmation of Life* (San Francisco: Glide Publications, 1972); Elizabeth Purdum and Anthony Paredes, "Rituals of Death" in Radelet, ed., *Facing the Death Penalty*, 139ff.

95. Van den Haag, *Death Penalty*, 115.

96. In the same way, to call someone a "drug addict" is a process of deviancy labeling by which a whole person is branded and limited by certain specific aspects of their behavior. For further on deviance labeling, see for example Paul Wilson and John Braithwaite, eds., *Two Faces of Deviance* (St. Lucia: University of Queensland Press, 1978); Joseph Gusfield, "On Legislating Morals: The Symbolic Process of Designating Deviance," *California Law Review* 56 (1968): 54; Howard Becker, *Outsiders: Studies in the Sociology of Deviance* (New York: Free Press, 1963).

97. Johnson, *Condemned to Die*, 23.

98. Caryl Chessman, extracted in ibid., 23–24.

99. Caryl Chessman, quoted in ibid, 23.

100. *McCleskey v. Kemp, Superintendent, Georgia Diagnostic and Classification Centre* (1987), 481 U.S. 279 at 309.

101. See Marvin Wolfgang and Marc Riedel, "Racial Discrimination, Rape, and the Death Penalty," in Bedau, ed., *Death Penalty in America*, 194–205; William Bowers and Glenn Pierce, "Arbitrariness and Discrimination under Post-*Furman* Capital Statutes," *Crime and Delinquency* (1980): 563. Bowers and Pierce assert categorically that "the probability that a difference [as to capital sentencing] of this magnitude . . . could have occurred by chance is so remote that it cannot be computed with available statistical programs. . . . The presence of differential treatment by race is unmistakable."

102. *Furman v. Georgia* (1972), 408 U.S. 238, 298; 250 per Justice Douglas; 293 per Justice Brennan; 309–10 per Justice Stewart. See also *Gregg v. Georgia* (1976), 428 U.S. 153, 222–26.

103. Foucault, *Discipline and Punish*, 1–5.

104. Arthur Koestler, *Reflections on Hanging* (London: Victor Gollancz, 1956), 14.

105. Hugo Bedau, "Background and Developments," in Bedau, ed., *Death Penalty in America*, 13.

106. In England executions took place at eight in the morning on the first Monday after the intervention of three Sundays since the signing of the writ. In New York, Thursdays at eleven in the evening was the normal time; in Louisiana, at midnight; this is typical of other American jurisdictions: Laurence, *History of Capital Punishment*, 27.

107. Steven Wilf, "Imagining Justice: Aesthetics and Public Executions in Late Eighteenth-Century England," *Yale Journal of Law and the Humanities* 5 (1993): 51, 53; see also the passages quoting Henry Fielding, 56–57, and William Paley, 75.

108. See David Cooper, *The Lesson of the Scaffold: The Public Execution Controversy in Victorian England* (Athens: Ohio University Press, 1974).

109. See Ariès, *Hour of Our Death*, Part IV; Cooper, *Lesson of the Scaffold*. See also Foucault, *Discipline and Punish*, 61–63. "In these executions . . . there was a whole aspect of carnival, in which the roles were inverted, the powerful mocked, and criminals transformed into heroes" (61). The popular festival culture of the lower orders was under threat more generally in Victorian England (and in America)—the making of a working class out of a peasantry was under way. See Blackwell, "Crime in the London District, 1828–1837," *Queen's Law Journal* 6 (1981): 528; Douglas Hay, Peter Linebaugh, and E. P. Thompson, eds., *Albion's Fatal Tree: Crime and Society in Eighteenth-Century England* (London: Allen Lane, 1977); Douglas Hay, "The Criminal Prosecution in England and Its Historians," *Modern Law Review* 47 (1984): 1; David R. Kelley, *Historians and the Law in Postrevolutionary France* (Princeton: Princeton University

Press, 1984); Randall McGowen, "The Body and Punishment in Eighteenth-Century England," *Journal of Modern History* 59 (1987): 651; E. P. Thompson, *The Making of the English Working Class* (Harmondsworth: Penguin, 1975).

110. Wilf, "Imagining Justice." Linebaugh has written of public execution as "a morality play," a suggestive metaphor not only in terms of the kinds of messages which were sought to be inscribed into these events but also in terms of the engagement and participation of the crowd in the unfolding spectacle: see Peter Linebaugh, "The Tyburn Riot against the Surgeons," in Hay, Linebaugh, and Thompson, eds., *Albion's Fatal Tree*, 65.

111. Foucault, *Discipline and Punish*.

112. Laurence, *History of Capital Punishment*, 42.

113. Recall Willie Francis, electrocuted but not killed in 1947. The heavy leather cap which covered his head made it virtually impossible for him to breathe. "Take it off. Let me breathe," he pleaded: *Francis v. Resweber, Sheriff, et al* (1947), 329 U.S. 459 at 480–81.

114. See for example Laurence, *History of Capital Punishment*, 68.

115. *Francis v. Resweber, Sheriff, et al* (1947), 329 U.S. 459, 460 per Justice Reed; Official Chaplain Maurice Rousseve, quoted, 481.

116. Ibid., 470 per Justice Frankfurter; 464 per Justice Reed.

117. The execution of Gee Jon took place on 8 February 1924: Bedau, "Background and Developments," in Bedau, ed., *Death Penalty in America*, 16.

118. Ibid., 17.

119. Ronald Reagan, master of euphemisms, put it this way (quoted in Prejean, *Dead Man Walking*, 216): "Being a former farmer and horse raiser, I know what it's like to try to eliminate an injured horse by shooting him. Now you call the veterinarian and the vet gives it a shot and the horse goes to sleep—that's it."

120. Ibid., 217–18.

121. Berns, *For Capital Punishment*, 25.

122. Johnson, *Condemned to Die*, 87.

123. Koestler, *Reflections on Hanging*, 139–40, and 18.

124. *Francis v. Resweber, Sheriff, et al* (1947), 329 U.S. 459; *Gregg v. Georgia* (1976), 428 U.S. 153.

125. See *Gregg v. Georgia* (1976), 428 U.S. 153, 182 per Justices Stewart, Powell, and Stevens; *Francis v. Resweber, Sheriff, et al.* (1947), 329 U.S. 459, 464 per Justice Reed, 470 per Justice Frankfurter, 476 per Justice Burton.

126. *Francis v. Resweber, Sheriff, et al.* (1947), 329 U.S. 459, 464 per Justice Reed.

127. Frequently, the question of worth is evaded by focusing instead on "acceptable" cases. The several case histories collected in Hugo Bedau's monumental *The Death Penalty in America* provide striking evidence of this, because, with few exceptions, these cases focus on the exceptional: on innocent men convicted, on "insane" people tried as if they were sane, on juvenile killers, and so on. In all these cases, the extenuating circumstances are addressed, not the

common humanity possessed by even the most ruthless killer. See also Michael Radelet, Hugo Bedau, and Constance Putnam, *In Spite of Innocence: Erroneous Convictions in Capital Cases* (Boston: Northeastern University Press, 1992).

128. See also the first-person accounts of life in the shadow of death contained in, for example, Johnson, *Condemned to Die,* and Levine, ed., *Death Row.*

129. Bedau, *Death Is Different,* 220. Neither is this the position only of those in favor of capital punishment. Bedau, too, emphasizes the fact of execution—"total activity smashing total passivity"—while expressing doubt about arguments that "waiting for it" constitutes a cruel and unusual punishment: see Bedau, ed., *Death Penalty in America,* 123–24, 168.

130. *Callins v. Collins* (1994), 114 S. Ct. 1127 per Justice Scalia.

131. Johnson, *Condemned to Die,* ix. For more on the distinction between pain and suffering, see Eric Cassell, *The Nature of Suffering and the Goals of Medicine* (New York: Oxford University Press, 1991).

132. Ariès, *Hour of Our Death.*

133. Caryl Chessman, quoted in Levine, ed., *Death Row,* 8.

134. *Callins v. Collins* (1994), 114 S. Ct. 1127 per Justice Blackmun.

135. Ibid., *passim.*

VARIATIONS ON A THEME

1. The many sets of variations on Paganini's theme provided me with a choice of models for the structure of this chapter. I finally settled on Sergei Rachmaninoff, *Rapsodie sur un thème de Paganini pour piano et orchestre,* op. 43 (1934). There were a number of reasons for this. Two in particular are worth mentioning. First, his use of a "precedent" variation before the first exposition of the theme seemed a good way of describing the structure of the first few pages of this chapter: a variation before I state my theme. Second, the famous inversion of Paganini's theme, the *Rapsodie* which is at the heart of his composition (Var. XVIII), provided an inspiration for one of the most important sections of this chapter, Var. VII, in which I discuss the idea of "inversion" in relation to metaphors and boundaries.

2. One may distinguish the "naturalness" of the theme and variations from those forms which were purely musical in origin, such as sonata or rondo form or the concerto. While these forms hardly survived the structural freedom of the nineteenth century and are, in the age of postmodern compositional techniques, rarely used in a recognizable fashion, the form of a theme and variations continues to provide a structural anchor to the most diverse compositional styles and intentions.

3. Johann Sebastian Bach, Chaconne in D minor from Partita No. 2, BWV 1004 (1720); Bach, *Goldberg Variations,* BWV 988 (1742). Of the symphonies of Ludwig van Beethoven, examples include the *Andante con moto* from Symphony No. 5 in C Minor, op. 67 (1809), and the *Allegretto* from Symphony No. 6 in F Major, op. 68 (1809). Significantly, the last three sonatas for solo piano, op. 109, 110, and 111 (1822–23), unparalleled in their depth and intensity,

are each centered on a theme and variations increasingly complex in nature. In fact, Beethoven's last word in the genre of a piano sonata, the final movement of the opus 111, is a theme and variations, mystical and expressive of an almost religious ecstasy.

For a survey of the development of variation form, and a detailed bibliography, see Stanley Sadie, ed., *The New Grove Dictionary of Music and Musicians,* vol. 19 (London: Macmillan, 1980), 536–56.

4. It is no exaggeration to say that the whole genre is built on the concept of a theme and variations: typically, the main theme is stated by the ensemble, and then a series of variations is developed, each variation demonstrating the capacities of a different instrument or performer, followed by a final variation-cum-recapitulation. The harmonic (nonmelodic) focus of jazz, and its special emphasis on extemporization, combine to make the form of a theme and variations particularly appropriate.

5. Paul Ricoeur, *The Rule of Metaphor: Multi-disciplinary Studies of the Creation of Meaning in Language,* trans. Robert Czerny (Toronto: University of Toronto Press, 1977); Hans-Georg Gadamer, *The Relevance of the Beautiful and Other Essays,* trans. N. Walker (Cambridge: Cambridge University Press, 1986).

6. For further on the distinction between procreation and creation, see Anton Schütz, "Sons of Writ, Sons of Wrath: Pierre Legendre's Critique of Rational Law-Giving," *Cardozo Law Review* 16 (1995): 979, 1015–17.

7. Niccolò Paganini, *Ventriquattro Capricci, Opera Terza (Dodici Capricci),* op. 1, no. 12 [XXIV] (1820); Johannes Brahms, *Variationen über ein Thema von Paganini, I und II,* op. 35 Heft 1 und 2 (1866) (there are fourteen numbered variations in each set, but the finale to each ought perhaps be counted another variation); Rachmaninoff, *Rapsodie sur un thème de Paganini pour piano et orchestre;* Robert Schumann, *Introduction and Variations on a Theme of Paganini* (1831); Franz Liszt, *Études d'exécution transcendante d'après Paganini,* op. 140, no. 6 (Theme and Variations) (1840); Witold Lutoslawski, *Wariacje na temat Paganiniego* (1941).

8. See Edward Shils, *Tradition* (Chicago: University of Chicago Press, 1981).

9. Janette Turner Hospital, *Borderline* (St. Lucia: Queensland University Press, 1985), 11.

10. J. Hillis Miller, *Versions of Pygmalion* (Cambridge, Mass.: Harvard University Press, 1990), 1.

11. Robert Samek, *The Meta-Phenomenon* (New York: Philosophical Library, 1981).

12. The absolute nature of the claim of aesthetic experience has been at the heart of both the force of its appeal and the fear it has generated: see Plato, *The Republic,* trans. D. Lee (London: Penguin, 1974); Immanuel Kant, *Critique of Judgment,* trans. W. Pluhar (Indianapolis: Hackett, 1987); Terry Eagleton, *The Ideology of the Aesthetic* (Oxford: Blackwell, 1990).

13. For example, Naomi Wolf, *The Beauty Myth* (New York: William Morrow, 1991); Edward Becker, *The Denial of Death* (New York: Free Press, 1973);

Philippe Ariès, *The Hour of Our Death,* trans. H. Weaver (New York: Oxford University Press, 1981).

14. Susan Sontag, *Illness as Metaphor/AIDS and Its Metaphors* (New York: Anchor Books, 1990), 83; see also Susan Faludi, *Backlash: The Undeclared War against Women* (London: Chatto & Windus, 1992); Tom Campbell and Charles Heginbotham, *Mental Illness: Prejudice, Discrimination, and the Law* (Aldershot, U.K.: Dartmouth, 1991); Richard Davenport-Hines, *Sex, Death, and Punishment* (London: Collins, 1990); Michel Foucault, *The Use of Pleasure,* vol. 2 of *The History of Sexuality,* trans. Robert Hurley (New York: Vintage Books, 1986).

15. *Ratté v. Booth* (1886), 11 O.R. 491; *W. Drysdale v. C.A. Dugas* (1895), 26 S.C.R. 20; and see *St. Helen's Smelting Co. v. William Tipping* (1865), 11 H.L.C. 642.

16. See Mary Douglas, *Purity and Danger* (London: Routledge & Kegan Paul, 1966); and see also the discussion of the meaning of bodily waste in Becker, *Denial of Death.* For further on the rhetoric of dirt, specifically in relation to racism, see Kendall Thomas, "Strange Fruit," in Toni Morrison, ed., *Race-ing Justice, En-gendering Power* (New York: Pantheon Books, 1992), 364–89; and more generally, Joel Kovel, *White Racism* (New York: Columbia University Press, 1984). On the psychological power of the idea of contagion in human societies, see Paul Rozin and Carol Nemeroff, "The Laws of Sympathetic Magic," in James W. Stigler, Richard Shweder, and Gilbert Herdt, eds., *Cultural Psychology* (Cambridge: Cambridge University Press, 1990), 207–24.

17. The distinction between a symbol and a sign is important here: in a symbol, A is conventionally taken to represent B (as an elephant represents the Republicans or the Red Flag communists); while in a sign, A necessarily points to the presence of B (as lightning points to thunder): Roberta Kevelson, *The Law as a System of Signs* (New York: Plenum Press, 1988).

18. Alan M. Kraut, *Silent Travelers: Germs, Genes, and the "Immigrant Menace"* (New York: Basic Books, 1994).

19. Haig Bosmajian, *The Language of Oppression* (Lanham, Md.: University Press of America, 1983), 41.

20. See, for extensive material, Anthony Yarwood and Michael Knowling, *Race Relations in Australia: A History* (North Ryde: Methuen, 1982); Eric Rolls, *Sojourners* (St. Lucia: University of Queensland Press, 1992); Ian McLaren, ed., *The Chinese in Victoria: Official Reports and Documents* (Melbourne: Red Rooster, 1985).

21. See for example *Chinese Restriction and Regulation Act, 1888* (N.S.W.), 52 Vict. No. 4, s. 2; N.S.W. Legislative Council, *Conference on the Chinese Question* (Sydney: Government Printer, 1888), 5–6. See also (S.A.) 51 & 52 Vict. No. 439; (Vic.) 52 Vict. No. 1005; (W.A.) 53 Vict. No. 3; (Qld.) 53 Vict. No. 22; *Immigration Act, 1901* (Cth.), No. 4 of 1901.

22. Yarwood and Knowling, *Race Relations,* 176 and 185.

23. See Manning Clark, *A History of Australia,* vol. 3, *God and Mammon* (Melbourne: Melbourne University Press, 1973).

24. *Bulletin* (Sydney), 12 January 1889, p. 6; 10 March 1888, p. 5.

25. "Humanity," *Sketches of Chinese Character* (Castlemaine: no publisher, 1878), 3–4.

26. *Bulletin*, 21 August 1886, pp. 11–14. See also Phil May, "The Mongolian Octopus-Grip on Australia," in ibid., pp. 12–13; and *Bulletin*, Supplement to 14 April 1888.

27. Sydney City and Suburban Sewage and Health Board, *Eleventh Progress Report*, in N.S.W. Legislative Assembly, *Votes and Proceedings 1875–765* (1875–76): 535–661.

28. Ibid., 568–69.

29. See also Kraut, *Silent Travelers*.

30. Archive Office of New South Wales (A.O.N.S.W.), Colonial Secretary Special Bundle, *Chinese 1888, 4/884.1*. See also the discussion in Rolls, *Sojourners*, 464–504; and my own discussion in Desmond Manderson, *From Mr. Sin to Mr. Big: A History of Australian Drug Laws* (Melbourne: Oxford University Press, 1993), 17–18.

31. Although the legislation in place at the time set a quota on the number of Chinese immigrants per ship which the *Afghan* certainly exceeded, the collector of customs refused to land any Chinese, including those who were British subjects (such as passengers from Hong Kong): *Influx of Chinese Restriction Act, 1881* (N.S.W.) 45 Vict. No. 11, ss. 4, 5, and 10 and cognate legislation.

32. *New South Wales Parliamentary Debates, Session 1887–88*, 51 & 52 Vict. 32 (1888): 4789 and 4793.

33. Sir Henry Parkes in ibid., 4787.

34. A.O.N.S.W., *Chinese 1888*.

35. *Bulletin*, 21 August 1886, p. 11; Phil May, "The Mongolian Octopus-Grip on Australia," in ibid., pp. 12–13.

36. Miller, *Versions of Pygmalion*, 1.

37. See N.S.W. Legislative Assembly, *Votes and Proceedings 1878*; William Young, *Report on the Conditions of the Chinese Population in Victoria* (Melbourne: Government Printer, 1868), in McLaren, ed., *Chinese in Victoria*, 33–58. By 1890, a Chinese population of about 21,500 in New South Wales and Victoria imported over 37,000 pounds of opium. In 1902, the Chinese population of Australia was 29,627; New South Wales imported 14,000 pounds of opium, Victoria 10,000, and Queensland, with over 10,000 Chinese working the canefields, 18,000 pounds. See Quong Tart, *A Plea for the Abolition of the Importation of Opium* (Sydney: ML 178.82 B2, 1887), 11, and Alfred McCoy, *Drug Traffic* (Sydney: Harper & Row, 1980), 72; N.S.W. Census of 1891 and Colonial Censuses of 1891 and 1901; *Commonwealth Parliamentary Debates 1905*, V Edw. VII, 26 (1905): 1773 and 1777.

38. Mrs. Winslow's Soothing Syrup, Bonnington's Irish Moss, Ayers' Sarsaparilla, and Godfrey's Cordial all contained opium, while Ayers' Cherry Pectoral was morphine based. Most other patent or proprietary medicines were alcohol based. See Royal Commission on Secret Drugs, Cures and Foods (Oc-

tavius Beale, Commissioner), *Report*, vol. 1 (Melbourne: Government Printer, 1907); Manderson, *From Mr. Sin*; McCoy, *Drug Traffic*, 52–70.

39. Dr. Scott in *Victorian Parliamentary Debates, Session 1893*, 73 (1893): 2640.

40. "The Chinese in Australia," in *Bulletin*, 21 August 1886, pp. 11–14.

41. See Manderson, *From Mr. Sin*, 20–58. *Sale and Use of Poisons Act of 1891* (Qld.), 55 Vict. No. 31, s. 13; *The Opium Act, 1895* (S.A.), 58 & 59 Vict. No. 644; *Opium Smoking Prohibition Act, 1905* (Vic.), 5 Edw. VII, No. 2003; *Police Offences Amendment Act, 1908* (N.S.W.), 8 Edw. VII, ch. 12, ss. 18–19. And see also its declaration as a prohibited import by *Commonwealth of Australia Gazette No. 64* (Cth.) 30 December 1905. In the United Kingdom, where there was never a large Chinese population, very different legal and medical approaches to the control of opiates developed: see Virginia Berridge, "War Conditions and Narcotics Control: The Passing of the Defence of the Realm Act Regulation 40B," *Journal of Social Policy* 7 (1978): 285.

42. Sydney City and Suburban Sewage and Health Board, *Report*, 568–69.

43. See in particular David Howes, "Olfaction and Transition," in David Howes, ed., *The Varieties of Sensory Experience: A Sourcebook in the Anthropology of the Senses* (Toronto: University of Toronto Press, 1991), 128–47; see also Alain Corbin, *The Foul and the Fragrant: Odor and the French Social Imagination* (Cambridge, Mass.: Harvard University Press, 1986); Constance Classen, David Howes, and Anthony Synnott, *Aroma: The Cultural History of Smell* (London: Routledge, 1994); David Howes, "Odour in the Court," *Border/Lines* (1989–90): 28.

44. I am sticking closely to my earlier discussion in Manderson, *From Mr. Sin*, 26–27, although there the discussion has a historical intent and not a theoretical one.

45. "Mr. and Mrs. Sin Fat," *Bulletin*, 14 April 1888, pp. 8–9.

46. Ibid., 8.

47. "The Chinese Invasion of Australia," *Bulletin*, 4 September 1886, p. 4. Further examples, from both popular literature and official reports, are to be found in Manderson, *From Mr. Sin*, 24–30.

48. *Bulletin*, 21 August 1886, pp. 11–14.

49. See in particular the evidence of a dozen European women who lived with the Chinese in Sydney's Chinatown, before the NSW Royal Commission on Alleged Chinese Gambling and Immorality, *Report and Evidence* (Sydney: Government Printer, 1892), 380–420.

50. In an extensive international literature, see David Musto, *The American Disease* (New Haven: Yale University Press, 1973); John Helmer, *Drugs and Minority Oppression* (New York: Seabury Press, 1975); Michael Green, "A History of Canadian Narcotics Control: The Formative Years," *University of Toronto Faculty Law Review* 37 (1979): 42; Neil Boyd, "The Origin of Canadian Narcotics Legislation," *Dalhousie Law Journal* 8 (1984): 102; Patricia J. Giffen et al., *Panic and Indifference: The Politics of Canada's Drug Laws — A*

Study in the Sociology of Law (Ottawa: Canadian Centre on Substance Abuse, 1991); Desmond Manderson, "The First Loss of Freedom: Early Opium Laws in Australia," *Australian Drug and Alcohol Review* 7 (1988): 439; idem, *From Mr. Sin;* Berridge, "War Conditions."

51. *Customs Act, 1901–1979* (Cwth.), s.235; *Drugs Poisons and Controlled Substances Act 1981–1983* (Vic.), s.71; *Controlled Substances Act, 1984* (S.A.), s.32(5); *Drug Misuse and Trafficking Act 1985* (N.S.W.), ss. 23(2), 24(2), 25(2) & 33; *Drugs Misuse Act Amendment Act 1990* (Qld.); *Drugs of Dependence Act 1989* (A.C.T.), s.164.

52. *Narcotic Control Act, R.S.C., 1985,* s. 4; Robert Solomon and S. J. Usprich, "Canada's Drug Laws," *Journal of Drug Issues* 21 (1991): 17.

53. Classen, Howes, and Synnott, *Aroma,* 203–5.

54. See Douglas, *Purity and Danger.*

55. Commonwealth and States of Australia (Commissioner: Justice E. S. Williams), *Australian Royal Commission of Inquiry into Drugs, Books A–F* (Canberra: A.G.P.S., 1980), Book A, plates following p. xx.

56. C. Pascal, "Intravenous Drug Abuse and AIDS Transmission: Federal and State Laws Regulating Needle Availability," in Robert J. Battjes and Roy W. Pickens, eds., *Needle Sharing among Intravenous Drug Abusers: National and International Perspectives,* NIDA Research Monograph 80 (Rockville, Md.: U.S. Department of Health and Human Services, 1988), 119–36.

57. *Harmelin v. Michigan* (1991), 115 L.Ed. 836, 874.

58. Jeremy Rayner, "Between Meaning and Event: An Historical Approach to Political Metaphors," *Political Science* 32 (1984): 537, 549.

59. Elaine Scarry, *The Body in Pain: The Making and Unmaking of the World* (New York: Oxford University Press, 1985), part II.

60. Rayner, "Between Meaning and Event," 549.

61. Sheigla B. Murphy, "Intravenous Drug Use and AIDS: Notes on the Social Economy of Needle Sharing," *Contemporary Drug Problems* 14 (1987): 373.

62. J. Bryan Page and Prince C. Smith, "Venous Envy: The Importance of Having Functional Veins," *Journal of Drug Issues* 20 (1990): 291, 300.

63. An informant quoted in Don Des Jarlais, Samuel Friedman, and David Strug, "AIDS and Needle-sharing within the IV-Drug Use Subculture," in Douglas Feldman and Thomas Johnson, eds., *The Social Dimensions of AIDS* (New York: Praeger, 1986), 115.

64. Murphy, "Intravenous Drug Use and AIDS"; Dan Waldorf et al., "Needle Sharing among Male Prostitutes," *Journal of Drug Issues* 20 (1990): 309; Harvey Feldman and Patrick Biernacki, "The Ethnography of Needle Sharing among Intravenous Drug Users," in Battjes and Pickens, eds., *Needle Sharing,* 28–39.

65. Murphy, "Intravenous Drug Use and AIDS," 383; Page and Smith, "Venous Envy," 300.

66. See Jon Howard and Philip Borges, "Needle Sharing in the Haight: Some

Social and Psychological Functions," in David E. Smith and George Gay, *It's So Good Don't Even Try It Once* (Englewood Cliffs, N.J.: Prentice-Hall, 1972). These generalizations remain largely true, but for a more contemporary and subtle analysis, see Avril Taylor, *Women Drug Users: An Ethnography of a Female Injecting Community* (Oxford: Oxford University Press, 1993).

67. Murphy, "Intravenous Drug Use and AIDS," 387.

68. Des Jarlais, Friedman, and Strug, "AIDS and Needle Sharing," 119.

69. Peter T. Furst, *Hallucinogens and Culture* (San Francisco: Chandler & Sharp, 1976), e.g., 194; Aldous Huxley, *The Doors of Perception* (London: Chatto & Windus, 1954).

70. Friedrich Nietzsche, *The Birth of Tragedy/The Case of Wagner*, trans. Walter Kaufmann (New York: Vintage Books, 1967).

71. Andrew Weil, *The Natural Mind* (Boston: Houghton Mifflin, 1972), 17–72.

72. See, for example, the compelling discussion of a peyote "hunt" in Furst, *Hallucinogens*, 133.

73. Rachmaninoff, *Rapsodie sur un thème de Paganini pour piano et orchestre*, Var. XVIII.

74. Carl Jung, *Man and His Symbols* (London: Aldus, 1964).

75. Michael Agar, *Ripping and Running: A Formal Ethnography of Urban Heroin Addicts* (New York: Seminar Press, 1973); Edward Preble and John Casey, "Taking Care of Business: The Heroin User's Life on the Streets," *International Journal of the Addictions* 4 (1969): 1–24.

76. Weil, *Natural Mind*, 72–97.

77. Preble and Casey, "Taking Care of Business."

78. See W. Pietz, "The Problem of the Fetish, Part I," *RES: Anthropology and Aesthetics* 9 (1985): 3, 10, discussed in Pamela E. Lee, "The Aesthetics of Value, the Fetish of Method," *RES: Anthropology and Aesthetics* 27 (1995): 133, 138.

79. Weil, *Natural Mind*, 194.

80. Pietz, "Problem of the Fetish"; Paul Wilson and John Braithwaite, eds., *Two Faces of Deviance* (St. Lucia: University of Queensland Press, 1978).

81. Stanton Peele, *The Meaning of Addiction: Compulsive Experience and Its Interpretation* (Lexington, Mass.: Lexington Books, 1985).

82. The phrase is often used to refer to the recurrence of the principal theme in every movement of Hector Berlioz, *Symphonie fantastique*, op. 14 (1845).

QUARTET FOR THE END OF TIME

1. Olivier Messiaen, liner notes to *Quartet for the End of Time* (1941): Erato, 1993, 12.

2. My own "Quartet for the End of Time" was also conceived and written in captivity. Any further resemblance to McGill University, Montréal, another

institution with 30,000 inmates set in an atrociously cold climate, is, of course, entirely coincidental.

3. "III. Abîme des oiseaux" and "VII. Fouillis d'arcs-en-ciel, pour l'ange qui annonce la fin du Temps," in Messaien, liner notes to *Quartet for the End of Time*.

4. Max Horkheimer and Theodor Adorno, *The Dialectic of Enlightenment* (New York: Continuum, 1982), 6; Arthur Koestler, *Darkness at Noon* (London: Hutchinson, 1973); the first chapter of Jürgen Habermas, *The Philosophical Discourse of Modernity*, trans. Frederick G. Lawrence (Cambridge, Mass.: MIT Press, 1991) presents very clearly the connections between "subject-centred reason," monism, and totalization.

5. I should note that François Ost, in characterizing the different sensibilities of time in law, connects postmodern law with what he calls "temporalité aléatoire." The aleatoric is a schematic form of modernism, for it represents a radical democratic notion of strict equality and a kind of systemization. The aleatoric is to be distinguished, therefore from the chaotic, which is the true temporality of postmodernism: see François Ost, "Les Multiples temps du droit," in J. J. Austray et al., eds., *Le Droit et le Futur* (Paris: Presses Universitaires de France, 1985), 115–53, 139.

6. See Richard Dawkins, *The Blind Watchmaker* (New York: Penguin, 1990); Ivars Peterson, *Newton's Clock: Chaos in the Solar System* (New York: W. H. Freeman, 1993).

7. See Jacques Attali, *Histoire du temps* (Paris: Presses Universitaires de France, 1982); Sebastian Grazias, *Of Time, Work, and Leisure* (New York: Twentieth Century Fund, 1962); John Riley, "The Hours of the Georgian Day," *History Today* 24 (1974): 307; E. P. Thompson, "Time, Work-Discipline, and Industrial Capitalism," *Past and Present* 38 (1967): 56; Stephen Toumlin and John Goodfield, *The Discovery of Time* (London: Hutchinson, 1965); Norbert Elias, *Time: An Essay*, trans. Edmund Jephcott (Oxford: Basil Blackwell, 1992).

8. See, in general, Michel Foucault, *The Order of Things: An Archaeology of the Human Sciences* (New York: Vintage Books, 1973).

9. Elias, *Time*, 45.

10. Boaventura de Sousa Santos, *Toward a New Common Sense: Law, Science, and Politics in the Paradigmatic Transition* (London: Routledge, 1995), xii, 400. See also similar reflections in Peter Fitzpatrick, *The Mythology of Modern Law* (London: Routledge, 1992), 93.

11. Elias, *Time*, 99–100.

12. See Michael Polanyi, *The Logic of Liberty: Reflections and Rejoinders* (London: Routledge, 1951), for a discussion of polycentricity in analysis.

13. After I had written several drafts of this chapter, I was astonished to discover remarkably similar arguments in Elias's *Time*. His ideas have helped me clarify the relevance of the "fifth dimension."

14. An object actually throws a three-dimensional shadow, although we observe it in only two dimensions. There is an easy test of this proposition: if

you hold an object between your hand and the sun, the object casts a shadow upon your hand no matter where you put it. The shadow thus exists at all depths, although we perceive it only when it strikes a surface. When we can see a shadow in all three dimensions, we call it a hologram.

15. Michel Foucault, *The Archaeology of Knowledge*, trans. A. M. Sheridan Smith (New York: Pantheon Books, 1972); idem, *Order of Things*.

16. Messaien, liner notes to *Quartet for the End of Time*, 14.

17. Roderick A. Macdonald, "Critical Legal Pluralism as a Construction of Normativity and the Emergence of Law" (paper prepared for Law and the Determinants of Social Order Programme, Canadian Institute for Advanced Research, Montréal, Que., 1994).

18. I am speaking here of legal theory as embodying particular conceptions of space rather than of how legal systems construct and organize particular spaces. It is the understanding of law as space rather than its application in, of, or to space that concerns me: for this, see the developing literature of "law and geography" discussed in Wes Pue, "Wrestling with Law: (Geographical) Specificity vs. (Legal) Abstraction," *Urban Geography* 11 (1990): 566, 576. Of this, the finest work is Nicholas K. Blomley, *Law, Space, and the Geographies of Power* (New York: Guilford Press, 1994). See also Joel Bakan and Nicholas K. Blomley, "Spatial Boundaries, Legal Categories, and the Judicial Mapping of the Worker," *Environment and Planning*, special issue (1991); Nicholas K. Blomley and G. L. Clark, "Law, Theory, and Geography," *Urban Geography* 11 (1990): 433; Paul Carter, *The Road to Botany Bay: Landscape and History* (New York: Alfred Knopf, 1988); Kim Economides, Mark Blacksell, and Charles Watkins, "The Spatial Analysis of Legal Systems: Towards a Geography of Law?" *Journal of Law and Society* 13 (1986): 161.

19. Saul Levinson and Jack M. Balkin, "Law, Music, and Other Performing Arts," *University of Pennsylvania Law Review* 139 (1991): 1597–1658.

20. Ibid., 1632–35; Eric Hobsbawm, "Introduction," in Eric Hobsbawm and T. Ranger, eds., *The Invention of Tradition* (Cambridge: Cambridge University Press, 1983).

21. See Edward Shils, *Tradition* (Chicago: University of Chicago Press, 1981); and see also Martin Krygier, "Law as Tradition," *Journal of Law and Philosophy* 5 (1986): 237; Jack M. Balkin, "Tradition, Betrayal, and the Politics of Deconstruction," *Cardozo Law Review* 11 (1990): 1613–30.

22. Even at times going so far as to advocate playing off pitch, or on badly tuned instruments: generally, see Levinson and Balkin, "Law, Music, and Other Performing Arts," 1601, 1616–22; see Nicholas Kenyon, ed., *Authenticity and Early Music* (Oxford: Oxford University Press, 1988); Peter Kivy, *Authenticities: Philosophical Reflections on Musical Performance* (Ithaca, N.Y.: Cornell University Press, 1995).

23. Messaien, liner notes to *Quartet for the End of Time*, 12.

24. I am grateful to Nicholas Horn for this point. He refers to John Eliot Gardner, the Kuijken brothers, Montserrat Figueras, Loeki Stardust, and examples of this more aestheticized generation of performers within the origi-

nalist tradition. The critique of originalism, which Balkin and Levinson argue somewhat by way of an exposé, is merely a critique of authority rather than of legitimate traditions. Even the most illegitimate authority can—and frequently does—give birth to a genuinely creative tradition. The authority of the origin is always a legitimating myth for contemporary practice: see Jacques Derrida, "Declarations of Independence," *New Political Science* 15 (1986): 7–15; idem, "Force of Law: The Mystical Foundation of Authority," *Cardozo Law Review* 11 (1990): 919; Drucilla Cornell, "The Violence of the Masquerade: Law Dressed Up as Justice," *Cardozo Law Review* 11 (1990): 1047; Dominick LaCapra, "Violence, Justice, and the Force of Law," *Cardozo Law Review* 11 (1990): 1065.

25. Lon Fuller, *Legal Fictions* (Stanford: Stanford University Press, 1967), 128. Note, however, that Fuller finds the idea, even as fiction, a useful means of describing reality.

26. Karl Llewellyn, "On the Good, the True, the Beautiful in Law," *University of Chicago Law Review* 9 (1942): 224.

27. John Austin, *The Province of Jurisprudence Determined* (London: Weidenfeld & Nicholson, 1971 [1834]); H. L. A. Hart, *The Concept of Law* (Oxford: Clarendon Press, 1961); Joseph Raz, *Authority of Law* (Oxford: Clarendon Press, 1979); idem, "Authority, Law, and Morality," *The Monist* 68 (1985): 295.

28. Hans Kelsen, *General Theory of Law and State*, trans. Anders Wedberg (New York: Russell & Russell, 1961).

29. See Ernest Weinrib, "Causation and Wrongdoing," *Chicago-Kent Law Review* 63 (1987): 407; idem, "Corrective Justice," *Iowa Law Review* 77 (1992): 403; idem, "Right and Advantage in Private Law," *Cardozo Law Review* 10 (1989): 1283. These themes roughly correspond to Perry's characterization of the "internalist thesis" and the "justificatory aspect" of Weinrib's formalism: Stephen Perry, "Professor Weinrib's Formalism: The Not-So-Empty Sepulchre," *Harvard Journal of Law and Public Policy* 16 (1993): 597, 598–99.

30. Ernest Weinrib, "The Jurisprudence of Legal Formalism," *Harvard Journal of Law and Public Policy* 16 (1993): 583, 594. Formalism in all its guises is precisely the opposite of the aesthetic interest in form which I have advocated, because it sees formal characteristics as a membrane, sealed rather than permeable, and because it sees the conversation among those characteristics as purely internal rather than as influenced by and evidence of the social processes around them.

31. Ibid., 583; Ernest Weinrib, "'Legal Formalism': On the Immanent Rationality of Law," *Yale Law Journal* 97 (1988): 984.

32. See Fitzpatrick, *Mythology*, 116; Ian Ward, "A Kantian (Re)Turn: Aesthetics, Postmodernism, and Law," *Law and Critique* 6 (1995): 171, 256; for a more enriched explication of Kant in this context, see Costas Douzinas and Ronnie Warrington, *Postmodern Jurisprudence* (London: Routledge, 1991), 163–69; Costas Douzinas, Peter Goodrich, and Yifat Hachamovitch, eds., *Politics, Postmodernity, and Critical Legal Studies: The Legality of the Contingent* (London: Routledge, 1994), 26; Paul Crowther, *Critical Aesthetics and Postmodernism* (Oxford: Clarendon Press, 1993).

33. See Weinrib, "Jurisprudence of Legal Formalism," 594. This of course raises several additional problems of its own: Kant and Hegel themselves cannot be treated as simply manifestations of self-evident rationality. As Perry ("Professor Weinrib's Formalism," 603) writes, "their arguments in support of agency-based rationalism are deeply controversial and cannot simply be treated as self-evidently correct."

34. Weinrib, "Jurisprudence of Legal Formalism," 586–87, 587–88. For a more detailed analysis of the meaning of coherence in formalism, see Ken Kress, "Coherence and Formalism," *Harvard Journal of Law and Public Policy* 16 (1993): 639. It is clear, for example, that although Weinrib claims that "coherence is the criterion of truth," he is not thereby appealing to the idea of coherence as it is commonly understood among modern philosophers, in partnership with relativism and pluralism, but, on the contrary, to an "extremely ambitious conception" which is deductive and monist in the extreme: see Kress, "Coherence and Formalism," 641, 649.

Weinrib's response to this critique equivocates; in claiming the inherent validity and desirability of coherence, arguing that "justifying coherence on incoherent grounds" would be "absurd," he confuses these two distinct meanings of coherence. There is in fact a complete failure to distinguish between coherence as a criterion of rational argument and coherence as an explanation of institutional form: the first is a normative claim for something and the second a descriptive claim about something which is said to exist in the world (Ernest Weinrib, "Formalism and Practical Reason, or How to Avoid Seeing Ghosts in the Empty Sepulchre," *Harvard Journal of Law and Public Policy* 16 [1993]: 683, 695).

35. See Kress, "Coherence and Formalism," 646; Weinrib, "How to Avoid Seeing Ghosts," 695–96.

36. Weinrib, "Jurisprudence of Legal Formalism," 593. Perry ("Professor Weinrib's Formalism," 617) also emphasizes the aesthetic dimensions of Weinrib's analysis.

37. For a critique of his use of language, which demonstrates both the unnaturalness of his terminology and the difficulties of interpretation this presents, see in particular Kress, "Coherence and Formalism," *passim*, and esp. 649, 668.

38. Ronald Dworkin, *Law's Empire* (Cambridge, Mass.: Belknap Press, 1986), 176–224, 214–16.

39. See Denise Réaume, "Is Integrity a Virtue?: Dworkin's Theory of Legal Obligation," *University of Toronto Law Journal* 39 (1989): 38, and Alan Hunt, ed., *Reading Dworkin Critically* (New York: Berg, 1992), for discussion.

40. Dworkin, *Law's Empire*, 214–15.

41. Ibid., 274; see also 272–75, and the notes, 440–44.

42. Weinrib, "How to Avoid Seeing Ghosts," 686, 693–95.

43. Ibid., 697, discussing Perry, "Professor Weinrib's Formalism," 620.

44. Weinrib, "Immanent Rationality," 972.

45. There are some exceptions: CLS literature from time to time intrudes

personal experience into legal discussion, although even here the narrative is often intended to contrast "law" with "life" rather than to allow one to inform the other: e.g., Patricia Williams, "Alchemical Notes," *Harvard Civil Rights-Civil Liberties Review* 22 (1987): 1401. For a rarer and more integrated approach, see Nicholas Kasirer, "Apostolat Juridique: Teaching Everyday Law in the Life of Marie Lacoste Gerin-Lajoie (1867–1945)," *Osgoode Hall Law Journal* 30 (1992): 427.

46. Weinrib, "Jurisprudence of Legal Formalism," 583, 591, 592, 593.

47. Roberto Mangabeira Unger, *Knowledge and Politics* (New York: Free Press, 1975), 236–37.

48. Dworkin, *Law's Empire*, 404–8.

49. Of the judge who is the star of *Law's Empire*, "Call him Hercules," says Dworkin: ibid., 239.

50. M. H. Hoeflich, "Law and Geometry: Legal Science from Leibniz to Langdell," *American Journal of Legal History* 30 (1986): 95; see the discussion of Gottfried Leibniz, 99–102; and see also Douzinas, Goodrich, and Hachamovitch, eds., *Politics, Postmodernity, and Critical Legal Studies*, 17.

51. Weinrib, "How to Avoid Seeing Ghosts," 684–85. The use of this metaphor in fact runs through this article.

52. Ibid., 696.

53. Weinrib (ibid., 685) claims for formalism a kind of pluralism, since he argues that law is but one "shape" of moral life, and "the requirement of coherence within a shape does not deny the existence of other shapes"—different geometries for different spheres. But this is hardly an adequate answer, since the impact of law is felt in every corner of our lives. The history of pink triangles and yellow stars, furthermore, are just two instances of the ways in which legal monism does indeed occasionally attempt to "deny the existence of other shapes."

54. See Morton Horwitz, "The Historical Contingency of the Role of History," *Yale Law Journal* 90 (1981): 1057; Harold Berman, "The Origins of Historical Jurisprudence: Coke, Selden, Hale," *Yale Law Journal* 103 (1994): 1651–1738; William Blackstone, *Commentaries on the Laws of England, 1765–69* (Chicago: University of Chicago Press, 1979).

55. *London Street Tramways v. London County Council,* [1898] A.C. 375.

56. See Brian Tierney, *Origins of Papal Infallibility 1150–1350,* Studies in the History of Christian Thought, vol. 6 (Leiden: E. J. Brill, 1972); J. J. I. von Döllinger, *The Pope and the Council* (London: Rivingston, 1869).

57. *Practice Statement (Precedent),* [1966] 1 W.L.R. 1234; see Anthony Kronman, "Precedent and Tradition," *Yale Law Journal* 99 (1990): 1029; Frederick Schauer, "Precedent," *Stanford Law Review* 39 (1987): 571.

58. Dworkin, *Law's Empire,* 228–38. The discussion of *McLoughlin v. O'Brien* (238–54) emphasizes the way in which present interpretations, to be legitimate, must reconcile precedent cases coherently.

59. Ibid., 273. The CLS approach to history, on the other hand, is not simply that law was constructed to serve certain vested interests—which appears to be

Dworkin's reading of it—but rather that the interests which history illuminates still govern the meaning and shape of law: see, for example, Morton Horwitz, *The Transformation of American Law, 1780–1860* (Cambridge, Mass.: Harvard University Press, 1977); idem, *The Transformation of American Law, 1870–1960: The Crisis in Legal Orthodoxy* (New York: Oxford University Press, 1992); idem, "History and Theory," *Yale Law Journal* 96 (1987): 1825.

60. Weinrib, "Jurisprudence of Legal Formalism," 594; Dworkin, *Law's Empire*, 275.

61. Levinson and Balkin, "Law, Music, and Other Performing Arts," 1641–46.

62. See Joseph Singer, "The Player and the Cards: Nihilism and Legal Theory," *Yale Law Journal* 94 (1984): 1; Mark Kelman, "Trashing," *Stanford Law Review* 36 (1984): 293; David Cole, "Getting There: Reflections on Trashing from Feminist Jurisprudence and Critical Theory," *Harvard Women's Law Journal* 8 (1985): 59; Allan Hutchinson, ed., *Critical Legal Studies* (Totowa, N.J.: Rowman & Littlefield, 1989); Robert Gordon, "Critical Legal Histories," *Stanford Law Review* 36 (1984): 57; Allan Hutchinson and Patrick Monahan, "Law, Politics, and Critical Legal Studies," *Stanford Law Review* 36 (1984): 199; Mark Tushnet, "The Critical Legal Studies Movement," *Stanford Law Review* 36 (1984): 623; Roberto Mangabeira Unger, "The Critical Legal Studies Movement," *Harvard Law Review* 96 (1983): 561. For further discussion of the scope and implications of "nihilism," see also Joseph Stick, "Can Nihilism Be Pragmatic?" *Harvard Law Review* 100 (1986): 332; David Couzens Hoy, "Dworkin's Constructive Optimism v. Deconstructive Legal Nihilism," *Journal of Law and Philosophy* 6 (1987): 321.

63. Staughton Lynd, "Communal Rights," *Texas Law Review* 62 (1984): 1417; Unger, *Knowledge and Politics*, 236–95; see Allan Hutchinson and Patrick Monahan, "The 'Rights' Stuff: Roberto Unger and Beyond," *Texas Law Review* 62 (1984): 1477.

64. Arthur Leff, "Unspeakable Ethics, Unnatural Law," *Duke Law Journal* (1979): 1229.

65. Unger, *Knowledge and Politics*, 290–91.

66. Ibid., 295.

67. Robin West, "Jurisprudence as Narrative: An Aesthetic Analysis of Modern Legal Theory," *New York University Law Review* 60 (1985): 145, 177–82. The difference is above all a question of timing. West's article appeared in 1985 and contains, of course, references to none of the material published in 1984 in which one begins to observe the development of a more tragic tone: for example, the works of Gordon, Kelman, Singer, Tushnet, and Hutchinson cited above.

68. West, "Jurisprudence as Narrative," 183; Roscoe Pound, *Justice according to Law* (1959), 90, quoted in West, "Jurisprudence as Narrative," 177. See Northrop Frye, *Anatomy of Criticism: Four Essays* (Princeton: Princeton University Press, 1957).

69. J. Griffiths, "What Is Legal Pluralism?" *Journal of Legal Pluralism and*

Unofficial Law 24 (1986): 1, 4; Marc Galanter, "Justice in Many Rooms: Courts, Private Ordering, and Indigenous Law," *Journal of Legal Pluralism and Unofficial Law* 19 (1981): 1, 21.

70. For a particularly helpful analysis, devoid of the opprobrious overtones that normally accompany the word "ideology," see Jack M. Balkin, "Ideology as Cultural Software," *Cardozo Law Review* 16 (1995): 1221–33.

71. Clifford Geertz, *Local Knowledge: Further Essays in Interpretive Anthropology* (New York: Basic Books, 1983).

72. See Pue, "Wrestling with Law," 576; see especially Blomley, *Law, Space, and the Geographies of Power.*

73. Griffiths, "What Is Legal Pluralism?" 8. Michael Walzer, *Spheres of Justice* (New York: Basic Books, 1983), is likewise evidently spatial in metaphor, although not postcolonial in origin. He argues that different ideas of justice are appropriate in different "spheres" of life and seems to see law exercising an overall supervisory role, defining and delegating "spheres of justice" according to its ultimate normative authority.

74. The first issue dates from 1962, and the characterization I am suggesting holds even until the very recent past—a random sampling of the table of contents of any issue will suffice to demonstrate the proposition.

75. A division between colonial and postcolonial pluralism, on the one hand, and capitalist pluralism, on the other, is dealt with in more detail in Sally Engle Merry, "Legal Pluralism," *Law and Society Review* 22 (1988): 869.

76. See Peter Fitzpatrick, "Law, Plurality, and Underdevelopment," in David Sugarman, ed., *Legality, Ideology, and the State* (London: Academic Press, 1983), 159; Peter Fitzpatrick, "Law and Societies," *Osgoode Hall Law Journal* 22 (1984): 115; idem, *Mythology;* idem, "'The Desperate Vacuum'": Imperialism and Law in the Experience of Enlightenment," *Droit et societé* 13 (1989): 347; Leopold Pospisil, *Law among the Kapauku of Netherlands New Guinea* (New Haven: HRAF Press, 1956); Boaventura de Sousa Santos, "The Law of the Oppressed: The Construction and Reproduction of Legality in Pasagarda," *Law and Society Review* 12 (1977): 5; idem, "Law, State, and Urban Struggles in Recife, Brazil," *Social and Legal Studies* 1 (1992): 235. It is an argument expressly confirmed in Santos, *Toward a New Common Sense,* 116.

77. See the excellent summary of these approaches in Griffiths, "What Is Legal Pluralism?" 15–36.

78. Galanter, "Justice in Many Rooms," 8, 23; Merry, "Legal Pluralism," 870. Thus when Galanter seeks to invert the hierarchy, and argues for "law in the shadow of indigenous ordering" rather than vice versa, the reified quality of his imagery is not diminished: he still conceives of law, formal and indigenous alike, as objects independent of our perception of them.

79. Robert H. Mnoonin and Lewis Kornhauser, "Bargaining in the Shadow of the Law: The Case of Divorce," *Yale Law Journal* 88 (1979): 950; Galanter, "Justice in Many Rooms," 8, 23; Harry Arthurs, *Without the Law: Administrative Justice and Legal Pluralism in Nineteenth-Century England* (Toronto: University of Toronto Press, 1985); Robert Ellickson, *Order without Law: How*

Neighbors Settle Disputes (Cambridge, Mass.: Harvard University Press, 1991); Jerold Auerbach, *Justice without Law* (Oxford: Oxford University Press, 1983).

80. Sally Falk Moore, "Law and Social Change: The Semi-Autonomous Social Field as an Appropriate Subject of Study," *Law and Society Review* 7 (1973): 719; Leopold Pospisil, *Anthropology of Law: A Comparative Perspective* (New Haven: HRAF Press, 1974), esp., 97–126; Walter O. Weyrauch and Maureen Anne Bell, "Autonomous Law-Making: The Case of the 'Gypsies,'" *Yale Law Journal* 103 (1993): 323; Auerbach, *Justice without Law.*

81. Boaventura de Sousa Santos, "Law: A Map of Misreading—Toward a Postmodern Conception of Law," *Journal of Law and Society* 14 (1987): 279; Santos, *Toward a New Common Sense,* 111–22.

82. Blomley, *Law, Space, and the Geographies of Power,* 27–51.

83. Messiaen, liner notes to *Quartet for the End of Time,* 16.

84. Gordon, "Critical Legal Histories," 57, 122.

85. Santos, *Toward a New Common Sense,* 57–60; Harold Berman, *Law and Revolution: The Formation of the Western Legal Tradition* (Cambridge, Mass.: Harvard University Press, 1983); Peter Stein, *The Teaching of Roman Law in England around 1200* (London: Selden Society, 1990).

86. *Supplement to New South Wales Government Gazette No. 120* (N.S.W.), 30 August 1927, r. 22; *Dangerous Drugs Regulations 1930* (Vic.), Gazette No. 12, r. 16.

87. I refer in particular to the realists' insight into the performative aspects of law and their consequent adoption of a pragmatic philosophy of meaning. But the realists, for their part, seemed to emphasize the authoritative pronouncements of the courts to the exclusion of all other loci of legal interpretation: see for example Jerome Frank, *Law and the Modern Mind* (New York: Brentano's, 1930); Karl Llewellyn, *The Bramble Bush: On Our Law and Its Study* (New York: Oceana, 1951); idem, "A Realistic Jurisprudence: The Next Step," *Columbia Law Review* 30 (1930): 431.

88. Obviously, I am echoing here the "internal aspect" discussed in Hart, *Concept of Law.*

89. R. H. Coase, "The Problem of Social Cost," *Journal of Law and Economics* 3 (1960): 1; Ellickson, *Order without Law,* 52, 92–103.

90. Galanter, "Justice in Many Rooms."

91. See Gunther Teubner, "The Two Faces of Janus: Rethinking Legal Pluralism," *Cardozo Law Review* 13 (1992): 1443; Santos, *Toward a New Common Sense,* 126–28.

92. See Llewellyn, "Realistic Jurisprudence"; Hart, *Concept of Law;* Dworkin, *Law's Empire;* Dragan Milovanovic, *Postmodern Law and Disorder: Psychoanalytic Semiotics, Chaos, and Juridic Exegeses* (Liverpool: Deborah Charles, 1992).

93. Harriet Hawkins, *Strange Attractors: Literature, Culture and Chaos Theory* (Hemel Hempstead: Prentice Hall/Harvester Wheatsheaf, 1995), 69, makes a similar point about the chaos of literature: "In our minds, as in every-

day life, we are all postmodernists, experiencing and fusing popular and classical and ancient and modern works in wildly eclectic and chaotic combinations."

94. Hart, *Concept of Law.*

95. Teubner, "Janus," 1457; see also C. Sampford, *The Disorder of Law* (Oxford: Basil Blackwell, 1989).

96. Coase, "Problem of Social Cost"; Mnoonin and Kornhauser, "Shadow of the Law"; E. P. Thompson, *Customs in Common* (New York: New Press, 1993); Galanter, "Justice in Many Rooms."

97. Ellickson, *Order without Law*; Arthurs, *Without the Law*; Peter Fitzpatrick and Alfred Rüegg, "Book Review, *Without the Law* by Harry Arthurs," *Journal of Legal Pluralism and Unofficial Law* 27 (1988): 135; Santos, "Law of the Oppressed."

98. See R. A. Macdonald, "Les Vieilles Gardes: Hypothèses sur l'emergence des normes, l'internormativité et le désordre à travers une typologie des institutions normatives," in J.-G. Belley, ed., *Le Droit soluble: Contributions québecoises à l'étude de l'internormativité* (Paris: L.G.D.J., 1996).

99. Fitzpatrick, "'Desperate vacuum'"; Peter Fitzpatrick, ed., *Dangerous Supplements: Resistance and Renewal in Jurisprudence* (London: Pluto Press, 1991).

100. Santos, "A Map of Misreading," 297–98.

101. Santos, *Toward a New Common Sense*, 385; see generally idem, "Law, the State, and Urban Struggles in Recife," 378–97.

102. Santos, "Law of the Oppressed"; idem, "The Law of the Oppressed," in *Toward a New Common Sense*, 124–248, esp. 176–84 and generally, 176–234.

103. James Gleick, *Chaos: Making a New Science* (New York: Viking, 1987); John L. Casti, *Complexification: Explaining a Paradoxical World through the Science of Surprise* (New York: Harper Collins, 1994). A further, if rather fragmentary, explication of the relationship of chaos to postmodernism and law is Milovanovic, *Postmodern Law and Disorder*, 117–18, 129, 228–40. Dragan Milovanovic, "Humanistic Sociology and the Chaos Paradigm: Review Essay of N. Katherine Hayles, *Chaos Bound,*" *Humanity and Society* 15 (1991): 135. And for other brief excursions, see Robert E. Scott, "Chaos Theory and the Justice Paradox," *William and Mary Law Review* 35 (1993): 329; Glenn H. Reynolds, "Chaos and the Courts," *Columbia Law Review* 91 (1991): 110. I would note, however, the largely peremptory nature of the discussion of chaos in these articles, despite their claims. Scott, in particular, fails to distinguish chaos theory as an explanation of "law" or "justice" from its value as an explanation of legal theories.

104. The seminal work is Benoît Mandelbrot, *The Fractal Geometry of Nature* (New York: W. H. Freeman, 1983).

105. Gleick, *Chaos*, 98. I use the word "tangled" with care, since it is typical of the descriptions of fractal geometry in Gleick, for example, and at the same time establishes a connection with the dense interwoven harmonic "tangles" in the linguistic and harmonic language of Messiaen's *Quartet for the End of Time.*

106. Milovanovic, *Postmodern Law and Disorder,* 235.

107. See, for example, the concept of "bio-power" developed in M. Foucault, *The Use of Pleasure,* vol. 2 of *The History of Sexuality,* trans. R. Hurley (New York: Vintage Books, 1986); idem, *The Care of the Self,* vol. 3 of *The History of Sexuality,* trans. Robert Hurley (New York: Random House, 1988), with its exploration of the replication of relations of power at the level of the body; see also the discussion of "the bodily hexus" as it instantiates social relations in Pierre Bourdieu, *Language and Symbolic Power* (Cambridge, Mass.: Harvard University Press, 1991).

108. Milovanovic, *Postmodern Law and Disorder,* 230–33, 242–45, relying in particular on Gilles Deleuze and Félix Guattari, provides a different interpretation. Focusing on the fractal as a fraction of a dimension, he treats it mainly as a metaphor for indeterminacy of meaning. The meaning of a text, he argues, is never either 0 (wrong) or 1.0 (right); rather, it lies in between as a "semiotic fractal," filling the space of meaning only partially. This interpretation of the fractal does not seem to me to capture either its shape or its meaning, let alone the reason for its aesthetic appeal (see below). A fractal is not simply another word for a *fraction.*

109. See Blomley, *Law, Space, and the Geographies of Power,* Chapter 3. See Mark S. Monmonier, *How to Lie with Maps* (Chicago: University of Chicago Press, 1991).

110. Compare the map by Saul Steinberg, "The View from Fifth Avenue," which attempts to map the perspective of the New Yorker, Fifth Avenue in sharp relief, then the Hudson River, New Jersey vaguely perceived in the distance, and India and Asia scarcely a speck upon the horizon.

111. Santos, "Law: A Map of Misreading," 298–99.

112. Ibid., 289–90.

113. Catherine MacKinnon, *Feminism Unmodified* (Cambridge, Mass.: Harvard University Press, 1987); Linda Nicholson, ed., *Feminism/Postmodernism* (London: Routledge, 1990); Angela Harris, "Race and Essentialism in Feminist Legal Theory," *Stanford Law Review* 42 (1990): 581; Marlee Kline, "Race, Racism, and Feminist Legal Theory," *Harvard Women's Law Journal* 12 (1989): 115. "Critical race theory" has provoked the same kind of debate within CLS.

114. The question of nonlinearity is returned to frequently in Gleick (*Chaos,* 23–24, 27) and others.

115. See Sampford, *Disorder of Law.*

116. See, for example, "Toward a Rational Drug Policy," *University of Chicago Legal Forum* (1994): 1–498; Australia, Parliamentary Joint Committee on the National Crime Authority (Commissioner: P. Cleeland), *Drugs, Crime, and Society* (Canberra: A.G.P.S., 1989); Judith C. Blackwell and Patricia G. Erickson, eds., *Illicit Drugs in Canada: A Risky Business* (Scarborough, Ontario: Nelson Canada, 1988); Ian Elliott, "Heroin: Mythologies for Law Enforcers," *Criminal Law Journal* 6 (1982): 6; David Hawks, "The Implications of Legalizing Heroin,"

Quadrant 34 (1990): 53; John Kaplan, *The Hardest Drug: Heroin and Social Policy* (Chicago: University of Chicago Press, 1983).

117. See for example Kettil Bruun, L. Pan, and I. Rexed, *The Gentlemen's Club* (Chicago: University of Chicago Press, 1975); Desmond Manderson, *From Mr. Sin to Mr. Big: A History of Australian Drug Laws* (Melbourne: Oxford University Press, 1993); David Musto, *The American Disease* (New Haven: Yale University Press, 1973).

118. It also suggests a suspicion of those theorists who claim to be interested in law as the science of prediction: "The prophecies of what the courts will do, and nothing more pretentious, is what I mean by law" (Oliver Wendell Holmes, "The Path of the Law," *Harvard Law Review* 10 [1897]: 457); or in the realists' assertion that law itself is "generalized predictions of what courts will do" ("Some Realism about Realism," *Harvard Law Review* 44 [1931]: 1222, in Llewellyn, *Bramble Bush*, 56).

119. See Peterson, *Newton's Clock*.

120. I do not mean, of course, that there is a one-to-one correspondence between action and transformation—one can imagine all sorts of different geometric progressions—but between the two there is a ratio that remains constant.

121. Geertz, *Local Knowledge;* Michael Polanyi, *Personal Knowledge* (London: Routledge & Kegan Paul, 1958). Clifford Geertz, *After the Fact* (Cambridge, Mass.: Harvard University Press, 1995), provides a fusion of personal knowledge and local knowledge in a narrative of richness and beauty.

122. Messiaen, liner notes to *Quartet for the End of Time,* 13.

123. In a rapidly expanding literature, see Douzinas, Goodrich, and Hachamovitch, eds., *Politics, Postmodernity, and Critical Legal Studies;* Douzinas and Warrington, *Postmodern Jurisprudence;* Alan Hunt, "The Big Fear: Law Confronts Postmodernism," *McGill Law Journal* 35 (1990): 507; "Deconstruction and the Possibility of Justice," *Cardozo Law Review* 11 (1990): 919; Seyla Benhabib, "Critical Theory and Postmodernism: On the Interplay of Ethics, Aesthetics, and Utopia in Critical Theory," *Cardozo Law Review* 11 (1990): 1435; Judith Butler, "Deconstruction and the Possibility of Justice: Comments on Bernasconi, Cornell, Miller, Weber," *Cardozo Law Review* 11 (1990): 1715; Costas Douzinas and Ronnie Warrington, "Posting the Law: Social Contracts and the Postal Rule's Grammatology," *International Journal for the Semiotics of Law* 4 (1991): 115; Drucilla Cornell, "Toward a Modern/Postmodern Reconstruction of Ethics," *University of Pennsylvania Law Review* 135 (1985): 291; "Law and the Postmodern Mind," *Cardozo Law Review* 16 (1995): 699; Anthony E. Cook, "Reflections on Postmodernism," *New England Law Review* 26 (1992): 751–82; "Postmodernism and Law: A Symposium," *Colorado Law Review* 62 (1991): 433; Pierre Schlag, "Introduction to Postmodernism and Law: A Symposium," *Colorado Law Review* 62 (1991): 439; Mary Joe Frug, "Law and Postmodernism: The Politics of a Marriage," *Colorado Law Review* 62 (1991): 483.

124. For example, Daniela Pacher, "Aesthetics v. Ideology: The Motives

behind 'Law and Literature,'" *Columbia-VLA Journal of Law and the Arts* 14 (1990): 587; Cornell, "Toward a Modern/Postmodern Reconstruction of Ethics," 291; Daniel Polsby and Robert Popper, "Ugly: An Inquiry into the Problem of Racial Gerrymandering under the Voting Rights Act," *Michigan Law Review* 92 (1993): 652; Wilf Stevens, "Imagining Justice: Aesthetics and Public Executions in Late Eighteenth-Century England," *Yale Journal of Law and the Humanities* 5 (1993): 51; Stephen Gey, "This Is Not a Flag: The Aesthetics of Desecration," *Wisconsin Law Review* (1990): 1549; Roberta Kevelson, ed., *Law and Aesthetics* (New York: Peter Lang, 1992); Costas Douzinas, *Justice Miscarried: Ethics, Aesthetics and the Law* (Hemel Hempstead: Harvester Wheatsheaf, 1994); Ward, "A Kantian (Re)Turn."

125. See for example Heinz-Otto Peitgen, *The Beauty of Fractals* (Berlin: Springer-Verlag, 1986); John Briggs, *Fractals: The Pattern of Chaos* (New York: Touchstone, 1992); John Briggs and F. David Peat, *Turbulent Mirror: An Illustrated Guide to Chaos Theory* (London: Verso, 1990).

126. Benoit Mandelbrot and Heinz-Otto Peitgen, quoted and discussed in Gleick, *Chaos*, 116–18. See the wonderful imagery reproduced in ibid., between 114–15; see also Peitgen, *Beauty of Fractals;* Briggs, *Fractals.*

127. Briggs, *Fractals*, 2.

128. Thomas Hobbes, *Leviathan* (Oxford: Blackwells, 1946), first published in 1651, and Sir Isaac Newton, *Philosophiae naturalis principia mathematica* (London: W. Dawson, 1966), first published in 1687. The closeness of these publications is of course by no means coincidental and reflects the emergence of just this shared modernist sensibility.

129. Carl Schorske, *Fin-de-Siècle Vienna: Politics and Culture* (London: Weidenfeld & Nicholson, 1979), 358–62.

130. See the discussion of Tom Wolfe, *From Bauhaus to Our House* (New York: Washington Square Press, 1981), which discusses the alienation of modernist architecture and housing, in Hawkins, *Strange Attractors*, 164–67.

131. Although I do not consider the matter here, the same message that comes from the conclusions of chaos theory also, to some extent, comes from the process of chaos theory—and, even more so, from quantum theory. Modern science in general has increasingly focused on the complexities and mysteries of the miniature. There could scarcely be a more extreme metaphor for the local and the particular than the subatomic particles that are today shattering our understanding of physics: see for a helpful summary, Roger Penrose, *Shadows of the Mind* (London: Vintage Books, 1994), 237–300.

132. Thus Nicholas Reschler, *Pluralism* (Oxford: Clarendon Press, 1993), 4, describes pluralism as "damage control" given the inevitable continuance of dissensus in society. It is an approach which finds echoes in classic works of liberalism such as J. S. Mill, *On Liberty* (New York: Liberal Arts Press, 1956 [1857]), and John Rawls, *A Theory of Justice* (Oxford: Oxford University Press, 1972).

133. It is a narcissism which the technology of the "news group" further facilitates by artificially limiting the subject matter of any communication and

by even denying us the capacity to see or hear our colleagues. Influenced only by the stream of words emanating from the screen, the fantastic projection of ourselves onto the other is encouraged. Even e-mail suffers from this problem. It encourages most intimate relations, but sometimes that intimacy is an illusion caused by the way in which the other is so easily reimagined in fantasy. Dialogue becomes a mutual soliloquy.

134. Roberto Mangabeira Unger, *False Necessity* (New York: Cambridge University Press, 1987), 531–32; Milovanovic, *Postmodern Law and Disorder*, 234–36; Santos, *Toward a New Common Sense*, 491–98. Santos most notably relates these ideas to chaos theory.

135. Santos, *Toward a New Common Sense*, 496–97.

136. Gleick, *Chaos*, 5.

137. See Hawkins, *Strange Attractors*, 51.

138. Plato, *The Republic*, trans. D. Lee (London: Penguin, 1974), 424c.

139. Jacques Attali, *Noise: The Political Economy of Music*, trans. Brian Massumi (Minneapolis: University of Minnesota Press, 1985), 3–4.

140. Walter Ong, quoted in Bernard J. Hibbitts, "Making Sense of Metaphors: Visuality, Aurality, and the Reconfiguration of American Legal Discourse," *Cardozo Law Review* 16 (1994): 229, 343.

141. Ibid., 295.

142. Ibid., 238–63, and sources there cited.

143. In particular, the ocular authority of modernity is developed throughout Michel Foucault, *Discipline and Punish*, trans. A. M. Sheridan Smith (New York: Vintage Books, 1979), and idem, *The Birth of the Clinic: An Archaeology of Medical Perception*, trans. A. M. Sheridan Smith (New York: Vintage Books, 1975). See in particular the analysis of this question in Martin Jay, "In the Empire of the Gaze: Foucault and the Denigration of Vision in Twentieth-Century Thought," in David Couzens Hoy, ed., *Foucault: A Critical Reader* (Oxford: Basil Blackwell, 1986), 175–204. Jay places Foucault's argument in the context of a variety of other writers, including Bergson, Bataille's *The Story of the Eye*, and the discussion of "le regard" in Jean-Paul Sartre's *Being and Nothingness*. I mention but do not discuss the central importance of the idea of masculinity of "the gaze" in much contemporary feminism.

144. Luis Buñuel and Salvador Dali, *Un Chien Andalou* (film, 1927).

145. Hibbitts, "Making Sense of Metaphors," Part III; Marshall McLuhan, *The Gutenberg Galaxy: The Making of Typographic Man* (New York: Signet, 1969).

146. There are interesting questions here about the operation and meaning of these senses in a differently constructed sensorium—in different cultures, for example (see David Howes, ed., *The Varieties of Sensory Experience: A Sourcebook in the Anthropology of the Senses* [Toronto: University of Toronto Press, 1991]), but also in the sense world of the blind or deaf. One might compare the clutter of noise which invades the world of the partially deaf from the almost visual acuity of the blind person's ear. My arguments about the differ-

ent sensory meanings of color and sound relate specifically to people with all their senses intact and not to these situations.

147. Vladimir Nabokov, "Sounds" (1923), trans. Dmitri Nabokov, in *The New Yorker*, 14 August 1995, p. 78.

148. See Koestler, *Darkness at Noon*; John Ralston Saul, *Voltaire's Bastards: The Dictatorship of Reason in the West* (Harmondsworth: Penguin, 1992), 41–47, 73–76.

149. Mayakovsky argues that the democratic individualism of the twelve-tone system is an aural representation of communism, but perhaps this is to look at the matter too narrowly and pedantically.

150. Theodor Adorno, quoted and discussed by Fredric Jameson in "Foreword" to Attali, *Noise*, x–xi.

151. Nabokov, "Sounds," 74.

152. James M. Curtis, *Culture as Polyphony: An Essay on the Nature of Paradigms* (Columbia: University of Missouri Press, 1978); Carol Weisbrod, "Practical Polyphony: Theories of the State and Feminist Jurisprudence," *Georgia Law Review* 24 (1990): 985.

153. We can find this distinction and this change in rhetoric in surprising places. In 1957, Karl Llewellyn wrote about "inter-racial peace": Llewellyn, "What Law Cannot Do for Inter-racial Peace," *Villanova Law Review* 3 (1957): 30. Now we would say interracial *harmony*.

154. Foucault, *Archaeology of Knowledge; Order of Things*.

155. Jacques Derrida, *Of Grammatology* (Baltimore: Johns Hopkins University Press, 1976); idem, "Scribble (Writing-Power)," *Yale French Studies* 58 (1979): 117; idem, *Positions*, trans. Alan Bass (Chicago: University of Chicago Press, 1981).

156. Attali, *Noise*, 121–42.

157. Susan McClary, "Afterword," in Attali, *Noise*, 158.

158. I am thinking here particularly of the extraordinary expansive semi-breves/whole notes played by the clarinet in the "Abyss of the Birds," and also the very end of the violin's part in "In Praise of the Eternity of Jesus."

159. Arnold Schoenberg, quoted in Schorske, *Fin-de-Siècle Vienna*, 362.

160. Ibid., chapters 6 and 7, esp. 351–52.

161. Messiaen, liner notes to *Quartet for the End of Time*, 13.

QUODLIBET

1. Jacques Attali, *Noise: The Political Economy of Music*, trans. Brian Massumi (Minneapolis: University of Minnesota Press, 1985), 26–31.

2. Ibid., 24. Edward P. Thompson provides an excellent example of the use of noise as a weapon and furthermore as a legal sanction in his discussion of social practices in defense of the moral code of eighteenth-century plebeian England: see his "Rough Music" in *Customs in Common* (New York: New Press, 1993), 467–531.

3. Peter Brooks, "What Happened to Poetics?" in George Levine, ed., *Aesthetics and Ideology* (New Brunswick, N.J.: Rutgers University Press, 1994), 165.

4. For an overview of the claims of different concepts of justice, see Tom Campbell, *Justice* (Basingstoke, Hampshire: Macmillan, 1988); Alisdair Mac-Intyre, *Whose Justice? Which Rationality?* (Notre Dame, Ind.: University of Notre Dame Press, 1988). For an eclectic sampling of the tradition of argumentation in justice, see Aristotle, *Nicomachean Ethics*, trans. D. Ross (Oxford: Oxford University Press, 1980); John Rawls, *A Theory of Justice* (Oxford: Oxford University Press, 1972); Julius Stone, *Social Dimensions of Law and Justice* (Sydney: Maitland, 1966); Michael Walzer, *Spheres of Justice* (New York: Basic Books, 1983); James Boyd White, *Justice as Translation* (Chicago: University of Chicago Press, 1990); Jacques Derrida, "Force of Law: The Mystical Foundation of Authority," *Cardozo Law Review* 11 (1990): 919; "Deconstruction and the Possibility of Justice," *Cardozo Law Review* 11 (1990): 919; A. Ross, *On Law and Justice* (Berkeley: University of California Press, 1959); Drucilla Cornell, Mark Rosenfeld, and David Gray Carlson, eds., *Deconstruction and the Possibility of Justice* (New York: Routledge, 1992); Costas Douzinas, *Justice Miscarried: Ethics, Aesthetics, and the Law* (Hemel Hempstead: Harvester Wheatsheaf, 1994).

5. Plato, Epistle VII in *Phaedrus and Epistle VII*, trans. W. Hamilton (London: Penguin, 1973).

6. Immanuel Kant, *Critique of Judgment*, trans. W. Pluhar (Indianapolis: Hackett, 1987), quoted in Albert Hofstadter and R. Kuhns, eds., *Philosophies of Art and Beauty: Selected Readings from Plato to Heidegger* (Chicago: University of Chicago Press, 1964), 280, 286.

7. Friedrich Nietzsche, *Beyond Good and Evil*, trans. R. Hollingdale (London: Penguin, 1990), e.g., 52–54; idem, *On the Genealogy of Morals and Ecce Homo*, trans. Walter Kaufmann (New York: Vintage Books, 1989), 87.

8. Quoted, for example, in Geoffrey Galt Harpham, "Aesthetics and Modernity," in Levine, ed., *Aesthetics and Ideology*, 124, 128. For further on the legal implications of Walter Benjamin, see also Fredric Jameson, ed., *Aesthetics and Politics* (London: NLB, 1977); Derrida, "Force of Law"; Rudolphe Gasché, "On Critique, Hypercriticism, and Deconstruction: The Case of Benjamin," *Cardozo Law Review* 13 (1992): 1115; A. Heller, "*Marche Funèbre* for a Century (1914–1989)," *Cardozo Law Review* 13 (1992): 1173; Samuel Weber, "Deconstruction before the Name," *Cardozo Law Review* 13 (1992): 1181; "Roundtable—The Call to the Ethical: Deconstruction, Justice, and the Ethical Relationship," *Cardozo Law Review* 13 (1992): 1219.

9. Jean Baudrillard, *Critique of the Political Economy of the Sign*, trans. C. Levin (St. Louis: Telos Press, 1981); Pamela E. Lee, "The Aesthetics of Value, the Fetish of Method," *RES: Anthropology and Aesthetics* 27 (1995): 133, 141.

10. W. Sauerländer, "Un-German Activities (Review of *Degenerate Art: The Fate of the Avant-Garde in Nazi Germany*, exhibition at the Los Angeles County Museum of Art)," *New York Review of Books*, 7 April 1994, p. 9.

11. See the discussion of Plato and Socrates in Costas Douzinas and Ronnie Warrington, *Postmodern Jurisprudence* (London: Routledge, 1991), 134–37.

12. See the excellent and thorough survey contained in Elizabeth Wilkinson and L. Willoughby, "Introduction" to Friedrich Schiller, *On the Aesthetic Education of Man*, trans. Elizabeth Wilkinson (Oxford: Clarendon Press, 1967). See also the discussion of the aesthetic philosophy of Montesquieu and the Earl of Shaftesbury in Oscar Kenshur, "The Tumor of Their Own Hearts," in Levine, ed., *Aesthetics and Ideology*, 57, 69–70. Here too there is a strong emphasis on this idea of the aesthetic as a mode of apprehension of truth, although, in typical eighteenth-century style, this "truth" is rendered absolute and statist: see also Terry Eagleton, *The Ideology of the Aesthetic* (Oxford: Blackwell, 1990).

13. Boaventura de Sousa Santos, *Toward a New Common Sense: Law, Science, and Politics in the Paradigmatic Transition* (London: Routledge, 1995), 52. See generally the discussion of emancipation and aesthetics, 52–54.

14. Ian Ward, "A Kantian (Re)Turn: Aesthetics, Postmodernism, and Law," *Law and Critique* 6 (1995): 256, discussing the postmodern interpretation of Kantian aesthetics in the work of Paul Crowther. See especially Douzinas, *Justice Miscarried*.

15. Roger Penrose, *Shadows of the Mind* (London: Vintage Books, 1994), 76; see generally 64–116. See Kurt Gödel, *Collected Works*, vol. 1 ed. S. Feferman (Oxford: Oxford University Press, 1986); idem, *On Formally Undecidable Propositions of Principia Mathematica and Related Systems* (New York: Basic Books, 1962). See also Douglas R. Hofstadter, *Gödel, Escher, Bach: An Eternal Golden Braid* (Hassocks, Essex: Harvester Press, 1979); John Casti, *Complexification: Explaining a Paradoxical World through the Science of Surprise* (New York: Harper Collins, 1994), 138–70.

16. Casti, *Complexification*, 122ff. Casti (138–43) puts Gödel's argument as a mathematical formulation of Epimenides' paradox.

17. This is to compress a very complex argument: see Penrose, *Shadows of the Mind*, 127–209.

18. Jacques Derrida, *Positions*, trans. Alan Bass (Chicago: University of Chicago Press, 1981); Peggy Kamuf, ed., *A Derrida Reader: Between the Blinds* (New York: Columbia University Press, 1991); Jacques Derrida, *Of Grammatology* (Baltimore: Johns Hopkins University Press, 1976). There is a reference to Gödel in Derrida's "The Double Session" (1972), but not, I think, one which does justice to the meaning or relevance of his theorem. On the contrary, Derrida, writing of "undecidability," appears to equate and even to some extent confuse Gödel's theorem with Heisenberg's uncertainty principle: see Kamuf, ed., *Derrida Reader*, 189. It is true that Gödel's theorem, understood as a systemization of paradox, can be neither "right" nor "wrong" within the framework of the system and is forever condemned by the system to a "grey zone" (Casti, *Complexification*, 139–41). But undecidability is only half the point, for the proposition, although undecidable within a formal system, is also true: Gödel's paper is not entitled *On Undecidable Propositions* but *On Formally Undecidable Propositions*.

19. Penrose, *Shadows of the Mind*, 72.

20. Lon Fuller, "Positivism and Fidelity to Law: A Reply to Professor Hart," *Harvard Law Review* 71 (1958): 630. See also the article to which this was the celebrated reply, H. L. A. Hart, "Positivism and the Separation of Law and Morals," *Harvard Law Review* 71 (1958): 593; and see also Kenneth Winston, "Is / Ought Redux: The Pragmatist Context of Lon Fuller's Conception of Law," *Oxford Journal of Legal Studies* 8 (1988): 329; Peter Read Teachout, "The Soul of the Fugue: An Essay on Reading Fuller," *Minnesota Law Review* 70 (1986): 1073.

21. Roderick Macdonald, "Whose Access? Which Justice? (Review of Allan Hutchinson, ed., *Access to Civil Justice* [Toronto: Carswell, 1990])," *Canadian Journal of Legal Studies* 7 (1992): 175; idem, "Theses on Access to Justice," *Canadian Journal of Law and Society* 7 (1992): 23.

22. Derrida, "Force of Law," 1023. See also Costas Douzinas and Ronnie Warrington, "Cases of Casuistry," in *Postmodern Jurisprudence*, 93–131.

23. Derek Attridge, "Literary Form and the Demands of Politics: Otherness in J. M. Coetzee's Age of Iron," in Levine, ed., *Aesthetics and Ideology*, 243, 248.

24. Derrida, "Force of Law," 961.

25. Santos, *Toward a New Common Sense*, 23–25.

26. See "On Popular Justice," in Michel Foucault, *Power/Knowledge: Selected Interviews and Other Writings 1972–1977*, ed. Colin Gordon (New York: Pantheon Books, 1980), 1–36.

27. Montesquieu, quoted in Kenshur, "Tumor of Their Own," 73. "Justice is eternal and immutable . . . and it is recognized aesthetically, by dint of its harmonious structure" (ibid.).

28. See the discussion of capital punishment in "Requiem," and in particular arguments concerning the lex talionis in Stephen Nathanson, *An Eye for An Eye?: The Morality of Punishing by Death* (Totowa, N.J.: Rowman & Littlefield, 1987); Ernest Van den Haag and J. Conrad, *The Death Penalty: A Debate* (New York: Plenum Press, 1983); Walter Berns, *For Capital Punishment: Crime and the Morality of Punishment* (New York: Basic Books, 1979).

29. William Shakespeare, *Othello*, Act iv, Scene 1, lines 203–5.

30. See Thompson, *Customs in Common*, esp. chapters 4 and 8.

31. From Jade Ngoc Quang Hu'ynh, *South Wind Changing* (St. Paul: Graywolf Press, 1994), quoted in Philip Gourevitch, "Vietnam: The Bitter Truth," *New York Review of Books*, vol. 41, no. 21 (1994), p. 55.

32. Michel Foucault, *Discipline and Punish*, trans. A. M. Sheridan Smith (New York: Vintage Books, 1979), John Baehre, "Origins of the Penitentiary System," *Ontario History* 69 (1977): 182; Michael Ignatieff, *A Just Measure of Pain: The Penitentiary in the Industrial Revolution 1750–1823* (New York: Macmillan, 1978); Joanna Innes and John Styles, "The Crime Wave: Recent Writings on Crime and Criminal Justice in Eighteenth-Century England," *Journal of British Studies* 25 (1986): 380.

33. Jonathan Culler, "Resisting Theory," *Cardozo Law Review* 11 (1990):

1565; Peter Fitzpatrick, ed., *Dangerous Supplements: Resistance and Renewal in Jurisprudence* (London: Pluto Press, 1991); Christopher Norris, "Law, Deconstruction, and the Resistance to Theory," *Journal of Law and Society* 15 (1988): 166.

34. Wilf Stevens, "Imagining Justice: Aesthetics and Public Executions in Late Eighteenth-Century England," *Yale Journal of Law and the Humanities* 5 (1993): 51; David Cooper, *The Lesson of the Scaffold: The Public Execution Controversy in Victorian England* (Athens: Ohio University Press, 1974); Douglas Hay, Peter Linebaugh, and E. P. Thompson, eds., *Albion's Fatal Tree: Crime and Society in Eighteenth-Century England* (London: Allen Lane, 1977); Thomas Laqueur, "Crowds, Carnivals, and the State in English Executions," in A. L. Beier, David Cannadine, and James Rosenheim, eds., *The First Modern Society* (Cambridge: Cambridge University Press, 1989).

35. Harold Berman, *Law and Revolution: The Foundation of the Western Legal Tradition* (Cambridge, Mass.: Harvard University Press, 1983).

36. Attridge, "Literary Form and the Demands of Politics," 248.

37. Susanne K. Langer, *Philosophy in a New Key*, new ed. (Cambridge, Mass.: Harvard University Press, 1978).

38. George Levine, "Introduction: Reclaiming the Aesthetic," in Levine, ed., *Aesthetics and Ideology*, 1, 21.

39. See White, *Justice as Translation;* James Boyd White, *Heracles' Bow: Essays on the Rhetoric and Poetics of Law* (Madison: University of Wisconsin Press, 1985).

40. Schiller, *On the Aesthetic Education of Man*, II.5, 9.

41. Martin Jay, "'The Aesthetic Ideology' as Ideology; or, What Does It Mean to Aestheticize Politics?" *Cultural Critique* 21 (1992): 41, 52.

42. Robin West, "Jurisprudence as Narrative: An Aesthetic Analysis of Modern Legal Theory," *New York University Law Review* 60 (1985): 145, 209–10.

43. Nietzsche, *Genealogy of Morals*, 20.

44. "What must be done, essentially, is to reveal to subjects that what they are asking for . . . in their values, ideals, conscious wishes and identifications is not the only expression or even the most truthful embodiment of what they really desire . . .": Mark Bracher, *Lacan, Discourse, and Social Change: A Psychoanalytic Cultural Criticism* (1993), 77, quoted in David S. Caudill, "Lacanian Ethics and the Desire for Law," *Cardozo Law Review* 16 (1995): 793–803. See generally "Law and the Postmodern Mind," *Cardozo Law Review* 16 (1995): 699; Dragan Milovanovic, *Postmodern Law and Disorder: Psychoanalytic Semiotics, Chaos, and Juridic Exegeses* (Liverpool: Deborah Charles, 1992), e.g., 9.

Bibliography

1. STATUTES (ARRANGED CHRONOLOGICALLY)

Magna Carta, 9 Hen. III (1225).
Carta Forestæ, 9 Hen. III (1225).
20 Hen. III (1235).
Statute de Anno et die bissextili, 21 Hen. III (1236).
Statute de Scaccario, 51 Hen. III, Stat. 5 (1266)
3 Edw. IV, c. 2 (1263).
Assisa Panis et Cervisiæ, 51 Hen. III, Stat. 1 (1266).
Statute de Marleberge, 52 Hen. III (1267).
Statute of Westminster the First, 3 Edw. I (1275).
De officio coronatoris, 4 Edw. I, Stat. 2 (1276).
Statute of Bigamy, 4 Edw. I, Stat. 3 (1276).
7 Edw. I, Stat. 1 (1278).
Statute of Rutland, 10 Edw. I (1282).
Statute of Westminster the Second, 13 Edw. I, Stat. 1 (1285).
Statutum Wynton, 13 Edw. I, Stat. 2 (1285).
An Ordinance for Ireland, 17 Edw. I, cc. 1–8 (1289).
Quia Emptores, 18 Edw. I (1290).
Statute of Money, 20 Edw. I, Stat. 4 (1292).
20 Edw. I (1292).
28 Edw. I (1299).
Articuli super Cartas, 28 Edw. I (1300).
De Tallagio non Concedendo, 34 Edw. I, c. 6 (1306).
7 Edw. I, Stat. 1 & 2 (1312).
7 Edw. II (1313).
10 Edw. III, Stat. 3 (1336).
36 Edw. III, Stat. 1 (1362).
1 Ric. II (1377).
2 Hen. IV, c. 15 (1400).

9 HEN. IV (1407).

27 HEN. VI (1449).

28 HEN. VI, c. 2 (1450).

33 HEN. VI, c. 2 (1454).

1 EDW. IV, c. 1 (1461).

22 EDW. IV, c. 7 (1483).

1 RIC. III, c. 2 (1483).

1 HEN. VII, c. 1 (1485).

7 HEN. VII (1491).

11 HEN. VII, cc. 4 & 12 (1495).

19 HEN. VII (1503).

3 HEN. VIII, cc. 11 & 14 (1511).

4 HEN. VIII, cc. 7 & 8 (1512).

14 & 15 HEN. VIII, cc. 2, 5 & 8 (1522).

20 HEN. III, c. 9 (1235).

4 GEO. II, c. 26 (1731).

Influx of Chinese Restriction Act, 1881 (N.S.W.), 45 VICT. No. 11.

Chinese Restriction and Regulation Act, 1888 (N.S.W.), 52 VICT. No. 4.

51 & 52 VICT. No. 439 (S.A.).

52 VICT. No. 1005 (Vic.).

53 VICT. No. 3 (W.A.).

53 VICT. No. 22 (Qld.).

Sale and Use of Poisons Act of 1891 (Qld.), 55 VICT. No. 31.

The Opium Act, 1895 (S.A.), 58 & 59 VICT. No. 644.

Immigration Act, 1901 (Cth.), No. 4 of 1901.

Commonwealth of Australia Gazette No. 64 (Cth.), 30 December 1905.

Opium Smoking Prohibition Act, 1905 (Vic.), 5 EDW. VII, No. 2003.

Supplement to New South Wales Government Gazette No. 120 (N.S.W.),
   30 August 1927.

Dangerous Drugs Regulations 1930 (Vic.), Gazette No. 12.

Georgia Criminal Code, §27–2534.1 (b).

Fla. Stat. Ann. §782.04 (1).

Texas Penal Code, Art. 1257 (b).

North Carolina General Statute, §14–17.

Police Offences Amendment Act, 1908 (N.S.W.), 8 EDW. VII, c. 12, ss. 18–19.

Customs Act, 1901–1979 (Cwth.).

Drugs, Poisons, and Controlled Substances Act 1981–1983 (Vic.).

Controlled Substances Act, 1984 (S.A.).

Drug Misuse and Trafficking Act 1985 (N.S.W.).

Narcotic Control Act, R.S.C., 1985 (Can.).

Drugs of Dependence Act 1989 (A.C.T.).

Drugs Misuse Act Amendment Act 1990 (Qld.).

2. CASES

Adams v. State 577 S.W. 2d. 717 (Tex.).
Barclay v. Florida (1983), 463 U.S. 939.
Barefoot v. Estelle, Director, Texas Dept. of Corrections (1983), 463 U.S. 880.
Berkey v. Third Ave. Ry. Co. (1926), 155 N.E. 58 (N.Y. 1926).
Blake v. State 239 Ga. 292.
Callins v. Collins (1994), 114 S. Ct. 1127.
Canterbury v. Spence (1972), 464 F. 2d. 772.
Del Ponte v. Del Ponte, New South Wales Court of Appeal, 6 Nov. 1987.
Donoghue v. Stevenson [1931] A.C. 231.
Eddings v. Oklahoma (1982), 455 U.S. 105.
Felder v. State 564 S.W. 2d. 776 (Tex.).
Fisher v. Lowe, No. 60732 (Mich.), (1983) 69 J. Am. Bar Assn. 436.
Francis v. Resweber, Sheriff, et al. (1947), 329 U.S. 459.
Furman v. Georgia (1972), 408 U.S. 238.
Gardner v. Florida (1977), 430 U.S. 349.
Godfrey v. Georgia (1980), 446 U.S. 420.
Gregg v. Georgia (1976), 428 U.S. 153.
Hinz v. Berry, [1970] 2 QB 40.
In re Kemmler v. (1888), 136 U.S. 436.
Jurek v. Texas (1976), 428 U.S. 262.
Lockett v. Ohio (1978), 438 U.S. 586.
London Street Tramways v. London County Council, [1898] A.C. 375.
Maynard v. Cartwright (1988), 486 U.S. 356.
McCleskey v. Kemp, Superintendent, Georgia Diagnostic and Classification Centre (1987), 481 U.S. 279.
McGautha v. California (1971), 402 U.S. 183.
Miller v. Jackson, [1977] 1 QB 976.
Natanson v. Kline (1960), 350 P. 2d 1093 (Calif.).
New Windsor Corporation v. Mellor, [1975] 1 Ch 380.
Nguyen v. Nguyen (1990), 91 A.L.R. 161.
Penry v. Lynagh (1989), 109 S. Ct. 2934.
Practice Statement (Precedent), [1966] 1 W.L.R. 1234.
Proffitt v. Florida (1976), 428 U.S. 242.
Ratté v. Booth (1886), 11 O.R. 491.
Reibl v. Hughes (1980), 114 D.L.R. 3d 1.
Roberts v. Louisiana (1976), 428 U.S. 325.
Shippy v. State 556 S.W. 2d. 246 (Tex.).
Smith v. State 540 S.W. 2d. 693 (Tex.).
Spinkellink v. State (1975), 313 So. 2d. 666 (Ga.).
St. Helen's Smelting Co. v. William Tipping (1865), 11 H.L.C. 642.
State v. Dixon, 283 So. 2d. 1 (Ga.).
Texas v. Johnson (1989), 109 S. Ct. 2533.

Trop v. Dulles (1958), 356 U.S. 86.
W. Drysdale v. C.A. Dugas (1895), 26 S.C.R. 20.
Woodson v. North Carolina (1976), 428 U.S. 280.
Young v. Woodlands Glenelg (1979) 85 L.S.J.S. 15.
Zant v. Stephens (1983), 462 U.S. 862.

3. OTHER PRIMARY SOURCES

References to volumes of the *Commonwealth Parliamentary Debates, Commonwealth Parliamentary Papers, New South Wales Parliamentary Debates, New South Wales Parliamentary Papers, Victorian Parliamentary Debates,* and archival material are completely sourced when cited.

4. BOOKS AND ARTICLES

"A Bibliography of Critical Legal Studies." *Yale Law Journal* 94 (1984): 461.
"Deconstruction and the Possibility of Justice." *Cardozo Law Review* 11 (1990): 919–1734.
"Postmodernism and Law: A Symposium." *Colorado Law Review* 62 (1991): 433–598.
"Closed Systems and Open Justice: The Legal Sociology of Niklas Luhmann." *Cardozo Law Review* 13 (1992): 1419–1770.
"Roundtable—The Call to the Ethical: Deconstruction, Justice, and the Ethical Relationship." *Cardozo Law Review* 13 (1992): 1219–1354.
"Toward a Rational Drug Policy." *University of Chicago Legal Forum* (1994): 1–498.
"Law and the Postmodern Mind." *Cardozo Law Review* 16 (1995): 699–1444.
Ackerman, Diane. *A Natural History of the Senses.* New York: Vintage Books, 1991.
Adams, Hazard, ed. *Critical Theory since Plato.* New York: Harcourt Brace Jovanovich, 1971.
Adler, Morton. *Desire — Right and Wrong: The Ethics of Enough.* New York: Macmillan, 1991.
Agar, Michael. *Ripping and Running: A Formal Ethnography of Urban Heroin Addicts.* New York: Seminar Press, 1973.
Alcoff, Linda. "Cultural Feminism v. Post-structuralism." *Signs* 13 (1988): 405.
Aldridge, David. "Aesthetics and the Individual in the Practice of Medical Research." *Journal of the Royal Society of Medicine* 84 (1991): 147.
Alexander, Gregory. "Talking about Difference: Meanings and Metaphors of Individuality." *Cardozo Law Review* 11 (1990): 1355.
Alexander, Larry. "Striking Back at the Empire: A Brief Survey of Problems in Dworkin's Theory of Law." *Journal of Law and Philosophy* 6 (1987): 419.
Aquinas, Saint Thomas. *Summa Theologiae.* Ed. T. Gilby. London: Eyre & Spottiswoode, 1963.

Arendt, Hannah. *The Human Condition.* Chicago: University of Chicago Press, 1958.

———. "Martin Heidegger at Eighty." *New York Review of Books,* 21 October 1971.

Ariès, Philippe. *The Hour of Our Death.* Trans. Helen Weaver. New York: Oxford University Press, 1981.

Aristotle. *Nicomachean Ethics.* Trans. D. Ross. Oxford: Oxford University Press, 1980.

Arnheim, Rudolf. *The Phenomenology of Aesthetic Experience.* Evanston, Ill.: Northwestern University Press, 1973.

Arthurs, Harry. *Without the Law: Administrative Justice and Legal Pluralism in Nineteenth-Century England.* Toronto: University of Toronto Press, 1985.

Attali, Jacques. *Histoire du temps.* Paris: Presses universitaires de France, 1982.

———. *Noise: The Political Economy of Music.* Trans. Brian Massumi. Minneapolis: University of Minnesota Press, 1985.

Auerbach, Jerold. *Justice without Law.* Oxford: Oxford University Press, 1983.

Austin, John. *The Province of Jurisprudence Determined.* 1834. London: Weidenfeld & Nicholson, 1971.

———. *Lectures in Jurisprudence.* London: John Murray, 1911.

Australia, Commonwealth and States of. *Australian Royal Commission of Inquiry into Drugs, Books A–F.* Hon. Just. E. S. Williams, Commissioner. Canberra: Australian Government Publishing Service, 1980.

Australia, Parliamentary Joint Committee on the National Crime Authority. *Drugs, Crime, and Society.* Peter Cleeland, Commissioner. Canberra: Australian Government Publishing Service, 1989.

Austray, J. J. et al., eds. *Le Droit et le futur.* Paris: Presses Universitaires de France, 1985.

Baehre, John. "Origins of the Penitentiary System." *Ontario History* 69 (1977): 182.

Bagnall, Gary. *Law as Art.* Aldershot, U.K.: Dartmouth, 1996.

Bakan, Joel, and Nicholas K. Blomley. "Spatial Boundaries, Legal Categories, and the Judicial Mapping of the Worker." *Environment and Planning,* special issue (1991).

Baker, C. Edwin. "The Ideology of the Economic Analysis of Law." *Journal of Philosophy and Public Affairs* 5 (1975): 3.

Balkin, Jack M. "Deconstructive Practice and Legal Theory." *Yale Law Journal* 96 (1987): 743.

———. "Ideology as Cultural Software." *Cardozo Law Review* 16 (1995): 1221.

———. "Tradition, Betrayal, and the Politics of Deconstruction." *Cardozo Law Review* 11 (1990): 1613.

Balkin, Jack M., and Sanford Levinson. "Constitutional Grammar." *Texas Law Review* 72 (1994): 1771.

Bardsley, J. "Vancouver's Needle Exchange Program." *Canadian Journal of Public Health* 81 (1990): 39.

Barthes, Roland. *Mythologies*. Trans. Annette Lavers. Frogmore, Hertsfordshire: Paladin, 1972.

———. *Image — Music — Text*. Trans. S. Heath. Glasgow: Fontana, 1977.

Bartlett, Katherine. "Feminist Legal Methods." *Harvard Law Review* 96 (1990): 743.

Bartlett, Katherine, and Rosanne Kennedy, eds. *Feminist Legal Theory: Readings in Law and Gender*. Boulder, Colo.: Westview Press, 1991.

Basho. *On Love and Barley: The Haiku of Basho*. Trans. L. Stryk. London: Penguin, 1985.

Battjes, Robert J., and Roy W. Pickens, eds. *Needle Sharing among Intravenous Drug Abusers: National and International Perspectives*. NIDA Research Monograph 80. Rockville, Md.: U.S. Department of Health and Human Services, 1988.

Baudrillard, Jean. *Critique of the Political Economy of the Sign*. Trans. C. Levin. St. Louis: Telos Press, 1981.

Baxi, Uppendra, ed. *The Right to Be Human*. New Delhi: Lancer International, 1987.

Bean, Philip. *The Social Control of Drugs*. London: Martin Robertson, 1974.

Beardsley, Monroe. *Aesthetics: Problems in the Philosophy of Criticism*. New York: Harcourt, Brace, & World, 1958.

Becker, Edward. *The Denial of Death*. New York: Free Press, 1973.

Becker, Howard. *The Outsiders: Studies in the Sociology of Deviance*. New York: Free Press, 1963.

Bedau, Hugo. *Death Is Different*. Boston: Northeastern University Press, 1987.

Bedau, Hugo, ed. *The Death Penalty in America*. Chicago: Aldine Publishing, 1964.

———. *The Death Penalty in America*. 3d ed. New York: Oxford University Press, 1982.

Belenky, Mary. *Women's Ways of Knowing*. New York: Basic Books, 1986.

Belley, J.-G., ed. *Le Droit soluble: Contributions québecoises à l'étude de l'internormativité*. Paris: L.G.D.J., 1996.

Bender, Leslie. "A Lawyer's Primer on Feminist Theory and Tort." *Journal of Legal Education* 38 (1988): 3.

Benhabib, Seyla. "Critical Theory and Postmodernism: On the Interplay of Ethics, Aesthetics, and Utopia in Critical Theory." *Cardozo Law Review* 11 (1990): 1435.

Bentley, Lionel, ed. *Law and the Senses*. London: Pluto Press, 1996.

Berman, Harold. *Law and Revolution: The Foundation of the Western Legal Tradition*. Cambridge, Mass.: Harvard University Press, 1983.

———. "The Origins of Historical Jurisprudence: Coke, Selden, Hale." *Yale Law Journal* 103 (1994): 1651.

Berman, Paul Schiff. "Rats, Pigs, and Statutes on Trial: The Creation of Cultural Narratives in the Prosecution of Animals and Inanimate Objects." *New York University Law Review* 69 (1994): 288.

Bernasconi, Robert. "Rousseau and the Supplement to the Social Contract: Deconstruction and the Possibility of Democracy." *Cardozo Law Review* 11 (1990): 1539.

Berns, Walter. *For Capital Punishment: Crime and the Morality of Punishment.* New York: Basic Books, 1979.

Berridge, Virginia. "War Conditions and Narcotics Control: The Passing of the Defence of the Realm Act Regulation 40B." *Journal of Social Policy* 7 (1978): 285.

Berridge, Virginia, and Griffith Edwards. *Opium and the People.* London: St. Martin's Press, 1981.

Black, Charles. *Capital Punishment: The Inevitability of Caprice and Mistake.* New York: W. W. Norton, 1974.

———. "Due Process for Death: *Jurek v. Texas* and Companion Cases." *Catholic University Law Review* 26 (1976): 1.

———. "Reflections on Opposing the Death Penalty." *St. Mary's Law Journal* 10 (1978): 1.

Blackstone, William. *Commentaries on the Laws of England.* 1765–69. Chicago: University of Chicago Press, 1979.

Blackwell. "Crime in the London District, 1828–1837." *Queen's Law Journal* 6 (1981): 528.

Blackwell, Judith C., and Patricia G. Erickson, eds. *Illicit Drugs in Canada: A Risky Business.* Scarborough, Ontario: Nelson Canada, 1988.

Blankenburg, E. "The Poverty of Evolutionism: A Critique of Teubner's Case for 'Reflexive Law.'" *Law and Society Review* 18 (1984): 273.

Blomley, Nicholas K. *Law, Space, and the Geographies of Power.* New York: Guilford Press, 1994.

Blomley, Nicholas K., and G. L. Clark. "Law, Theory, and Geography." *Urban Geography* 11 (1990): 433.

Bohman, James. "Complexity, Pluralism, and the Constitutional State: On Habermas' *Faktizität und Geltung*." *Law and Society Review* 28 (1994): 897.

Boodman, Martin. "The Myth of Harmonization of Laws." *American Journal of Comparative Law* (1991): 699.

Bosanquet, Bernard. *History of Aesthetics.* London: Allen & Unwin, 1922.

Bosmajian, Haig. *The Language of Oppression.* Lanham, Md.: University Press of America, 1983.

———. *Metaphor and Reason in Judicial Opinions.* Carbondale: Southern Illinois University Press, 1992.

Bottomley, Anne, Susie Gibson, and Belinda Meteyard. "Dworkin; Which Dworkin? Taking Feminism Seriously." *Journal of Law and Society* 14 (1987): 47.

Bottomley, Stephen, Neil Gunningham, and Stephen Parker, eds. *Law in Context.* Leichhardt, New South Wales: Federation Press, 1991.

Bourdieu, Pierre. "The Force of Law: Toward a Sociology of the Juridical Field." *Hastings Law Journal* 38 (1987): 805.

———. *Language and Symbolic Power.* Cambridge, Mass.: Harvard University Press, 1991.

Bowers, William, and Glenn Pierce. "Arbitrariness and Discrimination under Post-*Furman* Capital Statutes." *Crime and Delinquency* 26 (1980): 563.

———. "The Illusion of Deterrence in Isaac Ehrlich's Research on Capital Punishment." *Yale Law Journal* 85 (1975): 187.

Boyd, Neil. "The Origin of Canadian Narcotics Legislation." *Dalhousie Law Journal* 8 (1984): 102.

Boyle, Jamie. "Is Subjectivity Possible?: The Postmodern Subject in Legal Theory." *Colorado Law Review* 62 (1991): 489.

Bracton, Henry. *On the Laws and Customs of England.* Vols. 1–4. Ed. G. Woodbine, trans. S. Thorpe. Cambridge, Mass.: Belknap Press, 1968–77.

Brenner, Joel Franklin. "Nuisance Law and the Industrial Revolution." *Oxford Journal of Legal Studies* 3 (1974): 403.

Briggs, John. *Fractals: The Pattern of Chaos.* New York: Touchstone, 1992.

Briggs, John, and F. David Peat. *Turbulent Mirror: An Illustrated Guide to Chaos Theory.* London: Verso, 1990.

Brooks, Cleanth. *The Well Wrought Urn.* New York: Harcourt, Brace, 1947.

Brudner, Alan. "The Ideality of Difference: Toward Objectivity in Legal Interpretation." *Cardozo Law Review* 11 (1990): 1133.

Bruun, Kettil, L. Pan, and I. Rexed. *The Gentlemen's Club.* Chicago: University of Chicago Press, 1975.

Butler, E. C. *The Vatican Council, 1869–70.* London: Collins & Harvill Press, 1962.

Butler, Judith. "Deconstruction and the Possibility of Justice: Comments on Bernasconi, Cornell, Miller, Weber." *Cardozo Law Review* 11 (1990): 1715.

Campbell, Tom. *Justice.* Basingstoke, Hampshire: Macmillan, 1988.

Campbell, Tom, and Charles Heginbotham. *Mental Illness: Prejudice, Discrimination, and the Law.* Aldershot, U.K.: Dartmouth, 1991.

Campos, Paul. "Three Mistakes about Interpretation." *Michigan Law Review* 92 (1993): 388.

Carter, James. "They Know It When They See It: Copyright and Aesthetics in the Second Circuit." *St. John's Law Review* (1991): 773.

Carter, Paul. *The Road to Botany Bay: Landscape and History.* New York: Alfred Knopf, 1988.

Casebeer, Kenneth. "Paris Is Closer Than Frankfurt: The Nth American Exceptionalism." *Law and Society Review* 28 (1994): 931.

Cassell, Eric. *The Nature of Suffering and the Goals of Medicine.* New York: Oxford University Press, 1991.

Casti, John L. *Complexification: Explaining a Paradoxical World through the Science of Surprise.* New York: Harper Collins, 1994.

Caudill, David S. "Lacanian Ethics and the Desire for Law." *Cardozo Law Review* 16 (1995): 793.

Cavell, Stanley. *Must We Mean What We Say?* Cambridge: Cambridge University Press, 1969.

Chandler, David. *Capital Punishment in Canada.* Ottawa: McClelland & Stewart, 1976.

Chase, Anthony. "The Left on Rights: An Introduction." *Texas Law Review* 62 (1984): 1541.

Chytry, Josef. *The Aesthetic State*. Berkeley: University of California Press, 1989.

Clanchy, M. T. *From Memory to Written Record (England 1066–1307)*. Oxford: Blackwell, 1993.

Clarke, Jonathan. *New Times and Old Enemies*. London: Harper Collins, 1991.

Clarke, Shelley. "Note: A Reasoned Moral Response: Rethinking Texas's Capital Sentencing Statute after *Penry v. Lynagh*." *Texas Law Review* 68 (1990): 407.

Classen, Constance. *Worlds of Sense: Exploring the Senses in History and across Cultures*. London: Routledge, 1993.

Classen, Constance, David Howes, and Anthony Synnott. *Aroma: The Cultural History of Smell*. London: Routledge, 1994.

Coase, R. H. "The Problem of Social Cost." *Journal of Law and Economics* 3 (1960): 1.

Coleman, Jules. "Moral Theories of Torts: Their Scope and Limits: Part II." *Journal of Law and Philosophy* 2 (1983): 5.

Collins, H. "Roberto Unger and the Critical Legal Studies Movement." *Journal of Law and Society* 14 (1987): 303.

Cook, Anthony E. "Reflections on Postmodernism." *New England Law Review* 26 (1992): 751.

Cooper, David. *The Lesson of the Scaffold: The Public Execution Controversy in Victorian England*. Athens: Ohio University Press, 1974.

Cooter, Robert. "Introduction to Symposium: Void for Vagueness." *California Law Review* 82 (1994): 487.

Copleston, Francis. *Aquinas*. Harmondsworth: Penguin, 1955.

Corbin, Alain. *The Foul and the Fragrant: Odor and the French Social Imagination*. Cambridge, Mass.: Harvard University Press, 1986.

Corcoran, Marlena. "Aristotle's Poetic Justice." *Iowa Law Review* 77 (1992): 837.

Cornell, Drucilla. "The Philosophy of the Limit, Systems Theory, and Feminist Legal Reform." *New England Law Review* 26 (1992): 783.

———. "Toward a Modern/Postmodern Reconstruction of Ethics." *University of Pennsylvania Law Review* 133 (1985): 291.

———. "The Violence of the Masquerade: Law Dressed Up as Justice." *Cardozo Law Review* 11 (1990): 1047.

Cornell, Drucilla, Mark Rosenfeld, and David Gray Carlson, eds. *Deconstruction and the Possibility of Justice*. New York: Routledge, 1992.

Costonis, John. *Icons and Aliens: Law, Aesthetics, and Environmental Change*. Urbana: University of Illinois Press, 1989.

Cotterrell, Roger. *The Politics of Jurisprudence*. London: Butterworths, 1989.

Coulson, J. *Newman and the Common Tradition*. Oxford: Clarendon Press, 1970.

Courtwright, David. *Dark Paradise*. Cambridge, Mass.: Harvard University Press, 1982.

Cover, Robert. "The Bonds of Constitutional Interpretation." *Georgia Law Review* 20 (1986): 815.

———. "Violence and the Word." *Yale Law Journal* 95 (1986): 1601.

Crossman, Brenda. "The Precarious Unity of Feminist Theory and Practice: The Praxis of Abortion." *University of Toronto Faculty Law Review* 44 (1986): 86.

Crowther, Paul. *Art and Embodiment: From Aesthetics to Self-Consciousness.* Oxford: Clarendon Press, 1993.

Culler, Jonathan. "Resisting Theory." *Cardozo Law Review* 11 (1990): 1565.

Cunningham, Clark, Judith Levi, Georgia Green, and Jeffrey Kaplan. "Plain Meaning and Hard Cases (Book Review of L. Solan, *The Language of Judges*)." *Yale Law Journal* 103 (1994): 1561.

Currie, Greg. *An Ontology of Art.* London: Macmillan, 1989.

Curtis, James M. *Culture as Polyphony: An Essay on the Nature of Paradigms.* Columbia: University of Missouri Press, 1978.

Dallmayr, Fred. "Hermeneutics and the Rule of Law." *Cardozo Law Review* 11 (1990): 1449.

Danesi, Marcel. "Thinking Is Seeing: Visual Metaphors and the Nature of Abstract Thought." *Semiotica* 80 (1990): 221.

Davenport-Hines, Richard. *Sex, Death, and Punishment.* London: Collins, 1990.

Davis, Peggy. "Texas Capital Sentencing Procedures: The Role of the Jury and the Restraining Hand of the Expert." *Journal of Criminal Law and Criminology* 69 (1978): 300.

Dawkins, Richard. *The Blind Watchmaker.* New York: Penguin, 1990.

DeGregorio, Jorge. "The Unconscious and the Law/ The Law in the Unconscious." *Cardozo Law Review* 16 (1995): 1023.

de Man, Paul. *Blindness and Insight: Essays in the Rhetoric of Contemporary Criticism.* New York: Oxford University Press, 1971.

Derrida, Jacques. *Acts of Literature.* Ed. Derek Attridge. New York: Routledge, 1980.

———. "Declarations of Independence." *New Political Science* 15 (1986): 7.

———. "Force of Law: The Mystical Foundation of Authority." *Cardozo Law Review* 11 (1990): 919.

———. "For the Love of Lacan." *Cardozo Law Review* 16 (1995): 699.

———. *Margins of Philosophy.* Trans. Alan Bass. Chicago: University of Chicago Press, 1982.

———. *Of Grammatology.* Baltimore: Johns Hopkins University Press, 1976.

———. *Points . . . Interviews, 1974–1994.* Ed. Elisabeth Weber. Stanford, Calif.: Stanford University Press, 1992.

———. *Positions.* Trans. Alan Bass. Chicago: University of Chicago Press, 1981.

———. *The Post Card.* Trans. Alan Bass. Chicago: University of Chicago Press, 1987.

———. "Scribble (Writing-Power)." *Yale French Studies* 58 (1979): 117.

———. "TITLE: To Be Specified." *Sub-stance* 31 (1981): 5.

———. *The Truth in Painting.* Trans. G. Bennington and I. McLeod. Chicago: University of Chicago Press, 1987.

Dewey, John. *Art as Experience.* New York: Milton, Balch & Co., 1934.

Dickie, G. "The Myth of the Aesthetic Attitude." *American Philosophical Quarterly* (1964): 1.

Dix, George. "Administration of the Texas Death Penalty Statutes: Constitutional Infirmities Related to the Prediction of Dangerousness." *Texas Law Review* 55 (1977): 1343.

———. "Appellate Review of the Decision to Impose Death." *Georgetown Law Journal* 68 (1979): 97.

Döllinger, J. J. I. von. *The Pope and the Council.* London: Rivingston, 1869.

Douglas, Mary. *How Institutions Think.* Syracuse: Syracuse University Press, 1986.

———. *Purity and Danger.* London: Routledge & Kegan Paul, 1966.

Douzinas, Costas. *Justice Miscarried: Ethics, Aesthetics, and the Law.* Hemel Hempstead: Harvester Wheatsheaf, 1994.

Douzinas, Costas, Peter Goodrich, and Yifat Hachamovitch, eds. *Politics, Postmodernity, and Critical Legal Studies: The Legality of the Contingent.* London: Routledge, 1994.

Douzinas, Costas, Shaun McVeigh, and Ronnie Warrington. "The Alta(e)rs of Law: The Judgment of Legal Aesthetics." *Theory, Culture, and Society* 9, no. 4 (1992): 93.

Douzinas, Costas, and Ronnie Warrington. "On the Deconstruction of Jurisprudence: Fin(n)is Philosophiae." *Journal of Law and Society* 14 (1987): 33.

———. *Postmodern Jurisprudence.* London: Routledge, 1991.

Drahos, Peter, and Stephen Parker. "The Indeterminacy Paradox in Law." *University of Western Australia Law Review* (1991): 305.

Drew, Les, ed. *Man, Drugs, and Society.* Canberra: Alcohol and Drug Foundation Australia, 1981.

Dreyfus, Hubert, and Paul Rabinow. *Michel Foucault: Beyond Structuralism and Hermeneutics.* Chicago: University of Chicago Press, 1983.

Duncan, Martha. "In Slime and Darkness: The Metaphor of Filth in Criminal Justice." *Tulane Law Review* 68 (1994): 725.

Dworkin, Andrea. *Intercourse.* New York: Free Press, 1987.

Dworkin, Ronald. "Law as Interpretation." *Texas Law Review* 60 (1982): 527.

———. *Law's Empire.* Cambridge, Mass.: Belknap Press, 1986.

———. *Taking Rights Seriously.* Cambridge, Mass.: Belknap Press, 1977.

Eagleton, Terry. *The Ideology of the Aesthetic.* Oxford: Blackwell, 1990.

———. *Literary Theory: An Introduction.* Oxford: Blackwell, 1983.

Eco, Umberto. *The Limits of Interpretation.* Bloomington: Indiana University Press, 1990.

Eco, Umberto, Richard Rorty, Jonathan Culler, and Christine Brooke-Ros. *Interpretation and Overinterpretation.* Ed. Stefan Collini. Cambridge: Cambridge University Press, 1992.

Economides, Kim, Mark Blacksell, and Charles Watkins. "The Spatial Analysis of Legal Systems: Towards a Geography of Law?" *Journal of Law and Society* 13 (1986): 161.

Ehrlich, Isaac. "The Deterrence Effect of Capital Punishment." *American Economic Review* 65 (1975): 397.

———. "Deterrence: Evidence and Inference." *Yale Law Journal* 85 (1975): 209.

Elias, Norbert. *Time: An Essay.* Trans. Edmund Jephcott. Oxford: Basil Blackwell, 1992.

Ellickson, Robert. *Order without Law: How Neighbors Settle Disputes.* Cambridge, Mass.: Harvard University Press, 1991.

Elliott, Ian. "Heroin: Mythologies for Law Enforcers." *Criminal Law Journal* 6 (1982): 6.

Faludi, Susan. *Backlash: The Undeclared War against Women.* London: Chatto & Windus, 1992.

Farber, Daniel A. "The Jurisprudential Cab Ride: A Socratic Dialogue." *Brigham Young University Law Review* (1992): 363.

Feld, S. "Sound Structure as Social Structure." *Ethnomusicology* 28 (1984): 383.

Feldman, Harvey, and Patrick Biernacki. "The Ethnography of Needle Sharing among Intravenous Drug Users." In Robert J. Battjes and Roy W. Pickens, eds., *Needle Sharing among Intravenous Drug Abusers: National and International Perspectives.* NIDA Research Monograph 80. Rockville, Md.: U.S. Department of Health and Human Services, 1988.

Finley, Lucy M. "A Break in the Silence: Including Women's Issues in a Torts Course." *Yale Journal of Law and Feminism* 1 (1990): 41.

Finnis, John. *Natural Law and Natural Rights.* Oxford: Clarendon Press, 1980.

———. "On Reason and Authority in *Law's Empire.*" *Journal of Law and Philosophy* 6 (1987): 357.

Fish, Stanley. "Dennis Martinez and the Use of Theory." *Yale Law Journal* 96 (1987): 1773.

———. *Doing What Comes Naturally: Change, Rhetoric, and the Practice of Theory in Literary and Legal Studies.* Durham, N.C.: Duke University Press, 1989.

———. *Is There a Text in This Class?* Cambridge, Mass.: Harvard University Press, 1980.

Fitzgerald, Peter, and Alan Hunt. "Critical Legal Studies: An Introduction." *Journal of Law and Society* 14 (1987): 5.

Fitzpatrick, Peter. "'The Desperate Vacuum': Imperialism and Law in the Experience of Enlightenment." *Droit et societé* 13 (1989): 347.

———. "Law and Societies." *Osgoode Hall Law Journal* 22 (1984): 115.

———. *The Mythology of Modern Law.* London: Routledge, 1992.

Fitzpatrick, Peter, ed. *Dangerous Supplements: Resistance and Renewal in Jurisprudence.* London: Pluto Press, 1991.

Fitzpatrick, Peter, and Alfred Rüegg. "Book Review, *Without the Law* by Harry Arthurs." *Journal of Legal Pluralism and Unofficial Law* 27 (1988): 135.

Foucault, Michel. *The Archaeology of Knowledge.* Trans. A. M. Sheridan Smith. New York: Pantheon Books, 1972.

———. *The Birth of the Clinic: An Archaeology of Medical Perception.* Trans. A. M. Sheridan Smith. New York: Vintage Books, 1975.

———. *The Care of the Self.* Vol. 3 of *The History of Sexuality.* Trans. Robert Hurley. New York: Random House, 1988.

———. *Discipline and Punish.* Trans. A. M. Sheridan Smith. New York: Vintage Books, 1979.

———. *Madness and Civilization: A History of Insanity in the Age of Reason.* Trans. R. Howard. New York: Vintage Books, 1988.

———. *The Order of Things: An Archaeology of the Human Sciences.* New York: Vintage Books, 1973.

———. *Power/Knowledge: Selected Interviews and Other Writings 1972–1977.* Ed. Colin Gordon. New York: Pantheon Books, 1980.

———. *The Use of Pleasure.* Vol. 2 of *The History of Sexuality.* Trans. Robert Hurley. New York: Vintage Books, 1986.

Frank, Jerome. *Law and the Modern Mind.* New York: Brentano's, 1930.

———. "Say It with Music." *Harvard Law Review* 61 (1948): 921.

———. "Words and Music: Some Remarks on Statutory Interpretation." *Columbia Law Review* 47 (1947): 1259.

Frankfurter, Felix. "Some Reflections on the Reading of Statutes." *Columbia Law Review* 47 (1947): 529.

Friedman, Laurence. *A History of American Law.* New York: Simon & Schuster, 1973.

Frug, Mary Joe. "Law and Postmodernism: The Politics of a Marriage." *Colorado Law Review* 62 (1991): 483.

Frye, Northrop. *Anatomy of Criticism: Four Essays.* Princeton: Princeton University Press, 1957.

———. *The Great Code: The Bible and Literature.* Toronto: Academic Press Canada, 1982.

Fuller, Lon. *The Law in Quest of Itself.* Chicago: Foundation Press, 1940.

———. *Legal Fictions.* Stanford: Stanford University Press, 1967.

———. *The Morality of Law.* New Haven: Yale University Press, 1969.

———. "Positivism and Fidelity to Law—A Reply to Professor Hart." *Harvard Law Review* 71 (1958): 630.

Furst, Peter T. *Hallucinogens and Culture.* San Francisco: Chandler & Sharp, 1976.

Gabel, Peter. "The Phenomenology of Rights Consciousness and the Pact of the Withdrawn Selves." *Texas Law Review* 62 (1984): 1563.

Gadamer, Hans-Georg. *The Relevance of the Beautiful and Other Essays.* Trans. N. Walker. Cambridge: Cambridge University Press, 1986.

Galanter, Marc. "Justice in Many Rooms: Courts, Private Ordering, and Indigenous Law." *Journal of Legal Pluralism and Unofficial Law* 19 (1981): 1.

Gasché, Rudolphe. "On Critique, Hypercriticism, and Deconstruction: The Case of Benjamin." *Cardozo Law Review* 13 (1992): 1115.

Gasset, José Ortega y. *Phenomenology and Art.* Trans. P. Silver. New York: W. W. Norton, 1975.

Gay, Peter. *Style in History.* New York: W. W. Norton, 1974.

Geertz, Clifford. *After the Fact.* Cambridge, Mass.: Harvard University Press, 1995.

———. *The Interpretation of Cultures.* New York: Basic Books, 1973.

———. *Local Knowledge: Further Essays in Interpretive Anthropology.* New York: Basic Books, 1983.

Genette, G. "Structure and Function of the Title in Literature." *Critical Inquiry* 14 (1988): 692.

Gey, Stephen. "This Is Not a Flag: The Aesthetics of Desecration." *Wisconsin Law Review* (1990): 1549.

Gillers, Stephen. "Deciding Who Dies." *University of Pennsylvania Law Review* 129 (1981): 1.

Gilligan, Carol. *In a Different Voice.* Cambridge, Mass.: Harvard University Press, 1982.

Girard, François. *Thirty-two Short Films about Glenn Gould.* Montréal: National Film Board of Canada, 1993.

Gleick, James. *Chaos: Making a New Science.* New York: Viking, 1987.

Gödel, Kurt. *Collected Works.* Vol. 1. Ed. S. Feferman. Oxford: Oxford University Press, 1986.

———. *On Formally Undecidable Propositions of Principia Mathematica and Related Systems.* New York: Basic Books, 1962.

Goldberg, Arthur, and Alan Dershowitz. "Declaring the Death Penalty Unconstitutional." *Harvard Law Review* 83 (1970): 1773.

Goodhart, A. L. "The *Ratio Decidendi* of a Case." *Modern Law Review* 22 (1959): 117.

Goodman, Nelson. *Languages of Art.* Indianapolis: Hackett Publishing, 1976.

Goodrich, Peter. "The Antinomies of Legal Theory: An Introductory Survey." *Legal Studies* 3 (1983): 1.

———. "Historical Aspects of Legal Interpretation." *Indiana Law Journal* 61 (1985): 331.

———. *Languages of Law: From Logics of Memory to Nomadic Masks.* London: Weidenfeld & Nicholson, 1990.

———. "Law and Language: An Historical and Critical Introduction." *Journal of Law and Society* 11 (1984): 173.

———. *Legal Discourse: Studies in Linguistics, Rhetoric, and Legal Analysis.* Basingstoke, Hampshire: Macmillan, 1987.

———. "Literacy and the Languages of the Early Common Law." *Journal of Law and Society* 14 (1987): 422.

———. *Oedipus Lex: Psychoanalysis, History, Law.* Berkeley: University of California Press, 1995.

———. *Reading the Law.* Oxford: Blackwell, 1986.

———. "Rhetoric as Jurisprudence." *Oxford Journal of Legal Studies* 4 (1984): 88.

———. "The Rise of Legal Formalism; Or the Defences of Legal Faith." *Legal Studies* 3 (1983): 248.

———. "The Role of Linguistics in Legal Analysis." *Modern Law Review* 47 (1984): 523.

———. "Signs Taken for Wonders." *Law and Social Inquiry* 23 (1998): 707.

———. "Translating Legendre or, the Poetical Sermon of a Contemporary Jurist." *Cardozo Law Review* 16 (1995): 963.

Goody, Jack. *The Logic of Writing and the Organization of Society.* Cambridge: Cambridge University Press, 1986.

Gordon, Robert. "Critical Legal Histories." *Stanford Law Review* 36 (1984): 57.

Gottlieb, Gerald. "Testing the Death Penalty." *Southern California Law Review* 34 (1961): 268.

Gould, Glenn. *The Glenn Gould Reader.* Toronto: Lester & Orpan Dennys, 1984.

Gould, Stephen Jay. *Wonderful Life.* Harmondsworth: Penguin, 1989.

Gracyk, T. "Pornography as Representation: Aesthetic Representations." *Journal of Aesthetic Education* 21 (1987): 103.

Graham, H. "'Our Tong Maternall Maruellously Amendyd and Augmentyd': The First Englishing and Printing of the Medieval Statutes at Large, 1530–1533." *University of California Los Angeles Law Review* 13 (1965): 58.

Grazias, Sebastian. *Of Time, Work, and Leisure.* New York: Twentieth Century Fund, 1962.

Grbich, Judith. "The Body in Legal Theory." *University of Tasmania Law Review* 11 (1992): 26.

Greenhouse, Carol J. "Dimensions spatio-temporelles du pluralisme juridique." *Anthropologie et sociétés* 13 (1989): 35.

———. "Just in Time: Temporality and the Cultural Legitimation of Law." *Yale Law Journal* 98 (1989): 1631.

Grey, Thomas C. *The Case of Wallace Stevens: Law and the Practice of Poetry.* Cambridge, Mass.: Harvard University Press, 1991.

Griffiths, John. "What Is Legal Pluralism?" *Journal of Legal Pluralism and Unofficial Law* 24 (1986): 1.

Grimes, Ronald L. *Marrying and Burying: Rites of Passage in a Man's Life.* Boulder, Colo.: Westview Press, 1995.

Grout, Donald Jay. *A History of Western Music.* 2d ed. New York: W. W. Norton, 1960.

Habermas, Jürgen. *Between Facts and Norms: Contributions to a Discourse Theory of Law and Democracy.* Trans. William Rehg. Cambridge, Mass.: MIT Press, 1995.

———. *Knowledge and Human Interests.* Trans. Jeremy Shapiro. Boston: Beacon Press, 1971.

———. *The Philosophical Discourse of Modernity.* Trans. Frederick G. Lawrence. Cambridge, Mass.: MIT Press, 1991.

———. *Toward a Rational Society.* Trans. Jeremy Shapiro. London: Heinemann, 1971.

Haldar, Piyel. "In and Out of Court: On Topographies of Law and the Architecture of Court Buildings." *International Journal for the Semiotics of Law* 7 (1994): 185.

Halper, Louise. "Tropes of Anxiety and Desire: Metaphor and Metonymy in the Law of Takings." *Yale Journal of Law and Humanities* 2 (1990): 31.

Harding, Sandra, ed. *Feminism and Methodology*. Bloomington: Indiana University Press, 1987.

Harding, Sandra, and Merrill Hintikka, eds. *Discovering Reality: Feminist Perspectives on Epistemology, Metaphysics, and Philosophy of Science*. Dordrecht: D. Reidel, 1983.

Harris, Angela. "Race and Essentialism in Feminist Legal Theory." *Stanford Law Review* 42 (1990): 581.

Harrison, Frank L. *Music in Medieval Britain*. London: Routledge & Kegan Paul, 1958.

Hart, H. L. A. *The Concept of Law*. Oxford: Clarendon Press, 1961.

———. "Positivism and the Separation of Law and Morals." *Harvard Law Review* 71 (1958): 593.

Hartog, Hendrik. "Pigs and Positivism." *Wisconsin Law Review* (1985): 899.

Hawkesworth, M. "Knowers, Knowing, Known: Feminist Theory and Claims of Truth." *Signs* 14 (1989): 533.

Hawkins, Harriet. *Strange Attractors: Literature, Culture, and Chaos Theory*. Hemel Hempstead: Prentice Hall/Harvester Wheatsheaf, 1995.

Hay, Douglas. "The Criminal Prosecution in England and Its Historians." *Modern Law Review* 47 (1984): 1.

Hay, Douglas, Peter Linebaugh, and E. P. Thompson, eds. *Albion's Fatal Tree: Crime and Society in Eighteenth-Century England*. London: Allen Lane, 1977.

Hayles, N. Katherine. *Chaos Bound: Orderly Disorder in Contemporary Literature and Science*. Ithaca, N.Y.: Cornell University Press, 1990.

Hayles, N. Katherine, ed. *Chaos and Order: Complex Dynamics in Literature and Science*. Chicago: University of Chicago Press, 1991.

Hegel, George W. F. *Philosophy of Nature*. Trans. M. J. Petry. London: Allen & Unwin, 1970.

———. *Philosophy of Right*. Trans. A. M. Knox. Oxford: Oxford University Press, 1967.

Heidegger, Martin. *Being and Time*. Trans. J. Macquarrie and E. Robinson. New York: Harper & Row, 1962.

———. *History of the Concept of Time: Prolegomena*. Trans. Theodore Kisiel. Bloomington: Indiana University Press, 1985.

———. *Poetry, Language, Thought*. Trans. and ed. A. Hofstadter. New York: Harper & Row, 1971.

Helgerson, Richard. *Forms of Nationhood: The Elizabethan Writing of England*. Chicago: University of Chicago Press, 1992.

Helmer, John. *Drugs and Minority Oppression*. New York: Seabury Press, 1975.

Hibbitts, Bernard J. "Making Sense of Metaphors: Visuality, Aurality, and the Reconfiguration of American Legal Discourse." *Cardozo Law Review* 16 (1994): 229.

Highwater, Jamake. *Myth and Sexuality.* New York: Meridian, 1990.

Hobbes, Thomas. *Leviathan.* Ed. Michael Oakeshott. Oxford: Blackwells, 1946.

Hobsbawm, Eric, and T. Ranger, eds. *The Invention of Tradition.* Cambridge: Cambridge University Press, 1983.

Hoeflich, M. H. "Law and Geometry: Legal Science from Leibniz to Langdell." *American Journal of Legal History* 30 (1986): 95.

Hoffmann, Nigel. "Beyond the Division of Science and Art: Goethe and the 'Organic' Tradition." *Social Alternatives* 1 (1996): 46.

Hofstadter, Albert, and R. Kuhns, eds. *Philosophies of Art and Beauty: Selected Readings from Plato to Heidegger.* Chicago: University of Chicago Press, 1964.

Hofstadter, Douglas R. *Gödel, Escher, Bach: An Eternal Golden Braid; A Metaphysical Fugue on Minds and Machines.* Hassocks, Essex: Harvester Press, 1979.

Holmes, Oliver Wendell. *The Common Law.* Boston: Little, Brown & Co., 1963.

———. "The Path of the Law." *Harvard Law Review* 10 (1897): 457.

Horkheimer, Max, and Theodor Adorno. *The Dialectic of Enlightenment.* New York: Continuum, 1982.

Horn, Nicholas. "Tityrus." *Law/Text/Culture* 1 (1994): 48.

Horwitz, Morton. "The Historical Contingency of the Role of History." *Yale Law Journal* 90 (1981): 1057.

———. "History and Theory." *Yale Law Journal* 96 (1987): 1825.

———. *The Transformation of American Law, 1780–1860.* Cambridge, Mass.: Harvard University Press, 1977.

———. *The Transformation of American Law, 1870–1960: The Crisis in Legal Orthodoxy.* New York: Oxford University Press, 1992.

Howes, David. "Odour in the Court." *Border/Lines* (Winter 1989–90): 28.

———. "'We Are the World' and Its Counterparts: Popular Song as Constitutional Discourse." *Politics, Culture, and Society* 3 (1990): 315.

Howes, David, ed. *The Varieties of Sensory Experience: A Sourcebook in the Anthropology of the Senses.* Toronto: University of Toronto Press, 1991.

Howes, David, and M. Lalonde. "The History of Sensibilities: Of the Standard of Taste in Mid-Eighteenth Century England and the Circulation of Smells in Post-Revolutionary France." *Dialectical Anthropology* 16 (1991): 125.

Hoy, David Couzens. "Dworkin's Constructive Optimism v. Deconstructive Legal Nihilism." *Journal of Law and Philosophy* 6 (1987): 321.

———. "Interpreting the Law: Hermeneutical and Poststructuralist Perspectives." *Southern California Law Review* 58 (1985): 136.

Hoy, David Couzens, ed. *Foucault: A Critical Reader.* Oxford: Basil Blackwell, 1986.

Hume, David. *Treatise of Human Nature.* Oxford: Oxford University Press, 1978.

Hunt, Alan. "The Big Fear: Law Confronts Postmodernism." *McGill Law Journal* 35 (1990): 507.

———. "The Critique of Law: What Is 'Critical' about Critical Legal Theory?" *Journal of Law and Society* 14 (1987): 5.

———. "Foucault's Expulsion of Law: Toward a Retrieval." *Law and Social Inquiry* 17 (1992): 1.

———. *Governance of the Consuming Passions.* New York: St Martin's Press, 1996.

Hunt, Alan, ed. *Reading Dworkin Critically.* New York: Berg, 1992.

Hunt, Alan, and Gary Wickham, eds. *Foucault and Law.* London: Pluto Press, 1994.

Hutchinson, Allan. *Dwelling on the Threshold: Critical Essays in Modern Legal Thought.* Toronto: Caswell, 1988.

———. "From Cultural Construction to Historical Deconstruction." *Yale Law Journal* 94 (1984): 209.

Hutchinson, Allan, and Patrick Monahan. "Law, Politics, and Critical Legal Studies." *Stanford Law Review* 36 (1984): 199.

———. "The 'Rights' Stuff: Roberto Unger and Beyond." *Texas Law Review* 62 (1984): 1477.

Huxley, Aldous. *The Doors of Perception.* London: Chatto & Windus, 1954.

Ignatieff, Michael. *A Just Measure of Pain: The Penitentiary in the Industrial Revolution 1750–1823.* New York: Macmillan, 1978.

Illich, Ivan. *In the Vinveyard of the Text.* Chicago: University of Chicago Press, 1993.

Illich, Ivan, and Barry Sanders. *ABC: The Alphabetization of the Popular Mind.* London: Penguin, 1988.

Innes, Joanna, and John Styles. "The Crime Wave: Recent Writings on Crime and Criminal Justice in Eighteenth-Century England." *Journal of British Studies* 25 (1986): 380.

Jackson, Bernard S. *Semiotics and Legal Theory.* London: Routledge & Kegan Paul, 1985.

Jacobson, A. "Autopoietic Law: The New Science of Niklas Luhmann." *Michigan Law Review* 87 (1989): 1647.

Jameson, Fredric, ed. *Aesthetics and Politics.* London: NLB, 1977.

Jamieson, Dale. "The Poverty of Postmodernist Theory." *Colorado Law Review* 62 (1991): 577.

Jarlais, Don Des, Samuel Friedman, and David Strug. "AIDS and Needle-sharing within the IV-Drug Use Subculture." In Douglas Feldman and Thomas Johnson, eds., *The Social Dimensions of AIDS.* New York: Praeger, 1986.

Jay, Martin. "'The Aesthetic Ideology' as Ideology; or, What Does It Mean to Aestheticize Politics?" *Cultural Critique* 21 (1992): 41.

Johnson, Robert. *Condemned to Die: Life under Sentence of Death.* New York: Elsevier, 1981.

Jung, Carl. *Man and His Symbols.* London: Aldus, 1964.

Kamuf, Peggy, ed. *A Derrida Reader: Between the Blinds.* New York: Columbia University Press, 1991.

Kant, Immanuel. *Critique of Judgment.* Trans. W. Pluhar. Indianapolis: Hackett, 1987.

Kaplan, John. *The Hardest Drug: Heroin and Social Policy.* Chicago: University of Chicago Press, 1983.

Kasirer, Nicholas. "Larger Than Life (A Review Essay of *Broken Tablets* by Jonathan Ribner)." *Canadian Journal of Law and Society* 2 (1995): 185.

Katz, Jay. *The Silent World of Doctor and Patient.* New York: Free Press, 1984.

Keenan, Thomas. "Deconstruction and the Impossibility of Justice." *Cardozo Law Review* 11 (1990): 1675.

Kelly, Kevin. *Out of Control: The New Science of Machines, Social Systems, and the Economic World.* Reading, Mass.: Addison-Wesley, 1994.

Kelly, Michael, ed. *Critique and Power: Recasting the Foucault / Habermas Debate.* Cambridge, Mass.: The MIT Press, 1994.

Kelman, Herbert. "Violence without Moral Restraint: Reflections on the Dehumanization of Victims and Victimizers." *Journal of Social Issues* 29, no. 4 (1973): 25.

Kelman, Mark. *A Guide to Critical Legal Studies.* Cambridge, Mass.: Harvard University Press, 1987.

———. "Trashing." *Stanford Law Review* 36 (1984): 293.

Kelsen, Hans. *General Theory of Law and State.* Trans. Anders Wedberg. 1945. New York: Russell & Russell, 1961.

Kennedy, Duncan. "Form and Substance in Private Law Adjudication." *Harvard Law Review* 89 (1976): 1685.

———. "Legal Formality." *Journal of Legal Studies* 2 (1973): 351.

Kennedy, Duncan, and Peter Gabel. "Roll Over Beethoven." *Stanford Law Review* 36 (1984): 1.

Kenyon, Nicholas, ed. *Authenticity and Early Music.* Oxford: Oxford University Press, 1988.

Kestenbaum, V. *The Phenomenological Sense of John Dewey: Habit and Meaning.* Atlantic Highlands, N.J.: Humanities Press, 1977.

Kevelson, Roberta. *The Law as a System of Signs.* New York: Plenum Press, 1988.

———. "Semiotics and Methods of Legal Inquiry." *Indiana Law Journal* 61 (1985): 355.

Kevelson, Roberta, ed. *Law and Semiotics.* Vols. 1–3. New York: Plenum Press, 1987–92.

Kivy, Peter. *Authenticities: Philosophical Reflections on Musical Performance.* Ithaca, N.Y.: Cornell University Press, 1995.

Klinck, Dennis. "'This Other Eden': Lord Denning's Pastoral Vision." *Oxford Journal of Legal Studies* 14 (1994): 25.

———. *The Word of the Law.* Ottawa: Carleton University Press, 1992.

Koestler, Arthur. *Darkness at Noon.* Harmondsworth: Penguin, 1964.

———. *Reflections on Hanging.* London: Victor Gollancz, 1956.

Kramer, Lawrence. *Music as Cultural Practice, 1800–1900.* Berkeley: University of California Press, 1990.

Kramer, Matthew H. *Legal Theory, Political Theory, and Deconstruction.* Bloomington: Indiana University Press, 1991.

Kraut, Alan M. *Silent Travelers: Germs, Genes, and the "Immigrant Menace."* New York: Basic Books, 1994.

Kress, Ken. "Coherence and Formalism." *Harvard Journal of Law and Public Policy* 16 (1993): 639.

———. "Legal Indeterminacy." *California Law Review* 77 (1989): 283.

Kristeva, Julia. *Desire in Language: A Semiotic Approach to Literature and Art.* New York: Columbia University Press, 1980.

———. *Proust and the Meaning of Time.* Trans. Stephen Bann. New York: Columbia University Press, 1993.

Kronman, Anthony. "Amor Fati (The Love of Fate)." *University of Toronto Law Journal* 45 (1995): 163.

———. "Precedent and Tradition." *Yale Law Journal* 99 (1990): 1029.

Krygier, Martin. "Law as Tradition." *Journal of Law and Philosophy* 5 (1986): 237.

Kubie, Lawrence S. "The Fantasy of Dirt." *Psychoanalytic Quarterly* 6 (1937): 388.

Kuhn, Thomas. *The Structure of Scientific Revolutions.* Chicago: University of Chicago Press, 1962.

Küng, Hans. *Infallible?: An Inquiry.* Trans. E. Quinn. Garden City, N.Y.: Doubleday, 1971.

Lacan, Jacques. *The Seminar of Jacques Lacan, Book VII: The Ethics of Psychoanalysis.* Trans. Dennis Porter. New York: W. W. Norton, 1986.

LaCapra, Dominick. "Violence, Justice, and the Force of Law." *Cardozo Law Review* 11 (1990): 1065.

Lakoff, George. *Women, Fire, and Dangerous Things: What Categories Reveal about the Mind.* Chicago: University of Chicago Press, 1987.

Lakoff, George, and Mark Johnson. *Metaphors We Live By.* Chicago: University of Chicago Press, 1980.

Langbein, John. "Albion's Fatal Flaw." *Past and Present* 54 (1983): 96.

Langer, Susanne K. *Feeling and Form: A Theory of Art.* London: Routledge & Kegan Paul, 1953.

———. *Mind: An Essay on Human Feeling.* Baltimore: Johns Hopkins University Press, 1988.

———. *Philosophy in a New Key.* Cambridge, Mass.: Harvard University Press, 1942.

———. *Philosophy in a New Key.* New ed. Cambridge, Mass.: Harvard University Press, 1978.

Laurence, John. *A History of Capital Punishment.* New York: Citadel Press, 1960.

Lee, Pamela E. "The Aesthetics of Value, the Fetish of Method." *RES: Anthropology and Aesthetics* 27 (1995): 133.

Leff, Arthur. "Unspeakable Ethics, Unnatural Law." *Duke Law Journal* (1979): 1229.

Lefferts, Peter. *The Motet in England in the Fourteenth Century.* Studies in Musicology No. 94. Ed. George Buelow. Ann Arbor, Mich.: UMI Research Press, 1986.

Legendre, Pierre. "The Other Dimension of Law." *Cardozo Law Review* 16 (1995): 943.

Lehman, David. *Signs of the Times: Deconstruction and the Fall of Paul de Man.* New York: Poseidon Press, 1991.

Leppert, Robert, and Susan McClary, eds. *Music and Society.* Cambridge: Cambridge University Press, 1987.

Lesser, Wendy. *Pictures at an Execution: An Inquiry into the Subject of Murder.* Cambridge, Mass.: Harvard University Press, 1993.

Levenson, Thomas. *Measure for Measure: A Musical History of Science.* New York: Touchstone Books, 1995.

Levine, George, ed. *Aesthetics and Ideology.* New Brunswick, N.J.: Rutgers University Press, 1994.

Levine, Stephen, ed. *Death Row: An Affirmation of Life.* San Francisco: Glide Publications, 1972.

Levinson, Saul. "Law as Literature." *Texas Law Review* 60 (1982): 373.

Levinson, Saul, and Jack M. Balkin. "Law, Music, and Other Performing Arts." *University of Pennsylvania Law Review* 139 (1991): 1597.

Llewellyn, Karl. *The Bramble Bush: On Our Law and Its Study.* New York: Oceana, 1951.

———. *Jurisprudence: Realism in Theory and Practice.* Chicago: University of Chicago Press, 1962.

———. *My Philosophy of Law.* Boston: Little, Brown & Co., 1941.

———. "On the Good, the True, the Beautiful in Law." *University of Chicago Law Review* 9 (1942): 224.

———. "A Realistic Jurisprudence: The Next Step." *Columbia Law Review* 30 (1930): 431.

———. "Some Realism about Realism." *Harvard Law Review* 44 (1944): 1222.

———. "What Law Cannot Do for Inter-racial Peace." *Villanova Law Review* 3 (1957): 30.

Lorenz, Edward. "Deterministic Nonperiodic Flow." *Journal of Atmospheric Sciences* 20 (1963): 130.

Luban, David. "Legal Modernism." *Michigan Law Review* 84 (1986): 1656.

Luhmann, Niklas. "The Third Question: The Creative Use of Paradoxes in Law and Legal History." *Journal of Law and Society* 15 (1988): 153.

Lynd, Staughton. "Communal Rights." *Texas Law Review* 62 (1984): 1417.

Lyotard, Jean-François. *Libidinal Economy.* Trans. Iain Hamilton Grant. Bloomington: Indiana University Press, 1993.

———. *The Postmodern Condition: A Report on Knowledge.* Trans. Geoff Bennington and Brian Massumi. Minneapolis: University of Minnesota Press, 1984.

Macdonald, Roderick. "Academic Questions." *Legal Education Review* 3 (1992): 61.

———. "Critical Legal Pluralism as a Construction of Normativity and the Emergence of Law." Paper prepared for Law and the Determinants of Social Order Programme, Canadian Institute for Advanced Research, Montréal, Que., 1994.

———. "Legal Bilingualism." *McGill Law Journal* 42 (1997): 121.

———. "Office Politics." *University of Toronto Law Journal* 40 (1990): 419.

———. "Theses on Access to Justice." *Canadian Journal of Law and Society* 7, no. 2 (1992): 23.

———. "Whose Access? Which Justice? (Review of Allan Hutchinson, ed., *Access to Civil Justice* [Toronto: Carswell, 1990])." *Canadian Journal of Law and Society* 7, no. 1 (1992): 175.

MacIntyre, Alisdair. *Whose Justice? Which Rationality?* Notre Dame, Ind.: University of Notre Dame Press, 1988.

MacKinnon, Catherine. "Feminism, Marxism, Method, and the State: Toward Feminist Jurisprudence." *Signs* 8 (1983): 635.

———. *Feminism Unmodified.* Cambridge, Mass.: Harvard University Press, 1987.

MacNeil, William P. "Living On: Borderlines—Law/History." *Law and Critique* 6 (1995): 167.

Madry, Alan R. "Analytic Deconstructionism? The Intellectual Voyeurism of Anthony D'Amato." *Fordham Law Review* 63 (1995): 1033.

Maitland, Frederick, ed. *Bracton's Note Books.* Vol. 1. London: C. J. Clay, 1889.

Mandelbrot, Benoit. *The Fractal Geometry of Nature.* New York: W. H. Freeman, 1983.

Manderson, Desmond. *From Mr Sin to Mr Big: A History of Australian Drug Laws.* Melbourne: Oxford University Press, 1993.

———. "Metamorphoses: Clashing Symbols in the Social Construction of Drugs." *Journal of Drug Issues* 25 (1995): 799.

———. "*Statuta* v. Acts: Interpretation, Music, and English Legislation." *Yale Journal of Law and the Humanities* 11 (1995): 131.

Martin, Emily. *The Woman in the Body: A Cultural Analysis of Reproduction.* Boston: Beacon Press, 1987.

Mathews, Harry. *Immeasurable Distances.* Venice, Calif.: Lapis Press, 1991.

Matthews, Roger, ed. *Informal Justice.* London: Sage, 1988.

McCluskey, Lord. *Law, Justice, and Democracy: The Reith Lectures.* London: Sweet & Maxwell, 1986.

McCoy, Alfred. *Drug Traffic.* Sydney: Harper & Row, 1980.

McGowen, Randall. "The Body and Punishment in Eighteenth-Century England." *Journal of Modern History* 59 (1987): 651.

McIlwain, Charles H. *The High Court of Parliament and Its Supremacy.* New Haven: Yale University Press, 1934.

McLaren, Ian, ed. *The Chinese in Victoria: Official Reports and Documents.* Melbourne: Red Rooster Press, 1985.

McLaren, John. "Nuisance Law and the Industrial Revolution: Some Lessons from Social History." *Oxford Journal of Legal Studies* 3 (1983): 155.

———. "The Tribulations of Antoine Ratté: A Case Study of Environmental Regulation of the Canadian Lumbering Industry in the Nineteenth Century." *University of New Brunswick Law Journal* 33 (1984): 203.

McLuhan, Marshall. *The Gutenberg Galaxy: The Making of Typographic Man.* New York: Signet, 1969.

———. *Understanding Media.* New York: McGraw-Hill, 1964.

McLuhan, Marshall, and Q. Fiore. *The Medium Is the Massage.* Harmondsworth: Penguin, 1967.

Meltsner, Michael. *Cruel and Unusual.* New York: Random House, 1973.

Merry, Sally Engle. "Legal Pluralism." *Law and Society Review* 22 (1988): 869.

Mill, John Stuart. *On Liberty.* Ed. Currin V. Shields. New York: Liberal Arts Press, 1956 (1857).

Miller, J. Hillis. *Versions of Pygmalion.* Cambridge, Mass.: Harvard University Press, 1990.

Miller, James. *The Passion of Michel Foucault.* New York: Simon & Schuster, 1993.

Miller, Toby. *The Well Tempered Self: Citizenship, Culture, and the Postmodern Subject.* Baltimore: Johns Hopkins University Press, 1993.

Milovanovic, Dragon. "Humanistic Sociology and the Chaos Paradigm: Review Essay of N. Katherine Hayles, *Chaos Bound.*" *Humanity and Society* 15 (1991): 135.

———. *Postmodern Law and Disorder: Psychoanalytic Semiotics, Chaos, and Juridic Exegeses.* Liverpool: Deborah Charles, 1992.

Minda, Gary. *Postmodern Legal Movements: Law and Jurisprudence at Century's End.* New York: New York University Press, 1995.

Minow, Martha. "Learning to Live with the Dilemma of Difference." *Law and Contemporary Problems* 48 (1985): 157.

Mnoonin, R. H., and L. Kornhauser. "Bargaining in the Shadow of the Law: The Case of Divorce." *Yale Law Journal* 88 (1979): 950.

Moles, Robert. *Definition and Rule in Legal Theory.* Oxford: Blackwell, 1987.

Monmonier, Mark S. *How to Lie with Maps.* Chicago: University of Chicago Press, 1991.

Montaigne, Michel de. *Four Essays.* Trans. M. A. Screech. London: Penguin, 1995.

Moore, Michael. "A Natural Law Theory of Interpretation." *Southern California Law Review* 58 (1985): 277.

Moore, Sally Falk. "Law and Social Change: The Semi-Autonomous Social Field as an Appropriate Subject of Study." *Law and Society Review* 7 (1973): 719.

Mothersill, Mary. *Beauty Restored.* Oxford: Clarendon Press, 1984.

Motte, Warren F., ed. *OuLiPo: A Primer of Potential Literature.* Lincoln: University of Nebraska Press, 1986.

Mullins, Tom, ed. *The Nature of Chaos.* Oxford: Clarendon Press, 1993.

Münch, Richard. "Autopoiesis by Definition." *Cardozo Law Review* 13 (1992): 1463.

Munro, Thomas. *The Arts and Their Interrelations.* New York: Liberal Arts Press, 1949.

——. *Form and Style in the Arts: An Introduction to Aesthetic Morphology.* Cleveland: Press of Case Western Reserve University, 1970.

Murphy, David. "Plain English: Principles and Practice." Paper presented at the Conference on Legislative Drafting, Canberra, 1992.

Murphy, Sheigla B. "Intravenous Drug Use and AIDS: Notes on the Social Economy of Needle Sharing." *Contemporary Drug Problems* 14 (1987): 373.

Murray, James E. "Understanding Law as Metaphor." *Journal of Legal Education* 34 (1984): 714.

Nakell, Barry. "The Cost of the Death Penalty." *Criminal Law Bulletin* 14 (1978): 68.

Nathanson, Stephen. *An Eye for An Eye?: The Morality of Punishing by Death.* Totowa, N.J.: Rowman & Littlefield, 1987.

Nedelsky, Jennifer. "Law, Boundaries, and the Bounded Self." *Representations* 30 (1990): 162.

Newton, Isaac. *Philosophiae naturalis principia mathematica.* 1687. London: W. Dawson, 1966.

Nicholson, Linda, ed. *Feminism/Postmodernism.* London: Routledge, 1990.

Nietzsche, Friedrich. *Beyond Good and Evil.* Trans. R. Hollingdale. London: Penguin, 1990.

——. *The Birth of Tragedy/The Case of Wagner.* Trans. Walter Kaufmann. New York: Vintage Books, 1967.

——. *On the Genealogy of Morals and Ecce Homo.* Trans. Walter Kaufmann. New York: Vintage Books, 1989.

Nonet, Philippe. "What Is Positive Law?" *Yale Law Journal* 100 (1990): 667.

Nonet, Philippe, and Philip Selznick. *Law and Society in Transition: Toward Responsive Law.* New York: Harper & Row, 1978.

Norris, Christopher. *Deconstruction: Theory and Practice.* London: Routledge, 1982.

——. "Law, Deconstruction, and the Resistance to Theory." *Journal of Law and Society* 15 (1988): 166.

——. *Paul de Man: Deconstruction and Critique of Aesthetic Ideology.* New York: Routledge, 1988.

Nozick, Robert. *Anarchy, State, and Utopia.* Totowa, N.J.: Rowman, 1974.

O'Toole, L. "Dimensions of Semiotic Space in Narrative." *Poetics Today* 1 (1980): 135.

O'Toole, Michael. *The Language of Displayed Art.* Leicester: Leicester University Press, 1994.

Ong, A. *Orality and Literacy: The Technologizing of the Mind.* New York: Methuen, 1982.

Pacher, Daniela. "Aesthetics v. Ideology: The Motives behind 'Law and Literature.'" *Columbia-VLA Journal of Law and the Arts* 14 (1990): 587.

Page, J. Bryan, and Prince C. Smith. "Venous Envy: The Importance of Having Functional Veins." *Journal of Drug Issues* 20 (1990): 291.

Parsinnen, Terry. *Secret Passions, Secret Remedies*. Philadelphia: Institute for Studies of Human Issues, 1983.

Passell, Peter. "The Deterrence Effect of the Death Penalty: A Statistical Test." *Stanford Law Review* 28 (1976): 61.

Peele, Stanton. *The Meaning of Addiction*. Lexington, Mass.: Lexington Books, 1985.

Peitgen, Heinz-Otto. *The Beauty of Fractals*. Berlin: Springer-Verlag, 1986.

Penrose, Roger. *Shadows of the Mind*. London: Vintage Books, 1994.

Perry, Stephen. "Professor Weinrib's Formalism: The Not-So-Empty Sepulchre." *Harvard Journal of Law and Public Policy* 16 (1993): 597.

Peterson, Ivars. *Newton's Clock: Chaos in the Solar System*. New York: W. H. Freeman, 1993.

Philipson, Tomas, and Richard Posner. *Private Choice and Public Health: The AIDS Epidemic in an Economic Perspective*. Cambridge, Mass.: Harvard University Press, 1993.

Pinker, Stephen. *The Language Instinct: How the Mind Creates Language*. New York: William Morrow & Co., 1994.

Plato. *Gorgias*. Trans. W. Helmbold. New York: Liberal Arts Press, 1952.

———. *The Republic*. Trans. D. Lee. London: Penguin, 1974.

Plucknett, Thomas F. T. *Early English Legal Literature*. Cambridge: Cambridge University Press, 1958.

———. *Legislation of Edward I*. Oxford: Clarendon Press, 1949.

———. *Statutes and Their Interpretation in the First Half of the Fourteenth Century*. Cambridge: Cambridge University Press, 1922.

———. *Studies in English Legal History*. London: Hambledon Press, 1983.

Polanyi, Michael. *The Logic of Liberty: Reflections and Rejoinders*. London: Routledge, 1951.

———. *Personal Knowledge*. London: Routledge & Kegan Paul, 1958.

Pollock, Frederick, and F. W. Maitland. *The History of English Law*. Vols. 1–2. Cambridge: Cambridge University Press, 1895.

Polsby, Daniel, and Robert Popper. "Ugly: An Inquiry into the Problem of Racial Gerrymandering under the Voting Rights Act." *Michigan Law Review* 92 (1993): 652.

Popper, Karl. *The Poverty of Historicism*. London: Ark, 1957.

Porter, Roy. *England in the Eighteenth Century*. Harmondsworth: Penguin, 1975.

Posner, Richard. "Bork and Beethoven." *Stanford Law Review* 42 (1990): 1365.

———. *Law and Literature: A Misunderstood Relation*. Cambridge, Mass.: Harvard University Press, 1988.

———. "Law as Literature: A Relation Reargued." *Virginia Law Review* 72 (1986): 1351.

Pospisil, Leopold. *Anthropology of Law: A Comparative Perspective*. New Haven: HRAF Press, 1974.

Postema, Gerald. "On the Moral Presence of Our Past." *McGill Law Journal* 36 (1991): 1153.

Pound, Roscoe. "The Call for a Realist Jurisprudence." *Harvard Law Review* 44 (1931): 697.

———. *The Future of the Common Law.* Cambridge, Mass.: Harvard University Press, 1937.

Preble, Edward, and John Casey. "Taking Care of Business: The Heroin User's Life on the Streets." *International Journal of the Addictions* 4 (1969): 1.

Prejean, Helen. *Dead Man Walking: An Eyewitness Account of the Death Penalty in the United States.* New York: Random House, 1993.

Preziosi, Donald. *The Semiotics of the Built Environment.* Indianapolis: Indiana University Press, 1979.

Pue, Wes. "Wrestling with Law: (Geographical) Specificity vs. (Legal) Abstraction." *Urban Geography* 11 (1990): 566.

Purcell Jr., Edward. "American Jurisprudence between the Wars: Legal Realism and the Crisis of Democratic Theory." *American Historical Review* 75 (1969–70): 424.

Radelet, Michael, ed. *Facing the Death Penalty: Essays on a Cruel and Unusual Punishment.* Philadelphia: Temple University Press, 1989.

Radelet, Michael, Hugo Bedau, and Constance Putnam. *In Spite of Innocence: Erroneous Convictions in Capital Cases.* Boston: Northeastern University Press, 1992.

Radin, Margaret. "The Jurisprudence of Death: Evolving Standards for the Cruel and Unusual Punishment Clause." *University of Pennsylvania Law Review* 126 (1978): 989.

Rawls, John. *A Theory of Justice.* Oxford: Oxford University Press, 1972.

Raz, Joseph. *Authority of Law.* Oxford: Clarendon Press, 1979.

———. "Authority, Law, and Morality." *The Monist* 68 (1985): 295.

———. "Dworkin: A New Link in the Chain." *California Law Review* 74 (1986): 1103.

Réaume, Denise. "Is Integrity a Virtue?: Dworkin's Theory of Legal Obligation." *University of Toronto Law Journal* 39 (1989): 38.

Reid Jr., Charles. "Tyburn, *Thanatos,* and Marxist Historiography: The Case of the London Hanged." *Cornell Law Review* (1994): 1158.

Reynolds, Glenn H. "Chaos and the Courts." *Columbia Law Review* 91 (1991): 110.

Rhoden, Nancy. "Litigating Life and Death." *Harvard Law Review* 101 (1988): 375.

Ribner, Jonathan. *Broken Tablets: The Cult of Law in French Art from David to Delacroix.* Berkeley: University of California Press, 1993.

Ricoeur, Paul. *The Rule of Metaphor: Multi-disciplinary Studies of the Creation of Meaning in Language.* Trans. Robert Czerny. Toronto: University of Toronto Press, 1977.

Riley, John. "The Hours of the Georgian Day." *History Today* 24 (1974): 307.

Rolls, Eric. *Sojourners.* St. Lucia: University of Queensland Press, 1992.

Ronell, Avital. *The Telephone Book: Technology, Schizophrenia, Electric Speech.* Lincoln: University of Nebraska Press, 1989.

Rorty, Richard. *Contingency, Irony, and Solidarity.* Cambridge: Cambridge University Press, 1989.

Rosen, Richard. "The 'Especially Heinous' Aggravating Circumstance in Capital Cases: The Standardless Standard." *North Carolina Law Review* (1986): 941.

Rosenfeld, Michael. "Deconstruction and Legal Interpretation: Conflict, Indeterminacy, and the Temptations of the New Legal Formalism." *Cardozo Law Review* 11 (1990): 1211.

Ross, Thomas. "Metaphor and Paradox." *Georgia Law Review* 23 (1989): 1053.

Runnington, Christopher, ed. *Ruffhead's Statutes at Large.* Vols. 1–10. London: Eyre & Strahan, 1786.

Ruvin, A. "Does Law Matter? A Judge's Response to the Critical Legal Studies Movement." *Journal of Legal Education* 37 (1987): 307.

Sack, Peter, and Elizabeth Minchin, ed. *Legal Pluralism — Proceedings of the Canberra Law Workshop VII.* Canberra: Research School of Social Sciences, Australian National University, 1988.

Sacks, Oliver. *The Man Who Mistook His Wife for a Hat.* London: Picador, 1985.

Said, Edward. *Orientalism.* London: Routledge & Kegan Paul, 1978.

Samek, Robert. *The Meta-Phenomenon.* New York: Philosophical Library, 1981.

Sampford, Charles. *The Disorder of Law.* Oxford: Basil Blackwell, 1989.

Santayana, George. *The Sense of Beauty.* New York: Dover, 1955.

Santos, Boaventura de Sousa. "Law: A Map of Misreading—Toward a Postmodern Conception of Law." *Journal of Law and Society* 14 (1987): 279.

———. "The Law of the Oppressed: The Construction and Reproduction of Legality in Pasagarda." *Law and Society Review* 12 (1977): 5.

———. "Law, State, and Urban Struggles in Recife, Brazil." *Social and Legal Studies* 1 (1992): 235.

———. *Toward a New Common Sense: Law, Science, and Politics in the Paradigmatic Transition.* London: Routledge, 1995.

Sarat, Austin, ed. *The Killing State.* Oxford: Oxford University Press, 1998.

Sarat, Austin, and William Felstiner. "Law and Strategy in the Divorce Lawyer's Office." *Law and Society Review* 20 (1986): 93.

Saul, John Ralston. *Voltaire's Bastards: The Dictatorship of Reason in the West.* Harmondsworth: Penguin, 1992.

Saunders, David. "Approaches to the Historical Relations of the Legal and the Aesthetic." *New Literary History* 23 (1992): 505.

Scarry, Elaine. *The Body in Pain: The Making and Unmaking of the World.* New York: Oxford University Press, 1985.

Schauer, Frederick. "Precedent." *Stanford Law Review* 39 (1987): 571.

Scher, Steven Paul, ed. *Music and Text: Critical Inquiries.* Cambridge: Cambridge University Press, 1992.

Schiller, Friedrich. *On the Aesthetic Education of Man*. Trans. Elizabeth Wilkinson. Oxford: Clarendon Press, 1967.

Schlag, Pierre. "'Le Hors de Texte, C'est Moi': The Politics of Form and the Domestication of Deconstruction." *Cardozo Law Review* 11 (1990): 1631.

Schopenhauer, Arthur. *The World as Will and Idea*. Trans. Richard Haldane. London: K. Paul, Trench, Tubner & Co., 1927.

Schorske, Carl. *Fin-de-Siècle Vienna: Politics and Culture*. London: Weidenfeld & Nicholson, 1979.

Schütz, Anton. "Sons of Writ, Sons of Wrath: Pierre Legendre's Critique of Rational Law-Giving." *Cardozo Law Review* 16 (1995): 979.

Schwartz, Edward, and Warren Schwartz. "Deciding Who Decides Who Dies: Capital Punishment as a Social Choice Problem." Paper presented at the Law and Economics Workshop, Chicago, 1994.

Schwartz, Louis. "Justice, Expediency, and Beauty." *University of Pennsylvania Law Review* 136 (1987): 141.

Scott, Robert E. "Chaos Theory and the Justice Paradox." *William and Mary Law Review* 35 (1993): 329.

Sellin, Thorsten. *The Death Penalty*. Philadelphia: American Law Institute, 1959.

———. *The Penalty of Death*. Beverly Hills: Sage Publications, 1980.

Shils, Edward. *Tradition*. Chicago: University of Chicago Press, 1981.

Silas, Fay. "The Death Penalty: The Comeback Picks up Speed." *ABA Journal* 71 (1985): 48.

Silver, C. "Elmer's Case: A Legal Positivist Replies to Dworkin." *Journal of Law and Philosophy* 6 (1987): 381.

Simmonds, Nigel. *Central Issues in Jurisprudence*. London: Sweet & Maxwell, 1986.

Simon, Jonathan. "Between Power and Knowledge: Habermas, Foucault, and the Future of Legal Studies." *Law and Society Review* 28 (1994): 947.

———. "'In Another Kind of Wood': Michel Foucault and Sociolegal Studies." *Law and Social Inquiry* 14 (1992): 49.

Singer, Joseph. "The Player and the Cards: Nihilism and Legal Theory." *Yale Law Journal* 94 (1984): 1.

Smith, David E., and George Gay. *It's So Good Don't Even Try It Once*. Englewood Cliffs, N.J.: Prentice-Hall, 1972.

Smith, James Charles. "Review Essay: Law, Beauty, and Human Stability: A Rose Is a Rose Is a Rose." *California Law Review* 78 (1990): 787.

Solan, Lawrence. *The Language of Judges*. Chicago: University of Chicago Press, 1993.

Solum, Lawrence. "On the Indeterminacy Crisis: Critiquing Critical Dogma." *University of Chicago Law Review* 54 (1987): 462.

Somerville, Margaret. "Law as an 'Art Form' Reflecting AIDS: A Challenge to the Province and Function of Law." *University of Toronto Law Journal* 42 (1992): 287.

———. "'The Song of Death': The Lyrics of Euthanasia." *Journal of Contemporary Health Law and Policy* 9 (1993): 801.

Sontag, Susan. *Illness as Metaphor/AIDS and Its Metaphors.* New York: Anchor Books, 1990.

Stafford, Barbara, John LaPuma, and David Schiedermayer. "One Face of Beauty, One Picture of Health: The Hidden Aesthetic of Medical Practice." *Journal of Medicine and Philosophy* 14 (1989): 213.

Starr, Paul. *The Social Transformation of American Medicine.* New York: Basic Books, 1982.

Stein, Peter. *The Teaching of Roman Law in England around 1200.* London: Selden Society, 1990.

Steiner, George. *After Babel: Aspects of Language and Translation.* 2d ed. Oxford: Oxford University Press, 1992.

Sternfeld, F. W. *Music from the Middle Ages to the Renaissance.* New York: Praeger, 1973.

Stevens, Wallace. *Poems.* New York: Vintage Books, 1947.

Stevens, Wilf. "Imagining Justice: Aesthetics and Public Executions in Late Eighteenth-Century England." *Yale Journal of Law and the Humanities* 5 (1993): 51.

Stick, J. "Can Nihilism Be Pragmatic?" *Harvard Law Review* 100 (1986): 332.

Stone, Christopher. *Earth and Other Ethics.* New York: Harper & Row, 1987.

Stone, Julius. *Social Dimensions of Law and Justice.* Sydney: Maitland, 1966.

Sugarman, David, ed. *Law, Economy, and Society: Essays in the History of English Law.* Abingdon, U.K.: Professional Books, 1984.

———. *Legality, Ideology, and the State.* London: Academic Press, 1983.

Swain, Stella, and Andrew Clarke. "Negotiating Postmodernity: Narratives of Law and Imperialism." *Law and Critique* 6 (1995): 229.

Szasz, Thomas. *The Myth of Mental Illness: Foundations of a Theory of Personal Conduct.* New York: Hoeber-Harper, 1961.

Taylor, Avril. *Women Drug Users: An Ethnography of a Female Injecting Community.* Oxford: Oxford University Press, 1993.

Taylor, Charles. *Hegel.* Cambridge: Cambridge University Press, 1975.

———. *Sources of the Self: The Making of the Modern Identity.* Cambridge, Mass.: Harvard University Press, 1989.

———. "Understanding Modernity." Sprawle Lectures, McGill University, 1992.

Teachout, Peter Read. "The Soul of the Fugue: An Essay on Reading Fuller." *Minnesota Law Review* 70 (1986): 1073.

Teubner, Gunther. "Autopoiesis in Law and Society: A Rejoinder to Blankenburg." *Law and Society Review* 18 (1984): 291.

———. "Substantive and Reflexive Elements in Modern Law." *Law and Society Review* 17 (1983): 239.

———. "The Two Faces of Janus: Rethinking Legal Pluralism." *Cardozo Law Review* 13 (1992): 1443.

Teubner, Gunther, ed. *Autopoietic Law: A New Approach to Law and Society.* Berlin: de Gruyter, 1988.

Theweleit, Karl. *Male Fantasies.* Vols. 1–2. Minneapolis: University of Minnesota Press, 1987.

Thomlins, Thomas, ed. *Statutes at Large.* Vols. 1–10. London: Eyre & Strahan, 1811.

Thompson, E. P. *Customs in Common.* New York: New Press, 1993.

———. *The Making of the English Working Class.* Harmondsworth: Penguin, 1975.

———. "Time, Work-Discipline, and Industrial Capitalism." *Past and Present* 38 (1967): 56.

———. *Whigs and Hunters.* London: Allen Lane, 1975.

Tierney, Brian. *Origins of Papal Infallibility 1150–1350.* Studies in the History of Christian Thought, vol. 6. Leiden: E. J. Brill, 1972.

Toran, Janice. "'Tis a Gift to Be Simple: Aesthetics and Procedural Reform." *Michigan Law Review* 89 (1990): 352.

Toumlin, Stephen, and John Goodfield. *The Discovery of Time.* London: Hutchinson, 1965.

Turkel, Gerald. "Michel Foucault: Law, Power, and Knowledge." *Journal of Law and Society* 17 (1990): 170.

Turnbull, Ian. "Clear Legislative Drafting: New Approaches in Australia." *Statute Law Review* 11 (1991): 161.

Tushnet, Mark. "The Critical Legal Studies Movement." *Stanford Law Review* 36 (1984): 623.

———. "An Essay on Rights." *Texas Law Review* 62 (1984): 1363.

Unger, Roberto Mangabeira. "The Critical Legal Studies Movement." *Harvard Law Review* 96 (1983): 561.

———. *Knowledge and Politics.* New York: Free Press, 1975.

Usprich, S. J., and Robert Solomon. "Notes on the Potential Criminal Liability of a Needle Exchange Program." *Health Law in Canada* (1988/89): 42.

Utz, Stephen. "Rules, Principles, Algorithms, and the Description of Legal Systems." *Ratio Juris* 5 (1992): 23.

Van den Haag, Ernest. "In Defense of the Death Penalty: A Legal—Practical—Moral Analysis." *Criminal Law Bulletin* 14 (1978): 51.

Van den Haag, Ernest, and John Conrad. *The Death Penalty: A Debate.* New York: Plenum Press, 1983.

Waldorf, Dan, et al. "Needle Sharing among Male Prostitutes." *Journal of Drug Issues* 20 (1990): 309.

Waldron, Jeremy. "Vagueness in Law and Language: Some Philosophical Issues." *California Law Review* 82 (1994): 509.

Wallace, Robert. *Jane Austen and Mozart: Classical Equilibrium in Fiction and Music.* Athens: University of Georgia Press, 1983.

Walzer, Michael. *Interpretation and Social Criticism.* Cambridge, Mass.: Harvard University Press, 1987.

———. *Spheres of Justice.* New York: Basic Books, 1983.

Ward, Ian. "A Kantian (Re)Turn: Aesthetics, Postmodernism, and Law." *Law and Critique* 6 (1995): 256.

Warden, James. *A Bunyip Democracy: The Parliament and Australian Political Identity*. Political Studies Fellow Monograph No. 2. Canberra: Australian Government Publishing Service, 1995.

Weber, Max. *Law in Economy and Society*. Trans. M. Rheinstein. Cambridge, Mass.: Harvard University Press, 1954.

———. *The Rational and Social Foundations of Music*. Trans. Riedel Martindale and Neuwirth Martindale. Carbondale: Southern Illinois University Press, 1958.

Weber, Samuel. "Deconstruction before the Name." *Cardozo Law Review* 13 (1992): 1181.

Weil, Andrew. *The Natural Mind*. Boston: Houghton Mifflin, 1972.

Weinrib, Ernest. "Causation and Wrongdoing." *Chicago-Kent Law Review* 63 (1987): 407.

———. "Corrective Justice." *Iowa Law Review* 77 (1992): 403.

———. "Formalism and Practical Reason, or How to Avoid Seeing Ghosts in the Empty Sepulchre." *Harvard Journal of Law and Public Policy* 16 (1993): 683.

———. "The Jurisprudence of Legal Formalism." *Harvard Journal of Law and Public Policy* 16 (1993): 583.

———. "'Legal Formalism': On the Immanent Rationality of Law." *Yale Law Journal* 97 (1988): 984.

———. "Non-Relational Relationships." *Iowa Law Review* 77 (1992): 445.

———. "Right and Advantage in Private Law." *Cardozo Law Review* 10 (1989): 1283.

Weinsheimer, Joel. *Gadamer's Hermeneutics*. New Haven: Yale University Press, 1985.

Weisberg, Richard. "The Law–Literature Enterprise." *Yale Journal of Law and the Humanities* 1 (1988): 1.

Wellbery, David. *Lessing's Laocoön: Semiotics and Aesthetics in the Age of Reason*. Cambridge: Cambridge University Press, 1984.

Weisbrod, Carol. "Practical Polyphony: Theories of the State and Feminist Jurisprudence." *Georgia Law Review* 24 (1990): 985.

West, Robin. "Jurisprudence as Narrative: An Aesthetic Analysis of Modern Legal Theory." *New York University Law Review* 60 (1985): 145.

White, James Boyd. *Heracles' Bow: Essays on the Rhetoric and Poetics of Law*. Madison: University of Wisconsin Press, 1985.

———. *Justice as Translation*. Chicago: University of Chicago Press, 1990.

———. *The Legal Imagination*. Boston: Little, Brown & Co., 1973.

Wicke, Jennifer. "Postmodern Identity and the Legal Subject." *Colorado Law Review* 62 (1991): 455.

Williams, Bernard. *Ethics and the Limits of Philosophy*. Cambridge, Mass.: Harvard University Press, 1985.

Williams, Patricia. "Alchemical Notes." *Harvard Civil Rights–Civil Liberties Review* 22 (1987): 1401.

———. *The Alchemy of Race and Rights.* Cambridge, Mass.: Harvard University Press, 1991.

Wilson, David Fenwick. *Music of the Middle Ages: Style and Structure.* New York: Schirmer Books, 1990.

Wilson, Paul, and John Braithwaite, eds. *Two Faces of Deviance.* St. Lucia: University of Queensland Press, 1978.

Wimsatt, Wim. *The Verbal Icon.* Lexington: University of Kentucky Press, 1967.

Winston, Kenneth. "Is/Ought Redux: The Pragmatist Context of Lon Fuller's Conception of Law." *Oxford Journal of Legal Studies* 8 (1988): 329.

Winter, Steven. "The Metaphor of Standing and the Problem of Self-Governance." *Stanford Law Review* 40 (1988).

———. "Transcendental Nonsense: Metaphoric Reasoning and the Cognitive Stakes for Law." *University of Pennsylvania Law Review* 138 (1989).

Wittgenstein, Ludwig. *Tractatus Logico-Philosophicus.* Frankfurt: Suhrkamp, 1973.

Wolf, Naomi. *The Beauty Myth.* New York: William Morrow, 1991.

Wolfe, Alan. "Algorithmic Justice." *Cardozo Law Review* 11 (1990): 1409.

Wolff, Christoph. *Mozart's Requiem: Historical and Analytical Studies — Documents — Score.* Trans. Mary Whittall. Berkeley: University of California Press, 1994.

Woodman, Gordon. "The Alternative Law of Alternative Dispute Resolution." *Cahiers de droit* 32 (1991): 3.

Woodson, Gordon. "Book Review, *Legal Pluralism — Proceedings of the Canberra Law and Workshop VII.*" *Journal of Legal Pluralism and Unofficial Law* 27 (1988): 173.

Young, Robert. *White Mythologies: Writing History and the West.* London: Routledge, 1990.

5. SELECT MUSIC

Bach, Johann Sebastian. Partita in D Minor for Solo Violin, BWV 1004 (1720).

———. *Goldberg Variations,* BWV 988 (1742).

———. *Das wohltemperierte Klavier,* BWV 822–845 (1722); BWV 846–869 (1744).

Beethoven, Ludwig van. Symphony No. 5 in C Minor, op. 67 (1809).

———. Symphony No. 6 in F Major, op. 68 (1809).

Berlioz, Hector. *Symphonie fantastique,* op. 14 (1845).

Brahms, Johannes. *Variationen über ein Thema von Paganini, I & II,* op. 35 Heft 1 & 2 (1866).

Britten, Benjamin. *War Requiem,* op. 6 (1942).

Liszt, Franz. *Études d'exécution transcendante d'après Paganini,* op. 140, no. 6 (1840).

Lutoslawski, Witold. *Wariacje na temat Paganiniego* (1941).

Mendelssohn, Felix. *Songs without Words,* op. var. (1835–47).

Messiaen, Olivier. *Quatuor pour le fin du temps* (1942).

Mozart, Wolfgang Amadeus. *Requiem Mass*, K. 626 (1791).

Paganini, Niccolò. *Ventriquattro Capricci, Opera Terza (Dodici Capricci)*, op. 1, no. 12 (1820).

Rachmaninoff, Sergei. *Rapsodie sur un thème de Paganini pour piano et orchestre*, op. 43 (1934).

Schumann, Robert. *Introduction and Variations on a Theme of Paganini* (1831).

Shostakovitch, Dmitri. *Preludes and Fugues*, op. 87 (1950–51).

Tallis, Thomas. *Spem in alium* (1550?).

Index

Text: 10/13 Aldus
Display: Aldus
Composition: G & S Typesetters, Inc.
Printing and binding: Thomson-Shore, Inc.

ADX-1004

9/7/00
App